Documents on Contemporary British Government

II. Local government in Britain

Documents on Contemporary British Government

II. Local government in Britain

EDITED BY

MARTIN MINOGUE

Senior Lecturer, Department of
Administrative Studies, University
of Manchester

CAMBRIDGE UNIVERSITY PRESS

CAMBRIDGE
LONDON · NEW YORK · MELBOURNE

Published by the Syndics of the Cambridge University Press
The Pitt Building, Trumpington Street, Cambridge CB2 1RP
Bentley House, 200 Euston Road, London NW1 2DB
32 East 57th Street, New York, NY 10022, USA
296 Beaconsfield Parade, Middle Park, Melbourne 3206, Australia

First published 1977

Printed in Great Britain
at the University Press Cambridge

Library of Congress Cataloguing in Publication Data

Main entry under title:

Local government in Britain.

(Documents on contemporary British Government; v. 2)

Bibliography: p.

1. Local government – Great Britain. 2. Local
government – Great Britain – History – Sources. I.
Minogue, Martin. II. Series.

JS3095.1977.L63   352.041   76-43105

ISBN 0 521 21429 7 hard covers
ISBN 0 521 29147 X paperback

To my mother and father

Contents

List of Maps

Preface

This is the second volume in a two-volume selection of documents related to
government in Britain. This volume illustrates changes in local government in
Britain (construed to include Northern Ireland) in the post-1945 period; the first
volume deals with central government broadly defined, during the same period.

The past thirty years are taken as the principal reference period, but the majority
of documents in both volumes come from the past decade, which has witnessed a
remarkable and unprecedented series of reforming investigations across the whole
field of governmental activity, and into the system of government itself. The chief
reason for the concentration of these volumes on the formal structures of government is that the analysis and reform of these structures has occupied the centre of
the political stage in recent years. Moreover, the system of government more readily
lends itself to documentary analysis than the less formal parts of the political system, and it would have been impossible, for reasons of space, to deal adequately
with political parties, pressure groups, and elections within the scope of the present
volumes: it may be that a separate source book is needed to cover these areas.
Clearly an understanding of the political context of structural and constitutional
changes is essential to either description or analysis of those changes, and the
business of relating governmental structures and arrangements to political institutions and processes is part of the task of teachers and students of politics and
government everywhere. This documentary selection is, therefore, intended to be
complementary to the better existing texts and commentaries on British government and politics. The intention is to give students the opportunity to make more
direct acquaintance with the basic materials of British government than the
burgeoning supply of instant text-books either allows or encourages. Too often the
student thinks of official documents as dull, incomprehensible, or insignificant.
Sometimes they may be all of these things, but more frequently they are lively,
readable, and make crucial contributions to policy formulation. This selection is
published in the hope that students will be stimulated to turn towards these primary sources of information, and away from the easy 'crammer' which all too often
oversimplifies what is complex, renders anodyne what is fascinating, and imposes an
unreal order on a shifting, disorderly process. It is my view that if students become
accustomed to familiarity with the primary documents, they will not only learn to
make their own judgements about source material, but will derive from their
studies an enhanced enjoyment and enthusiasm for further enquiry.

Undeniably the attempt to select from a mass of documents has pitfalls for the
unwary. Documents cannot be properly understood if divorced from their political

and administrative context; extracts may give an incomplete or partial impression of the content of a particular document. The need to compress the selection into the confines dictated by the publisher and the market inevitably compels the editor to make arbitrary decisions about which documents, or parts of documents, to include or exclude. Accepting these strictures, I would emphasise that, firstly, the documents are intended to supplement the secondary reading material, and lecture programmes, which will provide the basis for any course in British government; secondly, that I have attempted to provide brief contextual material which will serve to link together the selected sources in a reasonably coherent manner, but would expect the more detailed interpretation of the sources, and their context, to be provided by lecturers responsible for courses (and this allows for differing interpretations of the same material, where textbooks frequently impose a particular approach); thirdly, in selecting from documents, I have tried to reduce the elements of arbitrariness by making lengthy rather than brief selections and by concentrating on documents which seemed to have a more permanent rather than an ephemeral character; and finally, I have tried to illustrate the wide range of sources which contribute to the formidable mass of official publications: white papers, green papers, departmental reports from special working parties, Royal Commission reports, parliamentary papers, commentaries by pressure groups, contributions from individual policy-makers — the range of sources is enormous, and fascinating. But the sheer volume daunts the average student, and even when it does not, considerable problems of access may remain. The present selection is intended to provide more convenient access to these sources, and at the same time to stimulate an appetite for more extensive use of the basic materials for the study of British government. (Note: 'British' and 'Britain' are taken to include Northern Ireland throughout these volumes, though technically they do not.)

I wish to offer my thanks to Roy Wallis for helpful advice on the section on local government finance; to the staff of the John Rylands Library, Manchester University, for help in locating documents; to Marjorie Marchant for her usual immaculate typing; to my publishers for sympathetic flexibility over deadlines; and to my wife Lizzie for considerable forbearance and moral support. Any faults are my own.

Martin Minogue
April 1976

Introduction

I

'Such an infinite variety of business has been heaped upon them, that few care to undertake and fewer understand the office.'

Blackstone, writing in 1765, referred to Justices of the Peace. His remark is equally apt to the local authorities which were the lineal successors to the Justices. Perhaps the most remarkable feature of our national system of government is the extent to which the central power has delegated the operations of the state to elective local bodies. Equally remarkable is the tight and careful control exerted by central authorities upon these local authorities, so that local government enjoys an infinite variety of business, but a highly restricted capacity for doing that business. We can discern in these arrangements, an uncomfortable conflict between the twin principles of democracy and efficiency embedded so deeply in our philosophy of public administration.

The shrine of local self-government occupies a central place in the British pantheon of constitutional gods; the ideology of British political institutions centres firmly on notions of democratic freedom, local autonomy, individualistic liberty. The extreme presentation even produces a demonology in which large-scale unified centralised government is intrinsically evil, and small-scale, fragmented, decentralised government is intrinsically good. These ideas are held to provide the very foundation of the whole system of government. Yet the history of local government in Britain, insofar as it can be freed from the weight of the democratic myth, shows the origins of the system to lie in the needs of the state. In medieval society, those needs were pre-eminently related to the maintenance of order and the preservation of social cohesion. In the modernising state, these needs remained, but were more closely linked to the effective expression of the mutual obligations of the state and its citizens, with emphasis later upon the economic and equitable provision of services by the state to the citizen.

The development of the need for effective governmental arrangements which could respond quickly to emerging pressures for social and economic change can be traced back to the industrial and commercial changes of the sixteenth century. Medieval political institutions began to be transformed by these pressures, though in functional rather than structural ways. For example, the lynchpin of local government was, during these three hundred years, the Justice of the Peace; but the Justices were thirteenth, not sixteenth century creations. The difference was that legislative changes in the sixteenth century expanded the role of the Justice far beyond the original conception of it. Similarly, the parishes, counties, and municipal boroughs all had medieval existence, but could in no sense be described as a 'system' of government. Yet parish, borough, and county survived into the mid-twentieth century, as basic units of local administration, though with greatly changed purposes and relationships. Up to the 1830s, these units of local administration must be discussed primarily in terms of their satisfaction of the requirements of the central administration of the state, expressed principally in terms of stability, law, order, and the collection of public revenue. After the Great Reform Act of 1832, the vocabulary changes significantly, and the concept of representative democracy moves into the centre of the stage. Yet this concept was quite limited in its initial application; and representation was primarily an instrument with which the commercial and industrial classes could bludgeon the state into providing a machinery of government more flexible in its response to economic and social pressures. Just as the 1832 Act was a first breach in the barrier of autocratic privilege, so the related 1835 Municipal Corporations Act was a blow at the corrupt monopoly of the old urban oligarchies; indeed, the 1835 Act introduced a broader franchise than the 1832 parliamentary franchise. The 1835 principle of elected councils, responsible to local ratepayers, was in 1888 extended to the counties, and so was laid down the principle of elected authorities which were representative of and responsible to a defined locality. At the same time, the 1834 Poor Law Amendment Act and subsequent regulative legislation in the social field, had established the conception of a systematic relationship between those elected authorities and a more streamlined central administration. The Justices of the Peace had been displaced, not merely by a new democratic ideology, but by their manifest ineptness as an instrument of modern administration.

The inrush of democracy did not, for some considerable time, dilute the elitist nature of political control of local activity; for instance, in 1889 half the elected representatives on county councils were local magistrates, the very dignitaries whom electoral reform was intended to displace; and 'half a century later, the same class of men still predominated'.[1] In 1939, the same authorities could still boast 34 peers of the realm. But electoral reform at least broadened the circle of elite groups which were to be regarded as the rightful guardians of public authority, and created the possibilities for that local and civic pride which was to be the hallmark of Victorian local government.

The Justices of the Peace had expanded through a constant redefinition of their powers, rather than through structural reform; so, too, did the new local government system grow, less through a process of structural reform than by the constant addition of new purposes and responsibilities. At first, local authorities were anxious to claim powers to ensure jurisdiction over local initiative and enterprise; in the twentieth century, the tendency developed for central government to use established local authorities as a convenient administrative instrument for the implementation of new social legislation, though always within the strict confines of central

---

1 B. Keith-Lucas ed. *Redlich and Hirst's History of Local Government in England* (Macmillan, 1970, p. 234).

financial and legislative control, and often in the face of local reluctance. The local government structure set up at the end of the nineteenth century showed itself capable of significant adaptation to new purposes. County boroughs could be extended and new county boroughs created. Between 1888 and 1926, the number of county boroughs in England went up from 59 to 78 while almost all the original ones expanded. But the process meant a steady erosion of the counties. In the mid-twenties the creation of new county boroughs was effectively stopped, while extensions became more difficult to secure. The Boundary Commission established in 1945 to review local government boundaries concluded that there should be some redistribution of functions between counties and county boroughs, but the government were not prepared for this, largely because the local authorities themselves resisted such a move, and nothing was done. And although they lost some responsibilities, notably the publicly maintained hospitals, gas and electricity, their responsibilities overall expanded, particularly in the fields of planning, education and housing.

One adaptive device which helped the system to respond to change was a shift of responsibilities from the district to the county councils. In 1945 the county councils became the sole education authorities within administrative counties, although boroughs and urban districts of 60,000 population or more had the right to claim delegation as excepted districts and the county councils were required to prepare schemes of decentralisation to divisional executives unless the Minister excepted an area, in whole or in part, from this requirement. In 1948 the county councils took over planning, but with the expectation that the exercise of some of the powers would be delegated back to the district councils. But these changes had a counter-productive consequence, of embittered relations between municipal and county councils, as county boroughs sought to expand and non-county boroughs struggled to acquire county borough status. The acrimonious conflicts of the 1950s and early sixties eventually produced in central government a weariness with the existing system and a determination to obtain radical reform.

Today, local government unquestionably has an infinite variety of business, and is responsible for services — for example, education and personal social services — which in many systems are regarded as a central responsibility. This principal owes a great deal to the notions, first, that bureaucratic response to the needs and demands of a mass population will be more effective if administrative and political powers are distributed outwards from the centre (or downwards from the top); and secondly, that decentralisation allows for variations in local circumstances. Is the principle soundly based? If the system really worked as a decentralised operation, there would be no difficulty in giving an unequivocal answer. But the relationships between centre and locality are defined principally by the considerable statutory and financial powers of central government; partly because of this, the relationship between the concepts of efficiency and democracy is, to say the least, ambiguous. It could be argued that a centralised system can provide more efficiently for people's wants than a decentralised system, and that any movement along the scale from centralisation to decentralisation brings a corresponding reduction in the ability of government to provide for people's wants. The democratic response is that efficient provision depends upon grass-roots knowledge, which can only be acquired and communicated through localised institutions, and in any case, that man cannot live by bread alone. A judgement between these positions becomes largely a matter of preferences and priorities; the problem for modern governments is that the complexity of modern life pulls government institutions outwards from the centre, while the scale of popular demand and the principle of equality pushes them inwards again.

It was, perhaps, the nature of these conflicts, and a growing awareness that in all probability the limits of the adaptiveness of existing institutions had been reached, that precipitated the scramble for reform in the post-war period. The 1920s and 1970s might well be compared with the 1830s and the 1880s in the history of British local government. But just as 1832 opened the way for a continuous reformulation of local institutions and power over half a century, it may be that 1972 will also, in the perspective of history, come to be seen as the starting point for reform, rather than its culmination.

II

'We do not delude ourselves into thinking that one can solve problems by projecting changes of machinery.'   Herbert Report, 1960

The General Introduction to Volume I discussed the historical context of recent constitutional changes in British government, and analysed the characteristics of the political process through which such changes emerge. The discussion hinged on three arguments which are as relevant to the process of local government reform as to other areas of reform in British government. First, that constitutional reform in Britain has been dominated by questions of structure; secondly, that the implementation of reform has been of an unco-ordinated, piecemeal nature; and thirdly, that the politics of the reform process itself constitute a partial explanation of these characteristics. I concluded from this line of argument that change in British government can largely be defined by what it is not: it is not radical, it is not planned, and it is not ideological. Nonetheless, change occurs steadily; changes in one part of the political system stimulate changes elsewhere in the system; and changes frequently reveal the ideological stances of the actors involved, though these may be implicit rather than explicit. The end result is rather like a comparison of two photographs of the same place, separated in time: the constitutional snapshot of Britain in 1975 gives the constitutional snapshot of 1945 a decidedly quaint appearance, but we are clearly looking at the same subject.

To what extent do these generalisations (as I freely admit them to be) about change in British government apply to the specific case of local government? Reform of English local government has consistently been regarded as a problem of structure. The question has always been, how to get the right relationship between the size, area, and number of authorities, and the functions which these authorities have to undertake. But analysis has consistently been constrained by the lack of freedom to consider whether or not existing functions were appropriately allocated to the local government system. Yet a fundamental explanation of the defects of the system lies in the process of historical evolution under which new purposes were constantly added to structures originally formed for a quite restricted set of purposes. This distortion of the relationship between structure and function is the principal structural defect of English local government, but one which the reforming bodies have never been allowed to tackle squarely, except in the case of Northern Ireland. Significantly, in Northern Ireland a review of the functions and structures of local government led to a solution more radical than emerged from local government investigations elsewhere in Britain: a regionally-based system of government for all major services, and a much reduced role for the local government system. It is not unrealistic to suggest that in England, Scotland and Wales, similar solutions will emerge within the next decade, because the current structures will demonstrate themselves to be defective not merely in relation to the responsibilities which at present belong to local government, but in relation to the changing political and constitutional relationships likely to emerge from the devolution of new legislative and executive powers to regional assemblies; currently to Scotland and Wales (and to Northern Ireland in principle), but potentially to new English regions too. From the standpoint of 1985, or even 1980, the local government reforms of the 1972—3 vintage may well be seen as limited, cautious, and inadequate, merely a prelude to the more fundamental constitutional review of the powers and procedures of Westminster-based government. Meanwhile, we are left with a system which, it is claimed, is a reformed system, but which remains strikingly similar to the unreformed system. Certainly, the number of authorities is significantly reduced but the two-tier principle established in the nineteenth century is undamaged; the criteria established for relating functions to populations are inconsistently applied; and central control is undiminished. To make confusion worse confounded, popular representation is reduced. All this argues that local government reform has fallen between the two stools of efficiency and democracy: seeking to create both, it has achieved neither.

It is not difficult to explain this unintended consequence, if we examine the processes by which reform was carried out. The initiatives for reform came from central government, and the procedures for achieving reform were fairly consistent: investigations by commissions independent of central authorities, a lengthy process of examination which relied both on partial evidence and impartial research, a report stage, and a political response which led to implementation. In this set of procedures, two questions stand out as significant. First, what evidence played a central part in the findings? Secondly, what considerations motivated the political response to these findings? If we consider the whole range of reforming activities in British government in the past thirty years, two conclusions emerge; first, that findings frequently reflected the evidence of interested parties; secondly, that the political response frequently reflected the pressures of interested parties. In local government the most interested parties were existing local authorities; and the political response to reform proposals invariably operated to dilute these proposals until they represented what the existing political interests would bear rather than what was needed. The reform of English local government offers the sharpest example: here, the new system owed relatively little to the principal reform proposal, and a great deal to the political sympathies between central and local political leaderships.

But it is possible that the real problem of local government reform lay in the piecemeal character of its implementation. We see that in England and Wales, in the 1960s, several bodies are required to examine the same or overlapping problems, but that agreed implementation takes fourteen years to achieve. Nevertheless, as the major reform commission in this process reports in 1969, a wider review on the constitution is initiated; and in 1972–3 the reform of local government in Wales and Scotland goes ahead, although the wider review will presently throw into the melting pot the whole system of decentralised government in Britain. That two such major reviews should proceed independently of each other suggests either stubborn determination to implement local government change at the first opportune moment, or else a more worrying inability on the part of political and administrative leaders to comprehend the essential relationship between the two types of reform. As a consequence, it is likely that the 'major' reform of 1972–3 will turn out to be yet another transitory phase in a much wider process of constitutional review. Indeed, the process is to some extent self-fulfilling prophecy, because the existence of the wider constitutional review was trotted out as a major argument against radical local government reform.

If we look back at thirty years of change or attempted change in the field of local government, it is manifest, first, that the pressures for change were inescapable; secondly, that the forces resistant to change were well-placed to resist, and relatively successful; thirdly, that changes were taking place in all parts of the political system without the possibility of systematic change ever being taken seriously; fourthly, that changes were ultimately incremental, rather than fundamental; and finally, rather dauntingly, that it is extremely doubtful that we have yet seen the final stage of the 'reform movement' in British local government. Much as our system of local government is in need of a period of stability, the political and anti-reforming rearguard fought by local government representatives probably means that local government has condemned itself to a continued period of uncertainty and upheaval.

Section I
England: Areas and purposes

The reform of English local government has a pedigree stretching back to the
immediate post-war period. Yet it can scarcely be seen as a reform movement. Up
to the late 1950s, alteration of the system was viewed as a matter for negotiation
between local authorities (represented by their collective associations) and central
government (represented by the Ministry of Housing and Local Government). In
what was essentially a bargaining process, central government was not disposed
towards any radical initiative, and the local authorities were more concerned to
protect and strengthen entrenched positions than to worry about the effectiveness
of the system. The Local Government Boundary Commission of 1947 foundered
against these rocks, and the ensuing period was marked by constant disputes
between authorities and a series of negotiations between local and central authorities which produced little more than a rationalisation of existing practice (1).

This period of extended negotiation did at least produce the Local Government
Commission for England (2), and agreement that the problems of governing the
capital city merited special analysis (see Section V). But the fruits of the Local
Government Commission were disappointingly meagre in relation to the effort
expended upon reviews of specific areas. The principal reason for this lay still in the
unwillingness of central policy-makers to grasp the stinging nettle of basic reconstruction. Vested local interests (with political support at the central level) were
allowed to dictate the response to the Commission's proposals. A sort of active
paralysis set in: there was no lack of analysis, or proposals, but a total hiatus when
it came to the implementation of proposals.

Only a firm act of political leadership could break this deadlock, and this came
from Richard Crossman, Labour's Minister of Housing and Local Government in
1966. Determined to drag local government into the twentieth century and convinced that the Local Government Commission (described in his *Memoirs*, rather
unfairly, as 'fussy old men') were unequal to the task, Crossman launched a new
initiative. This was a Royal Commission, given a membership calculated to produce
an informed but objective analysis, and terms of reference sufficiently explicit to
ensure positive proposals for reform (3). In the event, the Commission were divided,
and one of its members produced a strong dissenting report (4). The Majority
Report, with a curious confused logic, embraced a unitary principle (with single all-
purpose authorities), while proposing a two-tier system for three main conurbations. Significantly, these proposals emerged in a climate receptive to change.
While the Commission's findings were unwelcome to the existing local authorities,
and were not in line with the preferences expressed by central departments (5),

7

they were generally endorsed by the Labour Government (6). But another change of political fortunes brought in a Conservative administration more inclined to respond to the indignation of the Conservative-controlled counties; and their revised proposals (7), while keeping much of Redcliffe-Maud, abandoned the unitary principle. The two-tier principle was retained; so were many of the existing counties, and the whole parish system. The influence of Redcliffe-Maud showed in the retention (and extension) of the metropolitan system for conurbations, the abolition of the county boroughs and the population criterion of 250,000 to 1,000,000 for authorities providing the major services.

Given the political compromise embedded in the revised proposals, their statutory implementation (8) met with few difficulties. The Government made no concessions of principle, and reversed in the House of Lords its only defeat in the Commons (over the allocation of the refuse disposal function to the counties); there were some last-ditch, but insignificant, changes to metropolitan boundaries.

One of the defects of the previous two-tier system had been the uncertain and often acrimonious relationships between the two levels. The allocation of functions between two different levels, and the drawing of boundaries between different authorities, must inevitably have a degree of arbitrariness. The 1972 Act attempts to reduce this arbitrary element through what are known as 'agency arrangements', that is, arrangements by which one authority may act as an agent for another authority in the discharge of functions (9). These arrangements replace the old methods of 'delegation' and 'claiming' which caused so much controversy in the pre-1972 system. The intention of the agency provisions is to allow larger county districts to act as agents for county authorities in appropriate cases; but the provisions are permissive, and because of this, the precise allocation of functions between the two levels of local authority is not yet as clear as the final distribution of functions (Appendix B to this section) would suggest. But neither education nor social services can be the subject of an agency agreement, and it is expected that highways responsibilities will be the principal object of such agreements. Nowhere is the division of responsibility between the two tiers more blurred than in relation to planning functions. Essentially, counties are responsible for establishing the broad strategy through structure plans, and districts are responsible for detailed application and control in their areas. There is ample room for dispute about what constitutes a policy (or county) matter, and what can be left to local (or district) jurisdiction, and central government have laid down guidelines for co-operation between authorities in this field (10). The task of resolving where responsibilities lie could be eased by the implementation of the Dobry Report, which *inter alia* proposed procedures for the classification of development activities into routine and non-routine (38, Section II).

These complications aside, the distribution of functions between authorities is straightforward, but central government has taken the opportunity provided by the restructuring of local government to take away direct responsibility for certain functions. With the reorganisation of the National Health Service in 1973, local authorities lost their responsibility for a variety of personal health services (11). But the matching of Area Health Authority boundaries with county and metropolitan district boundaries, and the appointment of representatives of these authorities to the Area Health Authorities demonstrates a felt need for the continued association of local government with the health services. The continued involvement in water services is a much stronger one (**12**). While there is no correspondence between local authority boundaries and water authority boundaries, local authority representatives will form a majority on the new regional water authorities. Some water functions will be carried out by local authorities on an agency basis: notably, the districts are expected to undertake sewerage functions.

The appendices to this section set out the pre-1972 (A) and post-1972 (B) functions of local authorities (the new authorities came into being on 1 April 1974); the size of the new local authorities (C); and the pattern of non-metropolitan districts (D). The definition of these districts was the first task of the Local Government Boundary Commission for England, set up under the 1972 Act as a permanent review body. This first report was implemented in full, and it appears that central government intends to operate a convention whereby the Commission's proposals will normally be accepted by the Government without alteration. If such a convention is established structural reform will become a continuous activity, and this should help to produce a shift from the crisis mentality which has so dominated local government reform in recent years.

1 THE 1956 WHITE PAPER

From *The Areas and Status of Local Authorities in England and Wales* (Cmnd. 9831, 1956); by permission of H.M.S.O.

I. THE PRESENT STRUCTURE

The dual system

1. The pattern of local government in England and Wales was established on its present lines by the Local Government Acts of 1888 and 1894. Two separate systems were set up — one for the county boroughs and another for the counties. In the county boroughs a single authority was entrusted with the administration of all local government services in their area. On the other hand, the counties were organised on the so-called 'two-tier' system. Under this system the responsibility for some services lies with the county council, and for others with the councils of county districts (non-county boroughs, urban districts and rural districts). In rural districts, certain functions are performed by parish councils or parish meetings.

2. The Act of 1888 established 61 county boroughs and 62 administrative counties (including the County of London, which is organised somewhat differently). Under that Act, the Local Government Board (later the Minister of Health) was empowered to make Orders, subject to parliamentary confirmation, conferring

county borough status on non-county boroughs with populations of not less than 50,000. The Act provided a similar procedure for extending the boundaries of county boroughs. Alternatively, a borough council could seek to achieve either of these objects by promoting a Private Bill. By 1923, 21 additional county boroughs had been created and many of the original ones had been enlarged. This involved a considerable transfer of population and financial resources from administrative counties to county boroughs.

Onslow Commission

3. As a result of the First Report of a Royal Commission under the chairmanship of Lord Onslow, the procedure was altered by the Local Government (County Boroughs and Adjustments) Act, 1926. This provided that thenceforth the creation of new county boroughs could be effected only by Private Act, and that no borough could promote a Bill to achieve county borough status unless it had a population of at least 75,000. It provided also that the boundaries of a county borough could be extended by Order only where the other local authorities affected did not object to this course; otherwise the county borough council would have to proceed by Private Bill.

. . . . . .

5. Between 1926 and 1939, extensions of county borough boundaries on a substantial scale were made. This process was discontinued during the war years and during the lifetime of the Local Government Boundary Commission (1945—1949). Thereafter, a number of further extensions have been made, but these have been collectively much smaller than had been asked for by the county boroughs in their claims to the Commission.

6. Under the Act of 1888, adjustments to the boundaries of urban and rural districts and or parishes could be made on the initiative of county councils, as and when they thought fit, the final decision resting with the Local Government Board (later the Minister of Health). However, following the Onslow Commission's Second Report, the procedure was modified by the Local Government Act of 1929. This provided that county councils should carry out comprehensive reviews of their areas at specified intervals, and should recommend to the Minister desirable changes in county district boundaries.

7. The first series of reviews was carried out between 1931 and 1937. As a result, many authorities were amalgamated and the total number of urban and rural districts was reduced from 1,606 to 1,048. However, numerous very small authorities still remained.

Boundary Commission

8. During the war many claims for the creation and extension of county boroughs were held up, and a second series of reviews of county districts had become due. The problem was discussed by the Government with the Local Authority Associ-

ations; and, following the publication of a White Paper entitled 'Local Government in England and Wales during the Period of Reconstruction' (Cmd. 6579), a Local Government Boundary Commission was created by statute in 1945. The function of the Commission was to review the boundaries, and in certain cases the status, of local authorities.

9. After a comprehensive review, the Commission, in its Report for 1947, made proposals for far-reaching changes in the status and functions of local authorities. However, the Government did not adopt these proposals; and, in 1949, they dissolved the Commission and reinstated, with minor amendments, the previous procedure for effecting changes in local government areas.

. . . . . .

III. GOVERNMENT'S CONCLUSIONS

Need for reorganisation

15. The test of any system of local government in this country should be whether it provides a stable structure, capable of discharging efficiently the functions entrusted to it, while at the same time maintaining its local democratic character.

16. Since the present system of local government was established there have been far-reaching alterations in the distribution of population and industry, the scope and cost of services, the speed of communications, and the relationship between central and local government. But it does not necessarily follow that radical changes in organisation are needed. A fundamental alteration of the existing structure could be justified only if it had shown itself to be incapable of meeting present-day needs. That is not the situation. The present system has, over many years, stood up to the severest tests. It responded well to the abnormal demands made on it during the war and, despite certain weaknesses, has on the whole shown itself capable of adaptation to changing conditions. Moreover, the present system is firmly established and the local loyalties and civic pride which have grown up around it are a source of strength to local government which should not be underestimated.

17. There is, therefore, no convincing case for radically reshaping the existing form of local government in England and Wales. What is needed is to overhaul it and make such improvements as are necessary to bring it up to date.

18. It was laid down for the Local Government Boundary Commission in 1945 that the aim of all alterations in the status and boundaries of local authorities should be 'to ensure individually and collectively effective and convenient units of local government administration'. This broad objective was adopted in the proposals agreed by the representatives of the Local Authority Associations and is endorsed by the Government.

19. Leaving aside functions and finance, which can be considered separately, there are five main problems to be examined, namely:

creation of new county boroughs;

extension of existing county boroughs;
revision of county areas;
revision of county district areas; and
organisation of the conurbations.
But before these and other problems can be tackled, it is necessary to lay down
certain guiding principles and provide appropriate machinery to apply them.

Procedure for reviews

20. The first step is to establish satisfactory methods for determining what changes
need to be made. Apart from reviews of county districts, there is, at present, no
means of examining the organisation of local government comprehensively over
wide areas. For the creation of new county boroughs or the extension of existing
ones, the only machinery available (except where the authorities concerned accept
an extension by Order) is the promotion of a Private Bill. But in practice, this has
proved unsatisfactory, costly and often abortive.

21. Entirely new procedure is required. This must provide means for studying
problems comprehensively and for assessing the wider repercussions of proposed
changes upon other authorities affected. It must enable local circumstances to be
investigated and local opinion to be consulted. It must provide independent and
informed guidance, while leaving to the Government and Parliament responsibility
for ultimate decisions.

22. As the most effective means of fulfilling these conditions, it is proposed to
create two Local Government Commissions, one for England and one for Wales.
Their main task would be to make recommendations to the Minister in regard to
the creation and extension of county boroughs, any necessary alterations in county
boroughs, and the organisation of local government in the conurbations.

23. The Commissions' reports and recommendations to the Minister should be
published; and the Minister should submit to Parliament Orders giving effect to
them, with any amendments which he might consider desirable. Subject to certain
exceptions (see paras. 31 and 36), each Order presented to Parliament should cover
a substantial portion of the country, so that a comprehensive assessment can be
made of the effects of the changes proposed.

24. A serious disadvantage of the existing procedure is the anxiety caused to
county councils by the ever-present threat of further losses of territory through the
creation or extension of county boroughs; for even where a Private Bill has failed,
the fear remains that it may be re-introduced in a subsequent session. This puts a
strain on good relations between the authorities concerned and does not make for
smooth administration. It is accordingly proposed that, after the issues in a particular area have been settled, there should (apart from reviews of county districts) be a
standstill for a period of years, during which no further changes would normally be
made.

25. Since local government organisation in each conurbation needs to be considered as a whole, any review of county districts within those areas should be

carried out by the Commission. However, outside the conurbations, the county councils should continue to be responsible for reviewing their district areas and for proposing to the Minister any desirable changes, subject to the right of representation to him by the district authorities concerned. These reviews should be carried out by each county council as soon as the Commission's recommendations relating to their county have been considered, and the relevant Orders have been dealt with by Parliament.

26. Any changes in the areas and boundaries of county districts should, as at present, be effected by Order by the Minister. In any case where it should appear to the Minister that the proposals of the county council require radical alteration, he should be empowered to instruct the appropriate Commission to review the county districts concerned and make recommendations.

County Boroughs

27. One of the first tasks with which the Commissions would have to deal is the consideration of applications for promotion to county borough status, or, in the case of existing county boroughs, for the extension of their boundaries.

28. An essential qualification for promotion to county borough status must be the fitness of the authority concerned to discharge the functions of a county borough. In determining this, a number of factors have to be taken into account, such as population, resources and administrative record. Apart from the claimant's own fitness for promotion, consideration must also be given to the consequences which it would have for the county or counties concerned.

29. The Government agree with the representatives of the Local Authority Associations that, outside the conurbations, a town with a population of 100,000 or more should be assumed to be large enough to function effectively as a county borough; and that, while an authority with a smaller population should not be precluded from applying for promotion, it should have to make out a strong case to justify it.

30. In a conurbation, a multiplicity of autonomous local authorities is clearly undesirable. Therefore, the size of population required for promotion to county borough status should be higher there than elsewhere; and it should certainly not be lower than the minimum of 125,000 proposed by the representatives of the Local Authority Associations.

31. The adoption of the proposal that a local authority with a population of 100,000 (or, in a conurbation, of 125,000) should be presumed capable of discharging effectively the functions of a county borough council should not be deemed to imply that existing county boroughs with lesser populations are unfit to enjoy county borough status. (There are at present 34 county boroughs with a population below 100,000.) Nevertheless, it would not be right to exclude this issue in all circumstances. It should be open to the Commissions to recommend the withdrawal of county borough status if they are satisfied that a particular authority is unable to discharge its responsibilities effectively. However, to deprive a county

borough of its independent status would be a most serious step which should be contemplated only where it is plainly necessary for efficient administration. As a safeguard, any proposal to deprive a county borough of its status should be presented to Parliament in a separate Order, so that the question could be considered on its own.

. . . . . .

Counties

34. The representatives of the Local Authority Associations were agreed that the Commissions might have to consider 'the division, amalgamation, alteration and extension of counties'. There are undoubtedly anomalous features in certain county boundaries which cause administrative inconvenience and could with advantage be corrected. The Commissions should, therefore, be entitled to recommend adjustments of county boundaries, where they are satisfied that these are needed for efficient and economical administration.

35. Moreover, in exceptional circumstances, promotions and extensions of county boroughs might make such inroads into a county as to render it no longer a viable unit of administration. Such cases are likely to be rare. But where, for this or other reasons, the need arises, the Commissions should not be precluded from recommending the amalgamation of one county with another, or, even, the transfer of substantial territory.

. . . . . .

Conurbations

38. In the large built-up areas, known as 'conurbations', special problems of organisation arise. Six major conurbations have been defined by the Registrar-General for census purposes — Greater London, South-East Lancashire, the West Midlands, West Yorkshire, Merseyside and Tyneside. However, for purposes of local government organisation the conurbations would not necessarily be identical with these.

39. Local administration in the conurbations is usually divided between numerous authorities of different types and sizes. The effect is that autonomous county boroughs are intermingled with county districts belonging to counties, of which large parts lie outside the conurbation. There can be little doubt that these haphazard arrangements are not conducive to efficiency or economy.

40. There are various possible methods of improving the pattern of local government within the conurbations. One is to acquiesce in the continued existence of a patchwork of local authorities of different types and with different powers, but to endeavour to reduce their number. This could be achieved by amalgamating county districts, by expanding county boroughs and creating new ones, and by adjusting county boundaries so as to reduce the number of counties involved.

41. A second method is to reorganise the area on a uniform basis. The county borough is the normal form of government for a big town, and county boroughs do

in fact form the core of most of the conurbations. In the large conurbations, the creation of a single all-embracing county borough would not be practicable, but it might be possible to form a group of county boroughs which, between them, would cover the whole area.

42. Either of these approaches would still leave unresolved the problem of those local authority services which may need to be co-ordinated or administered in common for the whole conurbation. Such co-ordination or common administration might be secured by creating joint bodies, representative of the various authorities in the conurbation; though this course would have the disadvantages of any system of indirect representation. Alternatively, a directly-elected upper-tier authority might be created to deal with all the services requiring joint action.

43. It is thus clear that there is no simple or wholly unobjectionable solution to the problem of local government organisation in the conurbations. Moreover, conditions in the different areas are not identical; and the same treatment may not necessarily be appropriate for all. It may, therefore, be right that provision should be made for alternative solutions, and that the Commissions should be asked to recommend the one which seems most appropriate in each case.

. . . . . .

County Districts

48. In any review of county districts, the principal problem is that of reducing the number of unduly small authorities which still exist in many parts of the country. There are some 700 county districts in England and Wales with populations of less than 15,000, nearly 500 with less than 10,000 and over 200 with less than 5,000.

49. The extent of this problem varies from county to county. This is partly due to the differing manner in which the county councils carried out their reviews in the years before the war. As was stated in 1945 in the White Paper on Local Government in England and Wales:

'Some county councils undertook the work with vigour, and the resulting system of county districts and parishes in these counties was satisfactory and probably calls for little, if any, revision on a second review. Others met with strong opposition from interests concerned to maintain the *status quo*, and the proposals put forward were inadequate.

Another difficulty has been the problem of the small non-county boroughs.

50. When the next series of reviews takes place, it is essential that all county councils should tackle with determination the task of reviewing the areas and boundaries of their county districts and should recommend any changes necessary to secure administrative units with adequate population and resources. It might be helpful for some guidance to be given on the minimum population which is desirable in a county district. However, it would have to be recognised that local circumstances vary greatly, particularly in the more sparsely populated areas, and that consequently no standard could be rigidly applied.

Non-County Boroughs

51. One of the obstacles to the rational organisation of county districts has been the inability of county councils to deal with non-county boroughs in the same way as with other county districts. For example, a county council has the power to propose the transfer of a rural district to a non-county borough, but it may not propose the reverse. Therefore, where two such districts are amalgamated, the resultant unit must be a borough.

52. The Government agree with the associations' representatives that a county council should be free to recommend changes in the boundaries and status of any of its county districts, including non-county boroughs. Nevertheless, it must be recognised that these boroughs, by virtue of their Charters, history and traditions, are in a special position. The Government, therefore, consider that every effort should be made to preserve so far as possible their identity and dignities.

53. Where a non-county borough is amalgamated with another predominantly urban area, there is not normally any reason why the whole of the combined area should not have the status of a borough. But where the result of the amalgamation would be a predominantly rural area, the title to be accorded to the new unit and the retention of traditional dignities by any borough or boroughs included in it will need special consideration. Where it is decided not to accord the title, privileges and dignities of a borough to a predominantly rural area embracing an existing borough, provision should, wherever possible, be made for the identity and perhaps certain of the dignities of the borough to be preserved within the new unit.

54. In any case, no non-county borough should be deprived of its status without the specific consent of the Minister; and this should not be given until he has held an inquiry into any objections which the borough may wish to make.

2 THE LOCAL GOVERNMENT COMMISSION FOR ENGLAND

From *Ministry of Housing and Local Government, Annual Report, 1967–8*, by permission of H.M.S.O.

Reorganisation Under The Local Government Act 1958

Dissolution of the Local Government Commission for England When the proposal to appoint the Royal Commission was announced in February, 1966, the Minister suggested that it would be right to wind up the Local Government Commission. The Local Government (Termination of Reviews) Act 1967, accordingly dissolved the Local Government Commissions for England and Wales, the duties of which were deemed to have ceased on 10th February, 1966.

The Minister also said that where decisions had been announced before February, 1966, on proposals put forward by the Local Government Commission, these decisions would be implemented by orders. Proposals still awaiting decisions would be considered on their merits in the new situation. Decisions on all the outstanding recommendations of the Local Government Commission were taken in 1966 and 1967. In view of the appointment of the Royal Commission, further boundary changes were in the main restricted to land immediately required for housing purposes.

Tyneside The Local Government Commission had recommended in 1963 that the Tyneside Special Review Area should become a new continuous county comprising four most-purpose boroughs. Following a public local inquiry into objections to the Commission's proposals and consultations with the local authorities, the then Minister had announced his provisional decision not to accept the Commission's proposals and had put forward his counter-proposal for a single county borough for the Tyneside area. A second public inquiry had been held in 1966. Before reaching a conclusion, following the second inquiry, the Minister consulted the Royal Commission to ascertain whether the proposal for a single county borough was compatible with the broad thinking that the Commission were developing: they could not, however, express any views at that stage on how local government should ultimately be organised on Tyneside. In these circumstances the Minister announced in Parliament on 3rd May, 1967, his intention not to proceed with any measure of advance reorganisation there.

West Yorkshire In their report on the West Yorkshire Special Review Area the Local Government Commission recommended the retention of the main features of the existing pattern of authorities but with a substantial reduction in the total number of county boroughs and county districts in the area from 40 to 18. The county boroughs of Halifax, Bradford, Leeds and Huddersfield would have been extended under the Commission's proposals, a new county borough comprising Dewsbury and certain adjoining county districts would have been set up, and Wakefield would have been reduced to the status of a non-county borough. A series of local inquiries were held into objections to the Local Government Commission's proposals but, having consulted the Royal Commission (as in the case of Tyneside) the Minister decided not to proceed with reorganisation in West Yorkshire in advance of the Royal Commission's report.

New County Boroughs and County Borough Extensions During the two years under review the last fifteen orders resulting from the Local Government Commission's proposals completed their final stages.

Three of these orders resulted in the creation of new county boroughs: they had been made or were being prepared at the end of 1966 but were all approved by Parliament early in 1967. One amalgamated the former county borough of West Hartlepool with the borough of Hartlepool and part of the rural district of Stockton to form the new county borough of Hartlepool as from 1st April, 1967. Orders for the new county boroughs of Teesside and Torbay did not take effect until 1st April, 1968, to allow sufficient time for the new councils to become established. On

Teesside a single authority covering both sides of the river replaced the former county borough of Middlesbrough, the boroughs of Stockton-on-Tees, Redcar, Thornaby-on-Tees and parts of five other county districts. Most of the borough of Torquay and of the urban districts of Brixham and Paignton were united with small parts of adjacent rural districts to form the new county borough of Torbay.

Twelve other orders came into operation, extending the county boroughs of Bath, Darlington, Gloucester, Lincoln, Plymouth, Sheffield and Sunderland from 1st April, 1967, and of Derby, Grimsby, Kingston upon Hull, Norwich and York from 1st April, 1968.

County Reviews Section 28 of the Local Government Act, 1958, required county councils to carry out reviews of the county districts in their areas and to propose changes needed for the improvement of local government. However, this obligation was removed after the appointment of the Royal Commission by the Local Government (Termination of Reviews) Act 1967. Six counties — Shropshire, Cornwall, Worcestershire, Herefordshire, Bedfordshire and Warwickshire — had submitted their review proposals before this date. Shropshire had made their proposals long before the Royal Commission came into being and most of the review scheme had been implemented in the two Shropshire Orders of 1966. Of the other five counties, Warwickshire's review was rejected and for the rest, the Minister accepted only those changes which were generally agreed and urgently needed in advance of any wider reorganisation. Six further orders were made, all taking effect from 1st April, 1968.

Summary of changes resulting from the work of the Local Government Commission As a result of orders following from the various reports and proposals of the Local Government Commission for England a total of four administrative counties were abolished, and two new ones created (Cambridgeshire and Isle of Ely, and Huntingdon and Peterborough). Three county boroughs, thirteen boroughs, sixteen urban districts and three rural districts were abolished, and six new county boroughs (Solihull, Luton, Warley, Hartlepool, Teesside and Torbay) and two new urban districts (Aldridge-Brownhills and Leighton-Linslade) created. Twenty-four existing county boroughs were extended. These changes on balance increased by 1¼ million, the total population living in county boroughs in England.

Before they were dissolved the Commission completed their reviews and submitted final proposals covering six out of the nine General Review Areas which they had defined and three of the five Special Review Areas named in the Act of 1958. As the Minister decided not to proceed with any changes in the Tyneside or West Yorkshire Special Review Areas, changes were confined to six General Review Areas and to the West Midlands Special Review Area. The Commission submitted no final reports on the Merseyside or South East Lancashire Special Review Areas or on the North Western, Southern or South Eastern General Review Areas.

3 THE REDCLIFFE-MAUD MAJORITY REPORT

From *Royal Commission on Local Government in England, 1966–69* (Vol. I. *Report*, Cmnd. 4040, 1969; and *Short Version of the Report*, Cmnd. 4039, 1969); by permission of H.M.S.O. Hereafter referred to as *Redcliffe-Maud*. In this extract, the Commission analyses the defects of the existing system, states the general principles on which a new pattern of authorities should be based, sets out its recommendations, and describes the benefits likely to flow from these proposals.

The Present Pattern of Local Government

68. Leaving aside parish councils (and the Greater London authorities) the present operating units of local government in England are the councils of 79 county boroughs, 45 counties, 227 non-county boroughs, 449 urban districts, 410 rural districts – a total of just over 1,200. County boroughs and county councils are commonly referred to as first-tier authorities; they number together 124. The others, collectively known as county district councils, are the second-tier authorities; they number together 1,086 . . .

69. County borough councils are 'all purpose' authorities; that is, they are responsible for all local government functions. County councils are responsible only for some; notably for police (but most counties, as also most county boroughs, are now included in combined police authorities); fire, planning, roads and traffic (all roads, other than trunk, in rural districts, but only classified roads, other than 'claimed' roads, in boroughs and urban districts); education, health, welfare and children. Services for which they are not responsible include housing, water supply, sewerage and sewage disposal. Responsibility for some county services has to be shared with the county district councils (see next paragraph). In addition, of course, the district councils exercise a number of functions in their own right. Housing is probably the most important. Whether a particular authority carries responsibility depends, for a number of functions, on the size of its population . . .

70. The system by which county and district councils share responsibility for some functions is known as 'delegation', but a true delegation of power from one local authority to another is hardly possible, since both authorities remain responsible to their own electorates. There is a wide measure of agreement in local government that delegation is an unsatisfactory arrangement, though with good will it can be made to work.

71. All county district councils with a population of 60,000 or more can acquire delegated planning functions as of right. All borough and urban district councils of this size can similarly acquire delegated education, health and welfare functions. Other authorities can get these delegated functions if the appropriate Minister agrees. In addition, county councils can, if they so wish, delegate certain planning functions to any county district. In the education field there exists also provision

for the decentralisation of county administration to divisional executives (operated by 33 county councils). These executives are ad hoc bodies consisting mainly of members of the county and district councils for that division. For highways, the arrangements are that borough and urban district councils with a population of 20,000 or more can claim the power to maintain and improve classified roads as of right; and any district council can apply to the county council for the right to exercise delegated powers over county roads.

72. For other functions the position is even more complex. The councils of boroughs which had a population of 10,000 in 1881 can deal with diseases of animals; all boroughs and urban district councils with a population of 20,000 or more can enforce the Shops Act; borough and urban district councils between 20,000 and 40,000 can administer provisions regulating food and drugs if the Secretary of State for Social Services so directs, and at 40,000 they become responsible as of right; borough and urban district councils with a population of 40,000 can run libraries; at 60,000 they can administer the law on weights and measures. These are all elsewhere county services, and the total effect of all these arrangements is a sort of pock-marked administrative pattern.

73. The confusion grows when the sizes of authorities at different levels and performing different functions are considered. The populations of education authorities range from Canterbury with 32,790 to Lancashire with 2,428,040; and of housing authorities from Tintwistle rural district with 1,490 to Birmingham with 1,074,940. The area of the smallest planning authority, Bootle, is 3,330 acres and of the largest, Devon, 1,612,373 acres . . .

74. Forty-five non-county boroughs have populations between 50,000 and 100,000. So do 30 county boroughs and one county council. Twenty urban districts have populations of between 50,000 and 124,000, a band which also includes 43 county boroughs and three county councils. Thirty-three rural districts have populations of between 50,000 and 87,000. There are 24 county boroughs and one county council in this range.

75. Yet no non-county borough, urban district or rural district council, whatever the size of its population, carries more than a fraction of the responsibility that falls on a county borough council, or is entrusted directly by Parliament with the services that a county council must provide; and although 104 rural districts have populations of over 30,000, compared with 102 non-county boroughs and 63 urban districts, non-county borough and urban district councils have some responsibilities which no rural district county has.

. . . . . .

WHAT IS WRONG?

The division of town and country

85. Local government areas no longer correspond to the pattern of life and work in England. Population has long since over-run many of the old boundaries. But if this

were all, the Local Government Commission could have remedied it by creating new county boroughs, extending old ones and 'demoting' the smaller ones. (The Commission was instructed to regard 100,000 as the population qualifying for county borough status.) What it could not do was to recognise the interdependence of town and country. The failure to recognise this is the most fatal defect in the present structure.

86. Town and country have always been, and must be, interdependent. Even in 1888 there were some who thought that the split between county boroughs and counties was a mistake. Since then the enormous increase in personal mobility . . . has vastly increased the interdependence; and a local government structure which does not recognise this does not correspond with the realities of life. People from the countryside come into the towns for shopping, entertainment, higher education and many professional services; people who work in the towns increasingly live out in the country and commute; people who live in the towns increasingly go out to the country for recreation. Moreover, a great deal of the building needed now by the people living in overcrowded towns — and which will increasingly be needed as the population grows — will have to take place out in the present counties, in areas now rural or semi-rural.

The division between county boroughs and counties

87. The fragmentation of England into 79 county boroughs and 45 counties, each with its own independent authority concerned with its own interests, has made the proper planning of development and transportation impossible. It is obvious that town and country must be planned together, as the evidence given to us recognised. There being no provision for this under the present structure, central government has tried to fill the gap: by producing regional plans itself, by the appointment of regional economic planning councils, by persuading local authorities to work together on land-use and transportation surveys and on sub-regional plans, by taking power to establish passenger transport authorities. But none of these devices is satisfactory, since none puts responsibility squarely on local government or provides for continuous and comprehensive planning allied with power to implement the plans.

88. The division between county boroughs and counties meanwhile builds into the system a division of interest where, in fact, there is a common interest. The county councils are concerned, naturally, to defend their territory against the encroachment of the towns; the county borough councils, which must encroach, are concerned, equally naturally, to do it in the way easiest for themselves. Boundary ambitions and fears have dominated the work of local government for many years past. The needs of the population must be defined, and plans made to meet them, over the areas in which the needs have got to be satisfied; and the authorities which make the plans must be in a position to see that they are carried out . . . Further, there must be arrangements, rooted in local government, for planning the broad use of land over areas wider than those of the operating authorities, so that

needs which have to be met beyond their boundaries can be provided for. Nothing has been worse for local government than the fights between authorities over land.

Division of responsibility in the counties

89. Within the counties, the division of responsibility between county and district councils is a great weakness. The present district pattern, is, as we have shown, irrational. But even if that were cured by the creation of larger districts, the weakness due to the division of responsibilities would remain. One of the major difficulties in the present structure is that the county councils have no general development powers, and in particular no general house-building powers. This partly explains the negative attitude some of them have taken towards the needs of the municipalities; their powers are largely negative. The county councils which have tried to help the hard pressed towns have had enormous difficulties, since for many purposes they must work through the district councils. They can plan the use of land; they cannot see that their plans are implemented. They cannot do business with their powerful municipal neighbours on equal terms.

90. In the personal social service field the division of housing responsibility from the health, welfare and children's services is also a source of difficulty, as the Seebohm Committee showed. As one example, they pointed out that 'the counties through their welfare departments are responsible for homeless families but have no direct access to local authority housing . . . ' Any successful policy for the homeless therefore depends entirely upon good co-operation being established between a county and perhaps as many as twenty or thirty housing authorities in its area. With goodwill and effort it can be achieved but the hazards are considerable and not always surmounted.

91. We said, when describing the present pattern of local government, that the system by which some county district councils exercise some county council responsibilities results, in the counties, in a sort of pock-marked administrative pattern. This, of course, does not result only from the district council situation; it results too from the position of county boroughs as islands in the counties. The county councils must provide services over areas containing a series of holes. The county borough and county district councils for their part must stop short at boundaries which often have no meaning in practical terms. Local authorities do, in practice, work together in the provision of services, and a host of arrangements exist for mutual aid. But for those working in local government the pattern is often as frustrating as it is confusing to those whom local government serves. It was this situation in the north west which finally brought the Local Government Commission to recognise that they could not do a satisfactory job unless they could review both functions and areas over a much wider area than that of the two conurbations.

92. It is not only the physical manifestations of divided responsibility that are wrong under the present system in the counties. It is also the attitudes which the division necessarily engenders. No single authority is responsible for thinking about

the totality of related services and their adequacy for local needs; no single authority is responsible for considering the community as a whole. So county and district councils are, inevitably, providers of services rather than proper units of self-government.

Inadequate size of many local authorities

93. Perhaps the most frequently voiced criticism of the present structure is that many local authorities, whether county, county borough or county district councils, are too small in terms of area, population and resources, including highly qualified manpower and technical equipment. We have noted that the Local Government Commission was instructed to regard 100,000 population as qualifying for county borough status. That was, we understand, a figure painfully hammered out between the government and the associations of local authorities . . .

No examination, apparently, was at that time made of the size of population needed for efficient provision of the various services. So far as planning was concerned it was only in the conurbations that power was taken to establish wide-ranging authorities; and that did not extend to including much beyond the built-up areas. The discussions between central government and the local authority associations took place before it was realised what a sharp upward turn population growth was taking or what was going to happen to traffic. In fact neither central nor local government was then prepared for any radical changes in the structure of local government, outside the officially defined conurbations.

94. . . . We find that the minimum size for all the main services is, desirably, a population of some 250,000 . . . 9 out of the 45 counties, 65 out of the 79 county boroughs, and all the county districts, at present fall below it.

The relationship between local authorities and the public

95. The relationship between local authorities and the public is not satisfactory. The Committee on the Management of Local Government found that there is both ignorance of and indifference to local government on the part of the public; and indeed it is not uncommon to hear contempt expressed. This is partly, no doubt, the healthy attitude of any free society towards its governors, but it goes far beyond that and must be a cause of great concern to anyone who cares about the successful working of democracy in Britain. We think that the public's attitude to local government is largely due to the defects in the structure we have outlined.

96. Local government is, at present, apt to be irrelevant to people's problems, and often cannot solve them even though it has the responsibility for doing so. The irrelevance of local government was, essentially, the message of the Seebohm Committee: a family with related problems can nowhere get them seen and tackled as a whole. It can be very hard for the ordinary individual, especially in the counties, to understand which local authority does what. He will often find two 'town halls' next door to each other, one being the county borough, borough or urban district

office, the other the rural district office, and the county office may be somewhere else in the same town. There is no correspondence between this welter of authorities and the realities of people's lives, and too often a local authority which is concerned in a particular problem does not have the power to settle it.

97. Finding out where your problems can be settled is frequently difficult and sometimes impossible. In county boroughs the town hall, being the office of an all-purpose authority, will as a rule be organised to give advice — but you must go to the town hall. There are seldom, if ever, decentralised offices where the baffled citizen can either get an answer to his problems or at least be told where he can get it. In counties, where responsibilities are divided, the position is, obviously, very much more difficult . . .

. . . . . .

99. In short, what is needed is a clarification of the local government system. The system itself is hard enough for most people to understand, with county borough councils in some of the towns, county and county district councils elsewhere, and very little sense in the boundaries between the two. England needs a pattern of local authorities with clear responsibilities, big enough in area, population and resources to provide first class services, able to give decisions (subject to whatever control by central government is necessary), and determined to ensure that all their citizens have a reasonably convenient point of access where they can get answers to their questions and advice on how to get whatever help they need. We believe that the public would then become both more aware of local government and more interested in it . . .

The relationship between central and local government

100. Our general conception of the right relationship between central and local government will have emerged from what we said at the beginning of this chapter about the purpose and scope of local government. We do not believe that the right relationship exists today — or could exist while there are so many local authorities of such diverse sizes, and local government is unable because of the defects in its structure, to play its proper role. What is wrong in the relationship at present is partly that central government tries itself to do some of the things that belong properly to local government, and partly that local authorities are not given enough freedom to go their own way. In addition they are subject to a number of minor controls and requirements which detract from their ability to manage their own affairs and make their own decisions — controls and requirements which cannot, we believe, be justified as necessary in the national interest and some of which are simply relics of past history.

101. We recognise the responsibility of central government, to settle the policies to be followed in the provision of services of national importance, and to ask for minimum standards where some equality of standards is possible and there is a strong national interest in the quality of the service. We recognise also that central government must broadly determine the resources which can be devoted to local

government services and the priorities within them. It is reasonable too that central government should operate a check on the quality and cost of legal projects; and where there is a dispute between two authorities, or between an authority and private individuals, central government must act as arbiter — though the more such disputes can be settled locally the better for all concerned.

102. Accepting all this, however, local authorities must — and can — be given a real measure of freedom in reaching their own decisions and in settling, within broad national policies, their own priorities . . . They must be allowed to develop their own methods, to use their own initiative, to experiment. Central government should not intervene in what a local authority chooses to do unless some clear national interest is involved or there are local objections which must be heard . . . In general, control by central government should be limited to key points, and the better equipped and better staffed local authorities become, the fewer the key-points will be . . .

103. As soon as local government is reorganised, departments concerned with local government should be required to review, in consultation with representatives of the new local authorities, every point at which they control or regulate the actions of authorities. All rules or regulations, all requirements for consent or approval, which have no demonstrable value under the new local government system should be repealed.

104. Generally, local government suffers from much out of date law. Consolidation does take place, but amendment is more rare. The Ministry of Housing and Local Government is supposed, every 10 years or so, to give general effect to provisions in local Acts which have become common form, and which would be useful to all local authorities; but again it seems too difficult to find the Parliamentary time. We recognise that this is a real difficulty. But we hope that once local government is reorganised efforts will be made, by central and local government working together, to bring and to keep local government law up to date.

105. Another unsatisfactory feature of the relationship between central and local government is that the two parties sometimes seem to be at arm's length. The relationship has become much less formal in the last 30 years but sometimes decisions are handed down — or proposals are sent up — without any previous discussion or effort to reach agreement, or at least understanding. The normal practice should, it seems to us, be one of continuous consultation . . .

106. One serious weakness in the general relationship is that local government is not, at present, collectively effective. The associations of local authorities number five (not including the Greater London Council, which belongs to none of them, or the London Boroughs Association). The four main associations do take common action on many local government matters; but representing different types of authority and different kinds of area — counties, towns, urban or rural district — they seldom are able to present a united front in dealings with central government or to take a collective initiative in national policies. Local authorities ought to be able, on occasion, to present a common local government view and to take the lead in discussions with central government both nationally and in particular parts of the

country affected by common problems. As independent political bodies, representing local interests, they cannot always be agreed on the policies they want. But there are many matters on which they have a common interest and should be able to present it, and to do so forcefully. We said above that if local government, however reorganised, is to achieve its full potential, it will need a deliberate determination on the part of Ministers and Parliament, supported by the press, radio and television, both to make local authorities responsible for any services which ought to be provided locally and to allow local authorities to settle local issues for themselves. It will need an equally deliberate determination on the part of local government collectively to see that this is done.

107. What local government needs is a single, powerful association to look after its interests and to speak for it. Reorganisation will provide the opportunity . . . It would, we believe, be a disaster if, when the new system is established, separate associations of main local authorities were formed. We are convinced that if local government takes that road it will not achieve the right relationship with central government nor the independence and standing in the country that it ought to have.

108. Equally, a single department must be responsible, within central government, for looking after the well-being of local government and for seeing that the relationship between central and local government is right. The Ministry of Housing and Local Government already has a general responsibility for the well-being of local government. It has taken the lead in seeking to reorganise local government. If the government decides to go ahead with reorganisation it must take the lead in carrying the reorganisation into effect. Thereafter it must take the lead, with clear government support, in seeing that the new authorities have the conditions in which they can realise the full purpose of local government.

. . . . . .

OUR GENERAL PRINCIPLES

242. . . . we now consider the general principles on which a new pattern of authorities should be based.

Interdependence of Town and Country

243. The division between town and country in the present system has been very bad for local government. With the passage of time, it bears less and less relation to the changing distribution of population or to modern patterns of living, and it prevents problems from being considered over the areas necessary for their solution. The growing interdependence of town and country was widely recognised in the evidence. Our own researches confirmed the community of social and economic interest joining towns of various sizes with the countryside in a mutually advantageous relationship which the present pattern of local authorities fails to reflect. This community of interest must find expression in the local government of each part of the country. Each local authority should be responsible for a continuous

area that makes, so far as practicable, a coherent social and economic whole, matching the way of life of a mobile society and giving the authority the space it needs to assess and tackle its problems. Such areas are essential for effective planning and transportation policies. They will also suit other operational purposes. Whether an authority is resolving people's housing problems, settling the pattern of schools and colleges, or providing personal services for families and individuals in need of care or help, it is more likely to meet people's requirements and make most effective use of resources if its responsibility extends over the whole area that includes people's homes, the offices and factories they work in, the schools where their children are taught, the shops they buy their goods from and the places they go to for entertainment and recreation.

GROUPING OF SERVICES

The environmental services

244. In each area of the country, one authority should be responsible for land-use planning and the whole field of transportation. Decisions on the use of land shape the environment in which people live. They also generate the traffic which is increasingly part of that environment and sometimes dominates it. Only an authority responsible for both planning and transportation can tackle the tremendous problems created by the rapid growth in personal mobility. The places where people live, work, shop and enjoy themselves must be planned together with the roads, public transport and traffic management systems that enable them to move from one place to another.

245. Housing is of vital importance for planning and transportation. Deciding where new houses are to be built determines the pattern of settlement; and housing priorities, in terms of which people are in the greatest need and which areas should be tackled first, are central to planning authorities' policies for development, redevelopment and conservation. Furthermore the traffic problems that face authorities, and the transportation systems that should be evolved to deal with them, largely depend on the journeys that people make from their homes to their work during the week, and from their homes to shops and places of entertainment and recreation at the week-end. Housing is therefore a major instrument of planning policy and an authority responsible for planning and transportation must at least be in a position to assess housing needs and see that the necessary houses are built in the right places.

246. The argument for combining planning, transportation and development functions in one authority goes wider than housing and covers all forms of major capital expenditure by local government. It applies, for example, to water supply and sewerage. The rest of new development (including industrial development) depends on the provision of these services and they must be planned together with the pattern of settlement. Again, the timing and siting of new schools, clinics and all the other buildings needed for local government services will be better integrated

with an authority's general policy for its area if it can handle all forms of local government investment as part of a single programme.

247. But planning is not concerned only with land-use choices or questions of development. It is an instrument for satisfying people's personal and social needs. Because of their interaction on each other, the social environment and the physical environment in which people lead their lives must be planned together. The Seebohm Committee stressed that the social services must be involved in the preparation and execution of schemes that change people's physical environment, whether these schemes take the form of entirely new development, whose effect will be that people have to move into strange surroundings, or the radical alteration of old-established areas with which they have long been familiar. The Cullingworth Committee on the needs of new communities emphasised that social and physical planning should be parts of one process. It was particularly critical of the view 'that "the social" is a separate sphere which can be considered independently of physical planning and development'; and added that 'social planning must be an integral part of the whole planning and development process'. The Plowden and Newsom reports showed the relationship between policies and priorities in education and policies for dealing with the general environment. We endorse all these views on the interconnection between planning and the personal services. It is most desirable that these two major aspects of local government work should be more and more closely related to each other in future.

The personal services

248. It is in any case essential that the personal services provided by local authorities should be handled as a whole. The report of the Seebohm Committee has shown in the most authoritative way how close the relationships are between education, the personal social services and housing. We agree wholeheartedly with the committee's conclusion that one authority should administer them all . . .

249. One authority is already responsible, both in county boroughs and in counties, for education and the care of children, together with all the other personal social services. The Seebohm Committee drew attention to the difficulties that arise in inner London, where the Inner London Education Authority is responsible for education but the London boroughs are responsible for the personal social services. Leaving aside the special circumstances of inner London, which are not within our terms of reference, we endorse the committee's view that, in the rest of the country, it would be wrong for any new system of local government to divide responsibility for education and the personal social services between different authorities.

250. We have already explained how closely related housing is to planning and transportation. But its ties with the personal social services are equally strong. At present, however, only in county boroughs is housing the responsibility of the same authority as the personal social services. It is a major defect of the present system that, in the counties, housing and the personal social services are administered by

the district councils and the county council respectively. To discharge effectively its responsibility for the well-being of its citizens, an authority must be able to draw up a comprehensive social policy and have the means at its disposal to put that policy into effect. Housing is an essential part of social policy, since the home is the basis of family life. Much of the work of the personal social services stems directly from the conditions in which people live and depends for its success on housing policies designed to meet the most urgent social needs. The people and families who are the most likely to have severe housing problems also make the greatest demands on the personal social services — the young, the old, the poor, the fatherless, the handicapped, families with a large number of children and those who for one reason or another find the ordinary business of life too much for them. In the worst situation of all are the homeless. An authority responsible for the personal social services but not for housing lacks an essential means of dealing with the difficulties of those families and individuals who need its help; and a housing authority which does not administer the personal social services will not be aware at first hand of the social needs that should receive priority in its management policies and building programmes. For the links between housing and the personal social services do not lie only in house management. The heart of the house-building programme for local authorities is to provide the right number of houses and flats, of the right type, in the right places, for the people most in need of them. To be in a position to do this, an authority must be able to take a wide view of its housing responsibilities as part of a coherent social programme.

251. But we have already said that deciding where to build new houses, and whom to build them for, is a crucial element in planning policy. Here therefore is further evidence that the major groups of local government services are intimately related to each other and that services are likely to be best provided, both individually and collectively, if the organisation of local government reflects this fact.

The strength of the all-purpose authority

252. There is great strength in the all-purpose authority; and this has been shown in the county borough councils. Not all of them have exploited their potential strength to the full, partly because their areas have been inadequate, partly because their organisation has been fragmented. But where a county borough council under strong leadership has co-ordinated its services and set out to achieve objectives through the use of all its powers, it has been the most effective local government unit we have known.

253. A single authority has the great advantage that, through allocation of priorities and co-ordinated use of resources, it can relate its programmes for all services to coherent objectives for the future progress of its area considered as a whole. Being responsible for the total span of local government activity, it can see the full extent of the relationships between different services, what developments in each are necessary to meet people's needs and what gaps between services ought to

be filled. It is the local government of its area. There is no doubt where responsibility lies, no confusion over which authority does what. This is local government in its simplest, most understandable and potentially most efficient form.

254. We conclude that in an area where

(i)   geographic, social and economic circumstances allow,

(ii)   the different services can all operate on a scale appropriate to their functional requirements, and

(iii) the conditions necessary for effective local democracy are satisfied,

there are decisive advantages in combining the planning, transportation and development group of functions with the education, personal social services and housing group under a single authority.

Division of services where two tiers needed

255. We were clear, however, that concentrating the planning, transportation and development group of services in the same authority as the education, personal social services and housing group would not necessarily be the right solution everywhere. Conditions throughout England are too diverse for the same pattern of local government to be applied throughout the country. In those parts where the first ('environmental') group of services require authorities too large to be appropriate for the second ('personal') group, services should be divided between two tiers of authority and related services kept together. We recognise that this would be particularly likely to be the case where towns have spread or coalesced into huge urban masses and where wide areas with very large populations and extremely complex problems have to be planned as a whole.

MINIMUM SIZE OF AUTHORITY

256. To provide services effectively, an authority must serve a large enough population to employ the wide variety of qualified staff and the financial and material resources necessary . . .

257. We came to the conclusion that there is no such thing as a single 'right' size for any local government service — but that the area of an authority responsible for education, housing and the personal services should contain at least a population of around 250,000. We did not regard this as a rigid minimum to be applied regardless of local circumstances. But it is essential if full value is to be obtained from these services that they should be administered together by the one authority; and only an authority serving a population of some 250,000 or more will have at its disposal the range and calibre of staff, and the technical and financial resources, necessary for effective provision of the whole group.

258. Developments in education have made many authorities now responsible for the service too small. Out of 124 present education authorities, 45 are county councils and 79 are county boroughs (situated within geographical counties): 32 have a population of under 100,000; 35 are between 100,000 and 200,000; and a

further 7 have populations between 200,000 and 250,000, making a total of 74 with populations below a quarter of a million. For education authorities to be responsible in future for unbroken areas, each with a minimum population of around 250,000, should result in a great strengthening of the service . . .

259. A minimum population of around 250,000 also suits the personal services. It matches the Seebohm Committee's recommendation that an authority responsible for the personal social services should organise them in a number of decentralised area units, each serving a population of 50,000 to 100,000. We quoted in chapter IV the Ministry of Health's view that local health and welfare require a population of at least around 200,000 and the Home Office's view that child care requires a minimum of 250,000.

260. Some witnesses told us that the personal services should be administered by small authorities whose elected members are in close contact with the people for whose needs they cater. But the case for a wide and co-ordinated range of professional expertise is as strong in these services as in any other. We were unable to accept the view of the R.D.C.A. that a population of 60,000 would be large enough. Two conditions must be satisfied − the authorities providing the personal services must have adequate professional and other resources, and they must be in touch with the people who need their help. We endorse the Seebohm Committee's conclusion that a substantial authority operating through a number of decentralised units is the best method of achieving these objectives. A population of 60,000 or even 80,000 or 90,000, would be appropriate for a single decentralised unit, but not for a social service authority. So small a population would also make it impossible for education to be administered by the same authority as the personal services.

261. Housing is related both to the social services and to planning. A housing authority must be responsible for a sufficiently large population and a sufficiently wide area to be able to decide, in accordance with comprehensive social and planning policies, which housing needs have the highest priority and where the houses to meet these needs should be built. Authorities must also be large enough to build on a scale that will enable them to get rid of bad housing conditions within an acceptable time, undertake major development in the interests of their areas and take full advantage of modern building methods.

262. House-management must be in the hands of authorities which are both responsible for the social services and able to formulate rental and letting policies over wide areas on the basis of a coherent set of social and financial principles. For economic reasons too, there must be a single policy for the selection of tenants within any area that is largely self-contained for economic and social purposes. People must not be hindered from changing their jobs because of unnecessary difficulties in moving their homes.

264. We conclude that, where possible, housing should be administered over the same area as planning and for the same population as the personal services. The minimum population of 250,000 necessary for the social services should enable authorities to employ the resources needed to build and manage houses efficiently

on the scale required. In any part of the country where the best solution is to have two tiers of authority, with one administering the planning group of functions and the other administering the personal services group, both tiers should have housing powers.

265. For planning, it is a crucial consideration that authorities with acute housing problems or growing populations or both, must have areas big enough to meet more of their land needs. They need not be able to solve all their problems within their own boundaries. But they must have room for manoeuvre. Their areas must also match social and economic realities and should fit as closely as practicable the areas where people live, move, work, shop and find their recreation. No figure of population can be used as a yardstick for determining the size of a planning and transportation area. Density and distribution of population are more important than total numbers. But an area which needs planning as a whole will always contain a substantial population and sometimes a very large one. Authorities must in any event have the necessary range of experts and equipment and be able to carry out major development. An authority with a population much less than 250,000 is very unlikely to possess the resources needed.

MAXIMUM SIZE OF AUTHORITY

266. Should there be any maximum limit to the size of an authority? Every authority's area must satisfy the criterion of coherence. But some areas with very large populations would do this. In such cases, three main issues arise:
  (i)   though the areas in question may be necessary for planning and related functions, are they too big for the other services?
  (ii)   if units of this size were responsible for all services, would they suffer from diseconomies of scale?
  (iii) could they fulfil the democratic purposes which local government must serve?

267. . . . . It was implicit in the Ministry of Housing and Local Government's proposal for 30 to 40 city regions that several authorities would have populations of over a million, some well over; and it was the Ministry's view that such authorities would be suitable for most and perhaps all local government services. There was no strong body of opinion to suggest that for education and the personal services authorities of up to 1,000,000 would be too large. The Association of Education Committees thought that only in exceptional circumstances should an education authority be created with a population over 1,500,000; and the Ministry of Health hazarded a guess that where a population of 1,000,000 was spread over a wide area, difficulties might occur in the administration of the health and welfare services. Neither the Department of Education and Science nor the Home Office, however, was aware of any upper limit to the desirable size of an authority for the education or children's service. Their experience with the Inner London Education Authority and the old London County Council, which used to be responsible for

child care, did not suggest that 3,000,000 was too large for either service. On the whole, the largest present authorities have a good record in both services.

268. As for housing, the Ministry of Housing and Local Government did not consider that city regions, with populations ranging in our estimate from 300,000 to 3,000,000 would be too big; and the Institute of Housing Management suggested that housing authorities should have a population of between 1,000,000 and 3,000,000 or even more.

269. Our own conclusion is that there is no single service in which administration by a very large authority would have decisive disadvantages. Future developments in most services seem almost certain to favour much bigger operational units than most of the existing ones.

. . . . . .

271. There is no figure which clearly represents the maximum size of population, either for individual services or for all services together, but we concluded that, for organisational and managerial reasons, authorities responsible for running all local government services should not have populations of much more than 1,000,000. We believe that authorities with populations in the broad range of some 250,000 to around 1,000,000 would be the best equipped to run local government as a coherent whole, enjoying the advantages of size, unified control, co-ordinated use of resources and harmonised development of the main services.

272. Democratic considerations also point to an upper limit on the size of authorities running all main services. We do not believe that democratic control of services calls necessarily for a small functional unit. It is a basic requirement of effective local democracy that authorities should be in charge of areas within which they can provide efficient services. They must be able to assess alternative solutions to major problems, decide the best course of action and carry it out; and their areas must contain populations large enough for effective use of resources. These conditions can be met only by units larger than most present authorities. If, as we have said, a minimum population of around 250,000 is necessary for the efficient administration of services, it seems to us an inescapable corollary that local democracy will be ineffective unless organised in units of at least this size.

273. When the size of an authority goes beyond a certain point, however, the more difficult becomes the problem of reconciling the management of increasingly complicated services by able and powerful officials with democratic control by the elected representatives. For democratic control to be a reality, the size of unit must be such that the elected representatives can comprehend the problems of the area, determining priorities and taking decisions on policy in full understanding of the issues at stake.

274. It is also essential that they should maintain contact with their constituents. We agree with the Committee on the Management of Local Government that councils should not be too big if they are to manage their business with efficiency and establish sound relations between council-members and their officers (the committee suggested that 75 members should be the maximum). But if the size of

councils must for this reason be limited, then the larger the authority's area, the greater will be the number of citizens each councillor represents and the more serious will be the risk that he will lose touch with their problems, needs and wishes.

275. Moreover, the bigger the unit, the more doubtful it becomes whether the individual citizen can have a real sense of belonging to it. People should be able to feel that they are included in a particular unit for purposes of government because they share a common interest with the other inhabitants in the efficient administration of the public services provided. But when an authority is very large there is less chance that they will be willing to regard it as the only authority that ought to provide all their local government services. The distance between the people and their authority, therefore, must not be too great. This is particularly important for the personal service.

276. There can be no firm rule about the maximum size of an authority. But we concluded that the range of population, from about 250,000 to not much above 1,000,000 which we considered most suitable on functional and organisational grounds for authorities administering all local government services, was also appropriate on democratic grounds. Within this range the size of each particular unit should be determined by reference to all the local circumstances — the social, economic and geographic facts, the areas most appropriate for organising services, the accessibility of a suitable headquarters, the existing pattern of local government and other relevant considerations.

ONE TIER OR TWO: THE BASIS OF CHOICE

277. We thus reached the conclusion, for the reasons set out in this chapter, that wherever we could find coherent areas which made good units for planning and transportation and also contained a population of about 250,000 to about 1,000,000 we would combine responsibility for all services in a single authority for each area. We call such areas unitary and the authorities responsible for them unitary authorities.

278. Where, however, planning problems have to be tackled as a whole over an extensive area containing a very large population, as is chiefly to be expected in a great urban concentration with its surrounding territory, to make a single authority responsible for all local government services would put too heavy a load of work on it. The authority would run into difficult managerial problems; democratic control would be hard to achieve; and there would be a serious risk that people would feel remote from their local government. We therefore concluded that where an area

   (i)   has a population of substantially more than a million

   (ii)   must be planned as a whole, and

   (iii) can be divided into a number of units in the broad population range from 250,000 to 1,000,000 appropriate for education, the personal social services and housing

the right solution would be to have two operational tiers. Other services would be divided between the two according to which tier provides the more appropriate scale of operation.

RESPECT FOR PRESENT BOUNDARIES

279. Our conclusions mean the end of all present authorities responsible for administering local government services. County, county borough, non-county borough, urban and rural district councils will cease to exist. There will be no place in the new system for authorities dividing areas and functions between them as these authorities do now. We wish, however, to maintain wherever possible the momentum of the present local government system. It is a going concern on a large scale, supported by long tradition and many loyalties. We have therefore preferred, where we could, to form new units out of existing local government areas rather than draw completely new boundaries. In many instances, even where there are some social, economic and geographical arguments in favour of a new line, we have not thought them strong enough to justify discarding an existing boundary to which people are accustomed and within which there is a functioning organisation for the provision of services.

280. We would certainly not hold to a boundary dividing interdependent areas that ought to be administered as one coherent unit. But we decided that, generally, we would propose boundaries for the new units differing from those of present authorities only where the advantage appeared unquestionable.

281. Two other levels of local government will be necessary in the new structure in addition to the operational level. One is the level of the local community and the other is the province.

THE NEED FOR LOCAL COUNCILS

282. We always recognise that units of the size appropriate for the operation of services must be under-pinned and complemented by other representative bodies to express the interests and sense of identity of the more local communities. There must be a level of local government which fosters the pride and interest of local communities, or a vital element will be missing from the democratic pattern.

THE NEED FOR PROVINCIAL COUNCILS

283. We found persuasive the arguments in the evidence that favoured a provincial planning body. Our own investigations convinced us that some of the problems now facing local government already run wider than the limits of any unit appropriate for the operation of services. As population, mobility and the involvement of local government in economic questions increase, there will be growing need for a representative body capable of devising a strategy for the future development of a very large area. Provincial councils are required which can settle the broad econ-

omic, land use and investment framework for the planning and development policies of operational authorities. They should be rooted in local government and should work in closest touch with central government. They would replace the present regional economic planning councils . . .

THE THREE-LEVEL STRUCTURE

284. The structure of local government would thus consist of:
  (i)   an operational level for local government services (two-tier in some areas);
  (ii) a more local one to represent communities; and
  (iii) a provincial level to set the strategic framework for the operational authorities.

. . . . . .

NEED FOR LOCAL COUNCILS IN UNITARY AREAS

368. Responsibility for all local government services must lie with authorities commanding substantial resources, representing large populations and administering areas, in some cases wide-ranging, which combine town and country. Within each of these areas there are numerous distinctive communities: towns and villages of every size, all different from each other and many with strongly marked individual characteristics. All these communities have their special interests, in which their inhabitants feel deeply involved, and they must have their own local organs of representative government, especially in the areas where we propose a unitary form of government. They must have the means of expressing their own wishes and opinions, and of commenting on the policies and proposals of the main authorities; they must also have the opportunity of doing for themselves the many things that need communal action but can best be done on a scale smaller and more local than that of the unitary authority. The more varied the character of the unitary areas, and the further their centre from the periphery, the more important will it be to develop, within the new, broadly-based local government organisation, lively and effective institutions for local self-expression.

369. At present all these distinctive communities, even the smallest, have or can have their own organ of representative government: in the rural areas the parish councils and above them the rural district councils; elsewhere the urban district, borough and county borough councils. If all borough, urban district and rural district councils are to disappear, their areas being merged in bigger units, new representative bodies must take their place. We call these new bodies (and what are now called parish councils) local councils.

370. We do not think that there will be the same need for local councils in the metropolitan areas — where there will be metropolitan district councils as well as metropolitan authorities. In what follows we are referring to local councils in unitary areas . . .

. . . . . .

371. Our conclusion that local councils must be part of the new system is unanimous. We do not see them as having statutory responsibility for any local government service; but we do see them as contributing a vital element to democratic local government. Their key function should be to focus opinion about anything that affects the well-being of each community, and to bring it to bear on the responsible authorities; but in addition they should have a number of powers . . . to be exercised at discretion. It is clear that the bigger the main local authorities, the more an effective system of democracy will require local representative institutions capable both of rallying and giving expression to local opinion and of doing a number of things for themselves. We are fortified in our conviction about the need for such institutions by much of the evidence we received.

OUR MAIN CONCLUSIONS
[from Cmnd. 4039, 1969, Short Version of Report]

England (outside London which was not within our terms of reference) should be divided into 61 new local government areas, each covering town and country . . . In 58 of them a single authority should be responsible for all services. In the 3 very large and, for some purposes, indivisible metropolitan areas around Birmingham, Liverpool and Manchester, responsibility for services should be divided in each case between a metropolitan authority whose key function would be planning, transportation and major development, and a number of metropolitan district authorities whose key functions would be education, the personal social services, health and housing.

These 61 new local government areas should be grouped, together with Greater London, in 8 provinces, each with its own provincial capital. Provincial councils should be elected by the authorities for the unitary and metropolitan areas (including, in the south-east, the Greater London authorities), but should also include co-opted members. The key function of these councils would be to settle the provincial strategy and planning framework within which the main authorities must operate. They would replace the present regional economic planning councils and collaborate with central government in the economic and social development of each province. They will therefore play an essential part in the future adaptation of local government to the changes in ways of life and movement that time and technical progress will bring.

Within the 58 unitary areas, and wherever they are wanted within the 3 metropolitan areas, local councils should be elected to represent and communicate the wishes of cities, towns and villages in all matters of special concern to the inhabitants. These local councils would, at the outset, succeed the existing county borough, borough, urban district and parish councils, though provision should be made for later adjustment of their areas. The only *duty* of the local council would be to represent local opinion, but it would have the *right* to be consulted on matters of special interest to its inhabitants and it would have the *power* to do for the local community a number of things best done locally. It would also have the opportunity to play a part in some of the main local government services, on a scale appropriate to its resources and subject to the agreement of the main authority.

Thus in three metropolitan areas there will be two levels of authority, as in London. But the rest of the country will be covered by the unitary authorities. Their special feature is that they marry the planning and development of the area — where people will live and work and shop, how they will get about — with the education, welfare and personal services, so that *all* the main local government needs of *all* the people in the area can be considered from a single centre and provided for according to a single strategy.

THE MAIN GAINS

569. In this final chapter we summarise the main gains which seem likely to result from the establishment of the new local government system that we propose for England. This coherent and stable structure will itself constitute a major gain for English local government, ending the uncertainty which has hung over local governors since the last war with increasingly bad effect in recent years. But the full benefit will not come automatically from structural change. How far its potential value will be realised must depend on the use made of it in practice by citizens, the councillors whom they elect and the professional staff that councillors appoint. The value we shall get from time and money spent on local government will ultimately depend on the calibre and humanity of councillors and their staff, on the way they organise their work, and on the degree of mutual understanding they achieve between themselves and the communities they serve. The virtue of the new system is that it gives promise of the following main gains:

greatly improved service to the public, both in providing a better environment and in taking care of the needs of individual people and families;

more effective use of scarce resources of money and skilled manpower;

increased ability of local governors to meet the challenges of technological and social change;

more likelihood that people will recognise the relevance of local government to their own and to their neighbours' well being;

the revitalising of local self-government throughout the country, so that in England as a whole we have more sense of taking an active part in our own government.

BETTER SERVICES

570. Local government will be a more effective instrument for providing citizens with the particular services they need, for example:

(i)   In each part of England it will be possible for the various problems of the environment to be grappled with as a whole, within the appropriate local and provincial context of geography and common life. Decisions about places where people can live, work, shop and enjoy themselves, will therefore be

more likely to match real needs. As population and the number of cars constantly increase, questions of land use – for housing and schools, industry,
commerce and transportation – will continue growing in complexity; but in
the new and larger local government areas it will be possible to work out, and
apply, coherent plans for meeting the challenge of present and future local
problems. Among the chief of these are finding room for the new houses,
clearing slums, renewing urban centres, fostering new employment opportunities, deciding what additional roads are needed and what should be the
balance between public and private transport, reconciling development
demands with use of the countryside for agriculture and recreation.

(ii)   Education (outside universities) which we believe requires co-ordinated local
administration, will be in the undivided charge of one authority in each part
of England. These 78 authorities (58 unitary and 20 metropolitan districts)
will take the place of the present 124 education authorities, 31 excepted
districts and 125 divisional executives. Governors and heads will have more
scope to develop the individual character of their schools and colleges.

(iii)   Everywhere a single authority will be responsible, not only for all the various
personal social services (which the Seebohm Committee was convinced should
be in the hands of one department) but also for the intimately related services of education, health and housing. This will open the way for the development of a comprehensive family service.

(iv)   For house-building and house-management, 81 authorities will take the place
of more than a thousand. In the 58 unitary areas one authority will be responsible not only for all aspects of housing and the other social services but for
planning too. In each of the three metropolitan areas a single authority will
assess housing needs, decide how they can be met and secure a common housing policy; while strong district councils will be responsible for most of the
building and all of the management. Throughout England therefore, housing
output is likely to improve, thanks to the strength of the new housing authorities and their ability to place larger and longer orders, while those in need
of houses will have fewer authorities to deal with and tenants will have the
chance of moving house over wider, more comprehensive areas.

BETTER USE OF RESOURCES

571. (i) Structural change cannot of itself increase the supply of scarce and highly
qualified manpower, but it does make possible its better and more economic use,
thanks to the concentration of activities in fewer and larger councils.

(ii) The full use of new and developing management techniques, computers and
other equipment will be brought within the reach of all authorities.

(iii) Thus the public will be able to obtain increasing value for whatever money
they decide to spend on the services provided through local government. This will
make it easier to meet growing demands for services without spending proportionately more of the national wealth.

RESPONSIVENESS TO CHANGE

572. The new authorities have been designed to deal flexibly with the local problems of a dynamic society in which the present high rate of social and economic change may well grow faster still. This flexibility should ensure many years of stability for the new local government structure. But the new structure includes machinery for adjustment, either by local government itself or, where necessary, by central government, when and where this is called for by significant economic or social change.

4 SENIOR'S MINORITY REPORT

From *Redcliffe-Maud, Vol. II: Memorandum of Dissent by Mr. D. Senior* (Cmnd 4040 — I. 1969); by permission of H.M.S.O. This extract is Senior's own summary of his proposals for a two-tier system of 35 City Regions and 148 district authorities.

I cannot agree with my colleagues that a pattern of all-purpose local authorities conforming to a predetermined range of population size would enable essential functions to be effectively discharged or a viable system of local democracy to be sustained over the greater part of England. Especially in the more populous regions, the units they recommend would fragment planning and development problems; in most cases they would also be too remote for the democratic and responsive administration of the personal services and too unwieldy for the efficient co-ordination of the whole range of local government functions.

These unacceptable defects result, in my view, from a theoretical approach to the problem of local government organisation in which the requirements in population terms of administrative efficiency and democratic control are analysed in abstraction from the facts of social geography. My colleagues take account of these facts only as considerations to be weighed against others (including the present pattern of local government boundaries) in applying their population limits to the definition of all-purpose units in particular areas.

The right approach, in my view, is to analyse functional and democratic needs in relation to the patterns of settlement, activity and community structure in which a motor-age society organises itself. This analysis points to a general need to define units in terms of the potential service and commuting hinterlands of major centres for the functions associated with planning, transportation and development, and in terms of accessibility and population size for the personal services. In a few parts of the country the units so defined coincide and all criteria can be satisfied by a single all-purpose authority. Elsewhere a two-level structure is indicated as the only means of reconciling functional effectiveness with local democracy.

Accordingly I recommend a predominantly two-level system of service-running local government, comprising 35 directly elected regional authorities, responsible for the planning/transportation/development complex of functions (including water supply, sewerage, refuse disposal and other technical services), for capital investment programming and for police, fire and education; and 148 directly elected district authorities responsible for the health service, the personal social services, housing management, consumer protection and all other functions involving personal contact with the citizen. In four areas the same authority would exercise both regional and district responsibilities.

Where there would be two levels of local government, I recommend that they should be articulated in two ways: first, by the delegation of responsibility for the more personal and locally variable aspects of a regional authority's functions to district officers, dealing with areas coterminous with those of the region's component district units and advised by committees of the district authorities; and secondly, by the concentration of responsibility for the wider aspects of district functions in a joint organisation of the districts within each region. I indicate possible variations in the definition of both regional and district units in the less populous parts of the country, and hence in their total numbers, and recommend special arrangements for the London Metropolitan Region and for the northern tip of Northumberland.

I propose that these two levels of administrative local government should be complemented for other purposes, by directly elected common councils at 'grassroots' level, representing existing parishes and towns or parts of towns small enough to have a real feeling of community, and by five appointed provincial councils with members predominantly nominated by the regional authorities within their areas.

The primary function of a common council would be to act as a sounding board for community opinion on all matters affecting the local environment. It would also share with district and regional councils a greater *power*, superseding all existing permissive powers of local government, to provide as many social and recreational facilities, amenities and conveniences for the benefit of its area's inhabitants as they were prepared to pay for through a local precept on the rates. But it would play no part in the discharge of the statutory *duties* of local government.

The provincial councils would be responsible for long-term strategic planning and for bringing the needs and aspirations of each province as a whole to bear on the discharge by central government of its responsibility for the healthy growth of the national economy. They would have adequate staff, nationally financed, but no executive powers of their own. They would need as their executive counterparts province-based arms of central government responsible for the co-ordination at this level of departmental and regional investment programmes.

If central government prefers to transfer to local government the decision-making powers needing to be exercised at this level, I suggest as a second-best alternative the creation of 12–15 directly elected 'sub-provincial' authorities, which would take the place both of the regional and provincial councils I have recommended and of the province-based arms of central government I have postulated.

No system of local democracy can be viable unless its executive authorities are financially accountable to their own electorates. I therefore recommend that the district councils should be financed by rate revenue and that the possibility of handing over to regional authorities all forms of taxation on the use of private motor vehicles should be urgently examined. If that is not feasible, the whole of the education service should be taken out of local government.

5 THE MINISTRY VIEW

From *Written Evidence of the Ministry of Housing and Local Government* (to Redcliffe-Maud, 1967); by permission of H.M.S.O.

V. STRUCTURAL CHANGES

73. The Ministry have suggested in section II of this Part that town and country planning and transport planning should be entrusted to a fairly small number of large authorities — between 30 and 40 units of local government based in many parts of the country on city-regions. The size of local government unit, in terms of population and resources, is of importance for planning, but it is still more important that the unit should cover the area which embraces the total planning problem.

74. With major functions other than planning the primary consideration is that authorities should be large enough. Departments are indicating in their evidence the size of authority below which they think it would be difficult for the major functions to be efficiently performed; these minima are not optima. Given suitable arrangements for decentralisation, authorities could well be much larger. For education, for example, the Department of Education and Science suggest that the minimum population should be about 300,000 in sparsely populated areas and at least 500,000 in mixed urban and rural areas. In areas dominated by major urban concentrations there should be a single education authority for the whole area and no limitation need be set on size. For health and welfare the Ministry of Health recommend a population of at least 200,000, but considerably larger units would be preferable where population density allows, and a maximum population exceeding a million would be acceptable provided the area of the authority were not too great. The Home Office recommend a minimum population of 250,000 for the children's service and at the other end of the scale an authority as big as any existing authority would be satisfactory. For the police, they think units covering between half a million and two million population desirable, and comparable units may be needed for fire brigades, though the Home Office have reserved any definite opinion pending the report of the Departmental Committee on the Fire Service.

75. The evidence of many Departments draws attention to the important links which exist between different services. The especially important links between the planning of land use and transport, and between planning and housing, have already been mentioned in this evidence. There is a close connection between the health and welfare services, education and child care. There are also links between the personal health services and the environmental health services, including sewerage,

refuse and cleansing services. Policies for new highways, traffic management, car parking and public transport need to be worked out comprehensively. The police are responsible for the enforcement of traffic management schemes and need to participate in their preparation. Land use planning is concerned at some stage with most other local authority services, for example, housing, schools, water supply and sewerage − in the allocation of land, in providing information about trends for the future development of services, in coordinating the provision of different services to meet the needs of new development and in concerting decisions about the timing and phasing of investment in public works. Services are easier to coordinate if they are provided by the same authority; and where a comprehensive policy covering a number of functions needs to be worked out, a single local authority becomes very desirable.

76. Although geographical considerations are not so critical for most other functions as they are for planning, there are several functions for which they are important, and the optimum boundaries would not always correspond with what might be most suitable for town and country planning and transport planning. Nevertheless the considerations in the preceding paragraphs suggest that a structure of big authorities, perhaps 30 or 40, responsible for a number of major local government services, would be both practicable and desirable.

77. In order to prevent remoteness from parts of the services they administered and from the public, large authorities would need to maintain local offices, and to decentralise day-to-day administration; this would help to avoid delay and to take proper account of local factors. For some services it might be desirable to set up area committees. Other arrangements could also be made, which might take a variety of forms, to keep in touch with local opinion.

78. Although few other local government functions require units as big as do major functions, it would be possible to give them all to the same authorities as those discharging the major functions. This would help to avoid a multiplicity of authorities; and it would have the advantages of economy in the staffing of common services and of intelligibility to the general public.

. . . . . .

81. However, a local government structure consisting solely of 30 to 40 all-purpose units would reduce the opportunities for local participation in government, and for people to bring their problems to local elected representatives. It would, for example, drastically reduce the number of elected members of authorities. It could also be argued that no arrangements made by these authorities to decentralise their administration and to keep in touch with local opinion could be an adequate substitute for local government of the type to which this country has become accustomed. These considerations suggest that these main units of local government should be supplemented by a second tier of elected authorities entrusted with appropriate executive functions.

Second-tier authorities

82. The Ministry do not wish in this evidence to offer anything approaching com-

prehensive proposals for the form such a second tier of authorities might take. It is clear that most careful thought would need to be given to the differing structural patterns appropriate to different parts of the country, and to the considerations affecting different functions. For studying how to use to the best advantage the services of people who are prepared to give their time to work in local government, to give opportunities at the right points for the expression of local opinion and for local option, and at the same time to maintain functional efficiency, it is to be expected that considerable help will be gained from the work which has been conducted by the Committees on the Management and on the Staffing of Local Government, whose reports the Ministry understand are to be received in a few months. There are, however, certain general suggestions the Ministry wish to make at this stage.

83. Study of a second-tier structure should start from provisional conclusions about the number and functions of a first tier of authorities. The Ministry suggest above that authorities of a city-region type are indispensable for planning, and that there are strong arguments for giving major housing functions to the same authorities; and other Departments' evidence points to entrusting a number of other major functions to them also . . .

. . . . . .

85. The Ministry suggest that the differing circumstances of different parts of the country would call for a considerable diversity in the size and functions of second-tier authorities. The areas of such authorities might be biggish cities or urban areas down to quite small towns, or districts of the present type; and there may be parts of the country where all functions should be discharged by the first-tier authorities except for functions allotted to parishes (which need not necessarily be confined to the present range of parish functions).

86. It may well be right to join together, to form second-tier units, certain of the present units. For example, in some places rural districts might be combined with their urban centres. The Ministry suggest, however, that it would be a mistake to join places together with the sole object of creating second-tier units large enough in terms of population to enable particular functions to be allotted to them rather than to first-tier units. Amalgamation can serve the needs of local democracy only where the resulting unit is a real one in the sense that its people have common interests which may be different from the interests of other places. It is relevant here that local interests may be very local indeed. A small district may be too small to discharge efficiently functions calling for a staff of some size, while at the same time less useful than its component parishes as a piece of local democracy.

87. Although there are many functions which, viewed in isolation, can be efficiently discharged by reasonably small authorities, their discharge ought on occasion to take into account wider considerations that are the concern of first-tier authorities or of central government. For example, the timing of investment in capital works or equipment, or the scale and layout of new sewers and sewerage plant, ought on occasion to be influenced by considerations of which a second-tier authority might not be fully aware.

88. Government Departments have found it increasingly unsatisfactory that their relationship with local government should, in a number of fields, and in particular in the administration of loan sanctions and Exchequer grants, take the form of a relationship with nearly 1,300 English local authorities. Such an arrangement is a handicap to the exchange of information and of ideas. It leads inevitably to an undue centralisation of control in some respects. Because the purview of small authorities is confined to small areas, because they do not engage on large projects often enough to justify their maintaining specialist staffs, Departments are obliged to scrutinise their capital schemes in considerable detail. It also leads in other respects to serious inadequacies of control. The combined current and capital expenditure of local authorities accounts for an eighth of the gross national product. The control of public expenditure is one of the more important economic regulators available to central government; but the revenue or current element of local expenditure is, in practice, subject to very little central government control. Experience has shown that it may in total be seriously overestimated or under-estimated, and this handicaps central government in its management both of the national economy and of Exchequer monies, from which more than half of current local government expenditure is found. There is a clear need to reduce drastically the number of authorities with major financial responsibilities, so as to secure an improvement in their budgeting and control arrangements and in their relationship with central government in these matters.

89. This is not to say that all changes should be in the direction of transferring financial responsibility from local to central government. On the contrary, it is desirable that the first-tier authorities should give thought to the financial and economic problems of their areas, and decide, subject to control by central government over policy and over the aggregate of public expenditure, the priority and timing of capital projects within their areas. Central government should be relieved as far as possible of its present task of scrutinising individual items of local capital expenditure because it cannot trust a multitude of small local authorities to spend money wisely.

90. For these reasons, it seems desirable that if there are second-tier authorities they should be subject to a substantial degree of financial control by the first-tier authorities, and that their role in determining the level of local taxation should be limited. (It certainly seems right that the *collection* of local taxes should be conducted by the first-tier authorities rather than, as at present, by those of the second tier, which spend much the smaller share of the money collected.) It is also for consideration whether Exchequer grants should not, as a general rule, be paid to the first-tier authorities, although parts of these grants would be passed on to the second-tier authorities. There are admittedly difficulties in these concepts, particularly in their application to large free-standing towns, and they require further consideration. The Royal Commission may wish at a later stage to take further evidence on local finance and taxation from the Ministry and the Treasury.

91. There are other respects in which the relationship between first-tier and second-tier authorities will repay examination. There is much to be said for clear-

cut arrangements under which some functions are the concern solely of the first-tier authorities and others solely of the second-tier authorities (subject to whatever may be found appropriate about finance). Certainly a system under which general responsibility is allotted to first-tier authorities and executive responsibility in component parts of their area to independently elected or appointed bodies has been found unsatisfactory in several fields. However, there are some functions where the local knowledge of members of second-tier authorities can help the first-tier authorities to discharge functions assigned to them. Again, some functions allotted to one tier will have links with those allotted to the other. The control of development is a function where these factors apply . . . One possibility suggested there, under which responsibility could rest wholly with the first-tier authority, working through its own staff and taking its own decisions but using the help of some members of the second-tier authority, may be appropriate for other functions.

92. Finally, the Ministry suggest that since circumstances vary so much in different places and at different times, it would be desirable when the new structure is set up for Parliament to allow considerable flexibility in settling the relationships between first and second-tier authorities, and that it should be possible to modify them extensively without fresh legislation. It is arguable that the powers of second-tier authorities should often, and perhaps always, be assigned to them by the first-tier authorities rather than directly by Parliament, though within limits prescribed by Parliament. No doubt the relationships between first-tier and second-tier authorities in this and other respects should require the endorsement of Ministers, and be embodied in formal instruments; and should take account of the wishes both of first and second-tier authorities. However, if the first-tier authority is a strong, directly elected authority, with an area which is a real entity for a large proportion of the functions in which its electors are most interested, there must be a presumption in favour of arrangements which that authority thinks appropriate.

6 THE LABOUR GOVERNMENT'S RESPONSE TO REDCLIFFE-MAUD

From *Reform of Local Government in England* (Cmnd. 4276, 1970); by permission of H.M.S.O.

6. When the report of the Royal Commission (Cmnd. 4040) was published on 11th June 1969, the Prime Minister announced the Government's acceptance of its three main principles — that a major rationalisation of local government was called for, that a marked reduction in the number of units with executive responsibility was needed, and that the anachronistic division between town and country should be ended . . .

. . . . . .

8. The Commission proposed that

(a) the greater part of England should be organised in 'unitary areas', with populations of not much less than 250,000 and not much more than 1,000,000, in which a single authority would exercise all local government functions;

(b) certain areas, however, where planning, transportation and development require authorities which would be too large for other services, should be organised as 'metropolitan areas' in which functions would be divided between two tiers of authority;

(c) in the unitary areas, and in the metropolitan areas where the inhabitants wanted them, there should be 'local councils' whose most important function would be to express the views of local communities on any matters affecting them;

(d) the unitary and metropolitan areas should be grouped into eight provinces, each with a provincial council consisting of members elected by the main authorities together with some co-opted members, and with the prime task of creating a broad planning framework within which the main authorities would carry out their operational responsibilities.

The Government's general views

9. The Government broadly accept this structure (subject to what is said below about provinces). They do so after carefully weighing the views expressed in the consultations and elsewhere, the proposals put forward by Mr. Senior in his dissenting memorandum, and the results of their own studies. There is no 'right solution' to the problem of reorganisation. Whatever solution is chosen must sacrifice some things in the interest of others; and further changes will be needed from time to time to match the changing pattern of work, life, settlements and society . . . the Commission's analysis is sound in its broad essentials and their proposals provide the best basis for reorganisation. The Government differ only on the distribution of functions in areas where there are to be two tiers, the application of the Commission's structure in two parts of England, and certain aspects of the proposals for local councils.

10. The Government also share the Commission's view that unless local government is organised to meet the needs of the future, and in particular is organised in units large enough to match the technical and administrative requirements of the services which it administers, its power must diminish, and with it the power of local democracy. The Government intend, on the contrary, that it should be strengthened; and the proposals in this White Paper both for a new structure and for other important changes are directed to this end.

11. The choice of structure is not one of degree, of how far to go. It is a choice between a structure composed of large units — unitary ones, wherever conditions make this feasible — and something closely resembling what exists today. The Government are in no doubt of the tremendous service which existing local government has rendered to the nation — a service made possible by the devoted work of thousands of councillors and officers. Equally, they are in no doubt that if it is

adequately to meet the needs of the people, the system now requires fundamental change. In view of the time, effort and disturbance which such change involves, the new structure must be designed to last in its essentials for many decades.

. . . . . .

The unitary areas

18. The Government accept the Commission's belief in the advantages of making a single authority responsible for all services in a particular area, wherever geographical and other factors allow. Successful local government depends to a significant extent on the ability of authorities to co-ordinate a wide range of functions and services, and to develop links between them. Adoption of the unitary system, wherever it is practicable, will make local government stronger, more efficient and more comprehensible to the public.

19. The Government also accept the Commission's view that the unitary areas must cover both town and country. It is not that the interests of the two are identical. But they are complementary, and the social and economic interdependence of the towns and the countryside has increased to a point where only a single authority responsible for both can undertake the planned development of the main services to the maximum advantage of both.

20. The Government therefore accept, apart from the two major changes described below and subject to what is said in paragraph 39, the Commission's general recommendations both on the desirability and the size of unitary areas.

The metropolitan areas

21. The Government agree with the Commission that in some parts of the country — notably in certain actual or potential conurbations — the requirements of land-use planning and transportation demand planning areas of a size and population much larger than are necessary or desirable for some other services; and that a two-tier system is in these circumstances unavoidable.

22. [The Commission's proposed division of functions] . . . The Government dissent from this division in only one major respect, namely, education. This they believe should be entrusted to the upper-tier authority. The Commission preferred the lower-tier authority on the grounds that education should be administered by the same authorities as the personal social services concerned with children. There are, however, powerful arguments on the other side. In general, an authority which can command large resources, particularly in specialised manpower, can provide a more efficient education service. In particular, the proposed metropolitan areas contain heavy concentrations of institutions for further and higher education. These forms of education make exceptional demands on the resources of the administering authority, and involve the provision of facilities which have wide implications for the 'environmental services' of planning, transportation and development. Since students are mobile and catchment areas extensive, a high degree of

co-ordination is needed. It is true that under the Government's solution there remains the problem of co-operation in the field of child guidance and educational welfare between the education authority and the lower-tier authorities responsible for child care; but this need be no greater than the problem of co-operation in education matters between separate lower-tier authorities which the Commission's solution would involve. The choice is a difficult one, and the Government have weighed with great care the arguments both of the Commission and of the Seebohm Committee for entrusting education to the same authorities as the other personal services. But they have concluded that the balance of argument favours making it the responsibility of the metropolitan authorities.

23. The transfer of education to the metropolitan authorities requires, in the Government's view, that they should be the rating authorities in metropolitan areas, since the bulk of expenditure in these areas will now fall upon them.

24. The Government have devoted much thought to the Commission's proposals about housing. The Commission proposed that responsibilities should be divided as follows:

Metropolitan authority	*Metropolitan district council*
(a) metropolitan housing policy	(a) building (within framework of metropolitan policy)
(b) building in the interests of the metropolitan area as a whole	(b) house management
(c) building to ensure fulfilment of planning policies	(c) all other housing powers
(d) policy for selection of tenants	
(e) metropolitan rent policy	

The Commission were right in believing that the functions listed on the left must be carried out by the authorities responsible for planning, transportation and development; for they are among the most important ways in which planning is put into practical effect. It is arguable that the other housing functions should be entrusted to the same authorities in order to avoid division of responsibility. Nevertheless, the Government believe that the drawbacks of this division are outweighed by the advantages of giving the responsibilities on the right to authorities which are also responsible for the relevant personal social services; and they therefore accept in principle the Commission's proposals. When these proposals are translated into statutory terms, however, the power of the metropolitan authorities to undertake building should be widely drawn, and should include the power to supplement or reinforce the housebuilding programmes of the district councils.

25. The Government agree generally with the Commission's distribution of other functions in metropolitan areas . . .

. . . . . .

III THE MAP

29. The Commission proposed 58 unitary areas; and they explained at the end of their report what places each should include and why. They also proposed three

metropolitan areas — on Merseyside, in South-East Lancashire and North-East Cheshire, and in the West Midlands — and 20 districts within them . . .

Two-tier areas

31. The Government agree, as they have said above, that where, because of concentrations of population, the environmental group of services (planning, transport and development) need to be dealt with on an exceptionally large scale, the idea of a single authority for all services must be abandoned. There must be a large authority for some services, and several smaller ones for the rest.

32. The Government accept that the three metropolitan areas described by the Commission should be organised in this way. They recognise what this will mean for cities and towns in these areas which have throughout their history been accustomed to manage all their own local affairs. They regret that in the West Midlands it means further changes in an area which underwent reorganisation only a few years ago. But they believe that the environmental services above all need the comprehensive development which only a single authority can provide; moreover, joint work by several different authorities in practice involves too large an intervention by central government. For the same reason, the Government are satisfied that the Commission were right to draw wide boundaries for these areas, taking in parts of the surrounding country, though the actual line of the boundaries, in common with other boundary lines, will need to be considered in a further stage of consultations.

33. The Government have, however, reached the conclusion that, in addition to the three areas proposed by the Commission, the following additional two-tier areas should be created:

West Yorkshire

An area formed by combining the Commission's areas No. 7 (Bradford), No 8 (Leeds), No. 9 (Halifax), No. 10 (Huddersfield) and No 11 (Mid-Yorkshire).

South Hampshire

An area formed by combining the Commission's areas No. 57 (Southampton and South Hampshire) and No. 58 (Portsmouth, South-East Hampshire and the Isle of Wight).

34. In West Yorkshire, all the five unitary areas proposed by the Commission have interlocking problems. They have severe housing problems and, as urban renewal gathers speed, the pressure on land and in particular on the open wedges between the towns will increase. The pattern of employment is changing as the traditional textile industries come to occupy a less dominant position in the economy of the area. It is the Government's view that the allocation of land for housing and industry, the redistribution of population in relation to new employment, improvements in communications, and the co-ordination of programmes for dealing with derelict land, all demand a single planning authority for West Yorkshire.

35. South Hampshire presents a special problem. The area contains two major towns which are growing towards each other physically and in other ways. It

includes the Isle of Wight and other areas of outstanding scenic and amenity value. Population and industry in the area have been expanding exceptionally fast; this growth is likely to continue and even accelerate. In view of the nature of the area, and the size and speed of its development, the Government believe that there should, from the outset of the new system, be a single authority with full executive responsibility for planning the development of the area as a whole. The new authority will be able to build on the valuable work of the Joint Planning Advisory Committee established by the major authorities in the area.

36. It is the Government's view, after studying all the possibilities, that the three Redcliffe-Maud areas and the two now added are the only ones where a two-tier system should be adopted. There are, as the Commission noted, other areas where a two-tier solution may well be needed in the course of time. But this will depend on future developments which cannot now be adequately assessed. No pattern can be rigid for all time; and the Government propose to ensure that future changes in the structure of local government in any particular area can be made without the need for a further Act.

Districts in two-tier areas

37. The allocation of responsibility for education to the metropolitan authorities does not, in the Government's view, call for a radically different pattern of metropolitan districts from that proposed by the Commission. Districts of the general size which they proposed will still be needed to create effective housing and social service authorities. There will, however, be full opportunity to comment on the pattern and boundaries of the districts during the consultations which will take place on the boundaries of all the proposed new areas.

38. These consultations will of course include the pattern of districts in the two additional metropolitan areas. The Government's present view is as follows:

West Yorkshire

There should be five districts, corresponding to the five unitary areas proposed by the Commission. These are workable sub-divisions, and their sizes are suitable.

South Hampshire

There should be three districts. One would be the Commission's area No. 57; the second the Commission's area No. 58, less the Isle of Wight; and the third the Isle of Wight — a small district justified by exceptional circumstances.

The unitary areas

39. Leaving aside detailed boundary questions, on which several authorities have already tabled suggestions, the Government's present opinion is that the unitary areas proposed by the Commission, reduced in number to 51 by the additional two-tier areas, are of broadly the right size and shape . . .

7 THE CONSERVATIVE GOVERNMENT'S RESPONSE TO REDCLIFFE-MAUD

From *Local Government in England: Government Proposals for Reorganisation* (Cmnd. 4584, 1971); by permission of H.M.S.O.

Functions and Tiers

10. Local government reform must represent a balanced judgement based on a wide variety of considerations. There are certain points, however, which the Government regarded as specially important in reaching their conclusions about the operational authorities.

11. Land-use planning and transportation will increasingly be dependent upon the framework of a regional strategy, but the units responsible for these functions locally must be adequate in size and in resources to operate with a sensible external independence and internal cohesion.

12. With functions such as education and the personal social services — for the physically or mentally handicapped, the elderly and children — there is considerable advantage in having units of population sufficiently large to provide a base for their effective organisation and a high quality of service. The Government accept the view that the units appropriate to the provision of these services should have populations broadly within the range of 250,000 to 1,000,000. These limits should not be inflexible but it should only be in special circumstances that these services are provided by units with populations below this range.

13. In the Government's view, there will always be conflicts between those who argue for large scale organisation on grounds of efficiency and those, on the other hand, who argue for control by a body close to the people for whom the service is designed. The Government obviously must seek efficiency, but where the arguments are evenly balanced their judgement will be given in favour of responsibility being exercised at the more local level.

The Operational Authorities: Functions

14. The Government therefore intend that the reorganised system should everywhere be based on two forms of operational authorities. They do not, however, see the relationship between the two as implying that some authorities are answerable to others. The Government's concern has been to settle how functions can best be operated; some need wider areas of administration, while others are best dealt with by authorities more closely in touch with local conditions.

15. It would be quite wrong to use the terms 'upper' and 'lower' tier authorities and it is for this reason that the White Paper refers to 'counties', 'boroughs', 'districts' and 'parishes'. 'County' seems appropriate for the wider areas needed for some services. The more local areas will be 'boroughs' or 'districts'; purely for con-

venience the term 'district' is generally used here but without in any way
prejudicing how and to what extent the special attributes of boroughs should be
retained. 'Parish' appears to be the most generally acceptable name for the smallest
units of local government.

16. Two kinds of system are needed. In certain of the most populous parts of
the country the areas which must be treated as entities for major functions, such as
land-use planning and transport, will consist of a pattern of districts all of which
will be substantial units in terms of population and resources. Because services
should be administered as locally as possible, it would be right for the district councils here to be responsible for education and the local authority personal social
services. Being predominantly urban in character and generally compact, these districts would also be sensible and effective units for all local government functions
save those which require to be planned and administered over the wider area. For
these urban counties, the term 'metropolitan' is temporarily retained as a matter of
convenience, though it is not one to which the Government are committed.

17. Elsewhere, the districts are bound to vary considerably in size and resources
even after reorganisation. In these other counties, outside the metropolitan areas,
education and the personal social services must be the undivided responsibility of
the county authorities, each of whom must be in a position to organise and provide
these expanding services throughout the whole of their area. In education, it is the
intention to end the provisions for schemes of divisional education by which local
education authorities are compelled to delegate certain of their functions to
divisional executives. Similarly, excepted districts will have no place in the new
local government structure.

18. In the Government's view, responsibility for libraries should rest with the
education authorities — the district councils in the metropolitan areas and the
county councils elsewhere.

19. It is proposed that responsibility for highways, traffic management and
public transport should lie wholly with the county authorities, so as to end the
difficulties which arise through the present division of responsibility for highways
and traffic.

20. County responsibilities will also include police and the fire service. The
extent to which it may prove necessary to combine counties for the more efficient
operation of these services in particular parts of the country will be considered
when conclusions have been reached on the new county areas.

21. Planning control, however, raises issues of close local interest. All planning
applications should be made to the district councils, both within and outside the
metropolitan counties. The district councils should, as of right, take by far the
greater number of planning control decisions, provided that the professional advice
comes from officers who are part of a unified staff structure, serving both counties
and districts, so that local needs are reflected in the detailed implementation of
development plans. Responsibility for broad planning policies and for the development of both structure and local plans must, however, rest with the county councils.

22. Local authorities also provide an increasing range of services for the benefit

of their areas, many of which bear directly on local conditions, facilities and amenities. The district councils will have wide responsibilities here. The Government intend these councils to be genuine authorities, existing in their own right, and with responsibilities and powers sufficient to make service with them a reality for both members and officers. It would be a disservice to local government to establish authorities with functions which were inadequate to arouse public respect or interest.

23. One of the most important functions of local government is housing. The Government believe that the accurate assessment of housing requirements and the provision of housing and housing advice to the individual is of such paramount importance that the service should be operated as close to the citizen as possible. The management of council houses, slum clearance and the improvement of existing houses are all aspects of an essentially local service. Quality too is vital in this sphere, and it is in the districts that the expertise exists at the present time. For these reasons housing should be primarily the responsibility of the district councils. The counties will need powers to deal with those housing problems that transcend the boundaries of the districts.

24. The Government will consider the future responsibilities for water supply, sewerage and sewage disposal in the light of the report on these and related matters by the Central Advisory Water Committee which will be available shortly. The detailed allocation of environmental health services will need to be discussed with the local authority associations, as will functions in the field of consumer protection.

. . . . . .

26. In the Government's view, very little change is needed in the present statutory provisions governing planning functions in national parks. They intend that the two existing Planning Boards should be retained. They will, in due course, consider, with the new local authorities and other interested bodies, whether the establishment of further boards in multi-county parks is desirable. They consider that elsewhere planning functions in a national park should continue to be carried out by a special committee of the county council in whose area the park lies.

27. As already announced, the local authority personal health services will be transferred to the new health authorities to be set up on the reorganisation of the National Health Service.

The Operational Authorities: Areas

. . . . . .

29. It must be emphasised that the new counties will in no sense be a continuation of the existing county authorities. They will be entirely new authorities, binding together — in most cases for the first time — all of the urban and rural areas within their boundaries. Where possible, existing county boundaries will be retained in order to keep the maximum existing loyalties and to minimise the administrative problems.

30. *The Metropolitan Counties.* In the Government's view a metropolitan type

of structure would be appropriate in Merseyside, South-East Lancashire and North-East Cheshire (Selnec) and the West Midlands and, in addition, in West Yorkshire, South Yorkshire and the Tyne and Wear area. These six areas need to be treated as entities for purposes of planning, transportation and certain other services; at the same time the districts into which they divide would all be big enough in population and resources, and sufficiently compact in size to be responsible for education and the personal services, as well as the more local functions.

31. In other parts of the country there are big towns, now county boroughs, with distinguished records of service to the community in the fields of education, child care, welfare and the other personal social services. But if the new counties of which they will form parts were treated on the metropolitan pattern and divided into districts, with each district exercising responsibility for education and the personal social services, most of the districts would either have populations too small to support these major services or have areas too large for the other services. The metropolitan pattern is suitable only where a county is divisible into districts all of which are populous and compact. Alternatively, if responsibility for education and the personal social services were allotted to the large towns and, in the remainder of the counties concerned, to the county authority, a separation between town and country that experience has shown to be undesirable for these services would be perpetuated.

32. The Government are therefore of the view that the metropolitan type of structure should be adopted in the six areas referred to in paragraph 30, and not elsewhere. The boundaries of these areas should include all the main area, or areas, of continuous development and any adjacent area into which continuous development will extend. It may be right to include closely related built-up areas, too. But none of these proposed metropolitan counties can practicably contain the solution of all the planning problems of the conurbations and, where it is impossible to meet all housing and redevelopment needs within the county boundaries, the answer will lie in development well outside the metropolitan area, in accordance with a carefully worked out regional plan.

33. *Outside the Metropolitan Counties* there are now over 900 separate authorities. There is widespread opinion, particularly within the associations responsible for rural and urban district councils, that a sensible rationalisation should take place so as to provide districts with the resources to carry out efficiently the very considerable responsibilities that will continue to be placed upon them. The bigger cities and towns will retain their identities. In other places it would be right to reunite smaller towns with the rural communities associated with them. Where there is no clear centre to act as a focal point for a new unit, it may still be desirable to form a new district by the amalgamation of rural areas. The Government are anxious, in this structure, to ensure that the special interests of rural areas are not over-shadowed.

34. Even after the rationalisation of boundaries at this level the districts are bound to vary considerably in size, from the larger towns and cities down to much smaller populations in thriving rural counties. Where there is need for the creation

of larger units than exist at present, the Government would expect them to have populations ranging upwards from 40,000, save in sparsely populated areas.

Regions or Provinces

35. There are functions of both central and local government which need to be considered in a regional or provincial context — the process has already begun in the eight Economic Planning Regions. The most important of these is the formulation of the broad economic and land-use strategy which would be the regional framework within which services would be provided. The Government agree with the Redcliffe-Maud Commission in thinking that areas of this size would be too large to be appropriate for the operation of local government services.

. . . . . .

Parishes

38. The establishment of two operational forms of local authorities does not remove the need for authorities at the parish level. There has been a substantial revival of interest in recent years in the part that very small bodies or authorities can play in allowing local people themselves to get things done and in focussing local opinion on matters affecting the neighbourhood.

39. The Government wish to give every encouragement to the existing rural parishes outside the metropolitan counties. The general character of parishes should remain unchanged; they should remain bodies with powers rather than duties and as much a part of the social as the governmental scene. It would be desirable in due course to review parish boundaries, as there are many places where small parishes could, with advantage, be amalgamated to form fewer units.

40. The retention or establishment of parish councils in essentially urban areas raises different problems — in the metropolitan districts, for instance, or in town areas outside the metropolitan counties. It may be appropriate, if local people wish it, to provide for the equivalent of a parish council in a small town which is now a separate borough or urban district, where such a town is included in a new and enlarged district. But the views and wishes of neighbourhoods, or small communities within larger built-up areas, might preferably be represented by non-statutory bodies; district authorities should have powers to assist such bodies financially and in other ways. This is a matter which will be further discussed with the local authority associations as part of the preparations for legislation.

. . . . . .

60. The proposals set out in this White Paper constitute a major reform of local government in England, ambitious beyond anything attempted this century — but one which retains and improves the essential elements of the present system.

61. The Government are firm in their resolve that reorganisation should be centred on two tiers of local government throughout the country. They are

initiating further consultations on the boundaries and will consult the appropriate associations on details of the final distribution of functions.

62. In putting forward the changes set out in this White Paper, the Government have several linked objectives:

(a) they will establish a new pattern of areas within which the major services can be efficiently administered and developed in the future;

(b) by retaining important responsibilities at the more local level, too, they will give powers of decision and action to those who will be immediately affected;

(c) the total number of authorities is to be reduced, but the new and rationalised system will be founded upon the organisations of the existing authorities and will preserve wherever possible the loyalties attaching to ancient units of local government; the reduced number of authorities will permit the effective transfer of responsibility and power from central to local authorities;

(d) they accept the need for the operational authorities to be complemented at provincial and parish level.

PROPOSED ALLOCATION OF MAIN FUNCTIONS IN ENGLAND

County councils (outside metropolitan areas) and Metropolitan District Councils

Education
Personal social services
Libraries

All County Councils	**All District Councils**
Planning:	Planning:
Plan making	
Development control	Most development control
(strategic and reserved decisions)	
Acquisition and disposal of land	Acquisition and disposal of land
for planning purposes, develop-	for planning purposes, develop-
ment or redevelopment (1)	ment or redevelopment (1)
Highways, Traffic and Transport	
Housing:	Housing:
Certain reserve powers e.g. for	Including housebuilding
overspill	Housing management
	Slum clearance
	House and area improvement
Building regulations	
Weights and measures	
Food and drugs	
Clean air	
Refuse disposal	Refuse collection

All County Councils	All District Councils
Environmental health (2)	Environmental health (2)
Museums and art galleries (1)	Museums and art galleries (1)
Parks and open spaces (1)	Parks and open spaces (1)
Playing fields and swimming baths (1)	Playing fields and swimming baths (1)
Coast protection (1)	Coast protection (1)
Police (3)	
Fire (3)	

Notes:
(1) Concurrent powers exercisable by county councils and by district councils.
(2) Future administration of water supply, sewerage and sewage disposal to be considered in the light of the report of the Central Advisory Water Committee. Detailed allocation of other environmental services to be discussed with the local authority associations.
(3) Some counties will need to be amalgamated for police purposes and possibly for fire.

8 THE NEW SYSTEM: THE 1972 ACT

From (a) *Explanatory and Financial Memorandum on the Local Government Bill* (subsequently the Local Government Act, 1972); (b) *Local Government Act 1972* (Department of Environment Circular 121/72, 1972). Both by permission of H.M.S.O. These extracts summarise the provisions of the Local Government Act, 1972.

(a)

This Bill gives effect to proposals described in the White Paper 'Local Government in England: Government Proposals for Reorganisation' (Cmnd. 4584) and in the Consultative Document 'The Reform of Local Government in Wales'. It creates new structures for local government in England and in Wales, allocates the functions of local government among the new authorities, and makes provision for the working machinery of local government.

The Bill replaces the Local Government Act 1933 as the major Act in the field of local government. It also incorporates the provisions of the London Government Act 1963 which affect the constitution of authorities in Greater London; and the machinery provisions of the Bill apply to those authorities as to the new authorities.

Part I of the Bill provides for England, exclusive of Greater London and the Isles of Scilly, to be divided into local government areas known as counties and districts. Certain of the counties are to be metropolitan counties which are to contain metropolitan districts. (The allocation of functions under Part IX of the Bill will in some respects differ as between metropolitan and non-metropolitan counties.) The counties and metropolitan districts are defined in the Bill, but the non-metropolitan districts are to be defined by order on the advice of the English Boundary Commission to be set up under Part IV. Counties and districts are to have councils, consisting of a chairman, vice-chairman and councillors. A district council may petition Her Majesty for a charter conferring borough status; and if a charter is granted the council will have the name of the council of the borough and its chairman that of mayor. First elections to the new county and district councils are to take place in 1973. Members of county councils are to be elected for terms of four years and will be elected and retire together. Members of district councils are also to be elected for terms of four years but (subject to transitional arrangements for the first elected members) one-third of them will retire in every year which is not a year for the election of county councils. The existing position in Greater London with respect to the constitution and membership of the Greater London Council and London borough councils is maintained. Provision is also made for the continuance of rural parishes, parish meetings and parish councils, whose members are to be elected for terms of four years. On 1st April 1974, the date when councils for the new counties and districts assume their full responsibilities, all existing administrative counties, boroughs, urban districts, rural districts and urban parishes in England (outside Greater London and the Isles of Scilly), will cease to exist, together with their councils and corporations.

. . . . . .

Part III provides for changes in election arrangements which local government reorganisation in England and Wales makes necessary, and also repeats the substance of certain electoral provisions in the Local Government Act 1933. Provision is made for electoral registration to be undertaken by officers of the new district councils. Provision is also made for returning officers at parliamentary elections. The returning officer at county council elections is to be an officer of the county council and, at district, parish and community elections, an officer of the district council. All local elections are to be conducted under rules made by the Home Secretary. Local elections after 1974 are to be held on a day in April or May fixed for each year by the Home Secretary.

Part IV provides for the establishment of separate Local Government Boundary Commissions for England and Wales, and for their roles in the review of local government boundaries and local electoral arrangements. The Commissions will be advisory, their recommendations being given effect by orders made by the appropriate Secretary of State. Each Commission will have powers to make proposals for the alteration of local government areas, the creation of new areas and the abolition of areas. The powers of the English Commission will extend to Greater London. It is given the specific duty to carry out periodic reviews of certain local government areas and a general duty to review others; and it may be directed to hold or postpone the review of any area . . . It is also to be a duty of each Commission to carry out periodic reviews of counties and districts for the purpose of making proposals for changes in local electoral areas, and further for district councils to review electoral arrangements for their parishes or communities. Special provision is made for the alteration of the boundary between England and Wales, on the recommendation of both Commissions acting jointly and with the agreement of both county councils concerned.

Part V contains general provisions as to members and proceedings of local authorities. Existing provisions are re-enacted, modified as necessary to take account of the new local government structure; and the Part applies to Greater London as it applies to the rest of England and Wales. Matters dealt with include qualifications and disqualifications for election to and membership of a local authority; acceptance and vacation of office; restrictions on voting because of a pecuniary interest; and arrangements for the meeting and proceedings of local authorities.

Part VI deals with the manner in which local authorities may discharge their functions. It applies to Greater London as well as to the rest of England and to Wales. Authorities are given a wider discretion than they now enjoy to make arrangements and organise themselves for the discharge of their functions through committees, sub-committees, officers or other local authorities. There are certain limitations to this discretion. A local authority's functions with respect to levying, or issuing a precept for, a rate or borrowing money may be discharged only by the authority. Further, the position and responsibilities of certain committees specifically required to be set up by statute, and governed by their own special codes, are preserved. Provision is made for the appointment of joint committees of authorities, the appointment of advisory committees and sub-committees, and the co-option to committees of persons who are not authority members. A parish meeting for a parish without a parish council is enabled to arrange for a committee of local government electors for the parish to carry out the parish meeting's functions; and a district council may confer on a parish meeting the functions of a parish council.

Part VII is concerned with the ancillary powers of local authorities, such as the power to appoint staff and enter into land transactions. Where relevant the Part applies to Greater London as well as to the rest of England and to Wales. Authorities are given wide discretion in the appointment of staff, subject to the preservation of certain requirements to appoint particular categories of officer, or to follow prescribed procedures in their selection. County and district councils are to have general powers, effectively the same as those now enjoyed by county councils, for the purchase of land by agreement or compulsorily, for the appropriation of land and for the disposal of land. Parish and community councils will have similar powers with respect to land transactions to those now enjoyed by parish councils. Provisions in this Part of the Bill dealing with land transactions are subject, however, to specific provisions in certain other enactments (in this, following the pattern of the Local Government Act 1933). Local authorities will have power to incur expenditure equivalent to a rate of 2p in the pound for certain purposes not otherwise authorised. County and district councils are provided with clear powers to act without delay in the face of actual or imminent emergencies or disasters, and to incur expenditure for that purpose. County councils are to have a power to conduct or assist investigations into any matters concerning the county.

Part VIII deals with financial, audit and expenses provisions relating to authorities and to their members. Where appropriate it applies to Greater London as well as to the rest of England and to Wales. The effect of the provisions is that London borough councils and district councils will be the rating authorities; and the Greater London Council and county councils, and parish and community councils, will have power to issue precepts upon rating authorities. All local authority accounts are to be audited either by a district auditor, appointed by the Secretary of State with the consent of the Minister for the Civil Service, or by a private auditor. Private auditors can be appointed only by district councils, to audit accounts which are not specifically made subject under other legislation to district audit. The Secretary of State may order an extraordinary audit by a district auditor of accounts subject to either district or private audit. Provision is made for the initial expenses of the new county and district councils by way of contributions from existing rating authorities. Councillors of local authorities will receive an attendance allowance for the performance of approved duties; co-opted members and aldermen in Greater London will continue as now to be able to claim a financial loss allowance. Travelling and subsistence allowances will be generally available as now; and provision is made for expenses of attending conferences and making official visits.

Part IX is concerned with the allocation of functions in the new local government system in England and Wales. The new county and district councils will assume full responsibilities on 1st April 1974. A general formula provides for the allocation of existing county functions to the new county councils and for the allocation of the functions of existing urban district councils to the new district councils. This formula is, however, subject to the specific allocation of particular functions, and this Part of the Bill provides for the allocation of a number of major functions relating to the environment and social and welfare services, as well as of other miscellaneous responsibilities. Functions dealt with specifically include public health, town and country planning, town development, highways, traffic and transportation, education, libraries, housing, the personal social services, police, fire, food and drugs, and weights and measures. Related Schedules make consequential amendments to the legislation which confers these various functions.

Part X provides for the changes which local government reorganisation makes necessary in the administration of justice and in the arrangements relating to lieutenants and sheriffs of counties. There is to be a separate commission of the peace for each new county, and a separate magistrates' court committee for each metropolitan district and non-metropolitan county. Her Majesty is to appoint a lord-lieutenant for each new county and for Greater London, and may appoint one or more additional lieutenants. There is provision for the appointment of vice lord-lieutenants and for the nomination of sheriffs.

Part XI contains general machinery provisions relating to the exercise of the powers of local authorities. In the main, existing provisions are re-enacted or modernised. This Part of the Bill is in the main consolidation, but with some changes of minor substance. Local authorities are given power to initiate or take part in legal proceedings. Provision is made for the custody of records, and the service and authentication of notices, etc. Local authorities, other than parish or community councils, are empowered to promote or oppose local or personal Bills. Councils of counties or districts will be enabled to appointed honorary aldermen from among past members of the council and borough councils to appoint honorary freemen of the borough.

Part XII contains miscellaneous and general provisions, including clauses dealing with the transfer of staff and property to the new authorities . . .

Arrangements are provided for the transfer of staff and the conditions of transfer are laid down. There are to be separate Staff Commissions for England and Wales and provision is made for regulations for the compensation of staff suffering loss of office, or loss or diminution of emoluments, attributable to the Bill or other specified events . . . Provision is also made for the setting up of joint committees of existing authorities for the consideration of certain matters affecting new counties and districts.

. . . . . .

Financial Effects of the Bill Since the Bill is mainly concerned with altering the structure within which the existing powers and duties of local government are exercised, it will have little direct effect upon either local authority finance or expenditure overall. Costs to existing local authorities will arise from the need to meet the initial expenses incurred by the new local authorities before they assume their full range of functions. Costs will mainly arise for the new authorities from the introduction of a system of allowances payable to members for attendance at meetings and conferences. In addition the new authorities will be empowered to spend up to the product of a 2p rate on functions not covered by other statutory provisions. It is not possible to quantify the additional expenditure involved with any precision but it is not likely in total to be very large, relative to the overall level of local authority spending. On the basis of the present grant system, about 58 per cent. will fall on the Exchequer and the balance on local authority rates. Charges on central funds will arise from the operations of the Local Government Boundary Commissions for England and Wales and of the Staff Commissions. The amounts are unlikely to be large and in the case of the Staff Commissions will be for a limited period.

Effect on Public Service Manpower Reorganisation of local government will in the long run enable staff to be more effectively and economically deployed. The Local Government Boundary Commissions and the Staff Commissions will impose some additional requirements upon public service manpower.

(b)

Functions 10. . . . The chief difference between the distribution of functions in the metropolitan and non-metropolitan counties concerns education and the personal social services; these will be county responsibilities in the non-metropolitan counties but district functions in the metropolitan areas. The Act provides for a significant increase in the services which parish councils may provide concurrently with district councils. It also repeals, or designedly does not re-enact, a large number of Ministerial controls over the exercise of functions.

Constitutional and other changes 11. The Act makes changes in the constitutional and electoral arrangements of local authorities. There will be no aldermen as members of the new councils, but principal authorities . . . will have the power to recognise service to local government by conferring the title 'honorary alterman'.

12. The term of office of councillors is extended from three years to four. All county councillors will retire together every fourth year; one third of the councillors in metropolitan districts will retire in each of the years between the county council elections; non-metropolitan districts will be entitled to choose between all members of the council retiring en bloc every fourth year, or a third of the members retiring in each year in which metropolitan district councillors retire. After the initial elections local government elections each year will be held on the same day, which will normally be the first Thursday in May.

13. New provisions have been made for allowances for the members of principal authorities as from 1 April 1974. The new provisions do not represent a departure from the view that membership of local authorities should be essentially voluntary and should not attract a salary. The Act provides for a (taxable) flat-rate allowance for elected members, and a financial loss allowance (as in the present system) for the non-elected members. Rights to travelling and subsistence allowances remain. Arrangements will be made for members of the new authorities to receive the existing allowances from their election until 31 March 1974. From 1 April 1974 aldermen of London boroughs will be able to choose between the flat rate allowance and the financial loss allowance.

14. The existing rights of the public, including the press, to attend council meetings (except when the matters to be dealt with need to be treated confidentially) are extended by the Act to meetings of all committees of local authorities.

15. The provisions applying to the internal arrangements for carrying out functions are made more flexible, e.g. by the repeal of some of the existing statutory requirements for the appointment of specific officers and committees and by the introduction (except where existing requirements are preserved) of wider powers to delegate to committees, sub-committees and officers. In addition there are wide powers for local authorities to make arrangements between themselves for the discharge of many of their functions.

16. The Act includes a new provision (section 111) which puts beyond doubt that local authorities have power to do anything which is calculated to facilitate, or is conducive or incidental to, the discharge of any of their functions, even if they have no specific statutory power for that action. This proposition has long represented the law (see in particular *A.G. v. Smethwick Corporation* [1932] 1 Ch 562), but the section has been included for the avoidance of any doubt which might hamper local initiative.

17. The existing provisions affecting the audit of local authority accounts have been completely recast. In future principal authorities (and the Common Council) will be able to choose whether the audit of their accounts shall be undertaken by the district auditor or by an approved private auditor, and district councils will be able to decide which auditor should audit the accounts of the parishes in their areas. The district auditor's powers are substantially altered: notably, where he considers an item of account to be contrary to law, he can apply to the court for a declaration accordingly. However, where a sum is lost by wilful misconduct he can certify that an equivalent sum is due to the authority from the person responsible.

. . . . . .

55. In many areas, if not all, these joint committees of existing authorities have already been set up and have been operating for some time. They will no doubt be proceeding, as suggested in the Department's circular of 4 July 1972 (No. 68/72) with preparatory work on the great variety of matters which can usefully be considered in advance of the election of the new authorities. The Secretary of State would particularly commend for study and consideration the advice and proposals of the Study Group on Local Authority Management Structures appointed jointly by the Secretary of State and the local authority associations. Their report entitled 'The New Local Authorities: Management and Structure', was published in August of this year.

56. The report makes specific suggestions about committee and departmental structure and emphasises the need for a corporate approach to management, with overall central control over the major resources of the authority and their effective utilisation. The role of the Chief Executive, public relations and personnel management are amongst the other matters in respect of which the report makes important and far reaching recommendations, all of which will be of relevance to discussions in the joint committees.

9 RELATIONS BETWEEN LOCAL AUTHORITIES: AGENCY ARRANGEMENTS

From *Local Government Act 1972, Sections 101 and 110, Arrangements for the Discharge of Functions – 'Agency Arrangements'* (Department of Environment Circular 131/72, 1972); by permission of H.M.S.O. This circular sets out guidelines for local authorities as to the use of the (permissive) provisions of the 1972 Act by which an authority may act as an agent for another authority in the discharge of functions.

1. I am directed by the Secretary of State for the Environment to state that consultations have been held between the government departments and the local authority associations concerned to consider what advice might be given to local authorities about the establishment of arrangements between county and district councils for the discharge of their functions under section 101(1)(b) of the Local

Government Act, 1972. That subsection allows a local authority (subject to certain exceptions referred to in paragraph 18 below) to arrange for the discharge of any of their functions by another local authority. Such arrangements have already become widely known as 'agency arrangements' and for the sake of convenience that term will be used in the present circular.

2. A substantial measure of agreement emerged during the consultations on certain general principles within which agency arrangements might be considered. The advice given in this circular, which has been prepared in the light of those consultations, is directed to the situation in England; separate advice is being issued to Welsh authorities by the Secretary of State for Wales.

3. Arrangements made between local authorities for the discharge of functions need to be considered against the background of the general objectives of reorganisation. These include:

a. The establishment of two classes of executive authorities – the county and district councils – each of which should exercise a range of functions and responsibilities sufficient to attract and to provide worthwhile service for members and officers;

b. the clear allocation of statutory responsibility for each service to the class of authority at which that overall responsibility should most appropriately lie; but, within that allocation,

c. the provision of the widest and most flexible powers to enable authorities to combine with each other or to make joint arrangements for the exercise of functions in the light of the requirements of different services and changing circumstances.

4. During the debates in the House of Commons, the Secretary of State for the Environment said:

' . . . we have expressed two basic principles, first that we consider it will be in the interests of local government to organise sensible agency agreements, and . . . I think there is scope for agency agreements in both directions . . . Also secondly if one is to have the two levels in local government, then from the time this commences they should work together in a spirit of co-operation not of hostility and rivalry.'

The Act provides local authorities with a whole armoury of powers for co-operation not only between authorities of different classes, but also between district and district, or county and county. These include co-operation by way of joint committees; consortia; joint teams; loan of staff; and agency arrangements as contemplated in this circular. Further powers are contained in the Local Authorities (Goods and Services) Act, 1970. No one form of co-operation can be properly considered in isolation from the others; each is one of a range of devices which may be employed to deal with a range of problems and circumstances. Thus they are complementary to each other rather than alternatives for meeting the same problem.

5. But although the appropriateness of agency arrangements needs to be looked at as part of this comprehensive armoury of powers, it is particularly important that decisions about such arrangements should be taken early, especially for those

functions involving substantial numbers of staff. A decision to establish agency arrangements has obvious implications for the management structures of both the agent and the principal authority, and for this reason alone authorities will need to come to early conclusions . . .

6. Agency is quite distinct from the loan of staff under Section 113 in that it is the exercise of a function of one authority through another *authority*, involving the members and officers of the agent authority in genuine decision-making within whatever framework is laid down in the agreement.

7. It follows that although the precise terms of an agency agreement will vary with the service and with local conditions, the aim should be clearly to define the area of discretion of the agent, and the framework within which that discretion will be exercised. Within that framework agency arrangements should seek to give the agent authority the greatest measure of initiative in decision-making and the preparation of programmes of work, etc., subject, of course, to the statutory responsibility of the principal for the finance, overall standards and policy, and for the development of the service. A situation in which all decisions of substance would require to be made or reviewed by the authority with statutory responsibility for the function might suggest that some means of co-operation other than agency would be more appropriate.

8. Special considerations may apply to services undergoing radical change: subjects as diverse as refuse disposal and road safety are instances where it might be right for a measure of agency to apply to establish local functions (disposal of household refuse by existing treatment facilities in the one case and local aspects of road safety training, education and publicity in the other) while the newer and more specialised aspects of the function are developed by the authority with statutory responsibility.

9. The need for flexibility in applying the guidelines in this circular has been repeatedly emphasised by all the associations in the course of the consultations, and it is clear that the range of circumstances is so great that it is not practicable to lay down precise rules that will apply to a particular service in all circumstances; indeed an agency arrangement that may be appropriate for one district will not necessarily be appropriate for another district in the same county.

. . . . . .

11. Suggestions that agency arrangements might be made in particular cases should not be regarded as a reallocation of statutory responsibilities contrary to the way in which these are defined in the Local Government Act; nor, where the previous distribution of responsibilities has been modified by the Act, should they be regarded simply as a means for one authority to 'claw back' from another the services which were provided by its predecessor. Agency arrangements cannot alter the allocation of functions laid down by the Act and must not derogate from the ability of each authority to comply with its overall responsibilities, especially in connection with services which need wider areas for their planning and administration. Moreover an approach which envisaged county councils as having a role confined to the planning of services — leaving all execution in the hands of the

district councils — would be inconsistent with the purposes of reorganisation. But equally there should be no presumption against agency arrangements simply because the statutory responsibility is allocated to a particular class of authority. Agency arrangements should be considered on their merits as one of the ways in which the inter-relationship of all local authorities and of their functions can be accepted and given expression in a spirit of co-operation between authorities. The objective should be to improve the effectiveness and democratic discharge of local government functions, thus benefiting both local government itself and the public whom it serves.

12. On employment of staff there can be no rigid rule; much will depend on the volume of work involved in any particular agency arrangement and the availability of suitable staff. There will be many cases in which it will be appropriate for the staff required for the exercise of a function by an agent authority on behalf of a principal authority to be employed by the agent. In other instances, the need to make the fullest use of particular professional skills or to ensure the proper development and career structure of the officers involved will require that they should be employed by the principal authority.

13. The first consideration is the convenient and efficient operation of the function in question for the benefit of the public. In some instances, for example where detailed local knowledge is an advantage in carrying out the function, or where member involvement at the local level is particularly important, this may point to the desirability of county councils profiting from the local knowledge, organisation and expertise in the hands of district council members and officers. In the other direction, there may be particular functions which a county council could conveniently undertake, over a wider area, for several or all districts in their area. In the case of certain functions (eg urban conservation or the reclamation of derelict land) it will be important that specialist teams, wherever employed, continue in existence to avoid the fragmentation of specialist expertise. It will be for consideration in each such case whether, in the particular circumstances, the most appropriate arrangements will be by way of agency or loan of staff under Section 113.

14. Agency arrangements also require to be considered in relation to all the functions exercised by the authorities concerned and not in relation to a particular function in isolation. There may be managerial and staffing advantages (either for the county council or for the district council) if agency arrangements result in the exercise of related functions being concentrated in the hands of one authority. This will, for example, be particularly relevant where substantial expansion is proceeding under the Town Development Act, 1952, and where advantage lies in the concentration of operational responsibilities in a single body. If the package of activities with one authority is extended by agency arrangements and thus permits the employment of a stronger team of officers and a more balanced work force than would otherwise be the case, then benefits will be felt by all the functions exercised by that authority and not only those which are the subject of the agency arrangements.

. . . . . .

16. In some areas an organisation and a body of knowledge and expertise have been developed by an existing authority in relation to a particular function and either part of that function or a related function will be statutorily exercised as a district function after 1 April 1974. It may well be in the interests of the efficiency and effectiveness of the service in such areas for that organisation and expertise to continue in existence within the authority or authorities in whose area it will fall on reorganisation. Where the statutory allocation of functions under the Act would appear to lead to a contrary situation, consideration should be given to the advantage of concluding agency arrangements which would result in the least disturbance so far as the exercise of that particular function is concerned, subject to the need to ensure an effective service throughout the area of the principal authority.

17. With regard to certain functions, eg refuse disposal, there may be specific reasons for the establishment of short term arrangements between a principal and agent authority, but it should be recognised that such short term arrangements are likely to be unsettling for the staff concerned. Where it is necessary to adopt such short term arrangements it is therefore particularly important to keep staff fully informed at all stages and to consult them as proposals develop. The longer term interests of the officers concerned should be the subject of specific arrangements between the authorities.

18. Certain functions including education and social services are statutorily excluded from agency arrangements by subsections (7) and (10) of section 101 and others are likely to be regarded as non starters either on a commonsense basis (eg fire service) or because the Local Government Act clearly specifies that a particular function is to be directly exercised by an authority operating over a wide area (eg strategic planning and transportation). There will also be considerable variation in the functions for which, because of local circumstances, it will be appropriate to contemplate agency arrangements, and this circular cannot cover every case.

. . . . . .

20. Whilst there is no legal requirement that agency arrangements should be set out in a formal document it will normally be desirable for certain essential aspects to be considered and recorded in adequate detail for the avoidance of later doubt or dispute. The matters falling within this category will vary according to circumstances, but it is suggested that they include:

a. the functions to be exercised by the agent authority (defined by reference to the relevant statutory provision) and the extent of the agent's discretion;

b. staff and property arrangements;

c. duration of the agreement, machinery for its variation and consequential provision in respect of staff and property;

d. budgetary and financial control arrangements between the authorities involved.

21. In some instances agency arrangements between authorities will be of practical interest and importance to the public generally or to particular sections of the community. Steps should be taken to ensure that such arrangements are given suitable publicity.

22. Section 110 of the Local Government Act, 1972 empowers the appropriate Minister to make a direction either as to whether or not an agency arrangement should be entered into by particular authorities or as to the terms of such an arrangement, or both. The Act provides that such power shall not be exercised after 31 March 1974 and that any discretion made shall remain in force only to 31 March 1979.

23. The reason for the limitation is the transitional nature of the provision for Ministerial action and it is important to realise that the expiry of the direction will not, of itself, bring to an end the arrangements in respect of which it was made; nor does the limited duration of the power of direction in any way imply that agency arrangements generally should be similarly limited. The Act itself underlines the permanent interdependence of authorities and functions, and agency arrangements should be viewed in that context.

10 RELATIONS BETWEEN LOCAL AUTHORITIES: PLANNING FUNCTIONS

From *Town and Country Planning: Co-operation between Authorities* (Department of Environment Circular 74/73, 1973); by permission of H.M.S.O.

1. The effective discharge of planning functions under the Local Government Act 1972 depends on constructive working arrangements between authorities. The Secretary of State for the Environment and the Secretary of State for Wales wish therefore, following consultation with the local authority associations, to set out the general principles and considerations to which authorities should direct their attention.

2. The main statutory provisions are that

(a) County planning authorities will be responsible for the preparation of structure plans and development plan schemes in consultation with district planning authorities, who will, subject to any contrary provision in the structure plan or scheme, have the statutory responsibility for local plans.

(b) District planning authorities will deal directly with most planning control: the detailed arrangements for handling 'county matters' and other matters in which the strategic or highway interests of the county planning authority may be involved are set out in Schedule 16 of the Act.

3. The essential feature of this allocation of functions is that the new county planning authorities will have the statutory responsibility for establishing and maintaining the general strategic policies within their areas; while the new district planning authorities will bear the main general responsibility for the character of development within their individual areas. Both have thus the opportunity to play a part in the development and implementation of planning policies consistent with the overall strategic requirements of their areas. But although planning responsibilities are broadly distributed in this way planning is an inter-related process and this will

need to be reflected in the arrangements made between authorities. The test of the effectiveness of the arrangements will be the extent to which the public will receive the planning service it is entitled to expect.

4. It is likely that for some time authorities will not be able to obtain all the qualified and experienced staff they consider necessary to carry out their new duties. It is therefore essential that authorities assess their priorities and that available planning staff should be deployed and used in the most efficient and effective way, whichever authority is the employer.

5. Both counties and districts must therefore consider the planning process as a whole and set up the most effective arrangements they can devise for cooperation at both member and officer level. Circular 131/72 (Welsh Office Circular 277/72) drew attention to the range of powers for cooperation not only between authorities of different classes but also between district and district, or county and county — including cooperation by way of joint committees; consortia; joint teams; loan of staff; and agency arrangements. That circular noted that there was broad agreement that in town and country planning emphasis should be placed on the variety of flexible local arrangements and understandings, both formal and informal, open to authorities. The aim must be to produce constructive relationships between authorities which will help achieve their planning objectives and at the same time will form an integral part of the organisation within authorities for the corporate management of the whole range of local authority and related services.

. . . . . .

7. The main objectives are to secure a constructive relationship —

(i)   between county and district planning authorities (and, where applicable, between county and county and district and district);

(ii) between development plan and development control work;

(iii) between 'planning' and transportation together with the other services and functions directly linked to them.

8. The main requirements are —

(i)   to ensure a full understanding at member level of the respective planning policies of the authorities concerned and the coordination of their policies;

(ii) to maintain momentum in policy and plan making; to secure continuity and avoid delay — particularly in handling planning applications not decided on 1 April 1974; and to carry through schemes already initiated;

(iii) to decide on those arrangements which enable staff (particularly qualified and experienced staff) to be used to the best advantage (whichever authority employs that staff);

(iv) to make clear arrangements for the collection, use and exchange of information;

(v) to define and coordinate procedures so that duplication is reduced to a minimum and unnecessary misunderstanding or conflict at the formal stages is avoided.

. . . . . .

13. Both classes of authority will need planning staff in their own right. But it is important, and in the transitional stage vital, that staff — particularly those professionally qualified and experienced — should be deployed to the best advantage both to provide the service which the public and elected members are entitled to expect and also to produce attractive and worthwhile career structures. The support which professional officers can give to the partnership between authorities will largely depend on the extent to which their advice is available beyond their own authority — either on tasks for which teamwork is essential, where specialist advice is needed, or where an authority does not have professional town planning advice. In the short term senior officers with long experience in development control work though their qualifications are in other disciplines will often have a valuable part to play.

14. The fragmentation of existing teams is, of course, to be avoided; rather should they be strengthened and made available on a wider basis, both within and even beyond the county (e.g. for regional and sub-regional plan work) to bring together the best professional advice available. In addition consideration should be given to the establishment of new teams both on a longer term basis for continuing and related work or for specific projects — and in appropriate cases these teams should be able to draw on the services of all the authorities in the area and be available to them all. The prospect of covering the whole range of planning work should be a valuable incentive for career development and should enable officers to adopt a comprehensive approach to the planning process.

15. It is, of course, important that those officers in daily contact with the public — which in many cases will mean those primarily engaged on local planning and on development control — should have a high level of professional competence or have easy and immediate access to professional advice. Staff without specific professional qualifications need this access generally. Arrangements for professional advice will do much to avoid a scramble for the qualified staff available — which would be to the disadvantage of local government as a whole.

. . . . . .

18. Much of the effectiveness of cooperative working will depend on clear arrangements for the collection, use, sharing and exchange of information needed to carry out all parts of the planning process. These must ensure that both county and districts —

(i)   have access to existing survey and analysis material collected for development plan purposes;

(ii) have a consistent information base and coordinated methods for handling future survey and analysis material to avoid duplication;

(iii) have a regular exchange of information of changes taking place, so that both structure and local plans can be effectively monitored;

(iv) have access to an exchange of present and future development control records so that planning decisions are consistent.

. . . . . .

ANNEX 1: DEVELOPMENT PLANS

1. Even more than in the past, when the county was the one formal plan-making authority in their area, there will need to be, in readiness for the changeover at April and thereafter, close cooperation between county and districts.

2. District councils must be even more closely involved in structure plan work and committed to following it through in their local plan and development control work. The relationship between counties and districts must recognise the continuing structural role of counties as well as the important new role which districts will have as of right in local planning: and thus enable both authorities to make their contribution to plan-making.

3. It is not just a question of considering whether and, if so, what adaptations of existing machinery might suffice. Nor is it enough to rely simply on the formal consultation, important though this is, required by statute or regulations. To get the best from reorganisation, authorities will need to give considerable thought to the new allocation of responsibilities for a function which has to be seen as a whole.

4. The Secretaries of State look to existing and future authorities to adopt this approach. In the light of their discussions with the associations, they are confident that authorities will increasingly adopt it and welcome the fact that a number have already begun to plan on that basis. They expect authorities to be anticipating the problems, so that those formal and informal arrangements most appropriate for securing cooperation and collaborative working in their area can be adopted as soon as practicable.

5. The Act contains two specific pieces of machinery designed to promote effective cooperation in the planning field and to minimise delay, dispute and duplication.

(i) *The development plan scheme.* This is the document in which the county, following consultation with districts, will set out the allocation of responsibility for preparing local plans and the programme for them; and indicate their scope and, as appropriate, the relationship between them. It will need to be based on the arrangements, including those relating to the use of staff, agreed between the authorities. It may, in suitable cases, need to refer to these arrangements; but setting them out in the formal scheme, certainly in any detail, would make it less useful as the tool it is meant to be, as well as too elaborate and detailed. The setting out of these arrangements should be in a separate document from the development plan scheme; both can, of course, be readily revised as circumstances change.

(ii) *Certification.* The requirement for a certificate is designed to establish that any local plan which has been prepared is in general conformity with the structure plan. By cooperation and close working between them, authorities can secure that the request for a formal certificate results in its issue without delay.
The Secretaries of State have formal powers to settle disputes on a development plan scheme, or to determine questions about conformity referred to them. They

wish to use these powers only as a last resort: whether or not they have to exercise them will depend primarily on authorities.

ANNEX 2: PLANNING CONTROL

1. In planning control it will be of paramount importance that there be no doubt or misunderstanding on the part either of the authorities or the public about where the responsibility for decision rests. Subordinate legislation will provide that applicants should be entitled to be informed when responsibility for handling of applications has been transferred from one authority to another. Normally, however, the point of contact between the public and planning authority will be at district level; and it is open to authorities to agree that consultations should be in general carried out by the district planning authority and decisions issued through the district even where 'county matters' are involved. There will of course always be some cases where the advantage will lie in handling by the county planning authority throughout, e.g. mineral applications. But it will normally be convenient for the public to be able to get the maximum information about matters affecting their application from the district planning authority where otherwise an enquiry to a distant county or area headquarters could be involved.

2. Because development control arrangements are essentially matters to be settled between county and district planning authorities no provision was made in the Local Government Act 1972 for statutory development control schemes under which disputes could have been referred to the Secretary of State for arbitration. It is nevertheless considered that informal development control schemes should in general be drawn up in each area. While these schemes are unlikely to be of interest to the great majority of applicants for planning permission they should nevertheless be public documents available to the press and the public who have a right to know what arrangements have been made for joint working between authorities. Development control schemes should show clearly the range of matters covered and the way in which they are dealt with.

11 LOCAL AUTHORITIES AND THE NATIONAL HEALTH SERVICE

From *Local Government in England and Wales: a Guide to the New System* (Department of Environment, 1974); by permission of H.M.S.O.

1. The purpose of the reorganisation effected by the National Health Service Reorganisation Act 1973 was to bring within one organisation all the various parts of the health service. Thus the functions of Regional Hospital Boards in England, the Welsh Hospital Board, Hospital Management Committees and the Boards of Governors of Teaching Hospitals — with the exception of some London Post Gradu-

ate Teaching Hospitals — (which ran the hospital service); the local NHS Executive Councils (which looked after the services provided by family practitioners, dentists, pharmacists and opticians), and the local health authorities (which provided a variety of community health services, eg the district nursing and health visitor services, the ambulance service, maternity and child health care, family planning etc) are, together with the school health service, now administered principally by an organisation of *Area Health Authorities* (AHAs) and *Regional Health Authorities* (RHAs) with a direct line of accountability to the Secretary of State for Social Services. In Wales there is no regional tier and AHAs are directly responsible to the Secretary of State for Wales.

2. The areas of the AHAs are the same as the areas of the local social services authorities (ie the non-metropolitan and Welsh counties and the metropolitan districts), except that in London each AHA covers between 1 and 3 London boroughs. The RHAs each cover a group of AHAs; at least one University medical school is included in each region . . .

3. The RHAs are responsible for strategic planning and monitoring, allocation of resources and managing a small number of services. AHAs will plan and have responsibility for operating most services and for collaboration with local government.

4. An AHA may be divided into one or more health districts (not necessarily with the same boundaries as local government districts). In each Area there is a Family Practitioner Committee which, in accordance with regulations, administers on behalf of the AHA arrangements for the provision of Family Practitioner Services (general medical dental, ophthalmic and pharmaceutical services). Districts will be the basic management unit for planning and operating most services so that operational control is kept as close as possible to the point of direct patient care.

5. Close collaboration is required between AHAs and local authorities particularly in the areas of the school health service (which the AHAs will be providing for local education authorities), the social services (local social services authorities are now responsible for the hospital social work service as well as for the back up social care that a family may need while a parent is ill and at other times) and the environmental health services (which are the responsibility of the new district councils). This collaboration is made easier by the general use of the same boundaries for AHAs and local social services authorities. Each Area Health Authority includes, in addition to the Chairman appointed by the Secretary of State for Social Services, members appointed by the Regional Health Authority and some members appointed by the corresponding non-metropolitan county, metropolitan district or London borough council or councils; where appropriate members are also appointed by the Inner London Education Authority and the City of London. In Wales the Secretary of State for Wales appoints the Chairman and part of the membership. In addition Joint Consultative Committees are being established by each AHA and its associated local authority or authorities (ie the councils of the counties, districts, London boroughs or the City of London which are wholly or partly in the area of the AHA) to co-ordinate their interrelated activities.

6. The RHAs are required to establish 'community health councils' principally to

represent the local community's interest in the health services to those responsible for managing them. In Wales this function devolves on the Secretary of State. Generally one such council is being established for each health district with at least half its membership (total approximately 18–30) appointed by the appropriate local authorities for the area, at least one third by voluntary organisations and the rest by the RHA, or in Wales by the Secretary of State. AHAs are required to provide councils with such information about the planning and operation of health services in the Area as they may reasonably require; and to consult the CHC on any proposal which the AHA may have under consideration for any substantial development or variation of the health service in the CHC's district. CHCs have the right to enter and inspect hospitals and other health premises controlled by the AHA. CHCs are required to make annually a formal report to the establishing RHA on their activities, or in Wales to the Secretary of State, to send a copy to the relevant AHA and to publish it. The AHA is required to comment on these reports, to include a record of any steps taken on issues raised in them and to publish the comments.

7. Health Service Commissioners for England and Wales have been appointed (both offices are filled by Sir Alan Marre who is also Parliamentary Commissioner for Administration). The Commissioner is able to investigate complaints of injustices or hardship as a result of failure in, and a failure to provide, health authority services or of maladministration involved in other actions taken by health authorities, (but not complaints which relate to the exercise of clinical judgement by doctors and other staff nor complaints for which statutory procedures already exist). He will investigate complaints made within 12 months from the day the aggrieved person first had notice of the matters alleged in the complaint, but he will normally only undertake an investigation when he is satisfied that the health authority concerned has had a reasonable opportunity to deal with the complaint.

12 LOCAL AUTHORITIES AND WATER AUTHORITIES

From *Water Act 1973: Water Authorities and Local Authorities* (Department of Environment Circular 100/73, 1973); by permission of H.M.S.O. This circular sets out the working relationships between local authorities and the ten new regional water authorities created by the Water Act, 1973.

2. The reorganisation of water services is proceeding hand in hand with local government reorganisation. The Government have emphasised the important part which local authorities will play in the new system of organisation through appointing a majority of the members of each water authority and through the controlled function which district and London borough councils will retain in relation to sewerage. The present Circular is addressed both to the new water authorities and to local authorities. It is not intended to be a complete description of the Water Act 1973,

but concentrates on explaining those provisions which define or affect the relationship between the water authorities and local authorities . . .

. . . . . .

5. The composition of the regional water authorities is governed by section 3 of the Act. The essential feature of this section is that a majority of the members of each authority are to be appointed by the county and district councils in its area (in Greater London, by the Greater London Council and the London borough councils), while the remainder (including the chairman) are to be appointed by the Secretary of State or the Minister of Agriculture, Fisheries and Food as persons who have had experience of, and shown capacity in, matters relevant to the functions of water authorities . . .

6. In appointing members of water authorities, local authorities are not restricted by the Act to appointing one of their own elected members (section 3(12)): a particular authority might for example choose to appoint one of their officers to the water authority. But any member of a water authority who is at the time of his appointment an elected member of the local authority (or one of the local authorities) appointing him will automatically cease to be a member of the water authority (by virtue of section 3(13)) if he loses his seat on the local authority. The normal term of office for local authority members of water authorities will be 4 years ending on May 31 (paragraph 4 of Schedule 3 to the Act) . . .

. . . . . .

SEWERAGE

11. While the statutory responsibility for sewerage and sewage disposal will be transferred to the water authorities, section 15 of the Act contains specific provision for district and London borough councils to discharge sewerage functions as respects their area on behalf of the water authority. The scope of this controlled function is spelt out in some detail in subsection (2) of section 15. The main features are that the council will be required to prepare and submit annually to the water authority a programme for the discharge of sewerage functions as respects their area, having regard to any guidance given to them by the water authority; and to carry out the programme (in practice separate programmes for capital and recurrent expenditure, the latter being primarily maintenance) in the form in which it is approved by the water authority, exercising for this purpose the relevant powers of the water authority. The Council will also be required to provide such vehicles and equipment as may be necessary for maintaining the sewers which it is their function to maintain under the arrangements. All sewers provided by the council in pursuance of the arrangements will be vested in the water authority and the water authority will reimburse the council for the expenditure they incur by virtue of the arrangements.

12. Model heads of agreement have been worked out in consultation with the local authority associations, and are now being expanded into a model agreement, which will also be discussed with the associations. The intention is that district and London borough councils should retain a substantial degree of discretion in relation

to the maintenance and operation of sewers, and should also have a field of discretion in formulating the programme of future capital expenditure for approval by the water authority. Subsections (8) and (9) of section 15 of the Act extend the general powers of local authorities to arrange for the discharge of their functions by committees, sub-committees or officers so that these will also cover the sewerage functions which local authorities will be exercising on behalf of water authorities.
. . . . . .

15. The Act does however contemplate (subsection (6) of section 15) that there may be cases in which a water authority and a council come to the conclusion that it would be inexpedient in the interests of efficiency for the council to have a controlled function in relation to sewerage. If this occurs, provision is made for there to be no arrangements under section 15 and the executive responsibility for sewerage, as for other functions, will lie with the water authority . . .
. . . . . .

CO-OPERATION BETWEEN WATER AUTHORITIES AND LOCAL AUTHORITIES

34. The reorganisation will succeed only if there is close co-operation between water authorities and local authorities at all levels. The Act provides the necessary framework for such co-operation. Two elements in that framework, the appointment of a majority of the members of each water authority by local authorities and the retention by local authorities of a controlled function in sewerage, have been mentioned already . . . other important elements . . . are the relationship of planning by water authorities to the system of land use planning, co-operation in the provision of goods and services by one authority to another, and arrangements for emergencies and disasters.

35. Section 24 of the Act requires each water authority to carry out a survey of their area as soon as practicable after 1 April 1974, to prepare an estimate of the demand for the use of water in that area over the next 20 years, and to prepare a plan of action to meet the demand. The plan will cover all the functions of the water authority except land drainage (for which there is separate provision in subsection (5) of section 24) and the water authority are required to review it at intervals of not more than 7 years. They are also required to send every local authority in their area a copy of any report prepared by them in consequence of such a survey, and of any amendment to such a report (subsection (12)). These surveys and plans will, as soon as they become available, form the basis for the more detailed programmes covering a period of not more than 7 years which water authorities will be required to submit to the appropriate Minister or Ministers under subsection (6), and which when approved by the appropriate Minister or Ministers will be binding on them in respect to any project involving substantial outlay on capital account (subsection (9)).

36. This system of planning and programming implements the recommendations on this subject of the Central Advisory Water Committee in their report on 'The

future management of water in England and Wales' (HMSO, 1971). Clearly the water authority will have to work closely in this context with the local authorities which are wholly or partly within their area, and subsection (8)(a) of section 24 places a specific obligation on them to consult such authorities in formulating their plans and programmes. In addition paragraph (b) of the same subsection places a further obligation on them to have regard to the structure and local plans for their area or, as the case may be the old-style development plans.

. . . . . .

FINANCING OF WATER SERVICES

41. Part III of the Act makes important changes in the financing of water services. With the exception of exchequer grants and their land drainage functions, water authorities will derive their revenue primarily from charges for the services they provide. This means that a major service, sewerage and sewage disposal, will be transferred as from 1 April 1974 from the general rate to a charging basis; and the general rate will also cease to bear the cost of pollution control, which is at present financed by precept, and cease to meet deficits on water supply and fisheries accounts.

. . . . . .

45. It is envisaged that, in the case of domestic consumers, water authorities will move as quickly as possible to a system of levying a combined charge on each household for water supply, sewerage and sewage disposal. It is recognised however that it will be a considerable task, at least in rural areas, to identify those households who have main sewerage and on whom the charge for sewerage and sewage disposal should be levied. The Secretary of State therefore proposes to make provision by order under paragraph 5(2)(c) of Schedule 6 to the Act for a transitional system under which the charge for sewerage and sewage disposal will be expressed as a lump sum for a given local authority area and collected by the local authority with (but not as part of) the general rate. This will be in addition to, and distinct from, any arrangements which may be made under section 7 of the Act for a local authority to continue to collect charges for water supply on behalf of the water authority. The local authority associations have been consulted about this proposal and there will be further consultations about the details of the transitional system, which is expected to last for a period of the order of 2 years. At the end of that period the water authority might still find it convenient to arrange for the local authority to act as their agent in collecting the combined charge from individual households, but this would be achieved by mutual agreement under section 7 of the Act . . .

. . . . . .

LOCAL ADVISORY COMMITTEES

50. It is envisaged that the water authorities will have an extensive divisional organ-

isation, with offices at local points of contact for the convenience of the consumer. It may well be desirable in certain circumstances however for an additional channel of communication to be established between the water authority and local communities. This might take the form of advisory committees covering all the functions of the water authority (other than land drainage and fisheries, for which there is specific provision in the Act). Water authorities are empowered to establish such committees by section 6(8) of the Act. They may consist predominantly or entirely of persons who are not members of the authority and, although the case for establishing them and their composition will be something for each individual water authority to assess for themselves, it is to be expected that elected members of local authorities (appointed to the committee by the water authority in consultation with the local authorities concerned) will play a considerable role in them. In prescribing the form of annual report for water authorities under paragraph 49(2) of Schedule 3 to the Act, the Ministers intend to require them to provide information in that report about the local advisory committees which they have set up.

APPENDIX A PRE-1972 FUNCTIONS OF LOCAL AUTHORITIES

From *Written Evidence of the Ministry of Housing and Local Government* (to Redcliffe-Maud, 1967); by permission of H.M.S.O. Greater London is excluded from this list.

A. COUNTY BOROUGH COUNCILS

County borough councils have the functions of county and county district councils.

B. COUNTY COUNCILS

Children's Service

Care of children permanently or temporarily deprived of a normal home life.
Advice, guidance and assistance to promote the welfare of children by diminishing the need to receive them into or keep them in care or to bring them before a juvenile court.

*Civil Defence

Raising and training the Civil Defence Corps.
Functions in an emergency under regulations made by various Ministers.

Diseases of Animals

Except in certain boroughs (see Part D).

* Subject to delegation (see Part E).

*Education

Primary, secondary and further education.
Youth service and youth employment service.
Community centres and other recreational services.
School health service.
School meals service.

Fire Service ·

†Food and Drugs

Functions of a 'food and drugs authority':
    Enforcement of provisions relating to composition, labelling and description.
    Appointment of a public analyst.
(The other group of food and drugs functions — the enforcement of provisions
    relating to food safety and hygiene — is carried out by county district councils.)

Good Rule and Government Byelaws

In urban and rural districts only (see Part D).

*Health and Welfare

Personal health services
    Health centres.
    Care of mothers and young children.
    Midwifery.
    Health visiting.
    Home nursing.
    Vaccination and immunisation.
    Ambulances.
    Prevention of illness, care and after-care.
    Domestic help.
    Mental health.

Welfare
    Residential accommodation mainly for old people.
    Temporary accommodation for the homeless.
    Help for the disabled.

†Libraries

---

† Except where a borough or an urban district council qualifies on population to exercise the
functions (see Part D).

Police

Except where a combined police authority has been established by the amalgamation of county or county borough police areas.

Private Street Works

Only in rural districts (see Part D).

Registration and Licensing of Motor Vehicles; Issue of Driving Licences

As agents of the Minister of Transport.

Registration of Births, Deaths and Marriages; Civil Marriages

Appointment and payment of staff and provision of offices.

*Roads and Traffic

Highway authority for:
    All roads, other than trunk roads, in rural districts.
    Classified roads in boroughs and urban districts.
Trunk roads as agents of the Minister of Transport.
Traffic regulation.
Road safety information and training.

Shops Acts 1950 to 1965 — Enforcement

Only in rural districts and certain urban districts (see Part D).

Smallholdings

Provision of smallholdings to enable people with agricultural experience to farm on their own account.

*Town and Country Planning

Preparation of development plans.
Control of development (including tree and building preservation orders and control of advertisements).
Acquisition, appropriation and disposal of land for planning purposes.
Certain functions under the National Parks and Access to the Countryside Act 1949.

†Weights and Measures

Provision of standards of weight and measure.
Verification of traders' equipment and the protection of the buyer against short weight or short measure.

C. FUNCTIONS COMMON TO ALL COUNTY DISTRICT COUNCILS

Baths, Swimming Baths and Wash-houses

Bus Shelters

Caravan Sites

Cemeteries and Crematoria

Civil Defence

Functions in an emergency under regulations made by various Ministers.

Clean Air

Food and Drugs

Enforcement of provisions relating to food safety and hygiene.
Slaughterhouses — control and, where necessary, provision.

Housing

Provision and management of houses.
Slum clearance.
Abatement of overcrowding.
Improvement grants.
Loans for house purchase.
Enforcement of building regulations.

Litter Control

Offices and Shops

Enforcement of the Offices, Shops and Railway Premises Act 1963 (health safety
and welfare of persons employed).

Parking Places — Provision and Control

Parks and Open Spaces

Physical Training and Recreation

Provision of gymnasiums, playing fields, holiday camps, camping sites and community centres.

Public Health Functions — Miscellaneous

Control of communicable diseases.

Disinfestation.
Mortuaries.
Public conveniences.
Rodent control.
Suppression of nuisances.

Refuse Collection and Disposal

Sewerage and Sewage Disposal

Street Cleansing

Support of the Arts

Town and Country Planning

Acquisition, appropriation and disposal of land for planning purposes.
Certain functions under the National Parks and Access to the Countryside Act 1949.

Water Supply

In most cases through joint boards.

D. FUNCTIONS EXERCISED ONLY BY SOME COUNTY DISTRICT COUNCILS

Coast Protection

All maritime county district councils.

Diseases of Animals

Boroughs with a population of 10,000 in 1881.

Food and Drugs

Boroughs and urban districts with a population of 40,000 or more exercise the functions of a 'food and drugs authority' (see Part A) as of right; those with 20–40,000 only where the Minister of Health has given directions.

Good Rule and Government Byelaws

All boroughs.

Libraries

Boroughs and urban districts with a population of 40,000 or more (conferment and removal of powers requires ministerial action).

Markets

All boroughs and urban districts; rural districts only with the consent of the Minister.

Museums and Art Galleries

All library authorities and any local authority which was already maintaining a museum or art gallery when the Public Libraries Act 1964 came into force. Any other local authority, including a parish council, may provide one with the consent of the Secretary of State for Education and Science.

Offensive Trades — Control

All boroughs and urban districts; rural districts only by an urban powers order.

Private Street Works

All boroughs and urban districts.

Roads and Traffic

Boroughs and urban districts are the highway authority for unclassified roads. They are also responsible for road safety information and training. If their population is 20,000 or more, they exercise powers of traffic regulation.

Shops Acts 1950 to 1965 — Enforcement

All boroughs; urban districts with a population of 20,000 or more.

Street Lighting

Boroughs and urban districts; rural districts only by an urban powers order.

Weights and Measures

Boroughs and urban districts with a population of 60,000 or more can acquire the functions by resolution.

E. FUNCTIONS DELEGATED BY COUNTY COUNCILS TO COUNTY DISTRICT COUNCILS UNDER SPECIFIC STATUTORY PROVISIONS

Civil Defence

Counties commonly delegate to county districts functions relating to the local recruitment, organisation and training of sub-divisions of the Corps.

Education

Boroughs and urban districts with a population of 60,000 or more can acquire delegated functions as of right; other authorities can do so only if the Secretary of State is satisfied that there are special circumstances. 32 authorities exercise delegated functions. They are known as 'excepted districts', i.e. excepted from the scheme which many counties have prepared for decentralisation to divisional executives (ad hoc bodies consisting of members of the county council for that division of the county and of members of the district councils in the division).

Delegated and decentralised functions are mostly in the field of primary and secondary education. Functions in further education can, however, be devolved with the Secretary of State's approval, though in practice some are never devolved, for example, the training of teachers and awards to university students.

Health and Welfare

Boroughs and urban districts with a population of 60,000 or more can acquire delegated functions as of right; other authorities can do so only if the Minister is satisfied that there are special circumstances. 28 authorities exercise delegated functions.

All the main functions can be delegated without restriction *except*:

(1) ambulances;
(2) care and after-care of the mentally ill in residential accommodation;
(3) provision of residential and temporary accommodation.

(1) cannot be delegated at all; (2) and (3) only if the Minister is satisfied that there are special circumstances.

Roads and Traffic

Boroughs and urban districts with a population of 20,000 or more can 'claim' classified roads in their area and so become entitled to carry out maintenance and improvement. Most eligible authorities have claimed. In general the county council continues to meet the cost with the help of Exchequer grant.

Any county district council can apply to the county council for delegation of functions relating to classified roads. There is no appeal against a refusal. About 230 authorities exercise delegated powers, which may be in respect of particular roads only.

A rural district council can apply to the county council for delegation of functions relating to unclassified roads. There is a right of appeal to the Minister against a refusal. Delegation must cover all unclassified roads. Very few arrangements have been made.

Any county district council can apply to the county council to control free street parking.

Town and Country Planning

All county districts with a population of 60,000 or more ('excepted councils') can acquire delegated functions as of right; other authorities can be treated in the same way only if the Minister is satisfied that there are special circumstances. There are 30 'excepted councils' and 2 others.

County councils must delegate to 'excepted councils' nearly all their functions relating to the exercise and enforcement of planning control. They also have permissive powers to delegate any or all of these functions to any county district. Development plan functions cannot be delegated.

F. PARISH COUNCILS

Functions exercisable only by parish councils

Allotments.

Charities — right to appoint and act as trustees of and to receive accounts of parochial charities.

Maintenance of closed churchyards.

Maintenance of public footpaths and bridleways.

Appointment of school managers.

Parking places for motor cycles and bicycles.

Roadside shelters and seats.

Street lighting (a parish council can adopt powers if the rural district council has not acquired them by an urban powers order).

War memorials — power to maintain, repair and protect.

Functions common to parish and rural district councils

Baths, swimming baths and wash-houses.

Burial grounds and crematoria (powers in the Burial Acts can be adopted by a parish council); cemeteries and crematoria (powers in the Public Health (Internments) Act 1879 can be exercised by a rural district council).

Bus shelters.

Litter control.

Mortuaries.

Parks, recreation grounds and open spaces.

Physical training and recreation — gymnasiums, playing fields, holiday camps, camping sites and community centres.

Public clocks.

Rights of way — acquisition by agreement (rural district councils also have compulsory powers).

Delegation by rural district councils

A rural district council can delegate to a parish council or to a parochial committee appointed by it any of the functions which it is empowered to exercise in the area of the parish. (A parochial committee may consist either wholly of district council members or partly of such members and partly of local government electors, who must be parish councillors if a parish council exists.)

APPENDIX B POST-1972 FUNCTIONS OF LOCAL AUTHORITIES

From *Local Government in England and Wales: a Guide to the New System* (Department of Environment, 1974); by permission of H.M.S.O.

Notes (*for Tables on pp. 88, 89*)

a. In areas where there is a parish council that authority will be responsible.
b. Agency arrangements are not permissible.
c. The councils of non-metropolitan districts and inner London boroughs whose areas serve primary schools are minor authorities for the purpose of appointing managers of these schools except in areas where there is a parish or community council (or, in England, a parish meeting) which can act as minor authority. Where the area serving the school comprises two or more of the authorities mentioned above they act jointly as a minor authority.
d. Education is a borough function in outer London. In inner London education is provided by the Inner London Education Authority which is a special independent committee of the Greater London Council.
e. County councils have certain reserve powers to provide housing subject to a request by a district council and/or the approval of the Secretary of State.
f. The London boroughs are responsible for the provision of housing. The Greater London Council maintains a stock of housing which it inherited from the former London County Council and also has a strategic role (eg aiding the slum clearance programme of the inner London boroughs, provision of housing for Londoners outside London, re-housing GLC and London borough tenants whose accommodation needs change and providing accommodation through a nominations scheme for people on the borough waiting lists for housing).
g. Most local authorities collect local licence duties through the agency of the Post Office.
h. Some matters are reserved to the county councils but the district councils receive all planning applications initially.
j. Two joint planning boards have been set up to administer national park functions in the Lake District National Park and the Peak National Park. For other national parks these functions are administered by a special committee of the county council mainly concerned which may include representatives of the other county councils and the district councils for the area of the national park.
k. Greater London and certain areas immediately adjacent are policed by the Metropolitan Police force. This force is responsible directly to the Home Secretary.
l. Rate demands issued by the district councils include precepts from county and parish councils; those issued by the London borough councils and the City of London include precepts from the Greater London Council.
m. The function of licensing vehicles and drivers is now vested in the Secretary of State for the Environment. The issuing of licences is being centralised, but for the time being local authorities act as the Secretary of State's agents. For Greater London the local authority is the Greater London Council. Elsewhere,

Functions of Principal Authorities in England

Function	Metropolitan County	Metropolitan District	Non-Metropolitan County	Non-Metropolitan District	Greater London Council	London Borough
Allotments (a)		x		x		x
Arts and Recreation –						
Art and Crafts, support	x	x	x	x	x	x
Art galleries	x	x	x	x	x	x
Libraries		x	x	x		x
Museums	x	x	x	x	x	x
Recreation (eg parks, playing fields, swimming baths etc)	x	x	x	x	x	x
Tourism, encouragement	x	x	x	x	x	x
Cemeteries and Crematoria		x		x		x
Consumer Protection –						
Food and Drugs (composition)	x		x			x
Trade Description	x		x			x
Weights and Measures	x		x			x
Education (b)		x	x	(c)		x(c)(d)
Environmental Health –						
Building Regulations		x		x		x
Clean Air		x		x		x
Communicable disease control		x		x		x
Food safety and hygiene		x		x		x
Home safety		x		x		x
Litter control	x	x	x	x	x	x
Refuse collection		x		x		x
Refuse disposal	x		x		x	x
Rodent control		x		x		x
Street cleansing		x		x		x
Fire Service	x		x		x	x
Footpaths and Bridleways –						
Creation, diversion and extinguishment	x	x	x	x		x

Function						
Housing	(e)	x	(e)	x	x(f)	x
Local Licence Duties (eg dog and game licences)					x(f)	x(f)
Collection, (g)	x	x		x		x
Markets and Fairs	x	x		x		x
Planning –						
Advertisement Control	x	x	x	x		x
Building preservation notices	x	x	x	x	x	x
Conservation areas	x	x	x	x	x	x
Country parks	x	x	x	x	x	x
Derelict land	x	x	x	x	x	x
Development control (processing of planning applications) (h)	x	x	x	x		
Development plan schemes	x	x	x	x	x	x
Listed building control	x					
Local plans	x	x	x	x		
National parks (b)	x(j)	x(j)	x(j)	x	x	x
Structure plans	x	x	x	x	x	x
Police (b)	x	x	x	x	(k)	(k)
Rate collection (l)	x	x	x	x		x
Smallholdings	x	x	x	x	x	x
Social Services (b)	x	x	x	x	x	x
Traffic, Transport and Highways –						
Driver and Vehicle Licensing	(m)	(m)	(m)	(m)	(m)	
Highways (n)	x	(o)	x	(o)	x(p)	x(p)
Lighting – Footway	x	x	x	x	x	x
Highway	x	x	x	x	x(q)	x(q)
Parking – Off-street	x	x(r)	x	x(r)	x(s)	x
On-street	x		x		x(t)	
Public Transport	x(u)	x(v)	x(v)	(v)	x(u)	
Road Safety	x		x		x	
Traffic Regulation	x		x		x	
Transportation Planning	x		x		x	

the agent authority may be either a county or district council. Arrangements for the issue of licences at Post Offices are unchanged; if it is necessary to write to the local authority it is sufficient to write to the address shown on the licence concerned.

n. The Secretary of State for the Environment is highway authority for trunk roads.
o. District councils may claim the right to maintain unclassified roads in urban areas (this power is distinct from the powers to act under agency agreements).
p. The Greater London Council is highway authority for all principal roads in London other than trunk roads (ie the main strategic road network) while the London boroughs are highway authorities for non-principal roads.
q. Highway lighting responsibilities in Greater London are divided on the same basis as highway responsibilities.
r. Subject to the consent of the county council.
s. Subject to the consent of the appropriate London borough council.
t. On the application of the appropriate London borough council.
u. The metropolitan county councils and the Greater London Council are the passenger transport authorities and there are passenger transport executives responsible for day to day administration.
v. Non-metropolitan county councils are responsible for the co-ordination of public transport in their areas but in some cases district councils run transport undertakings.

FUNCTIONS OF PARISH COUNCILS IN ENGLAND AND COMMUNITY COUNCILS IN WALES

A. Powers to provide facilities and/or to contribute towards the provision of facilities by others

1. Allotments
2. *Arts and Recreation*
    Arts and Crafts, support and encouragement
    Community halls, provision
    Recreational facilities (eg parks and open spaces, playing fields, swimming baths etc)
    Tourism, encouragement
3. *Burials etc*
    Cemeteries and crematoria
    Closed churchyards, maintenance
    Mortuaries, provision
4. *Environmental Health*
    Cleaning and drainage of ponds etc
    Litter control
    Public conveniences
    Wash houses and launderettes
5. *Footpaths, Roads and Traffic*
    Bus shelters
    Footpaths — creation and maintenance;
                signposting

Footway lighting, provision
Parking facilities — cycle and motor cycle parks;
                      off-street car parks
Rights of way, acquisition and maintenance
Roadside verges, provision, maintenance and protection
6. Public Clocks
7. War Memorials

B. Specific powers to receive notifications and represent parish interests to other authorities

1. District councils must notify parish councils in England and community councils in Wales of the following —
   a. planning applications received by them where the parish or community council ask to be so notified;
   b. intention to make byelaws relating to hackney-carriages, music and dancing, promenades, sea shore, registry of servants and street naming;
   c. intention to provide a cemetery in a parish or community;
   d. proposals to carry out sewerage works.

APPENDIX C SIZE OF NEW LOCAL AUTHORITIES

From P. G. Richards *The Reformed Local Government System* (Allen & Unwin, revised second edn, 1975); by permission of the publisher.

SIZE OF LOCAL AUTHORITIES: ENGLAND

(i) Metropolitan counties

Name of county	1971 Census population (thousands)	Rateable value at April 1971 (£000s)
Greater Manchester	2,727	112,298
Merseyside	1,659	69,212
South Yorkshire	1,315	52,392
Tyne and Wear	1,209	48,809
West Midlands	2,790	137,440
West Yorkshire	2,053	73,178

(ii) Non-metropolitan counties

Name of County	1971 Census population (thousands)	Rateable value at April 1971 (£000s)
Avon	902	42,448
Bedfordshire	463	26,262
Berkshire	620	36,747
Buckinghamshire	476	26,410
Cambridgeshire	505	21,830
Cheshire	865	40,601
Cleveland	567	27,588
Cornwall	377	13,512
Cumbria	476	17,462
Derbyshire	886	34,867
Devon	896	39,034
Dorset	553	29,823
Durham	608	21,238
East Sussex	650	39,318
Essex	1,354	66,287
Gloucestershire	463	18,461
Hampshire	1,370	65,821
Hereford and Worcester	562	22,753
Hertfordshire	922	59,101
Humberside	838	35,185
Isle of Wight	109	4,441
Kent	1,396	60,404
Lancashire	1,341	53,150
Leicestershire	799	36,519
Lincolnshire	503	17,547
Norfolk	624	24,619
North Yorkshire	629	23,299
Northamptonshire	468	20,129
Northumberland	280	9,525
Nottinghamshire	973	42,171
Oxfordshire	504	23,150
Salop	337	14,414
Somerset	387	14,525
Staffordshire	963	36,942
Suffolk	537	20,240
Surrey	981	57,338
Warwickshire	456	19,138
West Sussex	610	36,015
Wiltshire	486	20,062

(iii) Metropolitan districts

Metropolitan county	Number of districts	Population range (000s)	Rateable value at April 1971 range (£000s)	Name of biggest district
Greater Manchester	10	174–542	5,699–29,330	Manchester
Merseyside	5	192–607	7,038–27,728	Liverpool
South Yorkshire	4	226–566	6,593–26,769	Sheffield
Tyne and Wear	5	177–308	6,372–16,180	Newcastle
West Midlands	7	192–1,096	8,902–58,667	Birmingham
West Yorkshire	5	194–738	5,841–30,621	Leeds

APPENDIX D PROPOSED PATTERN OF DISTRICTS IN NON-METROPOLITAN COUNTIES

From *Local Government Boundary Commission for England, First Report* (Cmnd. 5148, 1972); by permission of H.M.S.O.

4. The terms of reference for our initial task were:

In the light of the Government's general objectives for the reform of local government as set out in the White Paper (Cmnd 4584), and in accordance with the Guidelines for the Commission contained in the Annex to DOE Circular 58/71 – to consider the proposals made by local authorities and others in response to Circular 58/71 for a new pattern of districts in each of the English non-metropolitan counties proposed in the Local Government Bill; to prepare and publish draft proposals for such districts as a basis for the fullest practicable consultation with the existing authorities; and, having regard to any further representations from those authorities and from members of the public, to submit to the Secretary of State for the Environment recommendations for the pattern of districts in each county.

Local initiatives

5. The White Paper (Cmnd 4584) made it clear that the Government wishes 'to offer local authorities, communities and interests the greatest opportunity for local initiatives in drawing up proposals for the new pattern of districts', and that the Boundary Commission, in preparing their recommendations, should 'take account of local proposals and . . . consult fully with the authorities concerned'.

6. DOE Circular 58/71 invited local authorities to make representations regarding the future pattern of districts and these were forwarded to the Commission Designate. We received representations from nearly all the existing local authorities, together with some 2,500 representations from other organisations and members of the public. These proposals and observations greatly assisted us in preparing our draft proposals. When we published these draft proposals in April 1972, we said that we had been impressed by the care with which local authorities had prepared

proposals for our consideration, and by the extent of negotiation and discussion that had taken place between authorities, and that we had been glad to accept many of the proposals put to us.

Guidelines

7. The formulation of our recommendations for the new districts has been governed by guidelines issued by the Secretary of State. They were first published in DOE Circular 58/71 of July 1971, when the local authorities were requested to have regard to them in forwarding their proposals to the Commission Designate. As mentioned in paragraph 4 above, they formed part of our terms of reference for our preparatory work; and when the Commission was constituted under the Act it was confirmed that they should be the basis for our final recommendations. The text of the guidelines is as follows:

Population, the county patterns of districts and the identity of towns 1. The Boundary Commission should recommend a pattern of districts for the non-metropolitan counties ranging upwards in population from 40,000. Only very exceptionally should a district be proposed with a population under 40,000.

2. Except in sparsely populated areas the aim should be to define districts with current populations generally within the range of about 75,000–100,000. These figures are in no sense absolute limits: some districts will be larger or smaller, according to local circumstances; but regard should be had to the desirability of producing in each county a pattern of districts which are broadly comparable in population and conducive to effective and convenient local government throughout the country as a whole.

3. The identity of large towns should be maintained. The whole designated area of a new town, or the whole of an area defined for town development, should ordinarily fall within one new district.

4. Normally it will be necessary to take only current population levels into account in considering the size of district to be proposed. Account should be taken of a town's engagement in an approved programme of rapid expansion, e.g., under the New Towns Act or Town Development Act, but even in these cases regard must also be had to the population level needed to sustain efficient services in the meantime.

Definition of new districts 5. Wherever reasonably practicable a new district should comprise the whole of one or more existing county boroughs or county districts. Where this is not practicable, the new district should comprise whole parishes or wards. Because of the need to concentrate on the main pattern of the new districts, new boundaries which do not follow the boundary of an existing local government unit or electoral area should be proposed only in special circumstances. Once the new authorities have taken over, the Commission will be invited to carry out a thorough review of proposals for detailed adjustments of boundaries, including those of the counties and metropolitan districts.

General considerations 6. In formulating their recommendations the Commission should weigh all relevant considerations in the light of the general objectives of local government reorganisation as set out in the Government's White Paper, Cmnd 4584. Among other things they should have particular regard to the wishes of the local inhabitants, the pattern of community life, and the effective operation of local government services.

7. The Commission will also wish to take note of the pattern of Parliamentary constituencies in each county.

Consultations 8. The Commission should consider suggestions and proposals put to them by local authorities and other persons and bodies for the pattern of districts in each county, and should then make draft proposals. These should be published as a basis for the fullest practicable consultation with the existing authorities and so that, when formulating their final recommendations, the Commission can also have regard to any further representations and to representations from members of the public.

Timetable 9. The Commission's recommendations should be submitted to the Secretary of State for the Environment in time for them to be debated in Parliament in the autumn of 1972 and for the boundaries of the new districts to be established by order before the end of that year.

. . . . . .

15. The draft proposals envisaged the formation of 278 new districts to replace the 949 existing local authorities (county boroughs, municipal boroughs, urban districts and rural districts) in the non-metropolitan counties.

16. The population ranges of the existing local authorities and the draft new districts proposed in April 1972 were as follows:

Population Range (1971)	Existing Local Authorities	Draft New Districts
under 20,000	526	–
20,000–40,000	240	–
40,000–65,000	107	37
65,000–75,000	28	39
75,000–100,000	21	115
100,000–120,000	6	48
over 120,000	21	39
Total:	949	278

Thus only 21 of the existing local authorities are within the preferred population range of 75,000–100,000 indicated in guideline 2, whereas 115 of the draft new districts were within that range. 76 of the draft new districts were below that range and 87 were above it (the latter figure including the 27 existing authorities with a population of over 100,000). Almost three quarters of the draft new districts fell within the range of 65,000–120,000 population.

17. Of the existing authorities 766 were below 40,000 population whereas none of the draft new districts was below 40,000. We describe in paragraphs 37 to 40 the

process which subsequently led us to include 14 new districts below 40,000 population in our final recommendations.

. . . . . .

Recommendations

31. We set out our final recommendations for the pattern of new districts in Part 2 of this report. In the following paragraphs we summarise the main features and comment on some aspects of general interest.

32. We recommend the formation of 296 new districts, compared to 278 in our draft proposals. In terms of population range they are as follows:

	Draft Proposals	Final Recommendations
20,000–40,000	0	14
40,000–65,000	37	52
65,000–75,000	39	45
75,000–100,000	115	104
100,000–120,000	48	40
over 120,000	39	41
Total:	278	296

33. 212 of the new districts which we recommend are the same as those contained in our draft proposals. 41 new districts either involve minor modifications of our draft proposals – in most cases the transfer of a small district or parish from one area to another, where this reflected a clear expression of local wishes and where the change could be made without detriment to the overall pattern of new districts in the county – or are altered as a result of amendments to the Local Government Bill as it progressed through Parliament after the time when we published our draft proposals.

34. The remaining 43 new districts represent substantial modifications to the draft proposals. In general these changes involved either the division of a draft new district into two smaller districts, or the revision of two or more new districts to form a pattern that accorded more closely with local wishes and the views of the local authorities concerned . . .

35. It has been our aim to resolve the differences of view that were expressed in the response to the draft proposals. But this has not always been possible. In particular, we have not felt able to adopt solutions which might have been more acceptable to some of the local authorities concerned, or might have satisfied the more vocal expressions of local wishes, but were seen by us to be at variance with other evidence of local opinion and with the prospects for the efficient performance of local government services. In such cases we thought it fair that our tests of the validity of the proposed solution should include a comparison with the response of the great majority of local authorities, many of whom had settled local differences of view and perhaps conflicting interests and objectives in order to achieve solutions within the guidelines.

. . . . . .

New Districts below 40,000 population

37. . . . we have made it clear that an over-riding priority does not attach to guidelines 1 to 4, relating to the preferred population range for new districts of 75,000 to 100,000 and the scope for lower population figures. But given the link between these guidelines and the White Paper objective (also reflected in guidelines 4 and 6) of a system of fewer and stronger units of local government it was clear to us that the case for each district below the preferred population range would need to be tested and justified, with particularly vigorous tests for a proposed district with a population under 40,000, which guideline 1 instructed us to propose 'only very exceptionally' . . .

. . . . . .

40. In the event, our scrutiny of written representations and our visits and hearings in many of the areas concerned, have led us to include 14 new districts between 20,000 and 40,000 population in our final recommendations. Each was a case of exceptional treatment to meet special circumstances, so that rigid criteria would not have been appropriate and were not applied. As indicated in guideline 2, sparsity of population was a significant factor. But we took due account of other factors of significance such as distribution of settlements within an area, communications and travelling time, and local wishes. In general the basis upon which we have been able to recommend these new districts below 40,000 population is that these are cases where, very exceptionally, we consider that units of that size are appropriate to the topography of the area; that any alternative would make for less effective operation of local government; that local opinion was emphatically in favour of the smaller district; and that there was local capacity to operate it effectively.

Large towns

. . . . . .

42. One of the principal features of the Government's proposals for reorganisation related to the long-standing dichotomy between counties and county boroughs. The White Paper of February 1971 (Cmnd 4584) said (paragraph 6): 'The division between counties and county boroughs has prolonged an artificial separation of big towns from their surrounding hinterlands for functions whose planning and administration need to embrace both town and country.' The ending of this separation is not a job for the Commission. It is done in the Local Government Act itself, under which county boroughs as such will cease to exist. They will form part of the new counties and of the pattern of new districts within each county, and the old division between county and county borough — eg, for structure planning, education and personal social services — will be removed.

43. As regards the treatment of large towns in the new district pattern, the White Paper (Cmnd 4584) said (paragraph 33) 'The bigger cities and towns will retain their identities. In other places it would be right to reunite smaller towns with the rural communities associated with them.' Our guideline 3 repeats the White Paper with the instruction 'the identity of large towns should be maintained' and adds that 'the whole area of a new town, or the whole of an area defined for

town development, should ordinarily fall within one new district'. Accordingly we have proposed larger units for large towns on account of the special factors mentioned in the guideline 3. We have also proposed incorporation in a larger district where there have been residential areas which could not be accommodated in any other way. Otherwise we have proposed no change at this stage. The details are as follows.

44. Of the 45 towns already within or above the preferred population range of 75,000–100,000 (excluding those in Cleveland, where different guidelines applied) we have proposed that 10 should be extended or included in larger new districts. Three of these are engaged in new town schemes. For the other 7 towns, we decided that amalgamation with other authorities was necessary in order to establish a satisfactory pattern for that part of the county.

45. Of the other 35 large towns, 14 sought no extension of their areas at the present time and we have proposed none. The other 21 large towns sought some extension of their areas but we have proposed no change at this time.

46. The fact that we have proposed no change does not necessarily mean that the present boundaries are satisfactory. At this stage we have been concerned with establishing the general structure of the new district pattern. Within this general structure there will need to be detailed boundary adjustments at a later stage. The Commission's task is a continuing one, but it is one that has to be tackled in stages. As instructed in the guidelines we have 'wherever reasonably practicable' proposed new districts that 'comprise the whole of one or more existing county boroughs or county districts'. But, as stated in the guidelines, 'Once the new authorities have taken over, the Commission will be invited to carry out a thorough review of proposals for detailed adjustment of boundaries.'

47. We regard this detailed revision as an important part of the reorganisation process, but it clearly cannot be tackled effectively in the course of this initial review when the primary objective is to establish the broad pattern of new districts to enable reorganisation to proceed. The later adjustment of boundaries will have to be considered in detail case by case, after April 1974, taking account of the facts on the ground, the wishes of the local people, and the interests of convenient and effective local government.

Divided Areas

48. Guideline 5 requires that 'Wherever reasonably practicable a new district should comprise the whole of one or more existing county boroughs or county districts.' We have endeavoured to adhere closely to this guideline in the interests of facilitating the transition to the new system.

49. Our recommendations for new districts (listed in Part 2) include a number of cases where existing local authority areas are split, but most of these fall into one of the following categories:

    (*a*) Existing districts which are in two or more separate non-continuous parts. The recommended new districts eliminate all these anomalous areas.

    (*b*) Existing districts which are split between two or more new counties. There are 33 such districts, 11 split between non-metropolitan counties and 22 split between metropolitan and non-metropolitan counties.

    (*c*) Existing districts which are split by the boundary of a new town designated area and where, as the guidelines require, the draft proposals put the whole of the new town area into one new district (except in the case of the Central Lancashire New Town, where the new town area is divided between three new districts, two of which were wholly agreed amalgamations of existing authorities).

50. Apart from these categories there are some 20 cases where we decided, reluctantly, that it was necessary to split an existing district in order to establish a satisfactory pattern of new districts. But, in the great majority of cases, the new districts are amalgamations of the whole of two or more existing district authorities.

. . . . . .

Boundary Adjustments

55. As noted in paragraph 46 above, the guidelines state that 'Once the new authorities have taken over, the Commission will be invited to carry out a thorough review of proposals for detailed adjustments of boundaries, including those of the counties and metropolitan districts.' We are conscious of the need for such a review, and would wish to include in it a review of the boundaries of new districts especially where these, in following existing local authority boundaries, cut across areas of contiguous urban development. We are aware of a number of cases where these conditions occur and in some cases we have been urged to adjust the boundaries at this stage. But we have found that in many cases there is no unanimity of view among the local authorities concerned about the desirability of making the boundary change, and considerable room for argument as to where exactly the line should be drawn.

Summary Table: Numbers and Population Range of Existing Local Authorities in the Non-Metropolitan Counties

County	under 20,000	20,000–40,000	40,000–65,000	65,000–75,000	75,000–100,000	100,000–120,000	over 120,000	Total no of existing authorities
Avon	5	3	2	—	1	—	1	12
Bedfordshire	4	6	—	1	—	—	1	12
Berkshire	4	5	2	—	2	—	1	14
Buckinghamshire	9	3	2	2	—	—	—	16
Cambridgeshire	20	2	1	1	1	—	—	25
Cheshire	13	7	8	1	—	—	—	29
Cleveland	5	—	—	—	1	—	1	7
Cornwall	22	4	1	—	—	—	—	27
Cumbria	16	8	1	1	—	—	—	26
Derbyshire	17	10	1	2	—	—	1	31
Devon	34	6	—	—	1	1	1	43
Dorset	17	2	2	—	—	1	1	23
Durham	9	8	2	—	1	—	—	20
East Sussex	5	3	2	3	—	—	1	14
Essex	13	10	6	1	2	—	3	35
Gloucestershire	11	5	1	1	1	—	—	19
Hampshire	4	12	4	1	2	1	2	26
Hereford & Worcester	20	4	4	1	—	—	—	29
Hertfordshire	13	11	6	2	1	—	—	33
Humberside	13	5	2	1	1	—	1	23
Isle of Wight	3	3	—	—	—	—	—	6
Kent	17	17	11	1	1	—	—	47
Lancashire	29	15	4	—	2	1	1	52
Leicestershire	16	3	2	2	—	—	1	24
Lincolnshire	19	7	1	1	—	—	—	28

								Total
Norfolk	20	5	3	–	–	–	1	29
Northamptonshire	15	4	2	–	–	–	1	22
Northumberland	15	4	–	–	–	–	–	19
North Yorkshire	34	2	2	–	–	1	–	39
Nottinghamshire	4	8	5	1	–	–	1	19
Oxfordshire	12	6	1	–	–	1	–	20
Salop	6	7	1	–	–	–	–	14
Somerset	21	6	–	–	–	–	–	27
Staffordshire	6	8	7	–	1	–	1	23
Suffolk	22	6	1	–	1	–	–	30
Surrey	2	5	13	1	1	–	–	22
Warwickshire	5	4	3	1	–	–	–	13
West Sussex	8	7	2	1	1	–	–	19
Wiltshire	17	6	1	–	1	–	–	25
TOTAL	525	237	106	26	21	6	21	942

In addition there are 11 authorities divided between non-metropolitan counties, which fall in the following population ranges:

	2	6	1	2	–	–	–	11
TOTAL no of whole authorities	527	243	107	28	21	6	21	953

There are also 22 authorities divided between non-metropolitan and metropolitan counties

Summary Table: Numbers and Population Range of Proposed New Districts in the Non-Metropolitan Counties

County	Population range of proposed new districts						No of proposed new districts
	under 40,000	40,000– 65,000	65,000– 75,000	75,000– 100,000	100,000– 120,000	over 120,000	
Avon	–	–	1	2	1	2	6
Bedfordshire	–	–	–	2	–	2	4
Berkshire	–	1	–	2	1	2	6
Buckinghamshire	–	1	1	1	1	1	5
Cambridgeshire	–	2	–	3	1	–	6
Cheshire	–	–	1	3	2	2	8
Cleveland	–	–	–	1	–	3	4
Cornwall	–	3	3	–	–	–	6
Cumbria	–	1	1	3	1	–	6
Derbyshire	–	1	2	4	1	1	9
Devon	1	3	1	3	1	1	10
Dorset	2	3	1	–	1	1	8
Durham	1	1	1	4	1	–	8
East Sussex	–	–	4	1	1	1	7
Essex	–	2	3	2	3	4	14
Gloucestershire	–	1	2	3	–	–	6
Hampshire	–	1	2	5	2	3	13
Hereford & Worcester	1	3	1	4	–	–	9
Hertfordshire	–	–	2	5	2	1	10
Humberside	1	2	3	1	1	1	9
Isle of Wight	–	2	–	–	–	–	2
Kent	–	–	–	9	3	2	14
Lancashire	–	2	1	7	–	4	14
Leicestershire	2	2	2	1	–	2	9
Lincolnshire	–	2	3	2	–	–	7
Norfolk	–	–	2	3	1	1	7
Northamptonshire	–	5	1	–	–	1	7
Northumberland	2	4	–	–	–	–	6
North Yorkshire	–	2	3	1	1	1	8
Nottinghamshire	–	–	–	5	2	1	8
Oxfordshire	–	–	1	2	1	1	5
Salop	2	2	–	2	–	–	6
Somerset	1	–	–	3	1	–	5
Staffordshire	–	1	–	5	2	1	9
Suffolk	1	2	1	2	–	1	7
Surrey	–	–	2	5	4	–	11
Warwickshire	–	1	–	2	2	–	5
West Sussex	–	1	–	4	2	–	7
Wiltshire	–	1	–	2	1	1	5
TOTAL	14	52	45	104	40	41	296

Map 1 *The New Counties in England and Wales*

County boundary ───────

Metropolitan county ⋯⋯

National boundary ● ● ● ● ● ● ● ● ●

Northumberland

Tyne and Wear

Durham   Cleveland

Cumbria

North Yorkshire

Lancashire   West Yorkshire   Humberside

Greater Manchester   South Yorkshire

Merseyside

Cheshire   Derbyshire   Nottinghamshire   Lincolnshire

Clwyd

Gwynedd   Staffordshire

Salop   Leicestershire   Norfolk

West Midlands   Cambridgeshire

Powys   Warwickshire   Northamptonshire   Suffolk

Hereford and Worcester   Bedfordshire

Dyfed   Gloucestershire   Oxfordshire   Buckinghamshire   Hertfordshire   Essex

Gwent   GREATER LONDON

West Glamorgan   Berkshire

Mid Glamorgan   Avon   Wiltshire   Surrey   Kent

South Glamorgan

Somerset   Hampshire   West Sussex   East Sussex

Dorset

Devon   Isle of Wight

Cornwall

| 0 | 20 | 40 | 60 | 80 | 100 MILES |

| 0 | 20 | 40 | 60 | 80 | 100 | 120 KILOMETRES |

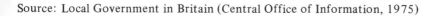

Source: Local Government in Britain (Central Office of Information, 1975)

Section II
England: Local democracy

The Redcliffe-Maud Commission, in formulating their recommendations, were obliged by their terms of reference to observe the need 'to sustain a viable system of local democracy'. It is the democratic element (rather than the notion of efficiency) which has dominated the philosophy of English local government, and provided the system with its chief justification (for us today, no less than for its Victorian architects), that local self-government is a necessary antidote to the centralising tendency of modern state bureaucracy (13, 14, 15). Yet the ideal is scarcely to be recognised in current practice and a variety of sources of evidence indicate serious constraints on the democratic operation of local authorities: close central control (20, 21, 22), extremely rigid political structures (27, 28), councillors motivated by self interest rather than community interests (29, 20, 31, 32, 33), and electorates characterised by ignorance and apathy (23, 24). The Redcliffe-Maud Commission believed that these were problems which could be identified and dealt with; in particular by the creation of strong local authorities which could resist central domination and so regain the respect and support of their electorates (26). They also called for revision of the electoral system to make it more comprehensible, and to ensure that representatives were directly responsible to local electorates. Their recommendations (16) were generally implemented under the 1972 Act (17); the abolition of aldermen, a standard four-year term of office for all councillors, simultaneous elections (on the first Thursday in May), and single-member-electoral divisions with only one election every four years (though this is only a permissive provision for non-metropolitan districts and does not apply in the metropolitan districts).

A major criticism of the new local government structure was that authorities created against a yard-stick of effective performance of functions were too large to retain contact with their citizens; there was much concern about the 'grass roots'. Government could point to the retention of parish councils: but these were principally a rural institution, and it was in the urban areas that a sense of community was so fragile, and where, particularly in the conurbations, the largest authorities were to be found. It must be doubted whether there is any necessary connection between size and inaccessibility — small authorities are quite capable of acting autocratically and secretively — but clearly the connection is generally thought to exist, particularly where reorganisation has produced fewer and larger authorities, and the risk of a gap between local citizen and local administrator. The proposal for neighbourhood councils (18) is intended to close this gap by creating in the urban areas local councils equivalent to the 'third level' of parish councils elsewhere. But

105

the proposal appears to have fallen on stony ground. The crucial local authority response, that of the Association of Metropolitan Authorities, is hostile to the idea of a new statutory level of local representation (19).

In local government as in national government, the concept of representation is inextricably tangled with the channelling of political activity through highly organised political parties (25, 27; and 44, 45 in Section III). Elections become at best a competition for political control of an authority, at worst, a mechanism for putting into office the nominees of a dominant or unopposed party. Moreover, parties in local government are largely pale reflections of the main national parties, and even adopt a similar organisational and 'parliamentary' style (28). It is unsurprising therefore, that local elections concentrate on national rather than local issues, and are frequently a test of the national strength of parties rather than of their local performance. But the effects of political organisation along party lines upon the operation of councils is even more significant: first, that the majority party group is the real decision-making body, rather than the full council, and secondly that the majority party can generally control all the important Committee chairmanships. It may be argued that arrangements of this kind are a practical realisation of the ground rule of British democratic politics, that effective power must lie with the elected majority; and the evidence to Maud (27) argues that authorities without organised party politics are not more (and probably less) democratic in character, than authorities dominated by a major party. Nonetheless, research, what little there is, into local committees and party politics suggests that local party hierarchies are not wholly representative of their electorates, and that majority group councils are characterised by excessive secrecy and lack of accountability.

Democratic theory assumes either that a candidate for political office is concerned to represent a part of the community to which he belongs, or to represent the interests of the whole community. It does not allow for the possibility that the candidate's concern might be limited to himself. Local administration, much more than central administration, offers to politicians opportunities for personal benefit, often of a financial kind; for example, the presence of significant numbers of estate agents, property developers, and builders on many planning committees is scarcely to be regarded as a coincidence. And although the law caters for this type of situation (29, 30) it is sufficiently tolerant that office-holders may obtain personal benefits without acting illegally. The problem of corruption is more clear-cut. Public and parliamentary disquiet over several instances of corruption in local government led to the appointment by the Prime Minister in 1973 of a Committee (chaired by the ubiquitous Redcliffe-Maud) to look at 'rules of conduct' in local government. The Committee found (32) that the incidence of corruption in local government was low and, while they recommended a tightening-up of the law in relation to the disclosure of pecuniary interests, their principal suggestion was the adoption by local authorities of a national code of local government conduct; such a code was subsequently agreed with the local authority associations, and commended to local authorities (33). The code applies only to members; officers are presumably regarded as bound by the 'code of ethics' contained in an agreement

governing the conditions of service of Senior Officers (**31**). Even before the publication of the report of the Redcliffe-Maud Committee (May 1974) a Royal Commission was appointed (April 1974) on Standards of Conduct in Public Life,
because of concern generated by the Poulson affair. The terms of reference apply to
local as well as central government, and the Commission will be able to review
matters already considered by the Redcliffe-Maud Committee.

Contemporary debate about the democratic responsiveness of government
centres increasingly on the view that the traditional democratic safeguards are no
longer effective in the face of the expanding scope and power of state bureaucracies. Citizens must therefore be given alternative means for the redress of
grievance. The device of the 'Ombudsman' — a special, independent investigating
body, with powers to investigate complaints against government — has been introduced in a number of areas of British public administration, including local government. When the Parliamentary Commission for Administration was established in
1967, local authorities were excluded from his jurisdiction; but in 1972 a scheme
for a separate system of investigation for local government was discussed between
central government and the local authority associations on the basis of a Consultative Document. The final proposals were given legislative form, despite opposition
from the associations, in Part III of the Local Government Act, 1974, which created
the Commission for Local Administration (**34**). Originally 10 Commissioners were
envisaged; so far, only 4 have been appointed (3 for England, 1 for Wales) but more
appointments are expected as work expands. The legislative provisions are stronger
in certain respects than for the Parliamentary Commissioner. Members of the public
may have direct access to the Commissioners if a local councillor refuses to refer a
complaint; and there are detailed arrangements to ensure maximum publicity for
reports. On the other hand, as with the Parliamentary Commissioner, Local Commissioners have no formal powers to compel redress, and significant areas are
excluded from investigation, notably police matters, and commercial and contractual transactions, both areas where concern about maladministration is frequently
expressed. Finally, the limitation of enquiry to maladministration (undefined, but
see **35**) as opposed to 'the merits of a decision taken . . . in the exercise of a discretion' repeats the cautious approach to redress of grievance so manifest in the
Parliamentary Commissioner system.

Another response to the problem of allowing the citizen access to government is
to create opportunities for effective two-way communication. The Bains Report
was at pains to link this process with efficiency in government (**40**). The need for
better communication between authorities and the public is most keenly felt in the
field of development planning and control, and the need for more effective public
participation in this field was the subject of an official committee of inquiry (the
Skeffington Report, *People and Planning*) in 1969. A partial response by government was evident in some of the provisions of the Town and Country Planning Act
1971 (**37**). The Dobry Report (*Review of the Development Control System*) in
1975 made further detailed recommendations in this area, but while government
accepted the need for improved procedures in relation to publicity and public

participation, they were not prepared to give these procedures the statutory foundation recommended by Dobry (38).

A criticism sometimes made of government is that they take 'participation' to mean no more than consultation after policy decisions have already been formulated, and that 'consultation' frequently is no more than an information process: in short, participation becomes little more than a public relations exercise, and the more uncomfortable possibilities inherent in a genuine involvement of people in the early stages of policy formulation are sidestepped. But if genuine popular participation is understandably difficult for local authorities to cope with, there is much less excuse for the tendency to closed, secretive government, and the possibility that the new authorities are not much better than the old in this respect, despite the 1972 provisions for improved public access to meetings, is underlined by the fact that central government felt it necessary to emphasise these new provisions in a circular (39).

Many commentators feel that, however important these various democratic issues — representation, political organisation, conduct, redress of grievance — they are not so crucial as the relationship between central and local government, and the degree of independence permitted by this relationship. Critics of the local government system have stressed the restrictive nature of central controls, whether legal, financial, or administrative. The Maud Report was only the first in a line of official reports to recommend a relaxation of these controls. Of the specific proposals in the Maud Report (20) only the plea for a reduction of statutory controls was ultimately met (in legislation in 1972 and 1974); and the generally disappointing character of central government response is exemplified by the 1970 White Paper (21) and also by the 1971 Green Paper on Finance (49, Section IV). Central government has not been unwilling to respond, but the increased need for central direction of public spending, and central maintenance of national standards of public service, militate against radical adjustment of the central—local relationship (22). In this context, Redcliffe-Maud's principal justification of large local authorities, that they could better stand up for themselves against the pressure of the central administration, can be seen to have some force.

It is clear from the range of material in this section that the practice of viable local democracy is hedged with serious difficulties; and it is doubtful whether the 1972 reforms are sufficiently radical to revive and nourish traditions which are in danger of becoming rituals.

13 THE PHILOSOPHY

From (a) *Royal Commission on Local Government in Greater London, Report* (Cmnd. 1164, 1960); and (b) *Redcliffe-Maud Vol.I. Report* (Cmnd. 4040, 1969). Both by permission of H.M.S.O.

(a)

230. This collective good-doing by local authorities can be beneficial, but it can also become oppressive. It consists partially in stopping people from doing things (e.g. throwing slops into the street), partially in forcing people to do things (e.g. sending the children to school), and partially in making people pay for services rendered whether they individually want them or not. Subject, of course, to the control of the Courts, these powers may go far in the restriction of individual freedom. Old people may be removed from home, or children from the care of their parents. It is impossible to carry out the vast range of local government services at the present day without the employment of an army of 'professional' people technically skilled in their respective activities.

231. The actual interfering with people's lives will be done mainly by the professionals; planning of services involves much work by professionals, contacts between citizens and authorities about personal matters will be largely contacts with professionals, and the more impersonal services (e.g. refuse disposal) will be performed entirely by professionals. So good professionals are indispensable; and an important criterion of size and area is the need to attract good professionals. This in practice means that (1) there must be scope for enough of them, organised by function in proper ranks and grades: (2) there must be the possibility of paying adequate remuneration: (3) there must be enough work to give full scope for the use and development of their professional abilities: (4) the 'hierarchy' must be large enough to offer some scope for advancement or promotion, even if promotion at or near the top is usually achieved by moves from one authority to another: and (5) one must not have more posts of such importance as to require exceptional ability than one may hope to fill from the relatively small number of exceptional people upon whose existence one can safely reckon.

232. But to provide scope for a full professional life for officers is not by itself enough. There must also be proper control of professional activities, since without such control (and the stimulation that comes with it when it is wisely exercised) the view of the expert can become too narrow. Professional enthusiasm can carry the expert beyond the bounds of good judgement, and 'Bumbledom' can be a real danger. Professional zeal on the other hand can run down and need renewing by the stimulus of frequently changing contact with the representatives of the 'consumer'. The desire of the experts (except the very good ones) to get as far away as possible from amateur control, administratively and even physically, is a factor to beware of.

233. The control of the expert by the amateur representing his fellow citizens is the key to the whole of our system of government. It is probably what people have at the back of their minds when they use the words 'democracy' or 'democratic'. It is therefore important that one should find the right sort of councillor, and another criterion of size, scope and area must be 'What is best to attract good councillors'? The best professionals readily agree that they do their best work when they can rely on the informed criticism, stimulation, counsel and support of good councillors.

Good professionals and good councillors need one another. Neither is likely to remain good for long without the other. The public need both, working in proper balance, each pulling his full weight in his own sphere and respecting the sphere of the other.

234. The sphere of the councillor includes these activities:

(1) He must know his people, those who have elected him, their needs, desires and fears. He must also remember that he represents not only those of his constituents who have voted for him but also those who have voted against him. Even where, as so often happens, seats are uncontested, a councillor usually represents some who would have voted against him if they had had the chance.

(2) He must be prepared to learn enough to participate effectively in policy decisions carrying out 'compulsory' functions and in policy decisions as to the extent to which 'voluntary' functions should be undertaken.

(3) He must learn how to utilise professional advice in coming to policy decisions without becoming a slave to it.

(4) He must learn to keep away from interference in the administrative execution of policy, leaving case work to the professionals.

. . . . . .

(b)

27. The questions that have dominated all our work are these. What is, and what ought to be, the purpose which local government serves; and what, at the present day, is its scope? Our terms of reference require us to consider the structure of local government in England (outside Greater London) in relation to its existing functions; and it was therefore on existing functions that we concentrated our attention. These are of immense scope and significance, covering as they do responsibility for the police, for the fire service, for almost all education other than university, for the health and welfare of mothers and infants, the old and the sick, for children in need of care, for public health, for housing, for sport and recreation, for museums, art galleries and libraries, for the physical environment and the use of land, for highways, traffic and transport, and for many other matters too numerous to mention [for a complete list of functions see Section I, Annex A]. But in considering the structure which will best enable local authorities to discharge these responsibilities, we have kept in mind the whole potential of local government, given the existing functions as the substance of what it does. This substance we see as an all-round responsibility for the safety, health and well-being, both material and cultural, or people in different localities, in so far as these objectives can be achieved by local action and local initiative, within a framework of national policies. It is in this light that we have considered the purpose and scope of local government.

28. Our terms of reference also require us to bear in mind the need to sustain a viable system of local democracy: that is, a system under which government by the people is a reality. This we take to be of importance at least equal to the importance of securing efficiency in the provision of services. Local government is not to be seen merely as a provider of services. If that were all, it would be right to consider whether some of the services could not be more efficiently provided by other means. The importance of local government lies in the fact that it is the means by which people can provide services for themselves; can take an active and constructive part in the business of government; and can decide for themselves, within the limits of what national policies and local resources allow, what kind of services they want and what kind of environment they prefer. More than this, through their local representatives people throughout the country can, and in practice do, build up the policies which national government adopts − by focussing attention on local problems, by their various ideas of what government should seek to do, by local initiatives and local reactions. Many of the powers and responsibilities which local authorities now possess, many of the methods now in general use, owe their existence to pioneering by individual local authorities. Local government is the only representative political institution in the country outside Parliament; and being, by its nature, in closer touch than Parliament or Ministers can be with local conditions, local needs, local opinions, it is an essential part of the fabric of democratic government. Central government tends, by its nature, to be bureaucratic. It is only by the combination of local representative institutions with the central institutions of Parliament, Ministers and Departments, that a genuine national democracy can be sustained.

29. We recognise that some services are best provided by the national government: where the provision is or ought to be standardised throughout the country, or where the decisions involved can be taken only at the national level, or where a service requires an exceptional degree of technical expertise and allows little scope for local choice. Even here, however, there is a role for local government in assessing the impact of national policies on places and on people, and in bringing pressure to bear on the national government for changes in policy or in administration, or for particular decisions. And wherever local choice, local opinion and intimate knowledge of the effects of government action or inaction are important, a service is best provided by local government, however much it may have to be influenced by national decisions about the level of service to be provided and the order of priorities to be observed.

30. We conclude then that the purpose of local government is to provide a democratic means both of focussing national attention on local problems affecting the safety, health and well-being of the people, and of discharging, in relation to these things, all the responsibilities of government which can be discharged at a level below that of the national government. But in discharging these responsibilities local government must, of course, act in agreement with the national government when national interests are involved.

14 THE ADVANTAGES OF LOCAL DEMOCRACY

From *Written Evidence of Ministry of Housing and Local Government* (to Redcliffe-Maud, 1967); by permission of H.M.S.O.

The advantage which the ordinary citizen derives from the provision of local government services

270. The services provided by local government are now an integral part of the life of the community; there may be scope for changes but it is difficult to imagine the broad range of functions being discharged more conveniently or in a way more responsive to people's needs than by elected local authorities or by some agency under their control. It is more convenient, where a local authority is responsible for most or all of the services in the area, for people to deal with one organisation than with a number of separate bodies. They can find out about services and apply for licences and consents, and they know where to complain when things go wrong. It may also be easier to pay for local services together rather than separately to a series of independent bodies.

271. One point about many local services is that there is little scope for personal choice. For instance, education is of such paramount importance that it is necessary for everyone to contribute towards it whether or not they are currently benefiting. Nor can people be allowed the choice of accumulating refuse on the premises and not paying for collection; everyone must pay and the service must be universal if public health hazards are to be avoided. The police and fire services are also needed by the community at large and cannot be organised on the basis of whether people wish to take advantage of the cover they provide; they must be paid for by the community as a whole. In other words, many services provided by local government are not commodity services to be supplied and paid for on a consumer basis; they are community services to which everyone ought to contribute.

272. There is scope for some degree of community choice, however, if not for personal choice; and it is one of the merits of local government that it allows for the exercise of local options, for the application of national policies according to local circumstances and for the provision of local facilities and amenities. A democratically elected body has a special incentive to take account of the varying needs of particular parts of its area, and to gauge the strength of local feelings when decisions about new developments and changes have to be taken.

273. Another strength of local government is that local authorities have a whole range of functions in addition to an implied general concern for the wellbeing of their districts. The variety of work is likely to prove more interesting to members and to encourage a balanced approach to decision making. More particularly, where services and functions are closely interrelated, it is a great advantage for them to be in the hands of a single body so that they can be planned and operated in a co-ordinated fashion.

274. There are, of course, wider democratic arguments in favour of entrusting the provision of public services and the regulation of some aspects of public life to elected local authorities. Local government provides a means for the ordinary citizen to take part in public affairs at local level: as electors people have an opportunity through their vote to exercise a decisive influence on the general direction of local affairs; as members of a local authority a small number of people have a chance to render an important public service, to take part in public and political life and to gain experience in administering what is often a very sizeable enterprise − not only has all this intrinsic value but it may serve to provide a very good training for other activities, including membership of appointed public bodies or of Parliament.

Local democracy

79. The Ministry suggest that the establishment of, say, 30 to 40 units of local government, of a fully adequate size for major functions and, in the key matter of planning, freed from the handicap that results from the separation of town and country, would substantially promote local democracy. It should help to check the present tendency for people to expect central government to deal with matters that ought to be dealt with locally, and to take less and less interest in their local authorities. Conversely, if the structure of local government is not adapted in this way to the functional needs of the present and still more of the foreseeable future, people may increasingly believe that it is central rather than local government that decides all issues of importance, even in local affairs. This would lead in turn to increasing apathy in local elections, to increasing difficulty in recruiting able persons as elected members of local authorities, and ultimately to the further extension of the functions of central government.

80. The existence of a relatively few major authorities would also open up the possibilities of greater independence for local government. It is reasonable to suppose that both financially and in other ways Departments would feel able to give to a small number of strong authorities more independence in the way they execute policies determined by central government. Parliament might also think it right to diminish the extent to which the approval of Ministers is required by statute for the exercise of local authority functions. Secondly, the powers of local authorities rest at present on a mass of general and local legislation, accumulated over many years. Any reform of local government should be accompanied by replacing the present powers, as soon as the mechanics of transition allow, by powers which would be much more uniform and which would be wide enough for Parliament to have to spend far less time in future on considering additions. This would be easier if authorities were fewer and stronger.

81. However, a local government structure consisting solely of 30 to 40 all-purpose units would reduce the opportunities for local participation in government, and for people to bring their problems to local elected representatives. It would, for example, drastically reduce the number of elected members of authorities. It could

also be argued that no arrangements made by these authorities to decentralise their administration and to keep in touch with local opinion could be an adequate substitute for local government of the type to which this country has become accustomed. These considerations suggest that these main units of local government should be supplemented by a second tier of elected authorities entrusted with appropriate executive functions.

15 THE STRENGTH OF LOCAL DEMOCRACY

From *Redcliffe-Maud, Vol. I: Report* (Cmnd. 4040, 1969); by permission of H.M.S.O.

573. There will be new opportunities for making local self-government a reality, both in relations between national and local government and within local government itself.

574. First, the position of local government in relation to central government will be strengthened:

(i)   Provincial councils will give the national government new opportunities for decentralising power and developing new methods of collaboration between central and local government.

(ii)   The new metropolitan and unitary authorities will be strong enough (in terms of area, population and resources) for Parliament and central government to trust them with increased responsibility and substantially relax the present detailed supervision.

(iii) It will be easier for local government to speak with a united voice.

(v)   The local government structure will be capable of organising and supplying new services to meet new national and local needs. There will no longer be the need to create unrepresentative machinery for special purposes.

(vi)   The scale of the new authorities will make it reasonable to consider bringing the national health service within the framework of local democracy and linking it with kindred social services.

575. Secondly, there will be fresh encouragement for citizens to take an active and effective part in their own local government, and new vitality can thus be breathed into our local life.

(i)   The main authorities will operate in areas linking town and country, more closely corresponding to the life and work of those they represent. They will have comprehensive powers to deal with the real problems that need solution now or will arise in the future. People will therefore have more reason to recognise the relevance of local government to their lives and to feel that it deserves their active interest, and it will be easier, if the new authorities actively collaborate, for press, radio and television to play their crucial parts in aiding two-way communication between the public and their local representatives. Thus people from a wide cross-section of society may be the readier to concern themselves with local government and to consider standing for election; a larger proportion of the electorate may feel it worthwhile to use their voting power; a better understanding of what local government can do will become possible.

(ii)   Within the wider framework of the main authority, local councils can put fresh life into the rural parish and give communities in city and town new kinds of opportunity to speak and take action for themselves.

(iii)   At the provincial level for the first time there will be representative councils enabling large areas of the country that share common interests to have a powerful say in their development.

REVITALISING ENGLISH LOCAL GOVERNMENT

576. (i) Local government is more than the sum of the particular services provided. It is an essential part of English democratic government, and reorganisation on the lines that we propose will make it a more powerful part than it has ever been before. Elected bodies will be far more able to resolve their problems – shaping the physical environment to meet human needs; seeking to reconcile traffic with civilised living and to make transport a better servant of the public; helping the individual, as national wealth increases, to become healthier and better educated; enabling neighbours to help each other more effectively.

(ii) These are the possible gains from a radical reorganisation of the existing structure. If we are not willing to face the pains involved the prospect for local government is bleak. Local governors under the present system, we are convinced, cannot grapple effectively with their problems; this indeed was generally admitted to us. Already the odds against success are heavy, but present problems are not going to stand still. During the next decade, unless the system is reformed, local government will be increasingly discredited and will be gradually replaced by agents of the central government.

(iii) Reorganisation of the system will make heavy demands on present local governors, both council-members and their officers. Many of them, while accepting that some reorganisation is needed, will disagree with our particular proposals. Most of them will regret disturbances of their own local authority. But if they believe that local government should have a long and fruitful future, can they resist the logic of the need for drastic and immediate change? Will not such change give them a better chance of serving effectively as local governors in years to come? There is room of course, for endless argument about what change; no one knows that better than we do. But we believe that our analysis points conclusively to the new system we propose.

(iv) Throughout the course of our enquiry we have become steadily more convinced that a powerful system of local government can in some crucial ways enhance the quality of English national life. The whole Commission is unanimous in its conviction that if the present local government system is drastically reformed, its scope extended to include functions now in the hands of nominated bodies and the grip of central government relaxed, England can become a more efficient, democratic and humane society.

16 REDCLIFFE-MAUD ON DEMOCRATIC STRUCTURES

From *Redcliffe-Maud, Vol. I: Report* (Cmnd. 4040, 1969); by permission of H.M.S.O.

456. . . . We now consider the number of members appropriate to a main authority. The Committee on the Management of Local Government recommended that, as part of any reorganisation of the structure of local government, councils should not have more than 75 members and that this should be regarded as the maximum for the largest authorities. We endorse that recommendation: in the new system 75 should be the maximum number of members for all main authorities — whether unitary, metropolitan or metropolitan district.

457. Though the Management Committee put its recommendation in the context of reorganisation — for we were already at work when the committee reported — its conclusion was drawn from study of local government within the present structural framework. Under our proposals, that framework will no longer exist. In particular, the system of operating services through two tiers of elected authorities will disappear over most of the country. In all unitary areas, operational responsibility for services will rest with one authority; and apart from the work of local councils in improving the convenience and amenity of life and sharing in the provision of certain services, the only councillors responsible for running services will be the members of the unitary authorities.

458. The reasons, however, that led the Management Committee to recommend that the number of members of a local authority should be limited to 75 will continue to apply under the new system. The new elected authorities, unitary, metropolitan and metropolitan district, must be effective instruments for the transaction of public business, and in particular for the control of policy. This they cannot be if they are so large that their internal organisation is influenced by the question of how to ensure that all members have worthwhile work to do . . . the elected members of the new authorities must have their minds free for the big issues and must not be preoccupied with detail. In the present system the size of councils, the number of committees and sub-committees and the disproportionate attention paid to minor questions have reflected the belief that members ought to be concerned with the details of their authority's work and that therefore councils must be large enough and committees numerous enough to allow most points of detail to be decided by elected members. The Management Committee considered that radical changes were necessary in traditional methods of organising the work of existing local authorities. We, for our part, say without qualification that the new main authorities — 81 of them responsible for the operation of all local government services in England outside London — will not work efficiently unless organised on

different lines from those followed in the past . . . The essential point here is that there must be a limit to the number of elected members. Otherwise the defects that exist now in the way that present authorities organise their work will reappear; and the scale and range of operation of the new authorities will make the consequences much worse and much more costly.

459. We stress that 75 should be the maximum for the largest authorities and not a norm to be aimed at for all. Many authorities will not need so large a number.

Aldermen

460. We agree with the Management Committee that the office of alderman should be abolished. The new main authorities and local councils should be wholly composed of members directly elected by the people. Many aldermen have given long and valuable service to local government. But the office of alderman blurs the principle of democratic control by the people's elected representatives.

461. Nor will there be any place for aldermen on local councils, whose basic function is to be directly representative of local people.

Co-option

462. There should, however, following present practice and the recommendation of the Management Committee, be power to co-opt outside persons to committees of a main authority. Local councils should also have the power of co-option.

SINGLE-MEMBER CONSTITUENCIES

Main Authorities

463. We recommend that the area of each main authority should be divided into single member constituencies. The direct relationship that ought to exist between electors and representatives is blurred when, as happens now in boroughs, there are three members for each ward. With single member constituencies each elected representative will have a clear, personal responsibility to his constituents.

464. The combination of single member constituencies with a maximum council-membership of 75 will mean that in those unitary authorities with a population in 1968 of over 750,000 (12 out of 58) each member will represent more than 10,000 constituents. Sheffield and South Yorkshire, with a population of 1,000,000 is the largest unitary authority. There, each member will represent 14,400 constituents. Compared with this, the position in some large, existing counties (where, unlike the boroughs, there are single-member constituencies) is as follows: the average size of a constituency is over 19,000 in both Kent and Lancashire, over 18,000 in the West Riding, over 14,000 in Cheshire and Essex, and over 13,000 in Hampshire, Hertfordshire and Surrey.

465. But constituencies in most unitary authorities will be smaller than 10,000.

In any case, if members are freed from the burden of detailed work and much of the operation of services is decentralised and delegated to local officers . . . they will have more time for the problems of their constituents.

466. The constituencies of metropolitan authorities will contain many more people than those of unitary authorities. The Selnec and West Midlands metropolitan areas will have populations of over 3,000,000, Merseyside one of over 2,000,000. Thus with a limit of 75 on the number of members, the average size of constituency will be over 40,000 for the Selnec and West Midlands metropolitan authorities and about 30,000 for Merseyside. These, however, are much smaller figures than the average number of people now represented by an elected member of the Greater London Council. Direct comparison is impossible because in Greater London each constituency is represented by three members; but there are 100 elected members on the Greater London Council serving a population of 7,764,000 — nearly 78,000 people for each member.

467. Moreover, as in Greater London there are the London borough councils, so in the three new metropolitan areas there will be the metropolitan district councils: four in Merseyside, nine in Selnec and seven in the West Midlands. London boroughs, whose populations range from 144,000 to 329,000 have a maximum of 60 elected members, but we do not propose a lower maximum than 75 for metropolitan district council membership. Many of these councils will not need as many members as 75. But the district containing Birmingham will have a population of 1,300,000 and those containing Manchester and Liverpool 979,000 and 936,000 respectively. Authorities with such populations should not have a smaller maximum than other main authorities.

Local Councils

468. Elected representatives will not of course be limited to the members of main authorities. In addition to their main authority, the citizens in every unitary area will have a local council to represent them, and in every metropolitan area, if they want a local council they will have it as well as the metropolitan authority and district council . . . a maximum of 50 members for a local council will serve. Wherever the area of a local council is big enough, members should represent single-member constituencies. In parishes, however, members should normally be elected, as now, to represent the community as a whole.

ELECTIONS

469. In the new local government system main authorities and local councils will be directly elected. Provincial councils will be indirectly elected by main authorities.

470. . . . confusion . . . results in the public mind from the present practice of holding elections for local authorities on different days and electing a third of the members of most councils each year. We endorse the view of the Management Committee that both practices should cease. In the new local government system,

all main authorities (unitary, metropolitan and metropolitan districts) should be elected on the same day throughout the country; and all the members of each authority should be elected on that day. Provincial councils should be elected by the main authorities immediately after they assume office.

471. But to refresh local interest and give the electors an opportunity to express their views at the polls more frequently than when they elect the main authorities, we suggest that elections for local councils should be held in the middle of the period of office of the main authorities. The same person should be able to stand for election both to a main authority and to a local council; and we hope that many members of main authorities will also be members of local councils.

472. We asked ourselves whether main authorities should hold office for three years or for four. Triennial elections − or a triennial cycle of elections − have been traditional in local government. But for an authority to hold office for four years would give it a better chance to work out and put into effect a coherent policy for its area. The increasing complexity of services and the scale often required for effective action mean that an authority's programmes need time to fructify. Only if an authority can look a reasonably long period ahead, can its financial − budgetary and investment − policies be wisely planned. Because a four-year term of office would provide a better time-scale than a three-year term for the work of a main authority, it would put the electors in a better position to judge the authority's degree of success or failure in carrying out its aims.

473. However, despite the advantages we see in holding elections to main authorities every four years, we do not specifically recommend a change to a system of four-yearly elections. With the abolition of present arrangements for electing a third of the members of most councils annually, the date when all members of all 81 main authorities are elected will provide electors with their only chance of passing judgement on the authorities responsible for local government services. From this standpoint an interval of four years between elections could be too long to be acceptable.

474. Our conclusion is that there should be further enquiry into the relative merits of three years and four years as the period for which main authorities should hold office. We believe that the case for four years is strong but until the results of the inquiry are known, the assumption should be that elections will be held every three years. If the eventual decision is that the balance of advantage lies with quadrennial elections, consideration should be given to holding elections for metropolitan districts in the middle of the term of office of metropolitan authorities.

17 DEMOCRATIC CHANGES: THE 1972 ACT

From *Local Government Act, 1972* (Department of Environment Circular 121/72, 1972); by permission of H.M.S.O.

Constitutional and other changes 11. The Act makes changes in the constitutional and electoral arrangements of local authorities. There will be no aldermen as members of the new councils, but principal authorities . . . will have the power to recognise service to local government by conferring the title 'honorary alderman'.

12. The term of office of councillors is extended from three years to four. All county councillors will retire together every fourth year; one third of the councillors in metropolitan districts will retire in each of the years between the county council elections; non-metropolitan districts will be entitled to choose between all members of the council retiring en bloc every fourth year, or a third of the members retiring in each year in which metropolitan district councillors retire. After the initial elections local government elections each year will be held on the same day, which will normally be the first Thursday in May.

13. New provisions have been made for allowances for the members of principal authorities as from 1 April 1974. The new provisions do not represent a departure from the view that membership of local authorities should be essentially voluntary and should not attract a salary. The Act provides for a (taxable) flat-rate allowance for elected members, and a financial loss allowance (as in the present system) for the non-elected members. Rights to travelling and subsistence allowances remain. Arrangements will be made for members of the new authorities to receive the existing allowances from their election until 31 March 1974. From 1 April 1974 aldermen of London boroughs will be able to choose between the flat rate allowance and the financial loss allowance.

14. The existing rights of the public, including the press, to attend council meetings (except when the matters to be dealt with need to be treated confidentially) are extended by the Act to meetings of all committees of local authorities.

15. The provisions applying to the internal arrangements for carrying out functions are made more flexible, e.g., by the repeal of some of the existing statutory requirements for the appointment of specific officers and committees and by the introduction (except where existing requirements are preserved) of wider powers to delegate to committees, sub-committees and officers. In addition there are wide powers for local authorities to make arrangements between themselves for the discharge of many of their functions.

16. The Act includes a new provision (section 111) which puts beyond doubt that local authorities have power to do anything which is calculated to facilitate, or is conducive or incidental to, the discharge of any of their functions, even if they have no specific statutory power for that action. This proposition has long represented the law (see in particular *A.G. v. Smethwick Corporation* [1932] 1 Ch 562), but the section has been included for the avoidance of any doubt which might hamper local initiative.

17. The existing provisions affecting the audit of local authority accounts have been completely recast. In future principal authorities (and the Common Council) will be able to choose whether the audit of their accounts shall be undertaken by the district auditor or by an approved private auditor, and district councils will be able to decide which auditor should audit the accounts of the parishes in their areas. The district auditor's powers are substantially altered: notably, where he considers

an item of account to be contrary to law, he can apply to the court for a declaration accordingly. However, where a sum is lost by wilful misconduct he can certify that an equivalent sum is due to the authority from the person responsible.

18 PROPOSALS FOR NEIGHBOURHOOD COUNCILS

From *Neighbourhood Councils in England* (Department of Environment Consultation Paper 1974); by permission of H.M.S.O. In this paper references to 'districts' include London boroughs.

Neighbourhood councils established on a non-statutory basis in individual urban neighbourhoods in different parts of the country have flourished in recent years, bringing substantial benefits to the areas they serve.

The scope, constitution and method of operation has varied from place to place, but typically a neighbourhood council has all or some of these basic aims:

(a) to organise or stimulate self-help within the local community to improve the quality of life for the residents as a whole (for instance by clearing dumped material from derelict sites);

(b) to help those in the community in need of special facilities (for instance by providing play-groups);

(c) to represent to operational organisations (central and local government, firms with factories in the area etc) the needs and wishes of the local community;

(d) in doing all these things, to foster a sense of community responsibility in the residents, particularly for children and adolescents whose potential for idealism it may help to harness.

The effect of local government reorganisation

The value of such initiatives is enhanced by the reorganisation of local government into larger units. The greater scale of the new districts means that in a metropolitan district or large non-metropolitan district there will be some 4,000–5,000 population per councillor, with 3-member wards of 12,000–15,000 people.

Moreover, current trends in management thinking in local government are liable to absorb the individual councillor into the general work of the council to a greater extent.

The councillor and those he represents are thus faced with heightened problems of communication to ensure that the ward councillor – and through him the council – fully appreciates what the people in the ward are feeling, what they want and what they need.

The difficulty works the other way too: how can the district council let the ordinary citizen know what their plans are; why some things must be done and others have to be left.

A neighbourhood council is not necessarily the only way to overcome these problems of communication, but in a number of places councils of this kind have already proved their value. Working in co-operation with the ward councillors (although not dependent upon them) they can reinforce their work, giving closer coverage to the needs and wishes of the people of the locality than it is physically possible for the limited number of ward councillors to do.

Neighbourhood councils, as the Prime Minister said (when speaking in Newcastle in February 1973 on 'Democracy in local affairs') would be an essential step in giving voice to 'individuals and families who feel themselves deprived of any say in the decision of, to so many of them, large and remote organisations who, week in week out, take the decisions which dominate so much of their world. They would be a vital step in making democracy articulate. For, if democracy means choice, that choice has to be so close to the individual that he can identify and express the issues on which he cares deeply and, having identified and expressed, to choose.'

Statutory status?

. . . What has been done so far has been on a non-statutory basis, and no doubt there are organisations that would prefer to stay non-statutory. If so, there is no reason why they should not. There is however a case for making statutory powers available where — and when — the local people want them. Potential benefits of doing so are:

(a) the council will be properly elected by the residents as a whole — not simply self-appointed or elected by members of an association. Thus it will both be representative and have the authority of a representative body with both the residents and the operational authorities;

(b) it will have some kind of stability and continuity,

(c) it will be easier for the neighbourhood council to employ the expertise it needs to help formulate its views and give weight to its representations; and

(d) it will make it possible to put the present informal consultation arrangements (eg on planning matters) on a formal basis.

Having considered these advantages, and the stimulus to further development of the movement which can be expected from statutory recognition, the Government is favourably inclined to legislation to this effect. The purpose of the present consultation paper is to seek reactions to this proposition and views on some of the detailed issues that would arise in the formulation of legislative proposals.

Issues raised by legislation

Diversity and local initiative are key features of existing successful neighbourhood councils, and it is important that any legislation should have full regard to these considerations. The Government therefore rule out from the outset any approach which would impose neighbourhood councils on all urban areas regardless of need and local wishes. They would also aim to keep the legislative framework as simple and flexible as practicable.

The basic characteristics of a statutory body for this purpose seem to be:

(a) formally elected, and responsive to their electorate;

(b) formal right to receive notification of planning applications (and perhaps other consultation rights);

(c) some limited finance, if only to pay for a newsletter;

(d) very local (say, 3,000–10,000 population, preferably nearer the lower end);

(e) essentially amateur;

(f) on good terms with district councillors, and with regular liaison, but no formal dependence;

(g) with, however, the possibility of co-operation with other bodies — eg by providing volunteer labour for community care activities, for which the district (or county) would provide premises and a paid organiser; and

(h) easy to establish quickly.

These considerations suggest the establishment of an entirely new kind of body, not a local authority in the normal sense, and devised with the needs of urban areas specifically in mind. This would be a rather simpler and more easily established body than a parish council, which has developed as an organ of executive local government, albeit normally in rural areas and on a very small scale. The new neighbourhood council could be set up in any area not covered by an existing parish, and would be wound up where a parish was subsequently established.

Issues that arise in devising such a body include:

Elections

A statutory council, with formal rights to consultation and to finance from the public, would clearly need to be representative. How should this be secured? Should it be by direct representation of individual electors on a geographical basis by the ballot-box in the normal way? If so, should the neighbourhood be warded with multi-member wards, or should there be single-member wards comprising a street or two each, so that representation would be truly local and non-political, with residents representing their immediate neighbours? If the latter, should candidates be eligible for election only for the actual ward in which they live?

What sort of election rules should be adopted for such elections? Is it essential to adopt for this purpose all the complexities involved in the safeguards felt necessary for election to local authorities? Should there be other divergencies from general electoral practice, such as mobile polling stations or the spread of an election over several days?

Who should be entitled to vote? Should the vote for this purpose be extended to resident aliens as well as to those on the electoral register? What should be the minimum age for election? Will representation by geographical location always be appropriate? Is there a case in some areas for at least some members to be representatives of particular organisations (such as churches, clubs, voluntary bodies) or minority communities, who might not otherwise seek election to the council? If this kind of representation is desirable what kind of safeguards would be needed, or would it be better to leave such matters to a right by the neighbourhood council to co-opt additional members for this purpose?

Answerability to electorate

Should there be a neighbourhood meeting (as in parishes)? If so, what powers should it have? Should there be provision for neighbourhood polls? . . .

Term of office

What should be the term of office? Should it be four years, as for local authorities, or say one or two years? Should elections (if held in static polling stations on one day) be held with the district elections, as in the case of parishes, or quite separately?

Powers and Finance

The purpose and functions of neighbourhood councils do not require, nor could they justify, substantial expenditure. But, clearly, such councils would need some limited source of finance to cover basic costs (within of course the overall need for restraint in public expenditure) . . .

Should neighbourhood councils have formal rights of consultation, eg on the local authority's planning and traffic proposals affecting the area? Should they have similar rights to those of parish councils in relation to planning applications? Should they have a right to nominate members of public bodies whose functions relate to the neighbourhood and, if so, which?

The references here to 'the neighbourhood' raise the further question how this should be defined. In many instances the area for a neighbourhood council will be in no doubt — where an area of an appropriate size (usually perhaps of the order of 3,000—10,000 population) is clearly defined geographically, it is regularly regarded as a particular and separate district of the town, and there is no controversy over its boundaries. But in other cases no such neat solution will present itself. How then should a neighbourhood be defined? Entirely by the sponsors of the petition for establishment of a council? Or by them, subject to some right of modification by the district council? Or should the district ward (not necessarily coinciding with an actual community) be taken where there is failure of district and local sponsors to agree?

Should there be any statutory minimum size, say an area with 1,000 electors, or should maximum and minimum sizes be left to convention?

How established and for what area?

This is perhaps the most difficult issue for a statutory scheme. Clearly, some practical steps to set up a council will need to be taken by the district council. But the starting-point needs to be local initiative, which suggests that a statutory neighbourhood council should only be set up when a certain number or proportion of the electorate of the area so wish. Should this be a relatively small number (say 100 signatories) or a relatively large number (say, 10% of the electorate of the neighbourhood) which might fit with a concept of statutory status coming normally only after a non-statutory neighbourhood council had developed a considerable basis of support in the area? Should there be provision for a petition to set up a neighbourhood council to be subject to challenge by way of a neighbourhood poll? Should conditions for establishment of a neighbourhood council be easier where the district council favour the move, and more stringent where they do not?

19 NEIGHBOURHOOD COUNCILS: A LOCAL GOVERNMENT RESPONSE

From *Association of Metropolitan Authorities Policy Committee Report, Appendix B* published in *Supplement to the Municipal Review* (January 1975); by permission of Municipal Review.

3. . . . The message which has come back from the over-whelming majority of metropolitan authorities replying is clear: that the new authorities have only just begun to function and should be permitted to make progress without new statutory bodies to add to the complications, the cost, the work (for members and officers), the confusion and the delays of administering local government. Some authorities consider the concept as weakening the influence of elected members of authorities. Others point out that on the basis of 3,000 inhabitants each they could be faced with up to 70 to 100 of these bodies in their areas. The proposals for compulsory formation of such bodies are claimed to be impracticable. This is the general view.

4. But there are in addition some welcomes for the idea and its possibilities, so long as the borough or district council can operate the concept on a voluntary basis where and how it fits the circumstances and with very limited finance in present circumstances.

5. The following paragraphs from replies seem to crystallise some of the issues: the result of the present proposals might be to set up another group of local representatives, adding further confusion to the majority of the public, reducing the power and credence of existing councillors, and creating a further source of confrontation between the public and authority which will slow certain procedures even further.

There is a danger that the development of neighbourhood councils, established to consider the needs of individual neighbourhoods, will obscure the broad role of the city as a whole, whose problems, potentials and responsibilities are greater than the sum total of its constituent parts (or neighbourhoods).

Further, the ward councillors will inevitably be drawn into any conflict between local or neighbourhood needs and city needs. They could be torn between policies demanded by their local neighbourhood council and the policies and constraints imposed by their elected colleagues, party policy, or committee decisions. Thus, in such a situation the neighbourhood council might be publicly seen to represent the interests of the neighbourhood, whilst the ward councillor might be discredited because he is seen to be powerless to effect necessary changes in decisions or to effect the re-allocation of resources in favour of the neighbourhood in question.

One of the aims of the Local Government Act 1972 was to create larger councils to provide better services. Before the new system has been in operation six months, and had a chance to prove itself, there are now proposals to modify the new structure. It is recognised that local authorities need to improve their links with the public, but the concept of neighbourhood councils as embodied in this consultation paper is not necessarily the only way of doing this. There is a danger in modifying a system every few months to meet particular demands that the system is never allowed to establish itself.

The Council is already in touch with the community at street level, through its own public participation arrangements, by means of numerous action and pressure groups, local organisations and through councillors' surgeries. Although channels of public participation could be improved, it is felt this is an internal matter for the Council, which is in any case constantly being refined in the light of practical experience.

. . . . . .

7. In so far as there is support for the proposals, the indications are that a ward basis would be best for boundaries, that perhaps the wish of 25 per cent of electors should be taken as the proportion required for forming neighbourhood councils, and that finance and staff might be found by a district central secretariat (but with very limited provision in present financial circumstances). One large city authority believes that if neighbourhood councils are to be established and elected, then that election should be 'total', i.e. representation should not be by pressure groups.

. . . . . .

9. Long memoranda received from two authorities refer to their extensive work in establishing community councils or groups of various kinds. One of these states:

My Council have considered in great detail the consultation paper on neighbourhood councils in unparished areas in England and have prepared a report giving detailed answers to the questions raised in the paper. The general feeling on the whole basis of the consultation paper is that there are many difficulties inherent in a statutory scheme. It is felt that the motivation and stimulation for the establishment of neighbourhood councils should come from within the community, given some preliminary input in most cases from staff appropriately versed in community development principles. It is thought that rules could not be established, unless they are drawn broadly to take account of different circumstances, and then it becomes questionable whether they are of any value at all. This Council see the establishment of such neighbourhood councils as a natural development, effected over a sometimes lengthy period with self-motivation characterising the process. Only after a council has been established in this way should the question of its status, i.e. statutory or voluntary be considered. It is felt that the discussion paper greatly over-stresses the formal processes needed to establish neighbourhood councils and that a variety of appropriate local arrangements unfettered as far as possible by regulations would be a much more satisfactory base on which to create these bodies. The question of the size of the neighbourhood for the purposes of creating a statutory council must be preceded by the question 'what is the structure being created for?' Is it to be another tier of local government, albeit with flexible and limited functions, or is it to create an extra dimension to urban life by establishing an organisation which is sensitive and adaptable to local needs and which can positively promote them? It is suggested that this structure should be aimed at the latter and that whatever arrangements are prescribed as regards the size of a neighbourhood they must be flexible to meet widely differing circumstances.

The authority indicate some support for the concept of enabling legislation for a permissive structure but the above comments show a very clear preference for evolution from the ground, leading to a statutory structure later.

20 CENTRAL–LOCAL RELATIONS: THE MAUD REPORT

From the *Committee on Management in Local Government, Vol.I. Report* (1967); by permission of H.M.S.O. Hereafter referred to as *Maud*. Of the specific proposals in this extract, only the one for a reduction of statutory controls was implemented (in 1972 and 1974 legislation). The 1972 Act retained the surcharge powers of district auditors, though it permits authorities to use private auditors, who do not have surcharge powers. The most radical recommendations, for a 'general competence', had little chance of acceptance: but under recent legislation, local authorities may take any action in realisation of their functions even if the action itself has no specific statutory basis; and may also spend annually an amount not greater than the product of a two-penny rate, in the interests of their area or its inhabitants.

CONCLUSIONS AND RECOMMENDATIONS

273. We are clear that there is a tendency for control and direction by the central government to increase, and for the financial independence of local authorities to decline still further, and that both these tendencies weaken local government as an organ of government and detract from its effectiveness. We are left in no doubt that both central government and local authorities accept, as part of the natural order of things, local government's role as a subsidiary instrument of public administration. We see a dangerous complacency amongst local government members and officers in their acceptance of the way in which the initiative of local authorities is sapped and in their acquiescence in growing government interference through regulations, directions and exhortations. We see this leading to a general impatience with the

democratic element in local government, and to pressure for local administration to be performed by organs untrammelled by popular representation, more amenable to central control and fitting tidily into a unified structure of public administration. The case for democratic local government is undermined if local authorities are reduced to complete dependence on the central government and if they are regarded as mere agents of the will of the central government with no life of their own.

. . . . . .

283. Our view is that *ultra vires* as it operates at present has a deleterious effect on local government because of the narrowness of the legislation governing local authorities' activities. The specific nature of legislation discourages enterprise, handicaps development, robs the community of services which the local authority might render, and encourages too rigorous oversight by the central government. It contributes to the excessive concern over legalities and fosters the idea that the Clerk should be a lawyer. Dr. Marshall refers to the following substantial advantages of the possession of a general competence:

(a) The local authority is encouraged to regard itself as responsible for the well-being of the community as a whole and not as a provider of specified services each regulated by specific statutes.

(b) There is the practical value of the freedom for local authorities themselves to expand their activities or to do so by participating in the efforts of other bodies.

(c) Dependence on statutory power for each function invites regulations, detailed scrutiny, comments, returns, inspections and the like . . .

284. The modification we would propose would not mean that local authorities would cease to be subject to the rule of law. The supremacy of Parliament is not in question. Nor are we advocating the abolition of the doctrine of *ultra vires* for local authorities would still have to work within the statutes. They would continue to have statutory duties and limitations imposed upon them and permissive powers granted to them, and their governmental and coercive powers would be regulated by law. They would however have, in addition to their specific statutory duties and permissive powers, general powers to meet the needs of the community.

285. In other words they would have a 'general competence' enabling them to undertake at their discretion services for the community additional to those provided for by specific legislation. We believe that this extension of power would in due time induce a much less negative outlook in those concerned with local government both at central and local levels, while at the same time the citizens' needs would be better catered for. The likelihood that, because of the comprehensive nature of local authorities' existing obligations, the new services would be marginal and supplementary, does not in any way detract from the benefit of what is, in our opinion, a much needed reform.

286. . . . . *We therefore recommend that local authorities should be given a general competence to do (in addition to what legislation already requires or permits them to do) whatever in their opinion is in the interests of their areas or their inhabitants subject to their not encroaching on the duties of other governmental*

bodies and to appropriate safeguards for the protection of public and private interests.

. . . . . .

290. There remains the power of the district auditor to impose a surcharge upon those responsible for illegal expenditure or loss of moneys. District audit does not apply to the whole of local government accounts: most accounts of most borough councils are audited by auditors with no power of surcharge. We are not aware that financial affairs not subject to district audit are conducted in an inferior way. The principle behind surcharge is in any case out of keeping with the autonomous and responsible local authorities we visualise for the future. We believe that fear of surcharge is an inhibiting feature, damaging to local government as much by its effect on the attitudes of members and officers as by the specific restraints it exerts. *We therefore recommend the abolition of the district auditor's power of surcharge.*

. . . . . .

Administrative relationship between central and local government

. . . . . .

295. Probably few in the central government would subscribe to the view of J. S. Mill that 'local representatives and their officers are almost certain to be of a much lower grade of intelligence and knowledge than Parliament and the national executive'. If the nature of central government controls is such as to suggest that local authorities are not competent to devise their own administrative machinery and methods it is hardly likely that people of calibre, either officers or members, will regard local government service as attractive. Further, the tendency for departments to assume responsibility for the administrative control of local authorities becomes self perpetuating and can only add to the burden of the departments and itself contribute to further delays and vexations. 'The continuous increase in the powers of Whitehall is . . . likely to reduce the quality and efficiency both of the central administration taken as a whole and of parliamentary control.' In addition 'over a wide range of services it can be shown that the greater flexibility and the opportunity for experiment give the system of local government important administrative advantages' . . . 'One of the great merits of local government is that it enables the tasks of public administration to be spread more evenly throughout the nation.'

. . . . . .

297. Our conclusions are that:
(*a*) Administrative control of local authorities by the central government is a consequence of:
  (i) the statutory and political responsibilities of ministers;
  (ii) the need for central control of the national economy and for the laying down of national policies;
  (iii) the financial dependence of local authorities on the central government;

     (iv) the prescription of minimum standards for services to be applied throughout the country;

     (v) the weaknesses of some local authorities which may involve instructions and restrictions applicable to all, irrespective of their capacities.

(*b*) Although national policies, the control of investment and of national resources and the need in some cases to secure minimum standards are the central government's responsibilities, administrative controls could be substantially diminished by recognition that local authorities are competent to make their own administrative arrangements and to be responsible for them.

(*c*) Any reorganisation of the structure of local government resulting in 'financially strong authorities' the need for which the government has recognised should be accompanied by a recognition that local authorities are competent to observe minimum standards without the need for detailed controls to secure them.

21 CENTRAL–LOCAL RELATIONS: THE 1970 WHITE PAPER

From *Reform of Local Government in England* (Cmnd. 4276, 1970); by permission of H.M.S.O.

60. As the Prime Minister made clear in his speech to the Association of Municipal Corporations at Scarborough on 17th September 1969, the Government believe unequivocally in greater freedom for local authorities within the framework of national policies laid down by Parliament. The reorganisation of local government creates an opportunity, which the Government intend to seize, for achieving this aim.

    61. Much of central government's intervention — more, perhaps, than is generally realised — consists of reconciling the proposals of different authorities and dividing between authorities that part of the nation's resources which is allotted to spending by local government. The extent of this intervention will automatically diminish with the reduction in the number of authorities — to less than half the present number in the case of education, for example, and less than a tenth in the case of housing. Moreover, the smaller number of authorities will make for a more intimate partnership and a more effective dialogue.

    62. Reform will thus bring greater freedom in its train. But the Government are also determined to take positive measures to reverse the trend towards centralisation. They are already planning to eliminate restraints that have become obsolete and, where control remains necessary for the furtherance of national objectives, to make this control more flexible and efficient. The new structure will facilitate this process; for with the best will in the world, no serious decentralisation is possible with the present mosaic pattern of authorities with populations varying from 1,500 to over a million . . .

Financial controls

63. The most irksome form of government control is the control over borrowing, under which in practice the Government's sanction is needed for the great majority of capital projects. Central government must of course, as the Commission accepted, be concerned with the total of investment, with its allocation among the major services, and with national standards in those services. However, control over borrowing in the form which it has taken under successive Governments for many years past is more restrictive and laborious than it should be. The Government therefore intend, with the help and advice of local government, to improve this system in two respects in particular — first, by replacing detailed control by control through programmes, where the more important sectors of the major services are concerned; secondly, by allowing a significant freedom of decision for local authorities in respect of the remaining services by way of an unallocated margin of expenditure. As the Prime Minister has already announced, the Government will pursue these means of enlarging the discretion of local authorities even before local government is reorganised.

. . . . . .

Non-financial controls

65. With controls that have little or no connection with finance, it is easier to see the principles on which the discretion of local authorities should be enlarged than to work out their detailed application. Scattered through the legislation of a century are controls which were appropriate when new functions were being introduced, but which are now clearly obsolete; while other controls exist which will be inappropriate when all authorities are large and can command comprehensive professional advice. The same is true of some statutory powers of Ministers to intervene in ways other than by exercising routine control: for example, some powers of enquiry and some default powers. Administrative means, such as 'blanket decisions', are not always a suitable method of adapting such powers to modern conditions. A statutory power of intervention is operative until it is removed by Parliament. To decide which powers of intervention should be removed will require a painstaking examination of provisions in many statutes to see which are obsolete, and which may still be needed either to provide for adjudication between authorities and individual citizens or to enable central government to discharge national responsibilities. The Government will undertake this examination in a positive spirit. Indeed, they have already asked the local authority associations to say which controls they think should be removed.

. . . . . .

Authorities' internal business

67. The Commission recommended, as did the Committee on the Management of

Local Government in still more specific terms, a reduction in statutory control over the internal administration of local authorities. The Government accept this recommendation. They agree that in general the statutory requirements that authorities should maintain separate committees for specific purposes are now obsolete — though this does not, of course, imply that the importance of particular committees has diminished; it means only that the services in question are now firmly established. The same applies, in general, to provisions requiring the approval of Ministers to the choice of officers for certain posts . . .

A general power for local authorities

68. The Commission recommended that the new main authorities should have a general power to spend money for the benefit of their areas and inhabitants. A power of this kind is readily available to local authorities under Section 6 of the Local Government (Financial Provisions) Act 1963, but it is limited in each area to the product of a penny rate. The Commission proposed that this financial limit should be abolished, so that the only limit on the use of the power to spend would be the wishes of the electors and such restrictions as may be placed on local government expenditure in the interests of national economic policy.

69. The Government are sympathetic in principle to this proposal. There are, however, practical difficulties; for example, unconditional powers, not restricted by any financial limit, might lead to wasteful duplication or to local action which conflicts with national objectives in important fields of policy. The scope of a revised and extended general power is therefore a matter which the Government will wish to discuss in detail with the associations as part of the preparations for the Reorganisation Bill.

22 CENTRAL–LOCAL RELATIONS: THE WHITEHALL VIEW

From Dame Evelyn Sharp: *The Ministry of Housing and Local Government* (Allen & Unwin, 1969); by permission of the publisher. This account by the former Permanent Secretary to the Ministry gives some useful, if guarded, insights into the role of the central department responsible for relations with local authorities. The Ministry was in 1970 absorbed into the new Department of the Environment.

THE ROLE OF THE MINISTRY

In a great deal of its work the Ministry's statutory role is largely negative. It is the local authorities which are expected to take the initiative. The Ministry's function is to approve, modify or disapprove their proposals or plans, usually after hearing the views or objections of rate-payers or citizens affected; to consent to capital expenditure — nowadays within the ambit of public investment programmes laid down by the Government; to hear appeals against their decisions. Default powers exist in some fields but are virtually never exercised. The Minister who is held responsible by Parliament for the conditions in which people live (not that this responsibility is anywhere expressed) is in the curious position that half the time he is acting as judge between the local authority trying to effect improvements and private citizens who would be injured by its proposals . . . But this does enable him to over-rule private interests where he is satisfied that the public interest ought to prevail. Nor, of course, does the Ministry limit itself to exercising its statutory role. It issues a constant stream of circulars and bulletins recommending the standards to be aimed at, telling local authorities what the Minister wants of them, advising how this or that problem might be tackled. Officers of the Ministry are in constant touch with their opposite numbers in local authorities, sometimes urging them to more vigorous action, sometimes holding them back; generally discussing their ideas with them before proposals are formally submitted. Where there is a difference of opinion between an authority and the Ministry – or where an authority is thought to need a vigorous push – a Minister will usually see a deputation, or, sometimes, will visit the area. A great deal is achieved simply by the persuasion of Ministers. Finally, the Ministry engages in an unending stream of legislation, much of which is designed to enlarge the powers of local authorities, sometimes to give general effect to powers which individual authorities have acquired by private Bill . . .

. . . . . .

RELATIONS WITH LOCAL AUTHORITIES

Different departments concerned with local government services have different attitudes to local authorities, owing partly to the nature of the services, partly to the character and history of the department. Some, concerned with what are essentially national services – e.g. the police, education – insist on certain standards of performance; and for this purpose have an inspection system (as both the Home Office and the Department of Education and Science do) and exercise a fairly close supervision over the work of the responsible authorities – even extending, in some cases, to a right to intervene in the appointments made to chief officer posts. The Ministry of Housing and Local Government has traditionally left the authorities to take the initiative in public health, housing, planning – though this is now changing; has no inspection system – though sometimes it will look back wistfully to the inspectors of the poor law; and would reject the idea that it should supervise what local authorities are doing . . . primarily the reason for the Ministry's belief that authorities should, largely, be allowed to go their own way has been that the services for which it is responsible have been seen as essentially local services.

While the Ministry ordinarily leaves the initiative to the individual authorities, it frequently exhorts authorities at large to particular policies by manual or circular; and sometimes urges individual authorities to particular action, e.g. to push up their house-building programmes. But the main work of the Ministry, outside the field of local government organization and finance, consists in approving, modifying or disapproving proposals made by authorities; and in a continuous stream of legislation, most of which alters or extends the powers of authorities, or puts new obligations on them. As remarked above, the departmental philosophy is — or at any rate has been — that the services with which it is concerned are local services; that the Ministry should see that authorities have the necessary tools and should help them with advice, often derived from initiatives taken by individual authorities; but that beyond this its main responsibility is to see that authorities keep within the law and do not over-stretch either their own or the national economy, and that the objections of rate-payers or others to what an authority proposes are given a fair hearing. This philosophy is, however, changing; and as it has become increasingly apparent that the old local government system is not able to do all that is now needed, so the Ministry has become increasingly interventionist. Intervention because of political disagreement is also becoming more common. This trend could be halted, and perhaps reversed, if the local government system is radically altered following the report of the Royal Commission on Local Government; but only if Governments will accept that local authorities should be allowed to follow their own policies even when these are disliked.

The traditional non-interventionist attitude of the Ministry is perhaps partly due to the inherited attitude of the Local Government Board; but it also owes something to the Ministry's responsibility for local government as such. Authorities are independent, responsible only to their electorate; and every officer of the Ministry is bred to respect this independence. It is true that the Ministry exercises a series of controls: controls which, in practice, severely limit the independence of authorities. Authorities have to get the consent of the Minister for all sorts of actions (some, it must be confessed, which they could well be left to decide for themselves); but consent has usually been forthcoming. The great exception to this is the strict control now exercised over the rate of capital investment by local authorities . . . Modern legislation tends increasingly to charge the Minister concerned with the duty to formulate and promote a national policy for the service; to enable him to give directions to the local authorities about their general administration of the service; to require his approval for all courses of action of any consequence which the local authority wishes to promote.

In practice statutory provisions of this kind are less important than they seem. Whatever may be inscribed on the legislative tablets, it is the tradition of British local authorities by and large to do what the Government of the day ask them to do, though they will do it at their own pace and in their own way. Head-on clashes do occur, but have been rare; though recently they have tended to increase. The personal prestige and influence of a Minister in his relations with local authorities is very great — even with authorities controlled by a party of a different political persuasion. For the Ministry, therefore, the theoretical nature of the Minister's powers is much less important than the practical state of its working relations with the authorities. The working relations are, nevertheless, shaped by the various provisions which require authorities to obtain certain consents from the Minister, or give aggrieved individuals a right to bring their objections or appeals to him . . .

. . . . . .

. . . the Minister's approval is required at various points to what local authorities want to do, e.g. to the compulsory acquisition of land, to closing streets or rights of way, to development plans. Here the function of the Ministry is twofold. Part is to form its own view of what is proposed — whether it fits with national policies, is not too expensive, is good of its kind. The other part (which bears on the first) is to hear the views of rate-payers who object to the cost entailed, and of owners or occupiers of land affected. Very often local authorities discuss their proposals informally with officers of the Ministry before submitting them formally, so that they can know that, subject to what may emerge on objection, the Ministry is likely to approve. Once a proposal is formally submitted the Ministry's function if there are objections becomes as already explained quasi-judicial, and thereafter discussion with the authority is at an end. A great deal of time, of the professional officers especially, is taken up with discussions of local authority proposals that will eventually need approval; but increasingly the real burden falls on the Ministry when it comes to consideration of objections. These, which can run to thousands in the case of a development plan, all need detailed scrutiny; and the unhappy result, all too often, is that many months or even, on occasion, years may elapse before an authority gets a final decision . . .

Personal Relationships Within these formal relationships are the personal relationships between the Ministry and the authorities. These are, in general, close and friendly. Officers of the Ministry know their opposite numbers in local government and are known to them. Many local government officers make it their business to know their way round the Ministry, whom to go to in order to find out how such and such a proposal is likely to fare, or why something seems to have stuck. Some will just drop in to find out what is cooking. Equally officers of the Ministry can turn to the officers of many local authorities for information, for help, for advice. Many members of local authorities also are well known inside the Ministry and never hesitate to go to the officer concerned with a particular question in order to push a point of view, to demand a quick decision, to talk over a problem. Departmental officers visit local authorities as much as they can, and though inevitably this is done most easily by the regional officers, some headquarters officers manage to make a point of regular visiting. Those who do manage it know that it is invaluable; for they get the feel of local government on its home ground as they never will from a series of deputations to Whitehall. But receiving deputations is a standard part of the work; and takes up a good deal of the time of Ministers. The real exchange of information and points of view is mostly made, however, in the more informal contacts.

23 LOCAL GOVERNMENT ELECTIONS: POPULAR ATTITUDES

From *Redcliffe-Maud: Research Study No. 9: Community Attitudes Survey, England, (1969)*; by permission of H.M.S.O. An interesting feature of the major enquiries into local government has been the willingness to examine not only evidence from interested parties (the time-honoured method), but the findings of objective research. This extract summarises research which revealed widespread apathy towards and ignorance of local government on the part of local government electors; see also **23**, below.

SUMMARY OF FINDINGS

Section A

1. Nearly four in five electors claim to possess some feelings of attachment to a 'home' community area. Propensity to have such a feeling is positively correlated with length of residence in the area.

2. The community area, as defined by electors, is not geographically extensive. In the majority of cases, it is considerably smaller than the size of the local authority area in which electors reside. In urban authority areas, approximately three-quarters of electors define their 'home' area as being of a size no larger than the equivalent of a ward; of these, the majority define its extent as being approximately the size of a group of streets or smaller. In rural areas, 85% of electors define the 'home' area as being of a size equivalent to a parish or smaller.

. . . . . .

Section C

1. Knowledge of the responsibilities for the local provision of public services is found to be slightly greater than average among men, younger and middle-aged informants (compared with those over 55), electors of a higher level of education and higher socio-economic status.

2. Generally speaking, there appears to be a slightly wider correct knowledge as to the authorities responsible for the administration of local government-provided services. There is some confusion as to the bodies responsible for hospitals and electricity supply, though less for social security.

3. Electors are, on balance, more disposed to mention public services in a favourable than a critical manner: 73% are able to quote at least one public service which they consider quite well run in their local authority area; 51% are also able conversely to think of at least one with which they can find fault.

4. There is some indication that the level of dissatisfaction with public services is higher among informants living in conurbation authorities, particularly municipal boroughs and urban districts.

5. The services most frequently singled out for praise are refuse collection and disposal, education and schools, libraries and hospitals. All these are mentioned by approximately 3 in 10 of the electors interviewed.

6. The services of which criticism is most often expressed (though by only

approximately 1 in 10 electors) are, once again, refuse collection and hospitals, in addition to recreational facilities, town planning and provision of housing.

7. It is possible that refuse collection, hospitals and recreational facilities are services over the administration of which electors are more sensitive. We might hypothesise that they have come to be seen as yardsticks for assessing the efficiency of local provision of public services, irrespective of the authority responsible in each case.

8. There is little conclusive evidence from the results of these questions to suggest that electors care whether public services should be the responsibility of local authorities or of other, central bodies.

Section D

1. The most frequent *primary* source which informants would consider contacting in order to deal with any enquiries or complaints is an administrative one — rather than an elected representative. The most frequently quoted source is a somewhat vague one — the 'council', or 'the town hall' — but the specific council department or head of department concerned with their enquiry often features in replies also.

2. Informants in rural districts, and those of a lower level of education and socio-economic status are more likely than others to think of contacting an elected representative — usually a local councillor.

3. Should primary contact with an office or department be unsatisfactory or inconclusive then a quarter of the electors would take no further action; of the remainder the majority would consider approaching some specific *person*: the head of the relevant department or, more likely, the elector's Member of Parliament or local councillor. It may be concluded in fact that while departments and officials are seen as the main primary point of contact for electors, elected representatives are then perceived as a second resort when a first approach has proved unsatisfactory.

4. More than one in four electors would not consider contacting their local councillor at all. The three main reasons for this were said to be his incompetence, the greater suitability of contacting someone else, and lack of knowledge as to who the local councillor actually is, or how to get in touch with him.

. . . . . .

9. Fifty per cent of all enquiries and complaints are considered to have been dealt with both fully and satisfactorily. Matters relating to refuse collection, health, and drainage are considered to have been dealt with most satisfactorily; those relating to education are considered to have resulted less frequently in a satisfactory outcome.

10. Thirteen per cent of electors say they have at some time contacted their local councillor(s). While the subjects of contact were, for the most part, miscellaneous complaints and grievances, the three main public services involved were provision of housing, town planning (i.e. planning permission), and streets and highways.

11. Eighty-five per cent of the sample know correctly the location of their respect-

ive town hall, or main local authority offices. Electors in rural districts are considerably less aware of the precise location than are urban residents. Distance of residence from the main office is seen to affect adversely both the level of correct awareness of the latter site, and the propensity to visit (as measured by the number of visits made in the last year). Overall, no more than 37% of electors have visited their respective town hall/main office during the previous year.

. . . . . .

Section E

1. Electors' opinions as to the optimum size of their local authority areas show a very marked preference for preserving the *status quo*.

2. The reasons given for keeping the present size are a mixture of satisfaction with the present system, and apprehension in the face of the consequences of any change. The latter comprises disbelief that change in the size of the area would lead to any functional, administrative or financial (i.e. rating) improvements, and fears that an *increased* size might have adverse effects upon community interests and, specifically, the surrounding countryside.

3. Reasons advanced in support of both an increase and a decrease in local authority area size are concerned very largely with the material gains which would accrue to the present area (or the electors' own part of it) from either sort of change.

4. Among those favouring a change, the balance of general opinion is clearly in support of a bigger authority area. Expansion is seen by those in favour of such a change as promoting greater efficiency and improving the facilities (especially in respect of housing) of the present area.

5. However, taking into consideration the views of all informants with fairly strongly-held opinions (irrespective of their basic attitude on this question), there is a slight balance of feeling that a smaller area would lead to improved accessibility and effectiveness. Many informants nevertheless consider that changes in the size of the authority area would have no consequences for either of these factors, nor for efficiency.

24 LOCAL GOVERNMENT ELECTIONS: THE ELECTOR

From *Maud, Vol.3: The Local Government Elector (1967)*; by permission of H.M.S.O.

ELECTORS' KNOWLEDGE OF THE LOCAL GOVERNMENT SYSTEM

1. Summary of findings

(1) There seems to be a certain level of general public ignorance concerning local

government and the services provided by the council. For instance, 20% of our informants were unable to name a single service provided by their councils at either the local or the county level.

(2) People know less about their county councils than they do about their local borough or district councils. Sometimes the functions of the one are confused with those of the other.

(3) People living in county boroughs tend to be better informed about some aspects of local government than the rest of the electorate.

(4) People living in rural districts and in metropolitan London know less about their councils than people living in other areas.

(5) To some extent women are less informed than men about local government.

(6) Informants with a higher degree of formal education know more about local government services than less educated people.

(7) Older people appear less informed than younger people about almost every apsect of council knowledge touched on in this survey.

(8) In some instances people in the youngest age group (21–34) are less knowledgeable than those in the middle age group (35–54).

(9) Younger people seem more aware of their lack of knowledge than older people and they want to get more information to a greater extent than do those in the older age groups.

ELECTORS' CONTACT WITH LOCAL GOVERNMENT

1. Summary of findings

1. Almost everyone has some 'contact' with the council in the sense that their household uses one or more council services, but (as chapter I has shown) not everyone is aware that the services they use are provided by the council.

2. 26% of the electorate had had some contact with the local town hall or council office in the last year; but only 6% of those living in areas served by the county council had had any contact with the county council office during the same period.

3. Younger people, more 'educated' people and people from socio-economic groups 1 and 2 were more likely to have contacted the town hall than older or less educated people or people from socio-economic groups 4 or 5.

4. 17% of the electorate had ever contacted a councillor of the borough or district in which they were living at the time of interview. 6% said they had done so in the last year.

5. Most contacts were by personal visit. People in socio-economic groups 1 and 2 and people who had lived in the area for a long time were more likely to have seen a councillor than people from socio-economic groups 4 or 5 or those who had recently moved into the area.

6. 7% of the electorate had ever been to a meeting of the local council of the area

in which they were living at the time of the interview. 1% said they had attended a meeting in the last year.

7. 8% of the electorate were able to say where and when the next meeting was to be held. People over 45 were more likely to know than younger people.

. . . . . .

ELECTORS' ATTITUDES TO LOCAL GOVERNMENT

1. Summary of Findings

1. Just over a quarter of our informants thought their local council was very well run and just under a quarter thought their county councils very well run. These are lower figures than might have been expected, as between a half to four-fifths said they were 'very satisfied' with other services and conditions on which they were asked their opinion during the course of the survey.

2. Younger people are less likely than older people to say they were very satisfied with either their local or their county council.

3. When asked for a definition of democracy, 39% were unable to give an answer, an additional 4% gave negative or derogatory definitions.

4. 64% of informants said they thought the democratic method a 'very good' way of running local areas although not all of them had been able to say what they meant by 'democracy'. The criticisms made by those who did not think it was a 'very good' method show that some electors appear to feel 'alienated' from their local council. Other criticisms made were of the party system, the system of representation, and the selection of representatives.

5. When asked a series of questions designed to measure their attitudes to voting in local elections, 6% gave answers to each question which expressed a negative attitude to voting. 20% gave answers to every question which expressed a positive attitude to voting. 74% gave answers which lay between the two extremes.

6. When informants were asked questions designed to measure their sense of their own ability to influence their local council, 12% gave answers which could classify them as 'confident', 34% were 'fairly confident', 18% thought themselves 'ineffective' and 36% were uninterested in local council affairs.

7. Women and older people (65 or more) tend to feel 'indifferent'. Men tend to feel 'confident'. More highly educated people and people in socio-economic groups 1 and 2 tend to feel 'confident', whereas people with only a primary type education and those from the socio-economic groups 3, 4 or 5 tend to feel 'ineffective' or 'indifferent'.

8. About 65% of the electorate in areas in which there were contested elections in 1964 said they had voted in the last main borough or district election. This is a higher figure than that calculated from returns made to the General Register Office for 1964 which is 42%.

9. About 50% said they had voted in county council elections in 1964. This is a higher figure than that provided by the G.R.O. of 41%.
10. The most often given reason for not voting in either local or county elections was 'not interested' or 'can't be bothered'. The second most often given reason for not voting in the last borough or district election was that the informant was unable to leave the house. In the case of county elections the main reason given was that the elector did not know the election was taking place.
11. Electors think their councillors spend about 16 hours a week on council work. The estimates grow smaller as the age of the informant increases, and also as the area they live in becomes less urban.
12. Over 90% agreed that their councillors spend some time going to and preparing for council or committee meetings, but only just under two-thirds thought their councillors spent any time on the problems of individual electors.
13. 53% of the electorate were aware that councillors were not at present paid for the work they did as councillors. When told the actual situation and asked what they thought the future situation should be, 42% thought it should be the same as at present, and 31% said they thought councillors should be paid a salary.
14. Most people thought their councillors were male, were local people, were party members and were 'older' or 'middle-aged'. However, only 29% thought they had 'above average' education. The ideal concept of a local councillor showed them as young, female, with 'above average' education and not belonging to a political party, to a greater extent than they were pictured to be in reality.

25 LOCAL GOVERNMENT ELECTIONS: THE COUNCILLOR

From (a) *Maud, Vol.2: The Local Government Councillor (1967)*, and (b) *Maud, Vol.5: Local Government Administration in England and Wales (1967)*. Both by permission of H.M.S.O. Research findings on the work and characteristics of councillors in local government.

(a)

SUMMARY OF CONCLUSIONS

Characteristics and Recruitment of Councillors

1. *How representative is local government?* The direct responsibility of local government for services designed to meet the needs of many sections of the population can only be effectively discharged if people with first-hand knowledge of all sections of the community are represented on councils. We find, however, that in some respects councillors differ widely from the general population. They are much older on average. Only one-fifth of male councillors are under the age of 45. More

than half are over 55. Only 12% are women. The proportion of councillors who are employers and managers of small businesses or farmers is four times that of these groups in the general population. On the other hand, manual workers, who form more than half of the male population over 25 are numerically very under-represented on councils.

2. Councillors are somewhat better educated than the general population. Forty-four per cent had only elementary edcuation or no formal qualifications, compared with about 70% of the general population. Fifteen per cent of councillors have had some form of further education. Amongst MPs 53% were in this position in 1964.

. . . . . .

5. Our constitutional guarantee of representative government is free elections, but thirty-eight per cent of all councillors were returned unopposed. Another 11% were appointed as aldermen, chairmen or mayors by their fellow councillors. In rural districts 69% were returned unopposed. Over half of all small businessmen and farmer councillors were returned unopposed . . .

6. *How do councillors come into council work?* About a third of all councillors were first brought into touch with council work, or asked to stand, by political parties. Twenty-eight per cent of councillors came into contact with council work through trade union, religious or welfare groups but only about 10% were *invited to stand* by such bodies. On the other hand 35% of councillors were invited to stand by private people or in other informal ways.

. . . . . .

Council Experience

12. *How much time do councillors spend on their public work?* On average councillors spend about 52 hours a month on all their public activities. Less than a quarter of this time is spent actually sitting in council or committees. But there are big differences between councillors. County borough and manual worker councillors spend much more time than the average on their public work and small employer and farmer councillors spend much less . . .

. . . . . .

14. About one-seventh of the councillor's public time on average is spent with electors but about a half of all councillors spend less than 5 hours a month on electors' problems. A small minority, however, spend 20 or more hours a month on electors.

15. *How do councillors feel about their council work?* In the opinion of councillors their councils had done most 'to help people and improve things' in 1964 by their work on housing, the public utility services and town planning. Housing was put high in the order of importance in all kinds of authority except county councils who put education first. The rural districts put work on developing public utilities first.

16. Councillors' main satisfactions arise out of particular council activities, amongst which housing and old people's welfare are prominent. In contrast the

frustrations of councillors' work arise mainly out of the way the machinery of local government works. Only 8% of councillors mentioned party politics as a cause of frustration.

. . . . . .

24. A majority of councillors thought that the present system of payment for loss of earnings, subsistence and so on was adequate although many would like to see some changes in this respect. Two-thirds of all councillors did *not* think that councillors should be paid. This was chiefly because they did not believe that payment would attract good or better qualified people.

25. About half of all councillors thought there should be a retiring age for councillors and three-quarters thought there should be a limit to the time anybody could be chairman of council or mayor.

26. Most councillors did not feel that the presence of aldermen had much effect on the standing of councils or their work or the willingness of people to stand. These views were shared by the majority of aldermen.

Councillors and their Public Relationships

. . . . . .

29. *What part does party politics play in local government? How essential is it to the system which now operates?* There are big differences in the extent to which councillors are involved in political organisations. Ninety-five per cent of county borough councillors are members of political parties but only about half of rural district councillors. Over 70% of rural district councillors describe themselves as 'independent' and so do nearly two-thirds of the smaller employers and farmers. Manual worker councillors, on the other hand, to an overwhelming extent think of themselves as politically organised.

30. According to the views expressed by councillors party politics plays a much smaller part in local government than is widely assumed and their views are supported by those of ex-councillors who no longer have the same kind of commitments. Three-quarters of all councillors said they did not think that party politics affected the *work* of their council very much. The extent to which councillors are themselves involved in party politics of course influences their views on how party politics affects the work of councils. County borough councillors were much more likely than others to say that the work was affected but only 16% of all councillors made critical comments about the effects of party politics on the work of councils.

. . . . . .

32. There are major differences between the views of different kinds of councillors on whether the party system is essential in local government or if the work could be better done without it. Eighty-nine per cent of rural district councillors, for example, most of whom are returned unopposed, thought the work could be done better without the party system. Only 24% of county borough councillors agreed with this view. Excluding the rural districts, just under half of the remaining

councillors thought the work could be better done without the party system. Manual worker councillors were the only group with a majority in favour of the party system. Small employers and farmers had the largest majority against. As a group, councillors who think party politics essential are likely to be the keener members of councils. Many of those councillors who are most opposed to party politics put in much less time than others on council work or with their electors.

. . . . . .

36. It seems clear that much better communication between councillors and electors is essential if public interest in local government is to reach a higher level. This is necessary both for the assurance and support it will give councillors and because it would then become more possible for the whole system to fulfil the purpose for which it exists.

(b)

Characteristics of Members

(*a*) *Age* . . . There is a high proportion of elderly members, and many of the councillors and chief officers were acutely aware of the problems this brought to their work — tolerance of senility, the inflexibility of some old and entrenched chairmen and other members with attitudes moulded many years ago . . . Amongst the officers and members we interviewed, three-quarters were in favour of an age limit. The average of the suggestions for a specific age limit was 72.

. . . . . .

(*c*) *Occupations and their representativeness* . . . If an authority's membership is unrepresentative of important groups in its area, there is a danger that it may be ignorant of the interests of important groups in the community. A situation can arise where the unrepresented elements become largely dependent on officers to explain their point of view to the committees — an unhappy situation fraught with difficulties.

The Social Survey figures show that in general the lower a group's occupational status the smaller its representation on councils. Farmer councillors (who tend to be older than the average member) are very strongly represented on rural district councils and on county councils where working-class representation is nil or minimal.

. . . . . .

Communication and influences between the councillor and the electorate . . . The councillor's public contacts may include:

(i)   his local community — a matter chiefly of informal relations;

(ii)   the organised groups to which he belongs — clubs, churches, trade unions, etc.;

(iii)   a second local authority;

(iv)   the electorate seen as individuals.

In the case of these there may be (i) communication of facts, promoting the flow of knowledge from the public to the council and from the council to the public; (ii) the use of the councillor as a 'sounding board' for public reactions by the council, or for council reactions by the public; (iii) influence exerted through the councillor by the public on the council or (perhaps rarely) by the council on the public.

(i) *The councillor as a link with the community* . . . In all these forms of relationship there is great variability from authority to authority. The information supplied to a council by members about their local communities may be considerable, or it may be little that the officers might not reasonably be expected to have available from their own sources. In total the information supplied by councillors to the public does not seem to be very great, although there is much variation between individual councillors in this matter.

. . . . . .

(iv) *The councillor as a link with individual electors* . . . In some authorities councillors have a close knowledge of individual electors and contribute much personal information to committee discussions. Councillors also pass information from the council to individual members of the public, but this can result in misunderstandings. Cases were found of councillors representing before committees and council the interests of electors by whom they had been lobbied.

. . . . . .

Concepts of the councillor's role . . . Two opposite views of the councillor's role which were mentioned to us were that of the councillor as a director and controller of policy and that of him as a 'watchdog' for the interests of his electors. Few members, even in some quite large authorities, seem to be conscious of making policy. Some officers thought that members should convey the public's views and decide on the advice tendered to them; that they should judge by results and spot checks. Appraisal and development of policy and control of administration without petty interference with executive work requires members of good calibre.

. . . . . .

Many chief officers in different types of authority thought that members were unable to grasp issues of any complexity. The general opinion was that only a minority, sometimes a very small one, made any real contribution in committee, although there were exceptions. Instances were found of abysmal standards of discussion. Cases of clear, purposeful discussion with a good level of understanding and contribution from all participants were rare.

. . . . . .

Recruitment . . .

(*a*) *Scarcity of candidates* . . . The problems of recruitment to local government service are indicated by the lack of competition for local government seats. Figures are given to show the high proportion of uncontested seats for the three-year cycle of elections for 1962—64, particularly in the counties (55%) and in the rural districts (70%). There is a notably higher proportion of contests for seats on county councils organised along party lines than for seats on non-party county councils. In some areas it seems that once a person becomes a councillor he is unlikely to have to fight another election; it is customary to return the sitting member unopposed.

In some areas parties are failing to recruit enough candidates whom the party leaders consider to be of adequate calibre. Some complacency was shown about being able always to find enough candidates. Several councillors thought recruitment difficulties were getting worse; none thought they were getting better. Particular mention was made of the difficulty of persuading relatively young candidates to stand.

. . . . . .

Co-option of members . . .

(a) *The aims of co-option* . . . Co-option is seen to aim at broadening the base of council decisions by adding to committees certain types of members with points of view which would otherwise be unrepresented and by enlisting the voluntary services of experts. It is also seen as a means of pooling information and fostering co-ordinated action with voluntary associations. The main statutory provisions relevant to co-option are reviewed, empowering authorities to appoint up to a third or under a half of members of committees, excepting the finance committee, and requiring in some cases the appointment of persons with special knowledge or experience.

(b) *The extent and nature of co-optative appointments* . . . All counties and county boroughs and nearly all urban authorities serving populations of over 60,000 use co-option to some extent. Below this level it appears that the smaller the authority the less it is likely to make any co-options.

. . . . . .

Political considerations obtrude into a significant proportion of co-optative appointments, both in the choice of individuals and of associations to appoint representatives. In some instances councils carefully protect their right to make appointments to represent outside groups without reference to any outside body; in other instances external nominations are sought partly to avoid political or group pressures within the council coming into play over such appointments. Elsewhere the arrangements embody a compromise between the two extremes. An agreement is often made between the majority party and the opposition on the sharing of the seats. 'Party' co-options are defended as a means of maintaining political balance amongst the co-opted members and as a 'proving-ground' for prospective councillors.

. . . . . .

(c) *The value of co-option* . . . Members rarely placed a high estimation on the value of co-opted members, and we formed no set views on their value as a result of our visits. Clerks of larger authorities were generally appreciative of the contributions by non-councillors, but in smaller authorities much less so. Some chief officers found co-opted members chosen by party bodies particularly disappointing;

elsewhere it had been found that experts from universities had made no impression, partly perhaps because the decision-making process had advanced too far by the time a matter reached them in committee and partly because they were often not supplied with enough information to give an informed opinion on a matter. Criticism was directed at representative members who spoke only to promote the self-interests of their groups and at their lack of responsibility and ignorance of local government procedures.

(*d*) *Suggestions for reform* . . . Suggestions included the replacement of all political co-options by requiring that the persons concerned be chosen by outside bodies; the appointment of a third of all members by central government; and appointments from the regional councils.

The appointment of non-voting advisers was thought by many officers and members a promising means of bringing in outside knowledge, opinions and advice, while obviating the political problems arising from co-options. A panel of experts for *ad hoc* consultation, and more extensive use of advisory committees made up partly of non-councillors, were other ideas put forward.

26 REDCLIFFE-MAUD ON DEMOCRATIC VIABILITY

From *Redcliffe-Maud Vol.I: Report* (Cmnd. 4040, 1969); by permission of H.M.S.O. No less than ten research studies were published by the Royal Commission on Local Government in England, which also considered research material generated by the Maud inquiry. This extract summarises the implications of all the research material.

. . . . . .

We had the great advantage of being able to draw upon the research and the findings of the Management Committee which covered a number of aspects in this field. We were also able to re-analyse some of their survey material and to draw upon the findings of other investigations. Nevertheless, there seemed to be five crucial subjects where existing knowledge was meagre or non-existent and on these we therefore concentrated most of our resources. They are:

(i)   the notion of community in relation to local government;
(ii)   accessibility and responsiveness of local government;
(iii)   decentralised administration;
(iv)   parish government;
(v)   public attitudes to local government and local leadership.

. . . . . .

Implications of these studies

233. Community: The results of the community aspects of the national survey were illuminating. The major finding was that more than three-quarters of those

interviewed were conscious of living in a local community which was defined as the 'home area'. This feeling was strongest among those people who had lived there longest, and it seemed to be most closely linked with the number of their relatives and friends living in the area. Within this aggregate response, there were substantial differences between different types of settlement in the extent to which the home area was identified with the existing local authority pattern. The two extremes were found in rural areas. Whereas no less than 85% of rural dwellers thought of their home areas as the civil parish or something smaller, only 2% of them thought of their home area as the rural district.

234. In urban areas, the smaller the town the more people tended to associate their home area with the town as a whole. In towns over 60,000 population, the majority thought of the home area in terms of a group of streets around their home and only 10% identified themselves with the whole town.

235. There seemed to be a number of implications in these findings. The first, and perhaps the most important, is that any redrawing of local authority boundaries to create larger units would do less damage to the sense of local community among the inhabitants than might be supposed, and would do least damage in rural districts. Only in the smaller towns below 60,000 population, it seems, would people's feeling of identification with their local authority be impaired.

236. The tendency for a sense of community in urban areas to vary, narrowing to a small group of streets in the larger towns, suggested that if there was a case on other grounds for elected bodies to represent the local community in towns, it might be best to allow such bodies to vary in size rather than insist on a permanent, uniform pattern. Finally, the evidence that, of all types of local authority, parishes are seen as natural communities by the overwhelming majority of their inhabitants, was a significant factor in determining a new local government structure.

237. *Accessibility and responsiveness.* On the question of accessibility neither the attitudes that were revealed nor the actual behaviour of those interviewed suggested that this was a highly-prized aspect of local democracy. Some 37% had visited their borough or district council offices in the preceding year and some 10% their county council offices. Only 13% had ever contacted their local councillor although most electors wanted him to live locally. Substantially more electors cited their council offices or an officer than cited their local councillor as their first point of contact about a complaint. It was difficult to find out people's preferences as between better services and more accessible town halls, but it can be inferred from the survey results that something between 35% and 45% of those questioned did rate the accessibility of their town hall or council offices highly. Answers to questions about public attitudes towards local government and non-local government services were mixed, but electors were inclined to mention public services of either kind favourably rather than unfavourably . . .

. . . . . .

In general, electors were better informed about local government services than about the others. The response to questions about a reformed system of local government made clear (what we suspect all Royal Commissions must bear in mind) that most people say they prefer the status quo.

. . . . . .

239. *Parishes*. The first thing these studies indicated was that parish councils are a feature of most rural areas: something like 95% of people living in rural districts live in a parish with a council. They also showed that, measured in terms of a series of indices of 'activity', most parish councils are active. The most active are the largest in terms of population and are usually those nearer to urban settlements. The chief activities, it seems, of parish councils are concerned with the environment and amenity. Only about 16% of parish councils could be definitely classified as inactive; and a clear relationship emerged between such inactivity and a parish's rural character.

240. *Representation and community attitudes*. Three important findings emerged from this analysis. First, elected local councils tend to embrace a more representative cross-section of the general population in terms of age, sex and occupation than do appointed voluntary local bodies. Secondly, of all the social characteristics of electors the level of education is the prime variable in determining their degree of interest in local government and their willingness to take part. This finding appears to hold true irrespective of the extent of population mobility. Finally, no relationship was found to exist between the level of interest in, or knowledge of, local government among electors and the size or type of their local authority.

241. The implications of these findings seem to us: first, that on the fairly safe assumption that more people will reach a higher level of education in the future, we may expect that interest in local government will steadily increase rather than fall off; and secondly, that although population mobility seems bound to increase in the future . . . this is unlikely to impair public interest in local government. These two conclusions apply also to people's interest in standing as candidates in future local government elections. Both, we believe, are hopeful signs.

27 LOCAL GOVERNMENT AND PARTY POLITICS: RESEARCH FINDINGS

From *Maud Vol.5 Local Government Administration in England and Wales* (1967); by permission of H.M.S.O. These extracts are from Chapter 5: 'Some Effects of the Presence or Absence of Party Politics on the operation of local authorities'. The reduced number of authorities in the post-1972 period is likely to reduce the number of authorities in which there is no organised party politics; and the increased number of larger authorities is likely to intensify political competition for control of these authorities.

The scope of party politics

2. The variety of practice in authorities and the different interpretations which can

be placed on definitions makes it extremely difficult even to determine the scope of party politics in local government. The Municipal Yearbook (1965) has an analysis of authorities based on replies given by Clerks to a questionnaire relating to party politics, but it is not clear how this information should be interpreted. According to whether or not authorities where the Clerk says the dominant 'party' is 'independent' and those where no party has an overall majority are regarded as operating on party lines, the percentages of 'party' authorities vary from 20% to 40% of counties, 75% to 92% of county boroughs, 45% to 88% of non-county boroughs, 40% to 77% of urban districts and 8% to 28% of rural districts.

. . . . . .

4. Whichever figures are taken, the high proportion of 'urban' areas which operate on a party basis, in contrast with the comparatively low proportion of counties and particularly of rural districts, is noteworthy. The replies to our postal questionnaire also show that the larger second-tier authorities (with populations over 30,000) are more likely than the smaller ones to be run on party lines. All county boroughs with over 200,000 population are 'party' authorities but it is only in counties with a population of over 600,000 (which are also the most urbanised) that the party system predominates.

5. Information about the party affiliations of councillors, as distinct from authorities, has been given by the Social Survey study, which shows that 39% of councillors do not consider themselves as part of any organised group. (For this purpose 'independents' are treated as a group if they are organised.) This applies to 27% of the councillors in counties, 4% in county boroughs, 2% in metropolitan boroughs, 28% in non-county boroughs and urban districts and 71% in rural districts.

. . . . . .

Types of 'party' authorities

. . . . . .

(a) Authorities where one party has an effective majority 13. The usual pattern in authorities where one party has an effective majority is for all the parties to be organised, to a greater or lesser extent, and to select for party controversy those issues which they regard as of political importance. These will of course vary from time to time. Notable examples are rent subsidies, the allocation of land for private building, the use of 'direct labour' employed by the council and comprehensive schools. On these issues the preliminary ground will have been prepared by both parties outside the committee structure but, by virtue of the fact that it is likely to hold the chairmanships of most, if not all, of the important committees and will usually have ensured that it has a majority of seats even on committees with a 'minority' chairman, the majority party will be able to secure a committee decision or recommendation on particular issues in its own favour and will also be in a position to initiate policy generally. The subtle and complex relationship between chief officers and committee chairmen . . . can have the practical effect of placing a majority party with a monopoly of important chairmanships in an advantageous position in drawing on professional advice, despite the fact that officers are acknowledged as the servants of the council as a whole . . .

14. It would nonetheless be a mistake to assume that the bulk of the business is transacted on party lines. Nearly all the evidence is to the contrary. In committees and sub-committees free discussion and even 'cross-voting' is quite common and on many issues there is little evidence of party discipline. It is possible for an observer to be present during meetings of important committees without being able to distinguish the party affiliations of any of the members present. On the other hand, individual councillors sometimes seize the opportunity to score 'party' capital on points of niggling detail which have little relevance to the main political issues. They may well be the least able members, often acting out of sheer ignorance, and can be an evident source of embarrassment to more responsible party leaders.

15. It is in full council meetings that party acrimony is most in evidence – and this can happen even in authorities where discussion in committees is almost invariably balanced and reasonable. It is sometimes difficult to believe that those who indulge in political antics in the council chamber are the same councillors who have shown considerable tolerance and good sense while plodding through the less spectacular committee agendas during the previous month.

16. No doubt in some authorities party bitterness is generally prevalent, but there is considerable evidence of reasonably good relations between parties (and particularly the leaders) in many others . . .

. . . . . .

17. Those authorities where majorities are short-term have special features. Sometimes the fluctuation of power is quite rapid. Examples have been quoted of changes of party control at regular intervals, even at each triennial election, and of a situation where over a period of twenty years no party has held a majority for more than four years. In these circumstances, it is not surprising if party rivalries are prominent; these are intensified when the majority party succumbs to the temptation to press their temporary advantage to the limit by monopolising both aldermanic seats and chairmanships. This action is particularly unfortunate in a situation where it is more than usually important that the minority party should be closely in touch with affairs, so that it is able to assume responsibility for the conduct of business if the party balance changes . . .

(b) Authorities where one party has a very strong, or overwhelming, majority
18. Where one party has a very strong, or overwhelming, majority (which is also almost inevitably long-term) this can have significant effects on both the majority and minority parties and on the ways in which business is conducted.

19. There is a danger that a high proportion of uncontested seats may lead to stagnation within the majority party and that some of its members – particularly its leaders – may develop autocratic tendencies. This is, however, by no means invariably the case. Security of tenure and length of experience can produce a remarkable political maturity and wisdom – in the words of one officer, 'they get sense and

sensibility'. They have little to lose from adopting a generous attitude towards the minority − for example, by granting them a proportionate share of chairmanships and aldermanic seats, a fair allocation of seats on important committees and representation on ceremonial occasions − and this in itself is likely to produce an amicable working arrangement between parties. In these circumstances the authority may acquire some of the characteristics of one which operates on a non-party basis, with the distinction that the majority party will presumably be subject to pressure and influences from party members outside the council.

. . . . . .

(c) Authorities where no party has an overall majority 23. Both councillors and officers are agreed that special problems arise in those authorities where party politics are significant but where no party has an overall majority. The most obvious difficulty is that there can be no clear direction of policy, since any fundamental political decision must depend on a temporary coalition between two of the parties and groupings could vary according to the particular points at issue. One party leader in this situation explained that if he and one of the other leaders agreed on any point it was settled, if not the final result was anyone's guess. The chief officers, particularly the Clerk, are in an extremely delicate position − in the words of one 'out on a limb' − and may well be forced into virtually controlling policy themselves.

24. Inevitably the committee and sub-committee chairmanships are shared between the parties and this again is a potential source of difficulty, particularly if important committees with closely linked functions have chairmen of different political persuasions . . .

25. There is likely to be an attempt to allocate seats on committees on a proportionate basis but, even so, in practice some committees may well not be an exact reflection of the party political strengths on the council as a whole; in one authority this is said to result in an unusual number of committee recommendations being rejected, or at least amended, at the council meeting . . .

. . . . . .

Party groups

27. The existence of the party group, or caucus, is generally acknowledged as fundamental to the influence of party politics in local government. We have deliberately made no attempt to attend group meetings; our information is based on our personal observations of the effects of group decisions on the conduct of business and on written or verbal comments by party leaders, other councillors (both party members and others) and officers. Inevitably, therefore, we have only limited information on such matters as the balance of forces within a group or the external influences upon it. However, those whom we have consulted have shown no reticence in referring to the existence, or discussing the function, of the group. In fact our experience confirms the view expressed by one committee chairman that

although, when he came into local government, there was 'a certain mystique about the group', this has now in most places disappeared. It is not unusual, for example, for councillors to ask in committee for a decision to be deferred, stating quite openly that this is a matter which must be settled by their party group, although in some authorities councillors in a similar situation still play for time by asking for a report giving 'further information' to be made at the next committee meeting. References to decisions made by party groups, as distinct from council committees, also appear in the press.

(a) Organisation and procedures 28. The organisation and procedures of Labour Party groups are the most specific and generally applicable, since they follow the model standing orders recommended by the national party organisation. Group meetings are held regularly (invariably before the council meeting) and attendance is regarded as a duty to the party. The dates of these meetings may even be included in an authority's official handbook and often meetings are held in the council offices. Their object is said to be to ensure that all members of the party have a voice in considering policy and action and that individual differences of opinion are thrashed out in private. All Labour Party aldermen and councillors attend, together with a small number of non-councillors, who can speak but not vote (these are variously referred to as representatives of the local Labour Party, of the local party executive committee or of the Trades and Labour Council). Where group decisions are made, members are expected to abide by these when speaking or voting in the council meeting, although some matters are left to a free vote. Individual councillors are not expected to submit resolutions or amendments at council meetings without the group's prior approval, although they may ask questions at their discretion, provided that their tendency is not likely to be in conflict with group policy. Groups normally elect a 'policy' committee and a number of officers.

29. In practice the standing orders are not strictly followed in every detail by all Labour councillors . . .

30. In general, however, on important political matters the 'whip' is imposed and Labour members vote solidly. This is one of the grounds on which Labour groups are most fiercely criticised by their political opponents, who feel that they are inflexible and impose quite unreasonable restrictions on their members . . . The Labour members themselves do not deny that the whip is imposed; they strongly defend the system. They stress that the process of discussion is entirely democratic and that decisions, having been taken on a majority vote, are accepted willingly.
. . . . . .

32. Conservative groups display more variety — inevitably so because their members do not necessarily even use the party name, being known also as Progressives, Moderates, Independents, Rate-payers, etc. The avoidance of the label 'Conservative' seems to be, for some, an article of faith. One, whose election address always includes a reference to support for the Conservative Party in national politics, explained that the use of the title 'progressive' on the local council was now a privilege reserved for the older members; it was obviously much prized. This is part

of a general tendency noticed among many councillors with Conservative leanings to play down the political aspects of their local authority work. Many claim that their groups came into existence reluctantly and merely to counteract the attempts at political organisation by Labour members. In some places group membership is limited to declared Conservatives; elsewhere it acts as an umbrella for those with Conservative leanings but with various labels. Sometimes, in addition to present councillors, prospective candidates attend, with no voting rights.

33. Conservative groups appear to follow the advice of the Conservative Central Office in holding a meeting before the council meeting, with the object of ensuring that members have full information about the business going forward, particularly that arising from committees on which they do not themselves sit. The official advice is that, although it is often possible to determine an agreed line of action, this does not mean that a member who does not agree with the majority should be pilloried for opposing. This emphasis on the absence of the whip and the right of the individual member to follow his conscience is reflected in the statements of Conservative group members . . .

. . . . . .

34. Many Labour members are extremely sceptical about the extent to which the Conservative group allows freedom of conscience, feeling that, since the group vote is normally unanimous, moral pressures must, for all practical purposes, have the same effect as the whip. They also imply that it is hypocritical for declared members of a national political party to suggest that they are not motivated by party considerations in local affairs . . .

. . . . . .

(b) Functions 37. Our information suggests that the precise function of party groups, as this affects the conduct of business, varies considerably more in practice than in theory. It has been noted that, almost invariably, party groups of all political persuasions meet before each council meeting, to receive information about the business and, in most instances, to decide on a party line (even though this may not be obligatory). The business consists, in the main, of considering reports from committees; the committee chairman or, if the chairman belongs to another party, one of the committee members has an opportunity of explaining to those councillors who are not members of that committee what lies behind its recommendations. However, the degree of detailed work in the group meeting apparently varies considerably . . .

. . . . . .

40. Since it is by no means the general rule for committee business to be discussed by the group in advance, decisions reached by committees with a majority party chairman are occasionally reversed by the majority group and, where a whip is imposed, a delicate situation is created. Sometimes, in these circumstances, a chairman will formally withdraw the committee report at the council meeting, giving no explanation. Sometimes, however, councillors are required to oppose in open council a motion, proposed by a chairman of the same party, which they have

previously supported in committee. The chairman himself abstains from voting or in some authorities votes against his own committee report. Naturally, their political opponents are likely to point to the absurdity of this procedure. It is contended, however, that this type of situation arises in practice only rarely, since committee chairmen should be sufficiently politically sensitive to seek guidance in advance on any item of committee business which is likely to impinge on group policy.

41. It seems that much of the time and energy of party groups is absorbed in vetting recommendations originating in committees. This enables the majority party to co-ordinate policy, but is in a sense a negative activity and quite different from the initiation of policy. There is certainly evidence of policy initiation by groups in some places. In one county borough, for example, majority party group meetings are held twice a month, one meeting to consider the council agenda and the other to deal with general policy. Some cases have been quoted of items being considered by committees at the request of the majority group and, as has been noted, some items are referred by chairmen for consideration by the group before being referred to a committee. Often the capital priorities programme is settled first by the majority party group, sometimes at a special meeting. The group may also fix the rate before the final approval of the revenue estimates. No doubt, too, in some authorities policy is initiated by the group's policy committee or by the party leader.

42. A considerable amount of scepticism has, however, been voiced as to the extent to which majority party groups as a whole are initiators of policy . . .

(c) The problem of action without professional advice 43. Since officers are regarded as the servants of the council as a whole and not of a particular party, there is a tradition that they do not attend party group meetings. No officer who has been consulted has stated that he does and most have specifically mentioned that they do not . . . It is not surprising, therefore, that some officers and occasionally councillors are extremely concerned in case important decisions should be made without adequate information or professional advice.

. . . . . .

49. There is no doubt that many officers, while accepting the convention of not attending group meetings, find . . . constitutional methods of ensuring that adequate information is available to party groups before they reach decisions. The devices adopted are various — for example, preliminary discussions of major policy with committee chairmen; giving chairmen an advance copy of committee reports; or making reports to committees at an early stage, with an indication that, although an immediate decision is not required, the matters raised will need to be resolved later. However, some of the less forceful officers may be unable to use such methods, which are at best ingenious devices to mitigate the worst effects of a basically unsatisfactory situation.

. . . . . .

Party leaders

52. It is usual for both majority and minority parties to have a group leader, some-

times referred to, if he represents the majority party, as 'the leader of the council'. We have not attempted to investigate systematically the basis on which leaders are selected, but suspect that this varies considerably. A leader will almost certainly have had long service in the party. Some are clearly the most able and influential of the party members, but this is not invariably the case . . .

53. The ways in which leaders interpret their position and exercise power also varies considerably . . . Eighteen authorities operating on a party basis had a member holding four or more chairmanships and in eight of these that member was the leader of the majority party . . . In the ten authorities where four or more chairmanships were held by another member, however, it is clear that the party leader is not the only member with considerable influence and it is certainly quite usual for the leader not to hold the key chairmanships.

54. The majority party leader is often influential in the selection of other committee chairmen . . .

. . . . . .

57. In addition to the party leaders, it seems that there are usually other members who exercise an exceptional influence. Officers and councillors when referring to these use such terms as 'inner caucus', 'party bosses', the 'big three' or the 'holy seven'. They will probably include party officers (the deputy leader, the party secretary, possibly the whip) . . . Some of the inner group may well be more able and in a sense more influential than the party leader himself. They will usually hold between them most of the important chairmanships or even constitute the entire membership of a key committee. Sometimes a small group of members, rather than the group leader alone, will discuss with a Clerk the implications of decisions reached in the group. The existence of an inner caucus is not necessarily overtly acknowledged and its membership can often not be precisely defined, there being some differences of opinion between commentators as to whether a particular alderman or councillor is included. Nevertheless it appears that in many authorities a small caucus may well be exercising a policy-making function for which the group as a whole is unsuited, although one Clerk pointed out that even his most influential members would drop an idea if it was provoking violent opposition from the group as a whole.

58. In general, the party system as it operates at present in England and Wales appears to be more likely to produce a group of influential members than a single autocrat; such references to autocrats as we have received have usually related to giants of the past.

. . . . . .

Attitudes towards party politics

78. In most of the non-party authorities we have visited many members and officers have expressed considerable relief that they are free from party politics, which they regard as an unmitigated evil . . . Even in those authorities which operate completely on party lines, the system has its critics. The almost apologetic

attitude of many Conservatives when discussing the existence of their party caucus and the reluctance of some of them even to use the party label seems to be symptomatic of a guilty feeling that party politics are inappropriate to local affairs. In the main, it is the members who belong to the Labour party who support the system wholeheartedly, on the grounds that it enables the electorate to know what they are voting for and ensures a consistent direction of policy.

80. The information which we have collected about attitudes towards party politics from written expressions of opinion and from our own visits is obviously not a fully representative sample. That collected by the Social Survey covers a much wider field, but as individual authorities are not distinguishable, it is not possible to relate a councillor's opinion to the atmosphere in which he is working. The findings were that 75% of councillors did not think that the main work of their council was affected by the fact that many councillors were attached to political groups. The differing percentages for different types of authority (for example 48% for county boroughs and 89% in rural districts) are no doubt related to the difference in the incidence of party politics as well as to the attitudes of councillors. Of those who said that the work was affected, 56% thought the most important effect was doctrinaire policies regardless of individual circumstances. It is interesting that 81% of ex-councillors thought this was the most important effect. In reply to a question whether the party system is essential to the work of local councils, 63% of all councillors said the work could be better done without; there was, however, a considerable variation in the replies from different types of authorities, the highest percentage (89%) being in rural districts and the lowest (20%) in the metropolitan boroughs. Of those who thought party politics were essential, 62% regarded their main advantage as getting things done more quickly.

28 LOCAL GOVERNMENT AND PARTY POLITICS: LABOUR PARTY ORGANISATION

From *The Labour Party: Model Standing Orders for Labour Groups on Local Authorities*; by permission of the Labour Party, Transport House.

1. GROUP MEETINGS

(*a*) Ordinary meetings of the Labour Group on the Council shall be held at an agreed time between the publication of the Council Agenda and the meeting of the Council. The Annual Meeting of the Group for the election of officers, etc., shall be held, on a date to be determined, prior to the statutory Annual Meeting of the Council.

(*b*) For the purpose of maintaining contact between the Group and the Central Labour Party, Constituency Labour Party or Local Labour Party, as the case may be, three representatives of the latter may attend Group Meetings in a consultative capacity and without voting power, provided that the number of such representatives shall not exceed one-third of the membership of the Group.

2. GROUP OFFICERS

The following Officers of the Group shall be appointed at the Annual Meeting:
  (*a*) Chairman and Leader (combined office).
  (*b*) Vice-Chairman and Deputy Leader (combined office).
  (*c*) Chief Whip.
  (*d*) Two Junior Whips.
  (*e*) Group Secretary.
The functions of a Group Secretary shall include the convening of Group meetings and the preparation of the Agenda.
  Note. As to whether this number of officers should be appointed will depend on the size of the Group. In some cases the functions may be combined.

3. POLICY COMMITTEE

The Officers, together with three other members of the Group to be appointed at the Annual Meeting, shall constitute the Policy Committee of the Group.
  Note. The appointment and size of the Policy Committee will depend on the size of the Group. Where the Group is small, it can itself perform the functions of a Policy Committee.

4. CASUAL VACANCIES

Casual vacancies among the officers or in the Policy Committee shall be filled at an ordinary or other meeting of the Group, of which appropriate notice shall be given.

5. DETERMINATION OF GROUP POLICY AND ACTION

(*a*) The Local Government Election Policy of the Party shall be determined by the Central Labour Party, Constituency Labour Party or Local Labour Party, as the case may be, in accordance with the terms of its Constitution as approved by the National Executive Committee of the Labour Party.
  (*b*) It shall be the responsibility of the Labour Group on the Council to take decisions on matters coming before the Council. If the Central Labour Party, Constituency Labour Party or Local Labour Party, as the case may be, desires to express a point of view upon any such matter, it may do so either by communicating with the Group Secretary or through the Party representatives at Group meetings.
  (*c*) The selection of nominations for mayoral, aldermanic and other Council offices shall be made by the Labour Group. The Central Labour Party, Constituency Labour Party or Local Labour Party, as the case may be, may submit names to the

Labour Group for consideration, but the final selection shall rest with the Labour Group.

(*d*) The policy of the Labour Group shall be determined by the Group Meeting, on the recommendation of the Policy Committee or otherwise; provided that in cases of emergency, where action requires to be taken by motion or otherwise, such action may be taken by the Policy Committee, which shall report its action for approval to the next Group Meeting; and provided that in cases of still greater urgency which do not admit of delay, the Leader of the Group, or in the absence of the Leader his deputy (in either case consulting, if possible, other officers or members of the Policy Committee), shall have power to act, and such action shall be reported to the next meeting of the Policy Committee and/or the Group for approval.

6. CHAIRMANSHIPS AND VICE-CHAIRMANSHIPS WHILE IN OPPOSITION

Members of the Labour Group, while in opposition, shall not accept chairmanships or vice-chairmanships of Council Committees or Sub-Committees, except with the consent of the Group.

7. ACTION BY INDIVIDUAL MEMBERS

(*a*) Individual members of the Labour Group shall not submit or move resolutions or motions or amendments at meetings of the Council, unless such resolutions or motions or amendments have first been submitted to, and received the approval of, the Policy Committee and/or the Group Meeting, or, in case of urgency, have received the approval of the Leader of the Group or his deputy.

(*b*) Individual members of the Labour Group may without consultation ask questions at meetings of the Council, provided the tendency of such questions is not likely to be in conflict with the policy of the Labour Group, in which case an officer of the Group shall be consulted.

(*c*) Members of the Labour Group are expected not to speak or vote at meetings of the Council in opposition to the decisions of the Labour Group, unless the Group has decided to leave the matter in question to a free vote. Where matters of conscience arise (*e.g.* religion, temperance, etc.), individual members of the Labour Group may abstain from voting, provided they first raise the matter at the Group Meeting in order to ascertain the feeling of the Group. In matters where the Council or its Committees or Sub-Committees are acting in a quasi-judicial capacity (*e.g.* licensing of theatres and cinemas, etc.), each member shall form his or her own judgement according to the evidence.

8. GROUPS ON COMMITTEES

The general principles embodied in these Standing Orders shall be applicable to

Labour Groups on, and members of, Committees and Sub-Committees of the Council, including co-opted members.

9. BREACH OF STANDING ORDERS

It is hereby declared that acceptance of these Standing Orders (as amended from time to time with the approval of the National Executive Committee of the Labour Party) is a condition of membership of the Labour Group on the Council. It shall be competent for the Group whip to be withdrawn from any member who violates these Standing Orders . . .

29 THE PURSUIT OF SELF-INTEREST: THE MAUD REPORT

From *Maud, Vol.I: Report* (1967); by permission of H.M.S.O. This extract comments on the legal and practical position relating to the self-interest of elected members.

. . . The Social Survey finds that when asked whether people become council-members because they want to make money for themselves, three-quarters of the sample of the electorate do not believe this to be the case; in reply to a further question, two-thirds say that they do not believe that they become members because they want higher positions at work. Generally the electors are more likely to credit members with 'community centred' than with 'personal centred' motives.

539. The research report comments that the general picture is of a high standard of honesty in council matters even when members are subject to strong local pressures. But the research report says that some disquiet arises from builders and developers being members of planning committees. The research report also refers to the special situation which exists where a large proportion of a council are tenants of their own authority and consider and vote upon rents and other conditions of tenure under a dispensation from the appropriate Minister, and concludes — 'sufficient was seen of such difficulties to emphasise that they should not be minimised'.

. . . . . .

542. The Ministers' powers under section 1(5) of the 1964 Act have, we understand, been liberally exercised. Under the Act they have power to remove a disability either indefinitely or for any period, and for any member or class of member. We understand that until the summer of 1964 dispensations were given for periods of three months, but that the present practice is for dispensations to be given for periods of up to a year. Dispensations to enable a member to speak are given quite readily, but dispensations for voting are given only where half, or more than half, of the council or any of its committees would otherwise be disabled, or where the number of members disabled and their distribution among the parties or groups on the council or committee are such that a decision might otherwise be

taken to which the majority of the council or the committee is opposed. In January 1967 the Ministers gave a general permission to members who are tenants of council housing accommodation to speak and vote on matters of general housing policy. Dispensation is not given, either for speaking or voting, if the matter to be dealt with is one solely affecting a particular member: for example, a member who owns property in a re-development area may obtain dispensation to speak and vote on the re-development proposals generally, but not on something affecting his own particular property alone. Dispensations do not absolve members from declaring their interest.

. . . . . .

544. There is little written evidence on this subject. Two distinct points of view are adopted; on the one hand there is the view that there should be no relaxation of the law and even that members with a pecuniary interest should be barred from the council. On the other hand, it is thought that the law relating to pecuniary interest deters some people from service, and that it should be amended to place members in the same position as members of Parliament. The evidence does not suggest to us that this issue is one which is a serious cause of embarrassment to members. We doubt whether it is a material factor in dissuading people from standing for election. Many witnesses do not seem aware of the practice in regard to dispensation to speak and vote.

. . . . . .

547. The law relating to pecuniary interest was drafted in the context of members' involvement or interest in contracts. Nowadays the difficulty lies primarily, we believe, in planning and development matters. We are concerned that there is a view that members do, or can, take advantage of their position as members and of the inside knowledge they may possess. It is abundantly clear to us that a member is in a position to take advantage of information which comes into his possession in his capacity as a member but that it is not easy to prove that the member has an interest which he has failed to declare. The probity of members and the pressure and interest of public opinion alone can defend the reputation of local government; but if there are pockets of disquiet, some people who might otherwise wish to serve local government may be deterred from so doing because of the reputation of the authority.

. . . . . .

549. *We recommend . . . that legal sanctions be retained which require a member to declare an interest and which prevent him from speaking or voting on a matter in which he has an interest unless dispensation is granted by the appropriate Minister.*

550. We find the present law cumbersome and difficult to understand and *we recommend that the law relating to pecuniary interest should be consolidated and simplified.*

30 THE PURSUIT OF SELF-INTEREST: THE LEGAL POSITION

From *Conduct in Local Government* (Department of Environment Circular 105/73,

Appendix II, 1973); by permission of H.M.S.O. This extract defines the existing legal position on pecuniary interests of elected members.

Summary of legal and administrative position

1. The law on pecuniary interests is set out in sections 94 to 98 and 105 of the Local Government Act 1972. This circular deals with the leading provisions only and is not a full exposition of the subject.

2. The essential requirement is that where a member of a council (or committee or sub-committee) is present at a meeting at which a matter in which he has a pecuniary interest is being considered:

 (*a*) he must disclose that he has a pecuniary interest; and

 (*b*) he must not speak or vote on the matter unless he has a dispensation from the Secretary of State (or from the district council in the case of a parish councillor in England and a community councillor in Wales).

3. Observance of the law is the member's responsibility. The Department cannot advise whether a member has a pecuniary interest in a matter. This is for the member himself to decide in the light of his own circumstances. Any member in doubt about the meaning of the law is recommended to consult the Chief Executive of the council or its legal adviser.

Disclosure of the existence of pecuniary interests

4. Under the Act disclosures must be made orally, as soon as practicable after the start of the meeting; except that in the cases specified in section 96 of the Act a member may make a general written disclosure of his pecuniary interest to the proper officer of the council. Where such a general disclosure has been made, further oral disclosures of the existence of the interest are not required.

5. The Secretary of State's dispensation to speak or vote does not remove the requirement to make either an oral or a general disclosure.

Applications to the Department for dispensation to vote and/or speak

6. An application may be made either by the member concerned or by the proper officer of the council acting on the member's behalf. It should specify the pecuniary interest and the matter coming before the council, in respect of which dispensation is sought. Where an application is received the Department acts on the basis that each member to whom it relates is satisfied that he has a pecuniary interest and that the application, if not made by him personally, is made with his approval.

7. Where more than one member of a council seeks dispensation to speak or vote on the same matter it makes for convenience and speed of handling if a joint application can be submitted.

8. Under the Act a dispensation may be given only where so many councillors

are disabled as to impede the transaction of business or where it appears to be in the interests of the inhabitants of the area to do so.

9. The Secretary of State's agreed policy is to give dispensation to speak unless the member's interest in the matter before the council appears so immediate that it would be wrong for him to take any part.

Dispensation to vote is given only where:

(*a*) at least half of the council or committee concerned are disabled; or
(*b*) disabilities would otherwise upset the elected party balance in the council or committee.

31 THE PURSUIT OF SELF-INTEREST: THE CONDUCT OF EMPLOYEES

From *Committee on Local Government Rules of Conduct, Report. Appendix G* (Cmnd. 5636, 1974); by permission of H.M.S.O. This extract from the Scheme of Conditions of the National Joint Council for Local Authorities Administrative, Professional, Technical and Clerical Services defines the standards of conduct expected of local government officials.

SECTION ONE: APPOINTMENT AND PROMOTION

. . . . . .

Relatives of Members of the Authority or Officers

Every candidate for any appointment under an employing authority shall, when making application, disclose in writing to the Clerk of the authority whether to his knowledge he is related to any member of the authority or to a holder of any senior office under the authority. Deliberate omission to make such a disclosure will disqualify the candidate and if the omission is discovered after appointment he shall be liable to dismissal. Every member and senior officer of the authority shall similarly disclose to the authority any relationship known to him to exist between himself and a candidate for an appointment of which he is aware. It shall be the duty of the Clerk to the authority to report to the authority or appropriate committee any such disclosure made to him.

The purport of this regulation shall be stated in any form of application issued
. . .

Canvassing of Members of the Authority

Canvassing of members of an employing authority, directly or indirectly, in connection with any appointment under the authority, shall disqualify the candidate. The purport of this regulation shall be stated in any advertisement and form of application issued. A member of the authority shall not solicit for any person any appointment under the authority, or recommend any person for such appointment or for promotion; but this paragraph shall not preclude a member from giving a written testimonial of the candidate's ability, experience, or character, for submission to the authority with an application for appointment.

. . . . . .

SECTION SEVEN: OFFICIAL CONDUCT

General

The public is entitled to demand of a local government officer conduct of the highest standard and public confidence in his integrity would be shaken were the least suspicion, however ill-founded, to arise that he could in any way be influenced by improper motives.

. . . . . .

An officer's off-duty hours are his personal concern but he should not subordinate his duty to his private interests or put himself in a position where his duty and his private interests conflict. The employing authority should not attempt to preclude officers from undertaking additional employment, but any such employment must not, in the view of the authority, conflict with or react detrimentally to the authority's interests, or in any way weaken public confidence in the conduct of the authority's business.

The officer should not be called upon to advise any political group of the employing authority either as to the work of the group or as to the work of the authority, neither shall he be required to attend any meeting of any political group.

Whole-time Service

Officers above AP. Grade 5 shall devote their whole-time service to the work of their Council and shall not engage in any other business or take up any other additional appointment without the express consent of the Council.

Proceedings of Committees

No officer shall communicate to the public the proceedings of any committee meeting, etc., nor the contents of any document relating to the authority unless required by law or expressly authorised to do so.

Interest of Officers in Contracts

If it comes to the knowledge of an officer that a contract in which he has any pecuniary interest, whether direct or indirect (not being a contract to which he is himself a party), has been, or is proposed to be, entered into by the authority, he shall, as soon as practicable, give notice in writing to the Clerk of the authority of the fact that he is interested therein . . .

32 THE PURSUIT OF SELF-INTEREST: THE 1974 REPORT

From *Committee on Local Government Rules of Conduct, Report* (Cmnd. 5636, 1974); by permission of H.M.S.O.

SUMMARY

Personal Honesty and Public Confidence

1. There is widespread current disquiet about conduct in local government, following recent prosecutions for corruption. Any general judgement on the honesty of local authorities is necessarily to a great extent subjective. The tenor of our evidence, which our own judgement endorses, is that British local government is essentially honest. But corruption spreads unless it is stopped; and the only acceptable standard is complete honesty.

2. The two essential safeguards for honesty in local government are (i) the honesty of the individual councillor and employee; and (ii) maximum openness on the part of all those concerned.

3. Rules of conduct cannot create honesty, but are indispensable. There are three present sources of rules of conduct; the law; standing orders; and conditions of service for employees. Changes are needed in all three. We propose, in addition, a new national code of local government conduct for all councillors.

4. Party political organisation of councils is increasingly widespread. The political parties must ensure that rules of conduct in party group meetings, which are not subject to local government law or standing orders, are no less strict than in those of the authority.

Conflicts of Interest

5. **Pecuniary Interests.** The law on disclosure of pecuniary interests should be strengthened. It should require councillors (i) to disclose an interest orally whenever it arises, without the present partial option of a general written notice; (ii) to withdraw from the meeting subsequently (except where they have a dispensation from the Secretary of State); and (iii) to enter certain interests in a register to be open to inspection by electors. Penalties for breach of these provisions should be increased. The corresponding provisions for officers should also be strengthened.

6. **Interest-related Committees.** Councillors should never serve as chairmen, nor in some circumstances even as members, of committees in whose subject they have

a substantial business, professional or other personal interest in the area of the authority.

7. **Contracts, Planning, Comprehensive Development.** Councillors have a particularly heavy responsibility for the proper conduct of business in three major areas where conflicts of interest can arise. These are the award of contracts, land use planning, and the comprehensive development or redevelopment of land.

8. **Non-pecuniary Interests** (such as kinship) cannot be covered by the law, but individuals should treat them on the same principles that the law requires them to treat pecuniary interests.

9. **Hospitality and Facilities.** Councillors and employees should ensure that hospitality given or received in connection with their official duties can always be justified in the public interest; and that official facilities to which they are entitled are used strictly for the purposes of their official duties and for no other.

10. **Attendance Allowances.** Authorities should ensure that their practice in the payment of allowances is clearly defined and made public.

11. **Outside Employment.** Local government employees should not undertake outside work for payment by members of the public on any matter within the scope of their official duties. Senior or professional employees wishing to take up other employment within two years of resigning or retiring from the local authority's service should be required to seek the authority's consent.

12. **Misuse of Information.** The use for private gain of information received through membership or employment in a local authority should be a criminal offence.

The Local Government Employee as Councillor

13. **Disqualification for Membership.** The present law disqualifies employees of a local authority for membership of it, but permits them to serve as members of another authority; and it disqualifies members of an authority for employment by it. There should be no change in the law. The arguments in favour of removing or relaxing the present disqualifications are outweighed by the need (i) to avoid conflicts of interest, (ii) to maintain political impartiality, and (iii) to secure sound internal relationships in the authority's organisation. There is no category of employees to which none of these considerations applies. No clear distinction can be made between employees who should remain disqualified and those who should not.

14. **Co-option of Teachers.** In view of the long history of the provision by which teachers are co-opted to education committees we do not recommend its abolition; but three of us dissent from this conclusion.

Responsibility for Maintaining Standards

15. The local authority must keep its own house in order and enable others to see whether it is doing so. It should (i) have a clear, and publicly known, machinery for

reviewing its own procedures and for investigating complaints; and (ii) pursue vigorous policies of two-way communication with the public. In this the press, radio and television also have important responsibilities.

16. **Central government** has a general responsibility for the well-being of local government and for the operation of procedures for its external review. Departments should now urgently consider the need to give fresh advice on procedures for the award of contracts and the management of comprehensive development. No new machinery for external review is required in addition to those already existing. There should be a new power for the inspection of financial records; and some detailed changes in the Prevention of Corruption Acts.

17. **The public** also has a responsibility for helping to maintain standards. Anyone who has evidence of misconduct by people in local government has a duty to take action; and we describe what he should do.

A National Code of Local Government Conduct

18. We propose the establishment of a new code of conduct for all councillors in the form of a short, simple and authoritative statement of principles and their application.

RECOMMENDATIONS

19. Our recommendations are summarised below.

I. THE LAW

Disclosure of Pecuniary Interests: Councillors

20. **Oral Disclosure**

(i) Councillors should be required to disclose a pecuniary interest orally whenever it arises. The present partial option of a general written notice should be abolished.

(ii) Councillors whose disability for speaking or voting has been removed by a dispensation of the Secretary of State should be expressly required to disclose orally both the interest concerned and the existence of the dispensation.

(iii) A councillor who has disclosed a pecuniary interest should be required to withdraw completely from the meeting, except where the Secretary of State has removed his disability.

(iv) Disclosures, withdrawals and dispensations should be required to be recorded (*a*) in the minutes of the meeting and (*b*) in a book to be kept for the purpose and to be open to inspection by any elector for the area of the authority.

21. A register of interests

(i)   There should be a compulsory register of certain pecuniary interests of councillors, to be additional to oral disclosure, to be revised annually, and to be open to inspection by any elector for the authority.

(ii)   The interests to be entered should be

      (*a*) all paid employments (omitting the amount of the income except in the case of sponsorship),

      (*b*) all land owned in the area of the authority,

      (*c*) companies in which the member has interest greater than a specified minimum, and

      (*d*) any tenancy of premises owned by the authority.

22. Penalties and Prosecution

(i)   Penalties for the offence of failure to disclose a pecuniary interest at a meeting should be strengthened.

(ii)   Failure to make an entry in the register should be an offence subject to the same penalties and time limits as failure to disclose an interest at a meeting.

(iii)   The time limit on prosecution for these offences should be extended.

Disclosure of Pecuniary Interests: Officers

23. (i)   Officers should be required to disclose an interest in a 'contract, proposed contract or other matter', not only in a 'contract' as under the present law.

(ii)   Officers should also be required to disclose a pecuniary interest orally at meetings.

(iii)   Offences by officers under (i) and (ii) above should be subject to the same penalties and limits on prosecution as those by councillors.

(iv)   The authority should be required to keep a record, open to inspection by councillors, of the pecuniary interests of chief and deputy chief officers and such other officers as the authority may require.

Misuse of Official Information

24. The use for private gain of information received through membership or employment in a local authority should be a criminal offence.

Disqualification of Employees for Membership

25. (i)   There should be no change in the present law disqualifying employees of a local authority for membership of it and members of a local authority for employment by it.

(ii)   There should be no change in the present law on co-option of teachers to education committees; but co-option should not be extended to other groups of employees.

Prevention of Corruption

26. (i)   There should be a power, available only on application by the Director of Public Prosecutions to a judge of the High Court (and on a corresponding procedure in Scotland) on proof of reasonable grounds for suspecting a corrupt act, for the police to inspect the financial records of persons or organisations before proceedings are started.

    (ii) Section 2 of the Prevention of Corruption Act 1916 should be amended so as to apply (a) to exercises of discretionary powers by local authorities as well as to the award of contracts; and (b) to councillors as well as to employees.

    (iii) Section 2 of the Public Bodies Corrupt Practices Act 1889 should be amended so as to give the court discretion to disqualify a person convicted of corruption for membership of a local authority for life on a first offence.

II. ACTION BY CENTRAL GOVERNMENT

27. (i)   Consultations should be urgently undertaken with the local authority associations about establishing an agreed national code of conduct for all councillors.

    (ii) The Departments concerned should urgently consider the need to give fresh advice on procedures for the award of contracts and the management of comprehensive development.

    (iii) When some experience has been gained of the operation of the Local Commissioners for Administration, consideration should be given to amending their power so as to enable them to transmit evidence of criminal conduct to the police.

III. ACTION BY LOCAL GOVERNMENT

Local Authority Associations

28. (i)   A national code of conduct for all councillors should be agreed in consultation with central government.

    (ii) The associations should together prepare a handbook on the law on disclosure of pecuniary interests.

Local Authorities

29. (i)   Local authorities should have clear arrangements for the systematic review of their internal procedures from the point of view of probity.

    (ii) Local authorities should have clear and well publicised arrangements for receiving and investigating complaints.

(iii)   Local authorities should pursue vigorous policies of public communication, on both general and specific subjects.

(iv)   In particular, local authorities should publicise the policies and procedures by which they carry out their statutory functions.

(v)   Local authorities should adopt standing orders prohibiting canvassing for appointments and requiring disclosure of kinship.

(vi)   Local authorities should not permit their employees to undertake outside work, for payment by a member of the public, on any matter connected with their official duties. A record of permissions given for approved kinds of outside work should be kept and should be open to inspection by councillors.

(vii)   Local authorities should require senior or professional employees, as a condition of service, not to take up within two years of retirement or resignation private employment in the authority's area without the authority's consent.

IV. ACTION BY THE POLITICAL PARTIES

30. The political parties at both national and local level should ensure that rules of conduct in local authority party group meetings are no less strict than in those of the authority itself.

V. ACTION BY INDIVIDUALS

Councillors and Employees

31. (i)   Councillors and employees should not let personal or private interests affect their judgement of the public interest.

(ii)   Councillors and employees should treat their non-pecuniary interests on the same basis that the law requires them to treat their pecuniary ones.

(iii)   Councillors and employees should ensure that hospitality given or received in connection with their official duties can always be justified in the public interest; and that official facilities or allowances to which they are entitled are used strictly for the purposes of their official duties and for no other.

Members of the Public

32. Members of the public should take action if they have evidence of misconduct on the part of any member or employee of a local authority.

. . . . . .

A NATIONAL CODE OF CONDUCT

The Need for a Code

. . . with the establishment of a new structure of local government some simpler and more general statement of principles is also urgently required. These principles already govern, we believe, the best practice among councillors. The purpose of stating them in writing would be twofold: to provide authoritative guidance for all councillors; and to provide an explicit public standard which those outside local government can expect from it. Such a statement should take the form of a code of conduct.

Contents

170. Our conception of a code of conduct for councillors is that it should be a short, simple and lucid statement of principles and of their practical application. It should be of such length and format as to enable the user to carry it about with him easily. It should serve as a supplement or extension to the law and standing orders and a reminder of their importance, but should not duplicate or replace them. It should constitute a frame of reference valuable to everyone serving in local government and especially to those doing so for the first time. It should be issued to all councillors on taking office and drawn to their attention periodically thereafter; it should also be generally available to the public and on sale in bookshops.

171. In addition to drawing attention to the law and standing orders, the code should deal with such matters as the distinction between public and private interest, membership of interest-related committees, the relationships between members and employees, the use of official facilities, and the handling of confidential information.

172. We have considered whether the code should be addressed to employees as well as to councillors. The principles governing their actions are fundamentally the same, and the spirit of the code's guidance applies to both alike. But we have previously mentioned the constitutional difference that councillors are responsible to the electorate and employees to the authority; and employees are besides subject to negotiated conditions of service which include guidance on conduct. We hope that, if an agreed code of conduct for councillors is adopted, the national negotiating bodies will consider whether any consequential changes are desirable in the standard conditions of service for employees.

173. This concept of the code differs from some others, notably that of the Association of Municipal Corporations, who saw the code primarily as a guide to the practical interpretation of the law on disclosure of pecuniary interests. We agree that a guide to these provisions would be useful, but the detailed treatment required would be more suitable to a separate handbook . . . than to the code of conduct.

Status

174. If a code of conduct on these lines is to achieve the two objects of helping to set a clear standard in areas of uncertainty, and of increasing public confidence in the integrity of local government, it needs to be uniform and to be applied in all types of local authority, including parish and community councils, throughout

England, Wales and Scotland. There may nevertheless be scope for local additions to the code to deal with particular local needs. We accordingly recommend that there should be a single national code of local government conduct which would apply everywhere and to which individual authorities could add further sections if they saw fit.

175. A permanent national code requires the authority of collective endorsement by both local and central government; and we recommend that consultations to this end should be undertaken without delay and completed as quickly as possible. The resulting code should then be promulgated as a national code, endorsed by Ministers and the local authority associations, without the need to wait for any legislative procedure. Some kind of Parliamentary approval, perhaps on the lines of that given to the Highway Code, would be an additional and desirable measure of endorsement for the code in due course, but we do not regard this as essential.

33 A NATIONAL CODE OF LOCAL GOVERNMENT CONDUCT

From *Conduct in Local Government* (Department of Environment Circular 94/75, 1975); by permission of H.M.S.O. This is the text of the national code of local government conduct agreed between the local authority associations and central government on the basis of a draft recommended by the Prime Minister's Committee in 1974.

NATIONAL CODE OF LOCAL GOVERNMENT CONDUCT

This Code is a guide for all councillors elected or co-opted to local authorities in England, Wales and Scotland. It supplements both the law enacted by Parliament and the Standing Orders made by individual councils. It has been agreed by the Associations representing local authorities in all three countries and by the Government.

CONTENTS

1. Law, Standing Orders and National Code
2. Public duty and private interest
3. Disclosure of pecuniary and other interests
4. Membership and chairmanship of council committees and sub-committees
5. Councillors and officers
6. Use of confidential and private information
7. Gifts and hospitality
8. Expenses and allowances
9. Use of council facilities

1. Law, Standing Orders and National Code

Make sure that you fully understand the rules of conduct which the law, Standing Orders and the national code require you to follow. It is your personal responsibility to apply their requirements on every relevant occasion. Seek any advice about them that you need from your council's appropriate senior officer or from your own legal adviser.

2. Public Duty and Private Interest

(i) Your over-riding duty as a councillor is to the whole local community.

(ii) You have a special duty to your own constituents, including those who did not vote for you.

(iii) Whenever you have a private or personal interest in any question which councillors have to decide, you must not do anything to let that interest influence the decision.

(iv) Do nothing as a councillor which you could not justify to the public.

(v) The reputation of your council, and of your party if you belong to one, depends on your conduct and what the public believes about your conduct.

(vi) It is not enough to avoid actual impropriety; you should at all times avoid any occasion for suspicion or the appearance of improper conduct.

3. Disclosure of Pecuniary and Other Interests

(i) The law makes specific provision requiring you to disclose pecuniary interests, direct and indirect. But interests which are not pecuniary can be just as important. Kinship, friendship, membership of an association, society, or trade union, trusteeship and many other kinds of relationship can sometimes influence your judgement and give the impression that you might be acting for personal motives. A good test is to ask yourself whether others would think that the interest is of a kind to make this possible. If you think they would, or if you are in doubt, disclose the interest and withdraw from the meeting unless under Standing Orders you are specifically invited to stay.

(ii) The principles about disclosure of interest should be borne in mind in your unofficial relations with other councillors — at party group meetings, or other informal occasions no less scrupulously than at formal meetings of the council, its committees and sub-committees.

4. Membership and Chairmanship of Council Committees and Sub-Committees

(i) You, or some firm or body with which you are personally connected, may have professional business or personal interests within the area for which the council is responsible; such interests may be substantial and closely related to the work of one or more of the council's committees or sub-committees, concerned with (say) planning or developing land, council housing, personnel matters or the letting of contracts for supplies, services or works. Before seeking or accepting membership of any such committee or sub-committee, you should seriously consider whether your membership would involve you (a) in disclosing an interest so often that you could be of little value to the committee or sub-committee, or (b) in weakening public confidence in the impartiality of the committee or sub-committee.

(ii) You should not seek or accept the chairmanship of a committee or sub-committee whose business is closely related to a substantial interest or range of interests of yourself or of any body with which you are associated.

5. Councillors and Officers

(i)   Both councillors and officers are servants of the public, and they are indispensable to one another. But their responsibilities are distinct. Councillors are responsible to the electorate and serve only so long as their term of office lasts. Officers are responsible to the council and are permanently appointed. An officer's job is to give advice to councillors and the council, and to carry out the council's work under the direction and control of the council and its committees.

(i)   Mutual respect between councillors and officers is essential to good local government. Close personal familiarity between individual councillor and officer can damage this relationship and prove embarrassing to other councillors and officers.

(iii) If you are called upon to take part in appointing an officer, the only question you should consider is which candidate would best serve the whole council. You should not let your personal or political preferences influence your judgment. You should not canvass the support of colleagues for any candidate and you should resist any attempt by others to canvass yours.

6. Use of Confidential and Private Information

As a councillor you necessarily acquire much information that has not yet been made public and is still confidential. It is a grave betrayal of trust to use confidential information for the personal advantage of yourself or of anyone known to you.

7. Gifts and Hospitality

Treat with extreme caution any offer or gift, favour or hospitality that is made to you personally. The person or organisation making the offer may be doing or seeking to do business with the council, or may be applying to the council for planning permission or some other kind of decision. Working lunches and other social occasions arranged or authorised by the council or by one of its committees or sub-committees may be a proper way of doing business, provided that no extravagance is involved. Nor can there be any hard and fast rule about acceptance or refusal of tokens of goodwill on special occasions. But you are personally responsible for all such decisions and for avoiding the risk of damage to public confidence in local government. The receipt or offer of gifts should be reported to the chief executive.

8. Expenses and Allowances

There are rules entitling you to claim expenses and allowances in connection with your duties as a councillor. These rules should be scrupulously observed.

9. Use of Council Facilities

Make sure that any facilities — such as transport, stationery, or secretarial services — provided by the council for your use in your duties as a councillor are used strictly for those duties and for no other purpose.

34 LOCAL COMPLAINTS: THE 1974 ACT

From *Local Government Act 1974, Part III: Local Complaints* (Department of Environment Circular 76/74, 1974); by permission of H.M.S.O. This Circular describes the provisions of the legislation which created separate local government 'Ombudsmen' (formally Local Commissioners for Administration) for England and Wales.

1. We are directed by the Secretary of State for the Environment and the Secretary of State for Wales to draw attention to Part III of the Local Government Act 1974, which received the Royal Assent on 8 February. This Part of the Act, with the Fourth and Fifth Schedules, sets up separate systems for the investigation of maladministration in local government in England and Wales.

Origins of Legislation

... The general purpose is to give a citizen who believes himself to be the victim of maladministration by a local authority or other authority within Part III the same kind of right to have his complaint independently scrutinised as he already has through the Parliamentary Commissioner for Administration in respect of alleged maladministration by central government.

Bodies covered by Part III

4. These are specified in *section 25*. The main category is local authorities, who are defined in *section 34(1)* as county councils, the Greater London Council, district councils, London borough councils, the Common Council of the City of London, and the Council of the Isles of Scilly.

Parish and community councils are not included. Joint boards of local authorities, police authorities (other than the Home Secretary) and water authorities (including the Welsh National Water Development Authority) are covered by Part III. Provision is also made for the list to be extended by Order in Council to other authorities having the power to levy a rate or to issue a precept.

The Commissions

5. *Section 23* provides for the setting up of two Commissions for Local Administration, for England and for Wales. Each is to consist of Local Commissioners appointed by the Crown on the recommendation of the appropriate Secretary of State after consultation with the representative bodies referred to in paragraph 6 of this Circular. England is to be divided into areas, with one or more Local Commissioners responsible for each, and this may be done in Wales if there is more than one Local Commissioner in Wales. Each of the Local Commissioners will be personally responsible for the cases he investigates and on which he reports. Apart from the reports on individual cases, Local Commissioners will make annual reports to their respective Commissions, and the Commissions each year will review the operation of the complaints procedure and may make recommendations or express conclusions to local or other authorities or to Government Departments. The Parliamentary Commissioner for Administration is to be a member of each Commission but will not be a Local Commissioner; accordingly he will not undertake investigations under the Act of 1974.

The Representative Bodies

6. *Section 24* provides for the designation, by the appropriate Secretary of State, of the 'representative bodies' which are to have general supervision of the complaints machinery. The bodies are to represent authorities within Part III of the Act. The intention is that they will be nominated on the basis of recommendations from the associations of local authorities and the National Water Council (in Wales the Welsh National Water Development Authority).

Matters subject to Investigation

7. The general provision set out in *section 26(1)* is that a Local Commissioner may investigate a complaint made by a member of the public who claims to have sustained injustice in consequence of maladministration in connection with action taken by an authority to which Part III of the Act applies, being action taken in the exercise of administrative functions. The generality of this statement is, however, subject to certain limitations. The chief of these are:

a. The procedural requirements described in paragraph 8 below must be observed.

b. A complaint must normally be made within 12 months of the day on which the person aggrieved first had notice of the matters alleged in it (*section 26(4)*).

(A Local Commissioner may, however, accept a complaint made out of time if he considers that there are special circumstances.)

c. The procedure will not normally be available where there is or was a right of appeal, reference or review to or before a tribunal constituted under any enactment; or a right of appeal to a Minister; or a remedy in a court of law (*section 26(6)*). In these circumstances, however, a Local Commissioner will have discretion to conduct an investigation if satisfied that it is not reasonable to expect the person aggrieved to resort or have resorted to the right or remedy.

d. A Local Commissioner is not to investigate any action which in his opinion affects all or most of the inhabitants of the area of the authority concerned (*section 26(7)*).

e. The matters set out in *Schedule 5* are also excluded from investigation.

f. Only matters arising on or after 1 April 1974 will be subject to investigation (*section 26(12)*).

g. A Local Commissioner is not authorised to question the merits of a decision taken without maladministration by an authority in the exercise of a discretion (*section 34(3)*).

Procedural Requirements

8. These are spelt out in *section 26* of the Act. A complaint is not to be entertained unless it is made in writing to a member of the authority concerned, specifying the action alleged to have constituted maladministration; and is then referred to the Local Commissioner, with the consent of the person aggrieved, by that member or some other member of the authority concerned, with a request to investigate. A Local Commissioner may, however, dispense with the requirement of reference by a member if he is satisfied that a member has been requested to refer the complaint and has not done so. Before proceeding to investigate, a Local Commissioner must satisfy himself that the authority concerned has been informed of the complaint and has been given a reasonable opportunity to investigate and reply to it.

Further provisions regarding Complaints and Investigations

10. *Section 28* deals with four miscellaneous procedural subjects concerning investigations by Local Commissioners:

a. *Section 28(1)* provides that where a Local Commissioner proposes to conduct an investigation he must give the authority concerned, and any person named in the complaint as having taken or authorised the action complained of, an opportunity to comment on the allegations . . .

b. *Section 28(2)* lays down that all investigations shall be conducted in private, but subject to that general principle it is left to the Local Commissioner to decide on the procedure. He is given a general power to make inquiries and obtain information, and to decide whether parties may be professionally or otherwise represented . . .

c. The Local Commissioners may make payments to persons who incur expense, or lose remunerative time, by attending or furnishing information for investigations (*section 28(3)*).

d. *Section 28(4)* makes it clear that the fact that an investigation is being carried out does not invalidate any action taken by the authority concerned, or inhibit them from taking further action in the matter.

11. *Section 29* provides for the obtaining of evidence in connection with local investigations. It also provides that obstruction of a Local Commissioner without lawful excuse may be treated as contempt of court and be dealt with by the High Court on the certificate of the Local Commissioner. The intention of these provisions is to make sure that inquiries into local complaints take place against the fullest possible background of information. *Section 29(3)* makes it clear that correspondence between a Government Department and an authority is not exempt from disclosure to the Local Commissioner. *Section 29(4)* reinforces the powers of Local Commissioners to obtain information from Government Departments, overriding the normal restrictions on the disclosure of such information, including the Crown privilege which may usually be pleaded as a bar to the production of evidence in legal proceedings . . .

Reports on Investigations

12. *Section 30* deals with reports on investigations by Local Commissioners, indicating to whom they should be sent and how they are to be made public. The general effect is that when a Local Commissioner conducts an investigation or decides not to do so, he is to report his results or his reasons to the person (if any) who referred the complaint, the complainant himself, the authority concerned and any other person alleged in the complaint to have taken or authorised the action in question. Reports are to be made available for public inspection for three weeks by the authority concerned, the fact of such availability for inspection being publicly advertised. The underlying principle here is that the best sanction against maladministration is the weight of public opinion, which is in turn dependent upon full information.

13. *Section 30(3)* directs that the report of a Local Commissioner's investigation shall not normally identify the officers or other persons concerned in the alleged maladministration. It is to do so only if, in the opinion of the Local Commissioner, the public interest so requires.

15. The general effect is that if a report finds that injustice has been caused to the person aggrieved in consequence of maladministration, the report must be laid before the authority concerned, which must then consider it and notify the Local Commission of the action which it has taken or proposes to take in the matter. The Local Commissioner must make a further report if:

a. he does not within a reasonable time receive a notification of what the authority has done or proposes to do by way of rectification; or

b. he is not satisfied with the action which the authority has taken; or

c. he does not within a reasonable time have confirmation that the authority has in fact taken the rectifying action which it proposed.

Any such further report will be subject to the same rules as to publication (with any necessary modifications) as applied to the first report.

17. Information obtained by a Local Commissioner in relation to an investigation is not to be disclosed except for the purposes of the investigation and report itself, or in connection with certain proceedings under the Official Secrets Act or for perjury or contempt of court. By *section 32(3)*, a Minister of the Crown or authority subject to Part III of the Act may give notice to a Local Commissioner that disclosure of particular documents or information would be contrary to the public interest; but a notice so given by an authority (as distinct from a Minister) may be discharged by the Secretary of State. Information derived from a Government Department and which has not been made public is not to be included in a Local Commissioner's report unless the consent of the Department has been obtained or at least one month's notice of the intention has been given, thus allowing time for the Minister concerned to consider whether he should prohibit publication (*section 32(5)*).

Law of Defamation, and Disclosure of Information

18. *Section 32(4)* provides that the powers of Ministers and authorities to prohibit, or seek to prohibit, the disclosure of documents or information by a Local Commissioner are not to affect the obligation under subsections (3) and (4) of *section 29* to furnish information required by a Local Commissioner. Accordingly, whatever restraint they may seek to impose upon disclosure by the Local Commissioner, they must nevertheless supply to him for his own use the information he requires of them.

Consultation between Local Commissioners, the Parliamentary Commissioner and the Health Service Commissioners

19. *Section 33* lays down a procedure for handling cases where there is a complaint of maladministration against both a Government Department (or a health authority) and a local authority in respect of what is essentially the same transaction, so that two or more Commissioners are or may be concerned. In this connection it will be borne in mind that the Health Service Commissioners for England and Wales were appointed from 1 October 1973 under the National Health Service Reorganisation Act 1973. At present the posts of Health Service Commissioner in both England and Wales are held by the Parliamentary Commissioner; but this is not a requirement of that Act. The general intention of *section 33* is that where there are complaints directed both at local government and at central government or the National Health Service about what appears to be the same matter, the Commissioners con-

cerned should be able to consult together about the handling — and also the substance — of the respective complaints.

Interpretation of Part III

20. Among the definitions in *section 34* the following points may be noted:
    a. the word 'action' is defined to include a failure to act;
    b. the definition of 'local authority' does not include parish or community councils;
    c. subsection (3) of *section 34* makes it clear that a Local Commissioner is not entitled to criticise the basic merits of decisions properly taken by an authority subject to his investigation. The Commissioner must distinguish between the substance of the decision reached and the manner in which it was arrived at.

Schedule 5 — Matters not subject to Investigation

22. *Schedule 5* lists the matters which are specifically excluded from the jurisdiction of Local Commissioners. (Other restrictions on their jurisdiction have been mentioned in paragraph 7 of this circular.) The main items in *Schedule 5* are court proceedings; matters concerning the investigation and prevention of crime; contractual or other commercial transactions; personnel matters; transactions connected with public passenger transport, entertainment, industrial establishments, markets, ports and harbours; and certain educational matters.

23. The following points may be noted in connection with these exclusions:
    a. The main reason for excluding the commencement or conduct of civil or criminal proceedings in any court of law is that the courts themselves have ample power to oversee their own proceedings. Administrative tribunals are not similarly excluded, so that if maladministration is alleged in relation to the commencement or conduct of proceedings by an authority before an administrative tribunal, there is nothing in the Schedule to prevent a Local Commissioner from considering it; but *section 26(6)(a)* precludes him from acting as an alternative tribunal to decide the very issue which went to the tribunal.
    b. *Paragraph 2* excludes action taken by any authority in connection with the investigation or prevention of crime. Police authorities are within the scope of the Act, so that their administrative actions are subject to investigation. But complaints against the police themselves are subject to investigation by separate machinery, and are accordingly excluded from the jurisdiction of Local Commissioners.
    c. The general reason for the exclusion of contractual and commercial transactions is that the Local Commissioners will operate in the field of relationships between authorities and members of the public as such — ie as ordinary citizens. Commercial transactions, where parties are at arms' length and on an equal basis, are in a different category. To allow the commercial judgements of authorities to be examined for 'fairness' to private interests would amount to putting them

and the ratepayers at a general disadvantage because the other interests themselves would not be subject to similar investigation.

e. *Paragraph 3(3)* excludes certain types of commercial transactions from the
general reference in paragraph 3(1), and thus brings them within the jurisdiction
of Local Commissioners. The first of these categories is transactions for or
relating to the acquisition or disposal of land — whatever the service concerned,
and whether or not compulsory purchase powers are used or are present in the
background. Secondly — with the exception of the transactions wholly excluded
in sub-paragraph (2), and except also for matters arising from the procurement
of goods and services — functions exercisable under any public general Act are
to be within the jurisdiction of Local Commissioners . . .

f. *Paragraph 4* excludes from investigation by Local Commissioners action taken
in respect of appointments, removals, pay, discipline, superannuation or other
personnel matters. This reflects the principle that Commissioners are intended to
deal only with relationships between government and the governed, and not with
the action of local authorities as employers. In both central and local government there is Whitley Council machinery for the consideration of remuneration
and conditions of service.

g. *Paragraph 5* excludes certain educational matters from the jurisdiction of
Local Commissioners. The general aim is to cater for the special circumstances
of schools and certain establishments concerned with further education, responsibility for the internal running of which rests largely with governing and managing
bodies. These specific educational exclusions are in addition to those of general
application such as actions by authorities in personnel matters or actions where
a complainant has an alternative legal remedy. The broad effect is to rule out
investigation of complaints about how and what pupils and students are taught,
and about the rules and conduct of the institution, including the imposition of
sanctions such as suspension or punishment. But the jurisdiction of Commissioners extends to complaints concerning actions by local authorities on all
other matters affecting the education service . . .

35 LOCAL COMPLAINTS: 'YOUR LOCAL OMBUDSMAN'

From *Your Local Ombudsman* (Commission for Local Administration in England
1975); by permission of the Commission. This is an explanatory pamphlet produced by the English Commission; the attempt to define maladministration is of
particular interest.

WHAT IS MALADMINISTRATION?

2. Maladministration is not defined in the Act and it will be for Local Commissioners to decide whether it has occurred. But it refers for example *to the way* in which
an authority's decision has been taken. Maladministration may be taken to cover

administrative action (or inaction) based on or influenced by improper considerations or conduct. Arbitrariness, malice or bias, including unfair discrimination, are
examples of improper considerations. Neglect, unjustifiable delay, incompetence,
failure to observe relevant rules or procedures, failure to take relevant considerations into account, failure to establish or review procedures where there is a duty
or obligation on a body to do so or the use of faulty systems are examples of
improper conduct. The Commissioner has no power to question the merits of a
decision taken without maladministration.

. . . . . .

COMPLAINTS

6. The Local Commissioner will not investigate any complaint until it has been
brought to the attention of the authority complained against, either by the person
aggrieved (or his personal representative) or by a member of the authority on
behalf of that person, and until the authority has had a reasonable time in which to
reply to the complaint.

7. A complaint intended for reference to a Local Commissioner should be made
in writing to a member of the authority complained against with a request that it
should be sent to the Local Commissioner. It should state the action which it is
alleged constitutes maladministration. If the member does not refer the complaint
to the Local Commissioner, the person aggrieved may ask the Commissioner to
accept his complaint direct. **A COMPLAINT SHOULD NOT BE ADDRESSED
DIRECTLY TO A LOCAL COMMISSIONER IN THE FIRST INSTANCE.**

INVESTIGATION

15. When a complaint is received it will normally be handled as follows:
   a) It will be examined to decide whether it is within the Commissioner's scope.
   b) It if proves to be outside his scope, a letter of explanation will be sent to the
      complainant and to the member who referred the complaint.
   c) If a complaint is received directly from a member of the public, or if further
      information about the complaint is needed, the matter will be taken up in
      correspondence.
   d) Before beginning to investigate a complaint, the Commissioner will tell the
      complainant and the member that he has accepted it for investigation. He will
      also notify the authority and any person named in the complaint as having
      taken or authorised the action complained of, giving them an opportunity to
      comment on any allegations contained in the complaint.
   e) If at any stage in the investigation the Local Commissioner decides that the
      action complained of also concerns a Government Department or part of the
      National Health Service (eg a hospital) he will consult the Parliamentary
      Commissioner or the Health Service Commissioner as the case may be. If he
      thinks it advisable that the complainant should ask for an investigation by

either of those other Commissioners he may inform him of the steps necessary to do so . . .

f) When the investigation is completed a report giving the Local Commissioner's findings will be sent to the complainant, the member, the authority or authorities concerned and any person complained against. A report will not normally give the name or other identifying details of the complainant or of any person involved in the matter.

FORM OF COMPLAINT

(to be given to a member of the authority complained against)

For the use of a person who claims to have suffered **injustice** as the result of maladministration by a local authority (except a parish council), a police authority or a water authority who wishes his or her complaint to be investigated by the Local Commissioner

1. Your name . . .
   and address . . .
2. Name of authority complained against . . .
3. Details of your complaint of injustice, stating the action which you consider to be maladministration . . .
4. An account of the way in which you have previously brought your complaint to the attention of the authority . . .
5. Particulars of any evidence which you wish to submit in support of your complaint (*see Note 1*) . . .
6. Date on which action complained of took place . . .
7. Date on which you first heard of the action complained of . . .
   Do not complete these sections [8, 9] unless you want to
8. Name (or title) of any individual employee, officer of member of the authority about whom you wish to complain (*see Note 3 below*) . . .
9. Your reasons for complaining about any individual at 8 above . . .
10. I want a member of the authority to refer my complaint to the Local Commissioner
    Signed (by aggrieved person) . . .
    Date . . .

Notes

(1) Any letters which you have from the authority concerned or other relevant documents should be referred to here and should be sent to the Commissioner with this form: he will return them to you.

(2) If the date on which you make your complaint is more than twelve months after the date on which you first heard of the action you should explain, on a separate sheet, why you have not complained earlier. The Commissioner may not consider your complaint unless he is satisfied with the reason for this delay.

(3) If you give the name (or title) of any individual the Commissioner must inform him and give him the opportunity to comment on your complaint.

36 PUBLIC PARTICIPATION: BAINS

From *The New Local Authorities: Management and Structure* (1972); by permission of H.M.S.O. Hereafter referred to as *The Bains Report.*

We believe that the forthcoming reorganisation of local government will bring into sharp focus the deficiencies of public relations within many local authorities. In our view the public have a right to information about the affairs of their local council and access to committee and council meetings may well stimulate the public's desire to be better informed.

A number of local authorities have of course, given specific recognition to the importance of public relations by the appointment of Public Relations Officers, the setting up of information centres, the publication of news sheets and other means, but our impression is that a great many authorities have paid insufficient regard to this function. This may be due to the doubt which exists in some areas about the propriety of some PR methods used in other spheres. We are in no doubt however that local authorities have a firm duty to inform the community of their activities and to put the Council's view on matters of concern to that community.

We suggest that all the larger local authorities should set up a full-time public relations and information unit, headed by a suitably qualified officer. We recognise that in some of the smaller authorities such a unit may consist only of one man and in the smallest even that might not be justified, but it is nonetheless important that the duty to provide information should not only be recognised but should be demonstrated. In those smallest authorities it should be one of the responsibilities of the Chief Executive to see that proper channels of communication are established in both directions and that both public and press have access to an officer of sufficient knowledge and authority to deal with their enquiries.

Above all we suggest that local authorities should themselves adopt, as far as possible, an outgoing and positive attitude to the members of the community which they serve and should provide adequate resources, both finance and staff, to facilitate this. It has been suggested to us that authorities should publish an annual report to their electorate each year. Such a report might contain not only factual information in relation to the utilisation of the resources of the authority but also a narrative section in which the authority would identify the major problems facing it and the plans it had for solving them. A report of this nature would enable the local electorate to judge the performance of the authority in relation to its declared plans and programmes.

Dissemination of information internally

It is not only in the dissemination of information to the public and Press that local authorities have a responsibility. They also have a responsibility to keep their own staff informed, particularly on matters which have, or are believed to have, a direct bearing upon them. This is important at a time of simultaneous organisational change within every authority such as is now facing local government staff.

We have been dismayed to see and hear how little staff have been told in the past about some proposed local reorganisations, as well as how little many authorities are doing to keep staff informed about progress on the present one. Some authorities have published news sheets, some have regular meetings either with the staff (in the smaller authorities) or with their representatives, but many appear to have done little or nothing. This is not just a question of the interests of the staff, important though these are. The success or failure of any organisational change depends largely on the willingness of the staff to make it work. If management neglects its responsibilities to keep staff informed it can hardly be surprised if they put their own interpretation on such information, probably inaccurate, as reached them through unofficial channels. We were told by an officer in one authority which had undergone a reorganisation that staff —

became apprehensive about their own positions. Ill-informed, insecure and confused, they became antagonistic to the whole reorganisation.

The responsibility for such an unhappy situation rests squarely with management and the remedy is in its own hands. There must be the fullest possible information to members of the staff; how this is done is relatively unimportant provided that it is done.

We have deliberately laid great emphasis on the particular circumstances of reorganisation, but much can and should be done to keep staff informed of what is happening within the authority in more normal times. Some authorities already do this through regular meetings between staff and senior officers or by circulation of brief synopses of news concerning the authority, and we commend such practices to all authorities.

We have referred earlier in this report to the importance of an adequate flow of information to the elected members. The need for this has become more and more apparent as our enquiries have progressed and we make no apology for referring to it again.

We have received evidence of a number of means by which elected members are either supplied with, or can obtain, information about specific matters. One authority publishes a brief synopsis of items of current interest covering not only internal affairs of the County Council, but also items appearing in the local and national Press and central Government decisions considered to be of particular interest. More detailed information is available on request in respect of any listed items. In another case each member has a supply of prepaid enquiry forms which enable him to raise enquiries on any facet of the Council's activities. Many authorities have set up members' information rooms in which detailed information about all matters concerning the work of the authority is available. All this, of course, is in addition to the normal circulation of appropriate committee reports and minutes.

It may well be a function of a Public Relations Unit to organise the provision of information to members, but if that is not the case we recommend that it should be a specific responsibility of one officer of suitable calibre.

37 PUBLIC PARTICIPATION: SKEFFINGTON

From *Town and Country Planning Act, 1971, Part II: Development Plan Proposals: Publicity and Public Participation* (Department of Environment Circular 52/71, 1972); by permission of H.M.S.O.

1. We are directed by the Secretary of State for the Environment and the Secretary of State for Wales to refer to the provisions in Part II of the Town and Country Planning Act 1971 about publicity and public participation in the preparation of structure and local plans; and to the report of the Committee under the chairmanship of the late Arthur Skeffington, published under the title 'People and Planning'.

2. The Act and Regulations lay down the formal statutory obligations with which local planning authorities must comply. The report of the Committee, whose terms of reference were 'to consider and to report on the best methods, including publicity, of securing the participation of the public', was intended to provide guidance to authorities on how they might consider carrying out their responsibilities: but it also ranged more widely.

3. The Secretaries of State believe that publicity and public participation are essential factors in the new development plan system and they fully support them. They take this opportunity to stress how important it is, in embarking on that new system involving new concepts, to seek the views of the ordinary citizen and to listen to them. If the policies to be embodied in the plans are to be understood and generally accepted, and if the proposals in them are to be implemented successfully, the authorities must carry the public with them by formulating, for public discussion, the aims and objectives of the policies and then the options for realising these aims and objectives. Giving the public the opportunity to participate in the formative stage will, when handled with skill and understanding, not only make the plan a better plan but also do much to improve relationships between the planning authorities and the public. Participation is a two-way process . . .

4. . . . . the Committee made it plain that in their view participation should not be a formalised or rigid process but should be flexible enough to meet all types of local need.

5. The Secretaries of State have adopted this approach by keeping to a minimum the provisions dealing with publicity and participation in the Structure and Local Plans Regulations. Public participation is a structural part of the statutory planning process. As the Report itself noted, participation has to work along with what are already complex procedures. There is a risk that by adding to these complexities, the implementation of the new development plan system will be spread out over an unreasonable length of time. But participation in depth does not need to be

unlimited in time. The overall time taken on plans is important: constructive participation should help both to improve their quality and relevance, and to keep the period for preparing and approving them within an acceptable timetable.

6. In this context, significant features of the new development plan system are that it has two tiers of plans, the structure plan and local plans — and that the Act provides for public participation in both . . .

7. With regard to the structure plan, the Government have proposed a new form of inquiry — an examination in public of the policies and strategies embodied in the plan. For the examination in public it will be important to ensure that the public has had full opportunity of participating in the formative stage of the structure plan and that, as a result, the important issues will have emerged in public debate — whether through the press, television and radio for the locality, public meetings, conferences and correspondence with elected members and officials and so on. The selection of issues and participants for that public examination will be closely linked with the thoroughness of the prior public participation. The Secretaries of State will be concerned with the effectiveness of public participation in this context when considering whether they are satisfied as to the adequacy of the steps taken by authorities on publicity and public participation.

8. Authorities should focus their attention on the ways in which they can best discharge the statutory duties placed on them in respect of publicity and public participation. In carrying out these duties it is for the local planning authorities to decide which of the suggestions and recommendations in the Report can usefully be adopted. The views which the Secretaries of State have formed at this stage on the Skeffington Committee's main recommendations are set out in the annex to this circular. The Secretaries of State wish to emphasise that the aim should be compliance in depth with the terms of the Act's provisions on public participation and the production of effective plans within a timescale which is acceptable overall.

THE PROVISIONS OF THE ACT

9. The basic provisions on publicity and public participation are in sections 8 and 12 of the Act. These provide that a local planning authority are to take such steps as will in their opinion secure that:

a. adequate publicity is given in their area to the report of survey (or to any relevant matters arising out of the survey) and to the matters they propose to include in a plan, and

b. people who may be expected to want an opportunity to make representations on matters to be included in the plan are made aware of their rights in this respect and are given an adequate opportunity to make representations.

The Act thus differentiates between the requirements for the report of survey, to which publicity has to be given; and for the matters it is proposed to include in the plan, for which both publicity and an opportunity to make representations are necessary. The local planning authority are to consider any representations made to them within the period prescribed by the regulations.

10. Regulation 4 of the regulations provides that, where the Secretary of State so directs, the local planning authority shall provide people, on request and subject to the payment of a reasonable charge, with a copy of any plan or other document which has been made public under these publicity requirements. There are various ways in which such material might be made available. Publicity arrangements are bound to vary considerably but should normally include not only the production of diagrams, illustrative material and explanatory documents but also the arranging of exhibitions and discussions . . .

. . . . . .

13. Regulation 5 prescribes a minimum period of six weeks which an authority must allow for representations to be made about the matters which the authority proposes to include in its plans. Authorities have discretion to choose a longer period than six weeks if they consider this appropriate. In reaching a decision they will doubtless consider such factors as the extent to which publicity has already been given to the proposals; the methods of publicity they intend to use; the extent to which they are going to give publicity concurrently in the areas to which the plan relates to all the matters they propose to include; the extent of the area to which the plan relates; and the complexity of its proposals. What is absolutely essential is that three things should be made known from the outset, (1) that the authority is encouraging comments, (2) the way in which such representations are to be submitted and (3) what timetable the authority has laid down for receiving representations.

14. The Act provides that a local planning authority shall, when submitting their structure plan or sending any local plan to the Secretary of State, accompany it by a statement . . . of the steps which the authority have taken to comply with the formal participation requirements. The prescribed forms of notice provide for this statement to be on deposit along with the plan. The regulations do not spell out what is to be contained in the statement, for circumstances will vary from plan to plan and from area to area. What is needed is an informative account of the ways in which the authority have publicised their survey material and their proposals, what issues have emerged and how they have taken account of the representations made or why they have not felt able to do so. The Secretaries of State are required by the Act to satisfy themselves that the purposes of the publicity and public participation provisions have been adequately secured: if not so satisfied, provision is made for them to direct further action.

COMMENTS ON THE MAIN RECOMMENDATIONS IN THE REPORT 'PEOPLE AND PLANNING'

Methods and techniques of public participation

Recommendation I 'People should be kept informed throughout the preparation of a structure or local plan for their area. A variety of methods should be used, and special efforts made to secure the co-operation of the local press and broadcasting.'

1. The supply of adequate and timely information to the press and local broadcasting organisations can be a valuable — and free — means of bringing information before the public. Authorities will wish to consider the advantages of regular press conferences and informal discussion with local editors and of establishing contacts with local broadcasting centres. This does not, of course, mean that there should be an unending flow of information which would inevitably make unreasonable demands on resources and could well defeat its own object. Co-operation between an authority's planning staff and their information department will help in selecting the appropriate material to publish and the appropriate time and technique for doing so. The aim should be to publish information about the survey and later the proposals for inclusion in the plan with, if the authority wishes, alternative proposals. Invitations to the public to make proposals, without having before them the provisional proposals of the authority, would not normally be purposeful.

Time given for participation

Recommendation II 'An initial statement should be published when the decision is made that a plan should be prepared. It should state how the authority propose to inform the public, and should contain a timetable showing the main opportunities for participation and the pauses for their consideration. Although there should be full opportunity for public debate, it should not run on endlessly.'

2. The preparation of a timetable for public participation will no doubt form an important element in the overall project report which authorities are preparing when starting out on development plan work. Authorities are most likely to gain the co-operation of the various interests able to contribute to plans by publicising their timetable. This will assist those concerned, ranging from the general public to the public authorities, local and central, to make their arrangements to contribute material at the appropriate times . . .

3. The Act envisages a 'pause' (to use the term introduced by the Report) for representations and views to be expressed and for these to be considered by the local planning authority. These representations and views are those made on the matters proposed to be included in the plan to which the authority have given publicity at the stage before they finally determine the content of the plan. Where authorities provide a pause at any other stage, the timetable should be so designed that the pause occurs at a point at which they will in any case be engaged on other work necessary for production of the plan.

Stages of participation

Recommendation III 'Representations should be considered continuously as they are made while plans are being prepared: but in addition, there should be set pauses to give a positive opportunity for public reaction and participation. Local planning authorities should concentrate their efforts to secure participation at two stages. These stages apply to both structure and local plans and are (a) the presentation following surveys of the choices which are open to the authority in deciding the main planning issues for the area in question and (b) the presentation of a statement of proposals for the area in question. Where alternative courses are available, the authority should put them to the public and say which it prefers and why.'

4. The Act provides for publicity for the report of survey, and publicity and the making and consideration of representations at the proposal stage. The overall effect of Recommendation III, which is more fully set out in Chapter VI of the Report, is to provide for additional stages and processes of publicity and participation in, for example, the authorities' process of selecting from the main possible strategies the chosen strategy to be incorporated in the plan. Authorities will need to consider to what extent additional stages are desirable and, where they are introduced, programme them carefully and keep them within a firm timetable so as to reduce as far as possible the additional time spent in producing the plan.

5. Public participation at the stage when real choices are available is likely to be well worthwhile; it could prove valuable to authorities in assisting them finally to select the appropriate strategy on which to base their plan and it may also help to reduce the amount of representations at the statutory participation stage. If, and at whatever stage, authorities decide to present alternatives, however, they should do so in a way which will cause the least possible danger of blight. It may be that in some cases the authority will reach the conclusion that blight is being increased by rumours in the absence of publicity upon feasible options. The danger can never be entirely eliminated whatever publicity course it adopted since it is inseparable from forward planning, publicity and public participation; it is one of the prices to be paid for them; but it should be minimised. Only realistic alternatives should be published and where the local planning authority have a clear preference they should indicate this. So far as possible alternatives should be described only in generalised terms, so that they cannot be related to precise areas of land. Once alternatives have been made public, any blight effect should be removed as quickly as practicable; first by the speedy submission of the structure plan containing the chosen strategy and secondly, once the structure plan has been approved, by publishing the local plan, which will define proposals with more precision . . .

Organisation of public participation

Recommendations IV—VI 'Local planning authorities should consider convening meetings in their area for the purpose of setting up community forums. These forums would provide local organisations with the opportunity to discuss collectively planning and other issues of importance to the area. Community forums might also have administrative functions, such as receiving and distributing information on planning matters and promoting the formation of neighbourhood groups.

Local planning authorities should seek to publicise proposals in a way that informs people living in the area to which the plan relates. These efforts should be directed to organisations and individuals. Publicity should be sufficient to enable those wishing to participate in depth to do so.

Community development officers should be appointed to secure the involvement of those people who do not join organisations. Their job would be to work with people to stimulate discussion, to inform people and give people's views to the authority.'

6. The Secretaries of State are of the opinion that it will often be advantageous if groups representing different interests could meet together to discuss their different views: but whether this is practical and how it should be done is essentially a local matter. There are a number of existing organisations which will be concerned with structure and local plans; and authorities will wish to enable them to play a constructive part in public participation. The form which any new organisations set up in response to major or local issues which emerge is bound to depend in large measure on these issues.

7. Local authorities themselves will be able to consider what methods, including publicity, are available to them to encourage those described in the Report as 'non-joiners' to interest themselves in the preparation of plans which are likely to affect them or the area in which they live. Much could usefully be achieved by ensuring that local councillors are kept fully informed about plans, contents and the steps for publicising the proposals concerning them. Where a significant or potentially contentious proposal arising from the needs of a Government Department, statutory undertakers or other public authority is to be included in a plan, the local planning authority should discuss with them the best ways of publicising the proposal and seek their co-operation in discussions with the public. The Secretaries of State are however of the opinion that the appointment of Community Development Officers is unlikely to be necessary solely in the specific context of development plans.

8. In the areas of county councils it will be particularly important for the district councils to be involved in the work of public participation on both structure and local plans . . . District authorities with their local knowledge will be able to assist the county council in suggesting the participation arrangements which would be most suitable for their areas, and they may be able to assist in the making and carrying out of these arrangements as well. They will also be able to report local opinion to the local planning authority, but it should be made clear that representations need not be submitted through the district council but may be made direct to the local planning authority.

9. Local planning authorities will no doubt associate both parish and rural district councils in the work of obtaining the views of people affected by plan proposals. It is perhaps most likely that the contribution of parish councils will be of particular value in the preparation of local plans . . .

Results of public participation

Recommendation VII 'The public should be told what their representations have achieved or why they have not been accepted.'

10. The main and most convenient way of providing this information would be by including it in the statement submitted by the local planning authority to the

Secretary of State setting out the measures taken to secure public participation in the preparation of structure and local plans (see paragraph 14 of the circular above). This statement is to be made available to the public.

Participation by activities

Recommendation VIII 'People should be encouraged to participate in the preparation of plans by helping with surveys and other activities as well as by making comments.'

11. This could prove a useful way of involving the public provided authorities ensure that people are not asked to do work for which they are not equipped.

Education

Recommendation IX 'A better knowledge of planning is necessary. Greater efforts should be made to provide more information and better education about planning generally, both through educational establishments and for the public at large. Only if there is a better public understanding of the purpose of planning and the procedures involved will a local planning authority's efforts be fully rewarded when they seek public participation in their own development plans.'

12. In order to provide basic information about the new planning system the Department of the Environment and the Welsh Office propose to provide publicity material which local planning authorities will be able to use in conjunction with their own publicity programme.

38 PUBLIC PARTICIPATION: DOBRY

From *Review of the Development Control System: Final Report by Mr. George Dobry Q.C.* (Department of Environment Circular 113/75, 1975) by permission of H.M.S.O. The Dobry Report, published in 1975, contained a number of recommendations for improved public participation in the system of development planning and development control. This Circular sets out the central government response. The effect (reinforced by a later circular, 9/76) is to reduce the strength of the Dobry proposals by refusing to give them a statutory basis, but the overall result should be some improvement of existing procedures.

3. When the then Secretary of State invited Mr Dobry in October 1973 to carry out his review, he did so against the background of an astonishing and unprecedented increase in the volume of work with which the development control system had to cope. For well over a decade the number of planning applications had remained much the same year after year at around the 400,000 mark. In 1972 it rose to over 600,000, an increase of more than half. My Department was faced not much later with an increase in the number of appeals of even greater proportions — from less

than 10,000 a year in the early seventies to more than 18,000 in 1973. The inevitable result was delay as the system strained to digest this massive influx. No administrative machine could be expected to cope with a sudden increase in workload of this order without creaking. It was a cruel coincidence that precisely when local authorities were labouring under such a burden they were faced with the upheaval of reorganisation.

. . . . . .

7. Mr Dobry concludes that the development control system is fundamentally sound — and I fully endorse this tribute to the architects of the 1947 Act — but that as operated it does not adequately meet current needs. He has made a number of recommendations designed to simplify and accelerate the handling of planning applications and appeals whilst maintaining the quality of decisions and the equity of procedures. I think this aim is right and I have kept it in mind in considering the report. But beyond this Mr Dobry has put forward the view that 'it is not so much the system which is wrong but the way in which it is used', and this I also accept.

8. I set out below my conclusions on each of the recommendations made by Mr Dobry, as they appear in the summary chapter of his Final Report.

Applications *2.1 The Report aims at:*
(i) giving greater freedom to harmless development; but
(ii) guarding against harmful development by retaining applications for all cases, as at present;
(iii) separating from the main stream all applications which might cause harm;
(iv) disposing of applications in the main stream by rapid and routine procedures; and
(v) applying the same approach to appeals.
The aim of distinguishing between minor and major applications and appeals in order to dispose of the former quickly and concentrate attention on the latter has my full support. This is entirely practicable within existing legislation.
2.2 To achieve these objectives a division of applications into two categories, Class A and Class B, is needed.
2.3 Class A should comprise:
(a) all simple cases;
(b) all applications conforming with an approved development plan;
(c) development which only just exceeds that permitted by the General Development Order, even when not allocated for that use in the development plan;
(d) the approval of reserved matters relating to cases classed as 'A' when outlined permission was sought.
Class B should comprise all other applications.
2.4 The planning officer should have the power to transfer an application between classes provided he gives reasons for the transfer.
2.5 A repetitive application might be refused on that ground alone or, if reconsideration is warranted, transferred to Class B.

2.6 There should be a uniform procedure for dealing with applications and a model code.

2.11 There should be a 28 day time limit for transfer to Class B.

2.40 There should be no appeal against a planning officer's decision to transfer a case between classes.

There are definite benefits in making a clear distinction between the treatment of what may be called for the sake of brevity 'major' and 'minor' applications. Applications for extensions and alterations to houses, domestic garages, infilling, lesser changes of use, development just beyond that permitted by the General Development Order and the like rarely raise important questions of planning policy. They should therefore almost invariably be decided quickly, with the minimum of fuss, either by officers under delegated powers or by planning sub-committee if it meets sufficiently frequently. Major applications, far fewer in number but of much greater significance, usually require consultation with other bodies, opportunuties for public comment, and the attention of the full planning committee. But they equally need to be decided as quickly as possible. It is essential that local authorities recognise this distinction and cater for it in their planning arrangements. Classification of applications in this way is a valuable management method of concentrating attention on important applications and ensuring that minor applications are disposed of quickly and without taking up the time of busy people.

I have, however, come to the conclusion that the disadvantages of enforcing classification by statute outweigh any benefits there may be by way of accelerated decision-making. First, applications are already classified to a considerable extent in that different publicity and consultation requirements apply according to the nature of the proposed development. Applications do not by any means all have to go through the same statutory procedures. Second, it would be impossible, as Mr Dobry has pointed out, to draw a hard and fast line between what be calls 'Class A' and 'Class B' applications. Applications do not fall at all readily into two groups but come in many varieties. 'Major' and 'minor' do not always mean the same as 'controversial' and 'uncontroversial' or as 'complex' and 'simple'. Moreover, as Mr Dobry recognises, what might be 'Class A' in one area could be 'Class B' in another. Wherever a line was drawn, many applications would cluster round it. The applicant would obviously favour 'Class A', as this would yield a faster decision with less publicity. But authorities would lean towards 'Class B' where there was any shadow of doubt about the appropriate class, in order to allow for unforeseen difficulties and to avoid reclassification later. Under pressure, some authorities might reclassify applications as 'B' on a very large scale. The only solution to this would be a right of appeal against reclassification. Such complications might generate much heat but throw little light on real planning issues and would not be conducive to speed of decision.

Third, and most important, a large number of authorities manage already to decide within the two month statutory period the 70% or so of applications which might fall into Class A. I conclude that it is not therefore the statutory requirements which need altering so much as the way in which some authorities operate within them, and that rather than try to oblige authorities by law to make decisions within fixed periods it is preferable to seek to ensure that those authorities whose performance falls below standard adopt the methods of the rest.

. . . . . .

2.89 In this report I use:

(1) 'Public involvement' to mean both public participation and public consultation;

(2) 'Public participation' to mean taking an active part – from the outset – in the formulation of development plans and the making of major planning decisions of strategic importance;

(3) 'Public consultation' to mean giving the public an opportunity to express views on planning applications already made;

(4) 'Interested parties' to mean all parties other than the applicant (or appellant) and the planning authority.

2.90 The best method of involving the public must be chosen for each set of circumstances.

2.91 Public consultation must be early. In ordinary cases it should begin as soon as the local planning authority receives the application; in especially controversial or major Class B cases, pre-application publicity can help to modify development proposals before attitudes harden.

2.92 The public needs to understand the nature and limits of planning control better: equally planners need a better grasp of the principles and techniques of public involvement. Public involvement must be (1) relevant, (2) more efficient, (3) constructive and selective.

2.95 The proper purpose of public involvement in planning is to guide, not dictate, the local planning authority's decisions.

2.97 Local authorities should be more active in providing planning design guides, planning briefs, explanatory leaflets and information sheets.

2.98 There should be greater, and perhaps more thoughtful coverage of planning in the local press, radio (including local radio), on television and in documentary films.

2.99 Publication of lists of applications and decisions is especially important.

2.100 Education is the key to efficient and effective public involvement. The schools, adult education institutes, universities and local societies can all make a valuable contribution.

I generally agree, and again emphasise that public involvement needs to be planned and subject to appropriate time disciplines. I shall touch on the recommendation at 2.97 in a forthcoming circular to local planning authorities.

2.9 There should be a standard procedure for publicity.

2.15 For Class A there should be the following publicity:

Compulsory	Discretionary
1 Site notice or neighbour notification.	1 Notification to local societies.
2 Notification of parish council.	2 Other compulsory items under Class B (see below).

2.16 Site notices should be of uniform design and size, distinctive in colour, and written in plain, non-technical language.

. . . . . .

2.20 For Class B there should be the following publicity:

Compulsory	Discretionary
1 *Site notice or neighbour*	1 *Notification to local societies.*
2 *Notification of parish council.*	2 *Advertisements for individual*
3 *Publication of lists of*	*applications in local newspapers*
applications in local newspapers	*or on notice boards (perhaps*
or on public notice boards and	*allocated for that purpose).*
to registered local societies.	

2.21 Some Class A applications transferred to Class B may require additional publicity.

2.22 For more important applications, a public exhibition and/or public meetings would be worthwhile.

2.111 Publicity. There should be the following publicity for appeals:

(a) notification to interested parties by the local authority;

(b) compulsory site notices for inquiries;

(c) discretionary publication of lists of appeals (and of the results) in local newspapers, by local authorities;

(d) in major cases, the appellants may be required to advertise.

. . . . . .

My view is that the present balance between the right of the public to be informed about proposed development in their area and the burden which this places on applicants and authorities is about right. As advised in Circular 71/73, most authorities carry out publicity beyond that required statutorily according to their local circumstances and opportunities. I should like them to continue to use their discretion in this respect.

Therefore, while I accept that some rationalisation of the present statutory provisions may be desirable, I do not propose — with one exception — to introduce any new publicity requirements. The exception is to amend the Town and Country Planning General Regulations in order to provide that local authorities' own proposals for development receive the same publicity as an equivalent application. The Department, in Circular 71/73, advised authorities to ensure this.

. . . . . .

2.61 The public and the press have a right to be admitted to committees. They should normally (but not always) be admitted to meetings of sub-committees.

2.62 Experience shows that no harm is caused by publication of officers' recommendations either before or after a decision is taken at a closed meeting.

I agree. Circular 45/75 deals at length with these and other aspects of openness in the conduct of public business. What is said there applies to the planning field as to any other.

2.103 Parish and community councils have a vital part to play in local planning.

2.104 In the large urban areas where they do exist, neighbourhood councils might be considered to fill the gap.

I agree that local bodies of this kind have a part to play in planning. I am considering the replies to a consultation paper from the Department about the possibility of a statutory framework for neighbourhood councils, and I welcome the initiative of local planning authorities who have been consulting non-statutory neighbourhood councils meanwhile.

2.101 Voluntary organisations receive insufficient help. There is a need in due course for a central national body (British Environment Council) provided with funds.

The Department makes discretionary grants to voluntary bodies in the environmental field. As well as those mentioned in the report, it has recently funded the appointment, on an experimental basis, of environmental liaison officers, to assist local groups' response to local authority proposals in planning and other fields. The extent of help has of course to be related to the amount of money the Government can make available for that purpose, but existing arrangements for consultation between the Department and voluntary bodies do not seem to be inadequate.

2.102 Local authorities should adopt more widely the practice of co-opting members of amenity societies and other bodies on to planning committees. This may co-ordinate consultation and help applicants.

Authorities are aware that they have this power, and of the advantages and disadvantages of co-option. It is best left to them to decide whether or not it would be useful in their particular circumstances.

2.75 A Planning Control Consultative Committee should be established (with representation from local authorities, developers, the construction industry, some amenity societies and the professions) as a combined national forum for consultations between DOE and the public.

I consider that the present flexible arrangements for consultation with these bodies work well, a view shared by most of them when giving me their views on the report.

. . . . . .

2.105 More local authority information centres and independent planning advice centres could reduce the number of abortive applications and appeals and enable objectors to present their case in proper planning terms.

2.106 There is a case for the introduction when resources permit of a Planning Aid scheme, similar to the Legal Aid scheme, for those who cannot afford professional help.

Giving information and advice freely to applicants and others is an important part of any planning department's work. Most authorities are aware of this, and seek to provide the necessary service to the public in the form most suited to local needs and resources.

I am considering whether Planning Advice Centres independent of local planning authorities have a useful role to play. In the meantime, I have made a grant to the

Town and Country Planning Association's Planning Aid Service to enable it to continue during 1975–6. A general Planning Aid Scheme is not possible in present economic circumstances.

. . . . . .

2.73 Guidance from central government is essential. Such guidance should have the following characteristics:

(a) It should be clear. Guidance contained in some circulars is hedged with so many reservations and savings as to be capable of being read as meaning anything.

(b) It should be comprehensive. The present welter of circulars, bulletins, etc should be pruned of obsolete material and published as one comprehensive and coherent whole.

(c) It should be up to date. This means that the publication just mentioned should be kept regularly up to date and the new policy should be published promptly.

2.74 The Department should publish the following documents:

(a) a single up-to-date consolidation of policy guidance as just explained;

(b) a simple 'popular' explanation of the more important plans and policy documents;

(c) a planning control leaflet;

(d) a quarterly bulletin of topical material of interest to planners;

(e) The Department's own Desk Training Manual.

I accept the importance of clear guidance from central government, and in response to the recommendations I have put in hand:

(a) a review of the many circulars and other guidance issued by the Department since the 1940s, with the object of cancelling that which is now out of date and consolidating what remains into a coherent form. Cancellation of a number of obsolete circulars will be notified in a few days and consolidated advice by subject will be issued from time to time in the coming months;

(b) the preparation of a leaflet for householders explaining when planning permission is needed and how to get it.

In addition, interested bodies are now being consulted about a new Departmental publication specially aimed to help councillors which will bring together information about all DOE activity, including planning, which affects local authorities.

39 PUBLICITY FOR THE WORK OF LOCAL AUTHORITIES

From *Publicity for the Work of Local Authorities* (Department of Environment Circular 45/75, 1975); by permission of H.M.S.O.

1. We are directed by the Secretary of State for the Environment and the Secretary of State for Wales to stress the need for all those concerned in local authority affairs

to take positive action to ensure the maximum degree of openness in the conduct of public business.

2. As explained in paragraph 7 below the Local Government Act 1972, under which the local government system in England and Wales was comprehensively reorganised, made an important extension to the scope of the legislation affecting the admission of the public to meetings of local authorities.

3. The Act is being observed both in the letter and the spirit by the great majority of authorities but in some cases the changes in the law seem not to have been accompanied by greater freedom in dealings with press and public. Indeed, reports have appeared alleging secrecy and lack of co-operation; such attitudes would, of course, be wholly out of keeping with the declared and generally accepted objective of greater public participation in local affairs.

4. Moreover, the report of the Redcliffe-Maud Committee 'Conduct in Local Government' (Cmnd 5636) has stressed the importance of maximum openness as an essential safeguard for honesty and public confidence in local government (paras 134–143).

5. The Secretaries of State therefore think it would be useful again to summarise the statutory provisions contained in the Public Bodies (Admission to Meetings) Act 1960, as amended, and to set out the principles and spirit in the light of which these provisions should be operated.

. . . . . .

7. The Act of 1960 gave a right of admission to full meetings of local authorities and the other bodies listed, but its application to committees of those bodies was limited. It covered only committees consisting of or including all members of the body concerned. The main effect of the Act of 1972 in this respect is to extend the provisions of the Act of 1960 (in its application to local authorities) to all committees. A summary of the law is set out in the Appendix to this circular.

8. It is important that people should be able – and know that they are able – to exert some influence on local decisions affecting their own lives: conversely, a local authority must respond as much as possible to the views and needs of those who live within its area. Perhaps even more importantly the public is entitled to know the reasons for the policy decisions of its elected representatives. This two-way process of communication should lead to more informed decision-making and a readier acceptance by the public of unpalatable decisions. It is to the common advantage of elector and elected. In short, if the democratic process is to flourish, there must be ready access to full information about a local authority's activities.

9. Many local authorities have their own arrangements for publicising their work – for example, through news letters and reports to ratepayers. But in practice, most people get this sort of information from local newspapers, and the relationship of the local authorities to the local press becomes a key factor. So, the Secretaries of State feel that local authorities should make special efforts to ensure that their lines of communication are in good working order and are regularly reviewed. Haphazard or ad hoc arrangements are hardly likely to prove adequate.

10. The particular methods adopted for keeping the press informed are best

settled locally; an important matter could justify a press conference while the issue of informative statements to the press may be suitable on other occasions. But, whatever the methods, it could be a valuable practice for local authorities to have fairly formal meetings from time to time with local newspapers or representative organisations in order to review progress and problems. Even if relations are generally considered satisfactory, such meetings could still be useful to both sides.

11. The Act of 1960 allows the public (which includes the press) to be excluded by resolution during the whole or part of a meeting on the ground that publicity would be prejudicial to the public interest. This is a necessary safeguard, as the Redcliffe-Maud Committee acknowledged, but it should not be abused. The types of cases in which it is necessary to invoke this power cannot readily be summarised. In certain situations, free and uninhibited discussion might well be impeded if conducted in public; in other cases it would be unreasonably damaging to individuals to publish information about their affairs. But the approach should always be that the debate should be full and open unless there are compelling reasons to the contrary.

12. The law says nothing either way about the admission of the public and press to meetings of sub-committees. The Secretaries of State recommend that meetings of sub-committees should be treated in the same way as other meetings, particularly where they have delegated powers. If decisions affecting the public are to be taken, the public ought to know what is decided and why; the status of the body taking the decisions is irrelevant.

13. If it is decided, on cogent grounds, that a sub-committee should not transact its business in public, it becomes the more important that, to the maximum extent permitted by the nature of the matter involved, its reports to the parent committee or council should be fully explanatory and should be available to the public and press.

14. Newspapers, newsagencies and organisations systematically engaged in collecting news for radio or TV are entitled to receive copies of the agenda of meetings of the bodies covered by the Act of 1960, together with such further statements or particulars as are necessary to explain the nature of the items. In the view of the Secretaries of State, the normal practice should be to let the press have copies of the documents circulated to council or committee members. These should usually reach the press at the same time as they reach members, but if this cannot be done, the press should still get them in sufficient time to form a clear understanding of the matters under discussion. This is as much in the interests of the council as of the press. There should be no embargo to prevent reports and comments being made in advance of the meeting.

15. If the reports contain confidential information which cannot be publicly disclosed, a separate statement should be prepared for the press and this should be in generously helpful terms. And, again, the reasons for withholding certain information should be made clear.

16. Under the Act of 1972, any local government elector for the area of the authority has the right to inspect, among other things, the minutes of meetings of that authority. These legal provisions should be regarded as setting only the mini-

mum requirements, however, and local authorities should make other documents available as widely as possible. For instance, documents available for inspection should include the minutes of committee and sub-committee meetings, especially where such bodies have been given delegated powers, and documents could be made available to representatives of the local press, whether or not they are electors.

APPENDIX

1. The Public Bodies (Admission to Meetings) Act 1960 replaced and extended the Local Authorities (Admission of the Press to Meetings) Act 1908. The 1960 Act has itself been extended by the Local Government Act 1972 and amended by other statutes.

2. The Act as amended applies to:

a. local authorities within the meaning of the Local Government Act 1972, the Common Council of the City of London and the Council of the Isles of Scilly;

b. joint boards and joint committees constituted to discharge functions of any two or more of those bodies;

c. parish meetings;

d. water authorities (by paragraph 14 of Schedule 3 to the Water Act 1973);

e. Regional Health Authorities, Area Health Authorities and Community Health Councils, and if the order establishing a special health authority so provides, that authority (by paragraph 99 of Schedule 4 to the National Health Service Reorganisation Act 1973); and

f. any other bodies (other than police authorities) having, within the meaning of the Public Works Loans Act, 1875, power to levy a rate.

3. The Act also applied to certain committees including education committees: these provisions have been supplemented by the Local Government Act 1972 (see paragraphs 10 and 11 below), and the Water Act 1973.

4. Section 1(1) of the Act lays down the general principle that meetings of the bodies to which the Act applies shall be open to the public; section 1(4)(c) enacts that while such a meeting is open to the public the body shall not have the power to exclude members of the public and makes special provision for newspaper reporters. These rights are extended to other agencies by section 1(7). The Secretary of State is advised that there is thus an obligation to admit both reporters and other members of the public; it would not be permissible for either category to be wholly excluded on the grounds that the available accommodation is fully occupied. The accommodation to be provided must, of course, depend on the circumstances. The Act cannot be regarded as placing an absolute obligation on each body to admit everyone who might wish to attend, but local authorities will clearly be expected to provide such accommodation as is reasonable having regard to all the circumstances — including the size and status of the body, its functions and the premises available to it.

5. Section 1(2) enables a body to which the Act applies to exclude the public by resolution during the whole or part of the proceedings on the grounds that publicity

would be prejudicial to the public interest. The need to exclude the public must arise, as the section makes plain, from the nature of the business to be considered or the nature of the proceedings. Although this power is similar to the power of exclusion contained in the 1908 Act it differs from the earlier provision in two important ways. First the Act of 1960 requires the body specifically to state in the resolution the reason why the public is to be excluded. Secondly it does not reproduce the provisions giving power to exclude where in the opinion of the majority of the members exclusion is advisable, and thus provides the possibility of challenge in the courts should the power to exclude be used unreasonably or improperly.

6. Section 1(4)(a) requires advance notice of a meeting to which the public have a right of admission to be posted at the offices of the body concerned or if it has no office, at some central and conspicuous place. This provision does not derogate from any other statutory provision dealing with advance notice of meetings (eg those contained in Schedule 12 to the Local Government Act 1972), though so far as public notices are concerned there is no objection to all requirements being met in a single notice.

7. Section 1(4)(b) gives certain statutory rights to newspapers, and newsagencies to receive advance copies of the gaenda as supplies to members, together with either the supporting reports and documents or such other statements and particulars as are needed to supplement the agenda in order that the press may be informed in advance of the matters to be discussed and to enable reporters at the meeting to follow the proceedings. There may be omitted from the agenda and supporting documents any item which will probably be considered by the body in private. While the statutory right to receive these documents is given only to the press the Secretary of State suggests that it is desirable also to hand them to other members of the public who attend a meeting in person so that they may follow the proceedings.

. . . . . .

[The Local Government Act, 1972]

10. Section 100 of this Act extends the provisions of the 1960 Act to any committee constituted under an enactment specified in paragraphs (c) to (h) of section 101(a) and to any committee appointed by one or more local authorities under section 102. The 1960 Act deals only with education committees (paragraph 1(d) of the Schedule) and with committees of the authorities indicated in that Schedule (as amended) whose members consist of or include all members of the authority.

Section III
England: Internal management and organisation

It is a central characteristic of local authorities that they are individually free to recruit their own staff and establish their own working methods. Although this freedom is limited in practice, not only by the overriding power of Parliament to intervene in any aspect of local government but by existing statutory requirements relating to internal organisation, this is an area where local government has some freedom of manoeuvre. Few authorities have used this freedom in a positive or innovative way, and the operational deficiencies of local bureaucracies have given rise to as much concern as the structural defects of the system as a whole.

The central problem of internal organisation can readily be located within the debate about the correct relationship between policy and administration, and therefore between members and officers (40). The confusion of the debate reflects confusion about the relationships. The Maud Committee on Management in Local Government (1967) provided the first thorough analysis of this problem by an official body (41), and showed clearly that organisational arrangements (committee structures, types of delegation, systems of co-ordination) would reflect whatever were the main assumptions about the respective roles of members and officers. Basing itself on research, as well as received evidence, the Maud Report found fundamental defects in the internal organisation of local authorities. The remedies proposed were a small directing Management Board responsible for all policy decisions; a reduced number of committees, which would lose their executive powers; and a streamlined managerial structure, with the traditional Clerk operating more clearly as an overriding chief executive (42). Many authorities responded to these suggestions in the post-Maud period, but not in such radical terms, preferring to retain the executive role of committees, and a central policy committee less powerful than the Management Board. In this they followed the dissenting proposals of Sir Andrew Wheatley (43), a member of the Maud Committee, rather than the main Committee proposals. Wheatley's version was more in sympathy with the existing reality of local authority operation; but Maud was more perceptive in seeing that the involvement of elected members in the detail of local administration prevented the development of a policy role which was arguably of greater democratic significance. Redcliffe-Maud (44) reflected the thinking of earlier reports (Maud on Management, and Mallaby on Staffing, both 1967); and given the same chairman, this is perhaps unsurprising. Redcliffe-Maud also suggested the need for a further review to consider appropriate organisational structures for the proposed new authorities. From this further review emerged the Bains Report on management and structure in the new local authorities, the work of a group of local authority representatives (45).

203

Though only advisory in nature, it appears to be established as an authoritative guide to local authority practice. Indeed, it was recommended as such to local authorities by central government (D of E Circular 121/72). But it has also been criticised for undue cautiousness (a result, perhaps, of the committee's membership), and for an uncertain grasp of the manner in which its ideas on corporate management would clash with the realities of local government politics. Nonetheless, most major authorities now have corporate planning, streamlined committee structures, a central policy committee, a single chief executive, and a management team of chief officers. Whether the various reports, running in a direct line from Maud, through Redcliffe-Maud to Bains, have merely reflected best existing practice, as has been suggested, or whether they have generated changes, there can be no question that substantial changes in the internal organisation and management of local authorities have taken place in the last decade. Meanwhile, local authorities continue to be free to experiment with new forms of organisation, and the concept of area management is one example (46) of the willingness of some authorities to continue the search for a system under which, to paraphrase Bains, the chief concern will be to make democracy efficient, rather than make efficiency democratic.

40 WHO ARE THE POLICY-MAKERS?

From B. Keith-Lucas: *Who are the policy makers?* (Public Administration, Autumn, 1965); by permission of the Editor and author. Professor Keith-Lucas, an academic specialist in local government, was also for some time an Oxford city councillor.

In theory, of course, according to the standard textbooks, the answer to the question 'Who are the policy makers in local government?' is delightfully simple. The councillors make the policy and the officers carry it out.

But can one really make such a distinction? It is all very well to say that policy making is the function of the councillor and carrying out the policy is the function of the officials, but surely the function of the councillor does go some way beyond just making policy. He has the functions of contact with the people, of seeing that administration is reasonably and properly carried out, of supervision.

There is of course provision for some form of appeal from many of the councillors' decisions (to the Minister in some cases, to County Courts in others and to tribunals of one kind or another in yet others). But there are many decisions against which there is no right of appeal except through this sort of Ombudsman function of the councillor.

So I think one has to reject the simple answer that the councillor's function is to make policy and the officer's to carry it out, and to admit that the officers have enormous influence on policy making, that the councillor plays a very big part in administration — and should rightly do so in seeing that the administration is fair, sensible and not biased in any way.

But what really happens in practice? Here we find the most bewildering and fantastic variety and this is why I feel very envious of the earlier speakers who were able to speak in such comparatively simple terms of a fairly standard pattern. They said that personalities can affect the pattern; so of course they can in local government. The personality of the Town Clerk probably varies very much more than that of the Permanent Secretary, if one looks up and down the whole range. At one end are the great and powerful Town Clerks who dominate their councils; at the other are those who are clerks in the true sense that they are the people who keep the records, prepare the agenda and just see that the business of the council runs smoothly. This of course is a consequence partly of the enormous variety of size in local government. There are some towns with a great tradition of powerful Town Clerks, where they have been as much or more the policy makers than any councillors; Nottingham is a case in point — it has had a succession of powerful Town Clerks — Sir Samuel Johnson, Sir William Board and onwards. These lions of local government are certainly not a thing of the past. There are lions roaring up and down Yorkshire today and I think one will find them in other parts of the country. There are also, however, mice — Town Clerks who take the completely opposite view of their function — that they are just the clerk.

There is a conflict here, I think, between two points of view. One says that the officer's function is basically to carry out the policy made by his council; the other says that the Town Clerk stands to some extent at least on his own feet — that he is not merely the servant of the council but that he is himself the holder of a statutory office which carries with it the responsibility for the good government of the town and that on occasion — an occasion which should, however, always be avoided — he should be ready to defy his council. The classical statement of this is of course in the famous deep shelters judgment during the last war; no doubt the Lord Chief Justice went too far in saying that the Town Clerk 'stands between the Council and the ratepayers', but it is clear that there is some such conception in the minds of some Town Clerks. They have a statutory duty to help in the making of policy and to see that there is good government, quite apart from their functions and duties as servants of the council. I know of one County Education Officer who was in very basic disagreement with his committee chairman; on being told to sit down at a committee meeting the officer retorted: 'I am the Education Officer of this county and I have a duty to advise, and I shall' — and he did. Of course that sort of conflict should never arise, but the mere fact that this is the view of some officers is significant.

Of course there is equal variety amongst councillors. Here again some towns have a tradition of powerful, single-man government . . .

Again, there is the extraordinary situation in some counties with the Chairman kept in office for ten, twenty or thirty years — fifty in one case. Though on paper such a man has the same powers as the Mayor of any small town, in the course of so many years he acquires a domination which makes it an utterly different type of appointment. In these cases one man, more than all the others put together, makes the policy by force of personal character and length of service. From those long serving and dominating Chairman down to the Mayor who hands over office after one year, there is as wide a range, or wider, than between the extremes of chief officer.

So far I have left out of account the political side of all this, and of course this is where one would naturally look for the policy making — in the political parties. One must remember that, apart from the parish councils (which do not work on a party basis), over half of our local authorities are not basically politically divided. Although practically all of the county boroughs work on a party basis, a very large number of the others do not. Many appear to work on a party basis at first sight; but although their members are elected as party representatives they have not got the machinery, the regular caucus meetings, the whips, the clear party line. Once they are elected many of these councillors do not really work as a political party. Others, however, who at first sight are non-political are in fact much more political; those who describe themselves as Independent are really, as often as not, the anti-Labour group . . .

Here again the picture must be very different from that of the central government, because, instead of having a Cabinet composed of only one party, local government normally works through committees composed of all parties, in more or less the same proportion as the membership of the council. A number of big cities have however got away from this to some extent. The L.C.C. under Herbert Morrison became more or less a replica of the machinery on the other side of the Thames, with a Cabinet and a Prime Minister — the Prime Minister of London. Leeds, as Professor H.V.Wiseman has shown, has been working on a very clear-cut and definite political basis with an advisory committee which has operated very much like a Cabinet, but with one big difference. It was not a committee of the council and was not therefore recognized by the officers. This advisory committee, composed entirely of the majority party, was where most policy decisions were really made — but the officers were not there to advise as they would be in an ordinary committee; it was a part of the party organization. A clear-cut distinction was drawn between the council committees at which the officers speak and at which members of all parties are present, and this advisory committee, the most important of all, where the real decisions are being taken without the presence of either opposition members or the officers. I think there are obvious dangers when policy decisions are made in this sort of group without the advice of the officers. Coventry have got over this by constituting their policy advisory committee as a committee of the council — a formal and official committee — and I believe a number of other places are doing the same. It is no longer a bit of party organization; it is a part of the council organization. There the officers and the councillors do meet and discuss policy. At the same time it is a party meeting in the sense that they do not admit to it members of the opposition party; unlike the majority of local government committees it is limited to 'the government' — the majority party and the officers. This is moving a little nearer the Cabinet concept and I believe on the whole the idea works well where it has been tried in local government, but there

are difficulties about it. One consequence of the Coventry system, I am told, is that
the other committees have a tendency to shirk major policy decisions and to leave
them to this 'Cabinet'. Another difficulty is that it tends to get involved in conflicts
between other committees and thus to be involved in co-ordination and smoothing
out this sort of disagreement, rather than with its primary function of policy
making.

41 MAUD ON INTERNAL ORGANISATION: RESEARCH FINDINGS

From *Maud, Vol.5: Local Government Administration in England and Wales* (1967);
by permission of H.M.S.O. The material here provided the foundation for Maud's
recommendations for a Management Committee, a single chief executive, and a
clearer definition of the respective roles of members and officers (and see **Doc. 42**,
below).

The initiation of policy

This section is based on the written comments of about 30 Clerks from all types of
authorities and on our discussions with officers and leading members in other authorities where we made our personal enquiries.

(*a*) *'Policy' committees.* Less than a third of the authorities consulted referred to
the existence of a committee which could be regarded as having in any sense
responsibility for the initiation of the policy of the authority as a whole; most of
those which did expressed some reservation about the extent to which the committee could be said to exercise this function. The committee most usually referred
to was the finance committee (which in some authorities includes other functions
also). This can in one sense be regarded as a general policy committee, as most new
policy proposals require expenditure and are therefore referred to it at some stage.
However, these proposals normally originate elsewhere and sometimes the finance
committee has a negative rather than a positive function, since its approval is necessary before proposals can be referred to the council. Even the finance committee's
function of assigning capital priorities is mainly a question of selecting from projects
initiated elsewhere. In one authority, however, the committee which deals with
finance and also a number of other major matters appears to be more than usually
concerned in the central direction of policy. Some authorities attributed an element
of policy initiation to the 'parliamentary' committee, which sometimes deals also
with other matters such as 'general purposes', 'selection' or 'finance', but these
committees also appear to be co-ordinators rather than initiators, since much of
their business has been raised in the first instance in other committees. Sometimes
the parliamentary committee deals with a specialised aspect of the central direction
of policy — questions affecting the boundaries, area and status of the authority — a

function stimulated in some places by the activities of a boundary commission. One Clerk referred to the part played by sub-committees of the general purposes committee in initiating policy in specialised fields. In one authority an *ad hoc* committee originally set up specifically to deal with the redevelopment of the town centre appears to be taking on other functions and to contain the germ of a general 'policy' committee.

(*b*) *The contribution of party groups and of groups of influential members in non-party authorities.* In many authorities operating on party lines the party group makes a more significant contribution to general policy initiation than any 'constitutional' committee. However, groups usually appear to spend much of their time and energy in what is in essence a negative function and quite different from policy initiation — vetting recommendations which originate in individual service committees. The group is in any event too large for the task of policy initiation and has the disadvantage of operating in the absence of professional advice. Policy initiation is more likely to be centred in an inner caucus consisting of a few leading members than in the group as a whole.

Similarly, in non-party authorities a dominating group can emerge which can sometimes be responsible for policy initiation and direction.

(*c*) *The initiation of policy in individual committees.* A large number of the Clerks who answered our enquiry stressed that policy ideas often originate in the individual service committees; this is not surprising in view of the fragmentation of local government services among separate departments. There are, however, a variety of ways in which a committee's contribution towards policy initiation is exercised, depending on the relative roles played by individual committee members, by committee chairmen acting either on their own initiative or in association with chief officers and by chief officers themselves.

(*d*) *The contribution of individual committee members.* In most of the authorities investigated the contribution of individual members towards the initiation of policy does not appear to be of great significance and is usually confined to narrow aspects of the service in which they have a particular interest.

. . . . . .

(*g*) *The contribution of officers.* In nearly two-thirds of the authorities consulted officers make a significant contribution and in nearly a quarter they play the major part in policy initiation. Various explanations are suggested in different authorities and in relation to different services — for example, because local government has become increasingly technical and less comprehensible to the layman, because no political party has an overall majority, because the average age of a council is high, because members become involved in so much detail that major issues are obscured, because policy tends to be conditioned by national legislation and central directives. It is clear that the practice in many authorities does not accord with the facile generalisation that members are concerned with policy and officers with its execution.

. . . . . .

THE WORK OF THE COMMITTEES – TYPES OF DECISION AND DELEGATION TO OFFICERS

Introductory

The appointment of committees, an obvious expedient to enable members to deal with matters collectively for which full council meetings are inappropriate, is provided for by statute. A council has wide freedom, despite certain statutory requirements, as to the type and size of committees and committee structure it sets up. The size of a committee affects the way in which it behaves, and the sub-committee structure the extent to which members specialise. The very large committee, without specialisation among its members, appears to be unsuitable for work on matters of complexity and unmanageable if a high level of general participation is attempted on a large number of items. Symptoms of the inadequate committee are the well-documented tendency to avoid discussion of major policy in favour of talk on minor matters, repetitiousness, 'hobby-horse riding' and perfunctory discussion of the latter part of the agenda. The typical local government committee, because of its cumbersome nature and its discontinuity, cannot administer in the normal sense of the word. Its limitations are overcome chiefly by the appointment of officers and of chairmen who take action on its behalf. In a large and growing authority the proliferation of sub-committees cannot keep up with the increase of business and the system would 'clog up' without selection of items for committee and extensive devolution.

The tendency of the law, however, is to force matters for decision towards the top level in the structure, in direct contradiction to the principle of good management that decisions should be taken at the lowest competent level in an organisation. This is sometimes seen as a conflict between efficiency and democracy, which, we argue, does not necessarily exist. The argument that undue resort to decision-making in committee is an escape from responsibility was made by some members and officers whom we interviewed. The frequently met distinction between policy and execution is mentioned in this connection.

Decisions before Committees

(a) *Towards a definition of policy*. Agendas are often heavily weighted with reports not requiring any specific decisions although action often arises from these, so that a committee agenda does not necessarily indicate in practice the balance between deliberative items and those put in only for the conveyance of information. Distinction between policy and executive decisions is more difficult, although it is often used to great practical effect in determining the members' sphere and that of the officers, and its importance was emphasised by a number of officers and members who gave us information and opinions. Some saw a firm distinction between policy and administration as a main road to reform.

The possibility of such a distinction is discussed, including the close relation of policy to the values of the members and the goals they wish to achieve. Policy-making, it seems generally accepted, involves laying down objectives and determining broad priorities, in such a way as to leave scope and freedom for officers to use their specialist skills and knowledge most effectively.

Examples are given of unquestionable matters of policy, all having significant social implications and possessing elements of controversy. Policy definitions often arise from specific cases or limited practical problems; committees sometimes proceed by a kind of case-law, a dependency on precedents arising from earlier decisions on particular problems. A succession of detailed decisions may eventually constitute a policy. (Consistency however can easily be lost unless there is a general formulation of policy, and in one authority the position was very confused because influential members refused to be bound in particular instances by their decisions on principles of planning.) Because administrative schemes for the execution of policy often bring out policy issues which had previously been overlooked, they sometimes form a stimulus for the members to make a clearer definition of objectives.

The distribution of resources between services is a matter of policy, or reconciliation of objectives. Allocation of benefits to localities can be governed by neutral criteria of local needs or each case can be argued as a matter of policy subject to political pressures. At what level the allocation of resources within a service ceases to be a matter of policy is perhaps impossible to define. It may be held that the most important policy issue is to define the most competent and efficient level at which this type of decision can be made in the interests of the service concerned. The fixing of the general level of expenditure is of course a pre-eminent issue of policy.

(*b*) *Executive matters*. Some committees we have attended have not formulated policy on any matters before them; all their decisions may be termed executive . . .

A wide range of specialist decisions are generally acknowledged to be within the competence of a specialist officer. In some authorities building plans are almost entirely the concern of the officers and in others much trouble is taken over putting them to the members for scrutiny. Aesthetic decisions are a doubtful field in which an officer's decision — although he may be an architect — is not always trusted, or in which members feel a great deal of interest and are therefore unwilling to leave in professional hands. Committees vary widely in the extent to which they participate in choosing furnishings. It is sometimes entirely a member's task and sometimes entirely an officer's . . .

Casework is a field where different committees, even within the same authority, interpret their responsibilities in widely varying ways. Committees or sub-committees in charge of old people's homes sometimes have specified powers of management over such matters as meal-times and fire-drills. Admissions to homes may be determined by committee, by a chairman or by officers. Some committees insist on having the names of welfare cases; elsewhere anonymity is the rule. Similar variations were found in the extent to which education special services committees, health committees and housing committees, were involved in decisions on individual cases. Casework is of high interest to many members, but discussion of individual problems in committee we found often uninformed and unsatisfactory, and it added little or nothing to the advice of the officers.

Like casework, planning decisions demand an intimate knowledge of particulars and a regard for personal rights. A large proportion of planning decisions are applications of defined policy and essentially executive. To treat applications differently and allow random personal considerations to enter into the process can lead to a dissolution of policy. Local interests, legal considerations and the failure to define planning policy with sufficient clarity keep business on all types of planning applications at committee level, and the members sometimes exercise a combined role of policy-maker, policy-executant and judge in each case.

(c) *The reasons for members' involvement in details of administration.* Observations are quoted from some authorities that members accustomed to dealing with matters of detail were often resistant to any suggestion that they should give this up. Concern with detail was explained as due to members' sensitivity to public reaction, a general wish to know 'what was going on', a retreat from problems of policy, the determination of larger issues outside the committee, a 'historical distrust of officials', the doctrine that a members' duties were to exercise power and watch the officers, the relatively slight amount of business in smaller authorities which gives members the time to discuss trivia, and the degree of inherent interest to members in certain types of subject. It can also be argued that dealing with detail enables members to keep policy under review in a practical way, and we noted cases of policy definition emerging from a routine consideration of executive action.

The placing of matters of detail before committees was also blamed upon the weakness of officers who failed to distinguish between policy and execution, who wished to boost their reputations or save their departments from appearing inactive, who were afraid to take responsibility and who erred on the side of timidity. It was also explained as a way of interesting members and necessary because it was difficult to decide what was contentious or what was a matter on which officers would eventually be glad of members' support. The importance of the influence of officers on this matter emerges from the great variation in the amount of detail going to parallel committees in the same authority and the influence of Clerks who have taken a strong lead in encouraging officers to cut down the detail they take to committees. The fear that delegation to officers is illegal is another important influence in this matter.

Officers' action

Devolution of minor matters to officers is opposed by members who find interest and satisfaction in considering these; it gives new definition to the jobs of both members and officers and therefore may be expected to have a direct effect on recruitment.

Many councillors and chief officers whom we interviewed emphasised the importance of increased delegation. The replies to questions we sent to a number of

Clerks indicated that only a minority felt members were interfering in executive matters. Some chief officers whom we interviewed felt that what authority they exercised should follow from the trust they inspired in members, and they had gained wide freedom of action in the confidence that their committees would back their actions retrospectively. Another wide area of action by officers covers informally assumed powers, regarded as reasonable by the members, which do not normally require confirmation by committee. In a very large authority problems of size make it less easy for chief officers to exercise assumed powers of this kind. Newly appointed officers may be reluctant to act on such an informal basis. In some authorities there is a tradition of hostility to allowing power to officers which is difficult to surmount.

Conclusion

We state our view, shared by many of those we interviewed, that the devolution of business to officers is a condition of efficiency and conducive to the recruitment of the type of member whom we would consider most valuable, although many existing members would, wrongly in our opinion, regard this as undemocratic.

. . . . . .

Co-ordination by committees

(a) **The need for co-ordination** Co-ordination may be seen as the task of keeping in check, through formal machinery and otherwise, the centrifugal tendencies of the committee system, or alternatively as the unification of policy, the achievement of a coherent set of objectives within the terms of which the different services are to work and of the general integration of development. This latter approach ideally involves planning from a view of the sort of life it is thought people should live and using the insights of social and administrative science to determine, as far as possible, what this involves for the different services. It may be argued against attempts at co-ordination of this kind that they reflect an impractical ideal since departmental policies are living things which cannot be subordinated to a 'super-policy' and that local government work is so subject to outside influences and contingencies that such integration is impossible.

. . . . . .

. . . Despite the varied arrangements for co-ordination of business there is hardly any systematic attempt at committee level to conceive and co-ordinate policy as a whole, and some members we interviewed thought there was no need for this. If it is admitted that there is a need for a consistent body of policy thought out in terms of the needs of the authority and the community as a whole, we think the case for a key policy committee strong. One aim would be to overcome fragmentation and to ensure that officers were brought together to report with common objectives in view and with the help of the most advanced effective planning techniques.

(*d*) *The idea of a policy committee.* The idea of a 'policy' or 'management' committee, or a local government cabinet, seemed familiar to most members and officers we questioned on the subject and in certain cases had been tried out without success. It had taken the form of a new horizontal committee parallel with the finance committee, and had developed no corporate loyalty and caused some dislike amongst members not included. A successful instance of the development of a finance committee to fulfil a general policy co-ordinating function causes us to wonder if, given no fundamental change in the present committee system, it would not be better to develop the functions of an existing finance or general purposes committee to fulfil this need rather than add a new horizontal committee.

In some authorities it was said that a group of influential chairmen or the majority party formed a kind of cabinet or executive committee, although we suspect that the claims were often exaggerated and in any event such a body is severely handicapped because of its dubious relation to the body of officers. In most authorities some members felt the creation of a new policy-defining committee was desirable. When this was not the case it seemed to be either on account of satisfaction with existing arrangements or fears on how it would work out in terms of personalities and human relations. Most members and officers who spoke of it were thinking of a body consisting at least in part of chairmen of service committees. There was emphasis on the fact that it should be a small committee and differences as to whether or not it should include members of the opposition.

Officers advocated it as a means by which they could ensure that full briefings could be given to a key decision-making body. Members thought the increased volume and complexity of business demanded a committee of this kind. It was seen as a way of speeding up procedure, of providing clear leadership and of making it possible for elections to be fought on clear issues of policy, as well as for co-ordination.

It was emphasised that the idea would meet strong opposition. Chairmen and members would resist because they would lose some of the satisfactions they found in the present system. A concentration of power was feared and it was suggested that there was not the basis of mutual trust for such a system. It was felt that if opposition members were admitted to such a committee the need for a private majority party caucus would remain and so one of the purposes of the institution would be frustrated. If opposition members were excluded it was feared that it would create a close association between the party in control and the officers, in sharp contradiction to the traditions of English local government. A minority party cut off from the main deliberations on policy would be ill-informed and therefore irresponsible, and inexperienced when it gained power.

There was a fear of full-time 'professional' chairmen and little confidence that the present machinery would necessarily select the right people for the jobs; that the chairmen selected would have more motives to interfere with the normal work of the officers, and that it would create a flow of work to the top which would be most harmful to efficiency. It was also suggested that in many authorities a 'cabinet' would not be strong enough to carry the support of the party group and that the result would be confusion. We conclude that some at least of these fears would be

groundless if members confined themselves to major decisions and allowed the
officers to play a full managerial role, subject to reasonable checks.

Co-ordination by officers

. . . . . .

(*b*) *Co-ordination by the Clerk.* When considering the ways in which officers
attempt to achieve co-ordination it is natural to begin with the contribution made
by the Clerk. Two different levels of co-ordination can be distinguished — co-
ordination of organisation and co-ordination of development; most of the methods
considered operate to some extent on both levels, although some are more closely
related to one than to the other.

In the large majority of authorities Clerks are concerned with preparing committee agendas, taking minutes and drafting reports from committees to the council, with the exception in some authorities of those relating to education committees. Many Clerks referred to this responsibility as an important element in their
co-ordinative role. It enables them to settle the general pattern of committee papers
and to exercise some control over the content as well as the form of the agenda.
However, the Clerk's position is rather different in the matter of written reports by
chief officers to committees, which are more often than not sent to members direct
by the officer concerned. Sometimes (but not invariably) a draft is seen in advance
in the Clerk's department and consultations often take place between officers
before reports are circulated. However, many committee clerks are dominated by a
succession of publication 'deadlines' and chief officers, to ensure that as much
business as possible is cleared by each committee meeting, tend to release reports
too late to give adequate time for discussion before despatch. Where Clerks do not
see draft reports before despatch they nevertheless have an opportunity of ensuring
that they are discussed with any other officers affected before the meeting; there
seems to be a variation in the extent to which the initiative in this is taken by the
Clerk or by the officers concerned. Examples are quoted of evidence seen in committee of lack of adequate prior consultation. There were, however, many other
occasions where it was clear that such consultation had taken place. The Clerk's
responsibility for committee work ensures that he has information which gives him
an opportunity of assessing major developments in all spheres of the authority's
activity. We saw little evidence of a deliberate attempt to preclude Clerks from
being consulted about the business of committees for which they have no such
responsibility.

The Clerk is normally present himself or represented (usually by a solicitor) at
the meetings of main committees at least. We received a few critical comments from
other chief officers on the part played by these representatives, but this was not a
subject on which many expressed an opinion. In a large authority the task of
ensuring that the Clerk is kept informed of significant developments in committee
business poses a problem of co-ordination within his own department.

Another factor generally regarded as contributing to his co-ordinative function is the recognition of the Clerk as the formal channel of communication with the outside world. If pushed to the limit, however, this can have the effect of antagonising other chief officers.

In many authorities the Clerk has responsibility for establishment matters; this is an aspect of co-ordination of the authority's administrative arrangements rather than its service to the community . . .

Another, rather different, aspect of the Clerk's co-ordinative function is his position as the leader of a team. The very varied views we have received about the use and value of chief officers' meetings are summarised; examples are also given of the different forms which such meetings can take. It seems that they are likely to be successful only if a willingness to co-operate already exists among officers; they appear to be particularly valuable where they give an opportunity for a constructive approach to major problems and are used to keep officers in touch with the thinking of political leaders. Reference is made to other, less formal, meetings with chief officers arranged by Clerks.

The Clerk's link with party group leaders or, in non-party authorities, leading members, is a vital factor in his co-ordinative function.

(*c*) *The idea of a chief administrative officer.* The views expressed to us about the idea of a chief administrative officer are summarised, bearing in mind that they did not relate to a clearly defined concept. There was a fair amount of support for the idea of having an officer whose position as leader and co-ordinator would be more clearly recognised than that of some present Clerks, on condition that the professional position of other chief officers was not prejudiced . . .

. . . the task of co-ordination would be simplified considerably if functions were grouped under a comparatively small number of departments and committees, since there would then be fewer units and these would be more nearly equal in scope and influence. Departmental grouping and committee grouping need not, however, necessarily coincide.

Despite the superficial attractions of the grouping of functions, there are many inherent difficulties. One is the existence of statutory committees and statutory appointments of officers, but there are also non-legal difficulties which are less specific and harder to overcome. There is the 'professionalism' of chief officers which makes them reluctant to work under the control of another officer. There is also, in some authorities, a practical difficulty in the dispersal of the council's offices. A further problem is to secure officers with the necessary knowledge and breadth of vision to be able to carry responsibility for a large department. It is significant that, in a number of authorities, the increasing complexity of business has in fact led to a proliferation of departments rather than to a reduction in their numbers.

The obstacles to the amalgamation of departments are matched by difficulties at least as acute in amalgamating committees. There is the practical problem of avoiding a situation where the scope of a committee's functions becomes too wide for comprehension by members; in some cases the increasing complexity of business in recent years has actually resulted in the establishment of extra committees. The

major obstacle to the amalgamation of committees is, however, said to be the existence of a host of committee and sub-committee chairmen who identify themselves
closely with 'their' committee and are reluctant to see it abolished, even if it has
ceased to fulfil a useful purpose.

Despite these difficulties, we received suggestions from a number of officers and
members that the grouping of functions would have much to commend it and that,
apart from simplifying co-ordination, it would have incidental advantages; it would
encourage members to dissociate themselves from detail and to concentrate on
more fundamental issues and would also further the interests of those services at
present controlled by officers of less administrative experience, power and influence
than their colleagues in larger departments.

42 MAUD ON INTERNAL ORGANISATION: PROPOSALS

From *Maud, Vol.1: Report* (1967); by permission of H.M.S.O.

PROPOSALS FOR REFORM

The basic principles for internal organisation

132. One of our criticisms of the present internal organisation of local authorities is
that it is bound too much by a pre-set pattern which cannot be easily adapted to
changing circumstances. It is not our purpose therefore to draw a blue print for the
internal organisation of local authorities complete in every detail and to recommend
its imposition on them all. But there are certain basic principles for the internal
organisation of local authorities which are as appropriate to the large county
borough council as they are to a district authority. Our aim is to devise a new
pattern of organisation which we can confidently commend to authorities leaving
them free to adapt it to suit individual circumstances. In recommending to local
authorities a new structure for their internal organisation we have in mind the
following principles:

  (*a*) effective and efficient management under the direction and control of the
         members;
  (*b*) clear leadership and responsibility among both members and officers;
  (*c*) an organisation which presents to the public an intelligible system of govern-
         ment;
  (*d*) responsiveness to the needs of the public.
. . . . . .

151 *We recommend that local authorities consider a division of functions and
responsibilities between members and officers as follows:*

  (*a*) *Ultimate direction and control of the affairs of the authority to lie with the
         members.*

(b) *The members to take the key decisions on the objectives of the authority and on the plans to attain them.*

(c) *The members to review, periodically, progress and the performance of the services.*

(d) *The officers to provide the necessary staff work and advice so that members may set the objectives and take decisions on the means of attaining them.*

(e) *The officers to be responsible for the day-to-day administration of services, decisions on case work, and routine inspection and control.*

. . . . . .

158. *We recommend that local authorities establish a managing body, to be called 'the management board' composed of from five to nine members of the council.*

. . . . . .

161. If the management board is superimposed on the present committee system there will be grave danger of the management board being overwhelmed by submissions from the committees. But we intend that the management board should be part of a new organisation in which the principle that committees administer the services is replaced by the principle that day to day management is the responsibility of officers. It will be (as we show later) the Clerk's responsibility to ensure that the organisation of the officers is such that wherever possible issues are dealt with by them, that agenda are short and that business is properly presented with matters of principle taken before those of secondary importance.

162. *We recommend that the functions of the management board be:*

(a) *To formulate the principal objectives of the authority and to present them together with plans to attain them to the council for consideration and decision.*

(b) *To review progress and assess results on behalf of the council.*

(c) *To maintain, on behalf of the council, an overall supervision of the organisation of the authority and of its co-ordination and integration.*

(d) *To take decisions on behalf of the council which exceed the authority of the principal officers, and to recommend decisions to the council where authority has not been delegated to the management board.*

(e) *To be responsible for the presentation of business to the council subject always to the rights of members under standing orders.*

163. *Committees.* In paragraph 100 we emphasise the present confusion between the functions and responsibilities of members and those of officers; it has been our purpose to disentangle them and to point to a division of labour between them. It is in the work of the committees that the confusion is most marked. Reference has been made to the value of the traditional committee system in keeping members informed and in giving them an understanding of the working of the various services. These values are not to be lightly set aside. To remove committees entirely would be to isolate the management board and to insulate it from the views, grievances and aspirations of the public and from the generality of members . . .

164. . . . . We are in favour of the retention of committees in local government, but with a different role.

165. *We recommend that:*
(*a*) *Committees should not be directing or controlling bodies nor should they be concerned with routine administration.*
(*b*) *No committee should have more than 15 members (including co-opted members).*

166. *We recommend that committees be deliberative and representative bodies in the sense that:*
(*a*) *They make recommendations to the management board on the major objectives of the authority and study and recommend the means to attain these objectives; they examine new ideas which they and other organs have formulated.*
(*b*) *They have a duty to review progress on plans and programmes and on the operation of individual services as the management board does for the whole range of services.*
(*c*) *They consider the interests, reactions and criticisms of the public and convey them to the officers and if necessary to the management board.*
(*d*) *They consider any matters raised by their own members or referred to them by the management board.*

167. *We recommend that committees take executive decisions only in exceptional circumstances when the management board requires them to do this. These fields of decision-taking should be strictly defined by the management board and it should be made clear that the committees issue instructions to the officers only on these matters.*

168. It will be necessary for committees with the functions we have prescribed to take a broad view of the subjects with which they are concerned. There are real advantages if each committee deals with a group of similar or related services; it will make co-ordination easier and reduce the present tendency for the authority's work to be dispersed amongst a large number of service committees. A management board, in making proposals to a council on the committee structure, should group similar or related functions under one committee. This will have the effect of reducing the number of committees, and we believe that in an all-purpose authority it should be possible to reduce their number to about six. A reduction in the size of committees together with a drastic reduction in their number may well mean that some members will not be on any committee of the council. We do not regard this as inconsistent either with the new form of organisation we have in mind or with the functions of members as we have defined them. The member who does not serve on any committee will have more time to devote to the problems of his constituents. His importance as a member of council will be enhanced as we believe that more frequent meetings of the full council may well be necessary and at these meetings he will have opportunities to question and challenge the administration.

169. *We recommend that the number of committees of a local authority should be drastically reduced and that similar or related services should be grouped and allocated to one committee.*

170. *The Clerk and the other principal officers*. Reference is made in paragraph 96 to steps which have been taken in some local authorities to create a post of chief executive for the authority, either by adding to, or setting aside, the traditional role of the Clerk to an authority. Many witnesses deal with this aspect in their written and oral evidence. There is a diversity of opinion. An extreme view stresses the need for a manager in local government who would act like the American City Manager or the manager of a commercial organisation, a man who would formulate policy, co-ordinate its execution and also direct the authority's business. A more moderate view proposes that the chief administrative officer should be secretary to the authority's policy or executive committee and should be the policy co-ordinator. At the other extreme, it is held that the Clerk should remain much as now but with a status which makes him, *vis-a-vis* the other principal officers, something more than 'first among equals'.

. . . . . .

174. No amount of change in the designation of the title of Clerk, no amount of reinforcement of his position by statutory provision or by redefinition in terms and conditions of service will make a weak Clerk a strong one. What is required is a fresh understanding of his position and an acceptance of it; this can best be done by changes in the terms and conditions of service of other principal officers whereby they are required to recognise his position and to assist him, by continuous co-operation and consultation, to discharge his duties efficiently.

175. Apart from his co-ordinating function, we see the Clerk as the leader of his team of specialist colleagues and with their assistance and advice surveying the whole range of his authority's activities. He should be active in promoting innovations in the procedure and organisation of the authority and of its services.

176. Some of the written evidence submitted to us resists the idea of an effective manager in a local authority for two principal reasons —

(*a*) it would be inconsistent with democratic local government;

(*b*) professional principal officers should not be in a position of subordination to the Clerk or to the officer who holds the position of overall responsibility whatever he may be called.

177. We do not accept these views for the following reasons. We do not see the Clerk with his position reinforced on the lines we suggest as in any way usurping political responsibility; it is not as if powers would be handed over to him as they are to the American City Manager or even to the Eire Manager. The council should have forward planning done for it; it should not be faced with unco-ordinated advice from a number of principal officers; it should have one officer to whom it can turn as the responsible man to give co-ordinated advice, to ensure that its decisions are conveyed to the appropriate department and are carried out. With regard to the second objection, in our view no efficient Clerk at present, nor any efficient Clerk with the added powers and status which we recommend, would seek to give instructions to professional officers on actions where their professional skills are involved. We see the principal officers working together on those matters which transcend the purely professional and departmental considerations under the Clerk's

leadership and producing agreed and co-ordinated recommendations. We would certainly agree that where a principal officer is in disagreement with recommendations being put to the management board his dissenting opinion should be made known to the board and further that the principal officer should be heard. We would regard it as unfortunate if dissenting opinions and appeals had frequently to be heard as this would imply that the Clerk was failing in his duties as a leader, or that individual principal officers were failing as colleagues in seeking for agreed solutions. The remedy must lie with the council and management board in deciding what changes such a situation calls for amongst their officers.

178. It is clear that the Clerk will not be able to act in the way we recommend unless he enjoys the confidencè of both the management board and the team of principal officers. The council must be mindful of this and of the degree to which they consider a candidate has the capacity to engender this in making appointments to the post.

179. *We therefore recommend:*

(a) *That the Clerk be recognised as head of the authority's paid service, and have authority over the other principal officers so far as this is necessary for the efficient management and execution of the authority's functions.*

(b) *That the Clerk be responsible to the management board and through it to the council.*

(c) *That the principal officers be responsible to the council through the Clerk and their terms and conditions of service be such that the Clerk's position and their own position are made clear.*

180. *We recommend that the duties of the Clerk include ensuring:*

(a) *The effectiveness and efficiency of the organisation and the co-ordination (and integration where necessary) of its activities.*

(b) *That the management board is adequately serviced to carry out its responsibilities by providing co-ordinated and integrated staff work and seeing that its decisions and those of the council are implemented.*

(c) *That effective control systems are devised and applied.*

(d) *That, under his leadership, principal officers work as a team, that able officers are given opportunities for self-development with responsibilities to match their talents, and that initiative and innovation are encouraged.*

(e) *That secretarial services are provided for all committees.*

(f) *That an effective establishment organisation is set up to secure economy in the use of manpower.*

181. . . . . We endorse the view of the Committee on Staffing and we join with them in *recommending that Clerkships should be open to people of all professions and occupations.*

182. *We recommend that the principal officers:*

(a) *Work as members of a team of managers and specialist advisers and see that the same approach is adopted by their staff at all levels.*

(b) *Be responsible to the council through the Clerk for the efficient and effective* running of the services provided by the departments of which they are the heads.

(c) *Execute the instructions of the council and of the management board and take such decisions as are necessary.*

(d) *Advise the management board and the committees as necessary and provide the necessary staff work together with professional and technical advice as requested.*

(e) *Be active in promoting innovation and improvements throughout the authority.*

. . . . . .

210. *We recommend that the members of the management board should not be regarded as responsible individually for the running of particular services or departments; this is the responsibility of the officers.*

211. *We further recommend that:*

(a) *Individual members of a management board have special spheres of interest and speak on them.*

(b) *Emphasis be placed on the collective responsibility of the management board for what they decide as a majority and not on the individual responsibility of a member.*

(c) *Provision be made for principal officers to consult members of the management board but this process must not be allowed to distort the organisation pattern we have suggested . . . The relationship between members of the management board and principal officers should not result in the Clerk being by-passed nor should the management board member break the unity of the board by acting independently . . .*

. . . . . .

Management board and party politics

234. At present committees are committees of the council and therefore they represent broadly the party composition of the council. The research report shows that the practice of appointing chairmen of committees exclusively from the majority party although not universal is frequent. It is a short step for the chairmen of committees under present arrangements to constitute a form of 'cabinet'. In paragraph 159 we imply that the management board should be selected or elected by the council. If our proposals for the internal organisation of a local authority are followed, there will be a change in the character of committees and a concentration of power in the management board. Many will see in this an invitation to the majority party to use its majority in the council to ensure that all seats on the management board are occupied by its members.

235. Two points of view emerge. On the one hand, it can be argued that party politics are part of the fabric of public life and the essence of party politics is conviction on certain principles, loyalty to a party's doctrines and the taking of sides.

The organization diagram

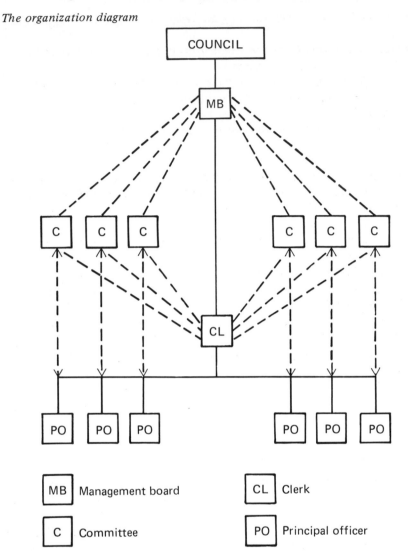

MB | Management board

C | Committee

CL | Clerk

PO | Principal officer

On this basis the members of the majority party might claim that they alone should serve on the management board where policy decisions will be taken. It can be further argued that as the management board would be an officially appointed committee of the council, the party leaders who form its membership could properly have the advantage of the advice of officers in taking decisions. At present, meeting as a party group, this is denied them. If the management board is composed of members of both the majority and minority parties, the real decisions are likely to be taken at private meetings of the leaders of the majority group and without the benefit of advice from officers.

236. On the other hand it can be argued that if the management board is monopolised by the majority party it will involve the Clerk and the other principal officers in association with and responsibility to a party majority and not, as now, to the council itself and all its members. If the majority party remains in power for a protracted period, members of the minority party will not be able to share in the responsibilities of the authority and able men and women sponsored by the minority party may be deterred from standing. Where the balance is fairly even, there are obvious advantages in the minority party being in touch with affairs so that they can assume responsibility when called upon. Moreover, as much of the work of a local authority is quite independent of party politics it can be strongly argued that the welfare of the community is best served and is seen to be best served if members of all parties are given an opportunity of contributing to its management. Such a development would remove one of the more divisive factors in local government.

237. The success of a management board will depend on its maintaining the confidence of the council. On balance we believe that the advantage lies in allowing minority parties to be represented on the management board, but the responsibility of the majority party for effective control must of course remain.

43 MAUD ON INTERNAL ORGANISATION: WHEATLEY'S ALTERNATIVE

From *Maud, Vol.1: Report: Memorandum of Dissent by Sir Andrew Wheatley* (1967); by permission of H.M.S.O.

FUNCTIONS OF THE MANAGEMENT BOARD AND OF COMMITTEES

Chapter 3, *paragraph* 162 (*d*) that the management board take decisions on behalf of the council which exceed the authority of the principal officers and recommend decisions to the council where authority has not been delegated to the management board.

Chapter 3, *paragraph* 162 (*e*) that the management board be responsible for the presentation of business to the council.

Chapter 3, *paragraph* 165 that committees should not be directing or controlling bodies.

Chapter 3, *paragraph* 166 that committees should be deliberative and representative bodies.

Chapter 3, *paragraph* 167 that committees only take executive decisions in exceptional circumstances when the management board requires them to do this.

In my view these proposals will vest far too much power in the small number of members who will be members of the management board, and will deprive the great majority of the members of the council of the opportunity of participating effectively in the formulation of policy and the development of the services which are the responsibility of local government. Local government is fundamentally a means of associating representatives elected by the people with government, and, so far from detracting from it, everything should be done to encourage it.

We are by our terms of reference called upon to consider how local government might best continue to attract people of the calibre necessary to ensure its maximum effectiveness. The elected members are by far the most important element in local government. In my experience most of them offer themselves for election because they wish to participate in, and contribute to the development of, services of great importance to the community which are entrusted to local government. Unless the members as a whole are given a worthwhile part to play, a function which must inevitably involve direct participation in formulation of policy, local government will not attract members of the quality that are needed. The prospect of becoming a member of the management board in ten or 15 years time is not a sufficient incentive. The local authorities which operate most effectively are those in which the responsibilities are shared as broadly as possible among the members as a whole. This gives the members both the feeling that the work to which they give their time is worthwhile, and a sense of belonging to the council. Indeed where dissatisfaction and discontent are found, the reasons are usually that a place cannot be found for a member on the committee whose work interests him most.

The committee system is characteristic of local government, and indeed by far the greater part of the work of local government is done in committees. Without the committee system local government could not work, and there is much in it which is excellent. The analogy with the central government is a false one, because it would be impossible to associate all the individual members of Parliament with decision taking, as has become the practice in local government. I accept the need for a strong management board to co-ordinate the whole range of activities of the council, something which has hitherto been lacking in many authorities. It seems to me however to be essential that the management board should not usurp the functions of the committees if local government is to operate satisfactorily.

I would retain standing committees, investing them with executive powers to manage the services for which they were responsible (but not to authorise every item involving revenue expenditure), with the duty to report to the council on the discharge of their functions; but on any major issue of policy or new scheme involving capital expenditure they should first report to the management board. It would be the responsibility of the management board to ensure that any new proposal of this sort did not conflict with the activities of the council in other directions. No doubt a standing committee, before reporting to the council, would consider any views that might be expressed by the management board, but I see no reason why, in the last resort, if agreement were not reached, both the standing committee and the management board should not report to the council, each expressing their views on the proposal, and explaining their reasons, leaving it to the council to come to a conclusion and take the decision on which view should prevail. Under the system which is recommended by my colleagues the management board would alone report to the council and none of the committees would have the opportunity of making their views known in writing before the meeting of the council. Fair though the management board would, no doubt, wish to be, in the case of a difference of opinion, they would start with the advantage of being the only body able to present arguments in writing for consideration by the members before the meeting of the council.

In associating committees of the council with the formulation and execution of policy, albeit effectively co-ordinated, a greater number of members of the council would be better informed of the issues which were involved and, instead of leaving the responsibility upon an individual member of the management board to carry an uninformed council with him, the chairman of the committee concerned would be able to look for the support of the members of his committee in seeking to persuade the council to come to the right decision. In the great majority of cases, he would have the support of the management board.

There is a very real danger in the scheme recommended by the Committee that the members of the management board may become too remote and detached from the members of the council as a whole.

The diagram . . . I would amend so that it takes the . . . form [shown] .

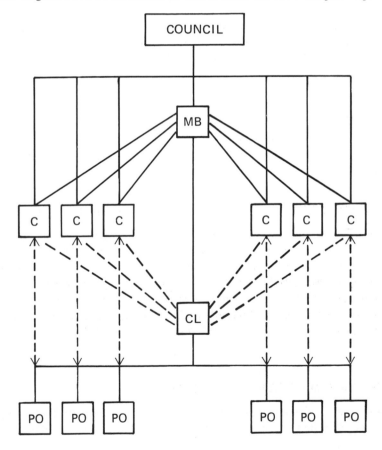

In my view this would have the following advantages:

(i)   It would enable the management board to play an effective part in co-ordinating the development and administration of the services as a whole.

(ii)   It would give the standing committees the opportunity of reporting direct to the council.

(iii)   It would enable the chairman elected by the committee to put the committee's point of view to the council.

(iv)   It would give the members of the committees a much greater sense of participating than would be the case if the committees were only advisory. The fact that members of the council had the opportunity of participating in this way would give them a far greater sense of belonging to and being members of a corporate body.

(v)   It would provide a much more healthy balance of power and prevent the management board becoming too autocratic and remote.

(vi)   It would be a much more effective method of spreading the burden of the work and would not overwhelm the members of the management board by compelling them to settle every question arising on the execution of the council's policy.

(vii)   It would enable committees, e.g. planning, to deal by delegation with statutory functions conferred upon the council.

(viii) It would lead to a much more healthy and successful system of local government.

44 REDCLIFFE-MAUD ON MANAGEMENT

From *Redcliffe-Maud, Vol.1: Report* (Cmnd. 4040, 1969); by permission of H.M.S.O.

THE NEW MAIN AUTHORITIES AND INTERNAL MANAGEMENT

482. The main authorities that we propose — unitary, metropolitan and metropolitan district — will be complex, large-scale organisations. Only five of the 61 unitary and metropolitan authorities and only four of the 20 metropolitan districts have populations below 250,000. Seven of the new authorities will have populations above a million, and 11 of them populations between 750,000 and a million. An authority of one million may well on present standards have a total staff of some 50,000 (including teachers) and one of 350,000 a staff of 18,000.

. . . . . .

THE CASE FOR SOME CENTRAL COMMITTEE

486. We are firmly of the opinion that the new main authorities must have a central committee, board or body of some kind, by whatever name it may be called. Local

Government has moved a long way from the days when its task was to provide a number of isolated services. Authorities are now responsible for a great deal of the context in which the lives of citizens are lived. Control of the physical environment, economic development, collaboration with other agencies of all kinds public and private, as well as the provision of local services, are now their business. They have a duty positively to promote the welfare of the community. Many of their decisions, therefore, transcend the interests of a single department. Thus, for example, physical planning determines the environment for all functions, while the close ties between planning, traffic and housing, between the various personal social services, and between them and education and housing, are of great significance. The determination of coherent objectives is of itself sufficient to make imperative a focal centre within each authority where a general view can be developed.

487. But this is only the beginning. Policy objectives have to be translated into programmes, priorities must be settled and projects dovetailed. Local authorities are constantly faced with the need to curtail schemes and with choices between competing claims. Settled programmes have to be controlled, adapted and eventually appraised – processes which themselves call for a central vantage point.

. . . . . .

489. Each local authority should work out the form most suited to its particular requirements, but the case is surely cast-iron for a central body to advise the council on its strategy and priorities, co-ordinate the policies and work of the service committees, and ensure that the best managerial methods are adopted in each department and in the work of the council as a whole.

FUNDAMENTAL FEATURES OF A CENTRAL COMMITTEE

490. The central committee should have positive functions and should not merely scrutinise and harmonise proposals coming from elsewhere. It should be reponsible for advising the council on general development, the physical plan and the allocation of resources (i.e. the revenue and capital budgets). As watchdog of the corporate point of view, it would effect co-ordination and where necessary unify procedures. It would work out the internal administrative arrangements, including the duties of departments. Establishment matters would fall to it, though with maximum delegation to departments, especially in making appointments. It would be responsible for providing departments with all necessary management aids and for seeing that these were fully used.

491. However, the nature of local government's work sets limits to the degree of centralisation which is either possible or desirable. The greater part of the effort within a local authority must be concerned with individual services. It is within the departments that the technical work is done, and technical progress generated; it follows that it is in the committees with which departments work that a great deal of the pressure for improvements must develop.

492. Working in conjunction with the central committee there must therefore be a number of committees. They should be many fewer in number than at present but

they would be highly influential. Each committee would have a specialist interest in the services under its wing. All business of importance relevant to its services would be first discussed at its meetings and it would be informed of all proposals, whatever their origin, that might affect its business. Subject to the council's general objectives, committees would thus be the main initiators of policy for individual services . . .

. . . . . .

494. We believe that each of the new authorities should work out for itself the precise position of the central committee and the division of duties between that committee and the service committees. Some may prefer the model put forward by the Management Committee which, in addition to covering the points we have put forward, provided for chief officers to refer the day-to-day problems upon which they needed advice to the central committee (which they termed a board) or to one of its members, rather than to the service committee. Others, while adopting a central committee, may wish to make chairmen of service committees the point of reference for officers needing advice. The largest authorities might lean more towards the quasi-ministerial system of the Greater London Council. No universal method of applying the principle of a central committee can be prescribed. The size of the authorities, their nature, the social and other circumstances of the area and local political traditions will all play a part in determining the solution. We hope that there will be a wide variety of experiment.

. . . . . .

THE TEAM OF CHIEF OFFICERS

500. As recommended by the Management and Staffing Committees, each authority should have a clerk or chief executive who should be the official head of its staff. The clerk should be chosen solely on the grounds of his ability, and the post should be open to members of all professions, including the lay administrator. We would hope and expect that appointments would sometimes be made from the civil service and from industry.

501. The clerk would act as the leader of a team of chief officers, which would form the central management group at official level. Few major decisions about the development of services can be taken in isolation. Besides applying their special knowledge in the administration of their own departments, chief officers should be jointly responsible, under the clerk's chairmanship, for considering the council's general problems and for co-ordinating action to solve them. This team of chief officers will be the counterpart, at official level, of the central committee at councillor level. Its success will depend on harnessing the enthusiasm of the specialist to the needs of central management.

45 THE BAINS REPORT

From *The Bains Report* (1972); by permission of H.M.S.O. For a full account of the impact of Bains on local authority practice, see '*The Organisation of Local Authorities in England and Wales, 1967–75*', Institute of Local Government Studies, University of Birmingham.

THE ELECTED MEMBERS AND OFFICERS

The Maud Committee exploded the myth of policy being a matter for the elected members and administration for officers and it is disturbing to find, five years later, that many members and officers still see this as a sufficient description of their respective roles and one behind which they can shelter as occasion requires. It is perhaps even more disturbing to see how a rigid interpretation of the role of one or the other defeats any attempt to create a sense of unity of purpose within an authority.

We believe that if local government is to have any chance of achieving a corporate approach to its affairs members and officers must both recognise that neither can regard any area of the authority's work and administration as exclusively theirs.

Officers must accept that members have a legitimate interest in the day to day administration of cases involving their constituents and that it is frequently only a lack of information which causes them to pursue such matters into the administrative machine.

Members must equally realise that the skilled professional officer is not just a servant who is paid to do as he is told. We do not dispute that the major policy decisions must be taken by the elected members, but the officers have a role to play in the stimulation and formulation of policy and in seeing that the members have available the necessary advice and evaluation to enable them to make the best decisions . . .

. . . . . .

The elected member – his aims and objectives

The Maud Report recognised . . . that members do not all achieve satisfaction from the same type of role within the authority and drew attention specifically to the distinction between broad policy matters and work relating to individual persons.

We believe that members of local authorities have a wide diversity of aims and interests. In addition to those who wish to take part in broad policy decisions there are, for example:

(i)   those interested in the welfare type of activity;

(ii)   those who see it as their role to 'manage' the local authority, often by rigid application of commercial principles;

(iii) those who wish to serve the community, in the general sense;

(iv) those whose main objective is to limit spending by the authority.

. . . . . .

If members have these diverse aims, it seems to us to be impossible to cast them all in the same role. We suggest that the structure of the authority should be such as to provide members with work of the appropriate type and should encourage them to identify for themselves the area in which they wish to work.

We have received a considerable volume of evidence about the role of the elected member, much of which follows the general principles outlined in the Maud Report that:

(a) ultimate direction and control of the affairs of the authority should lie with the members;

(b) the members should take the key decisions on the objectives of the authority and on the plans to attain them;

(c) the members should keep under review the progress and performance of the services.

We would not wish to dissent from the view that all of these are functions proper to members, but, as we have already implied we doubt whether it is possible to divide the total management process into two separate halves, one for members and the other for officers. If it is to the community that local government is accountable for the effectiveness of its operations, then it is unlikely that one can rule out the elected representatives of that community from any particular part of the management process.

Delegation to officers

It has been suggested that extensive delegation to officers is in some way undemocratic, but we do not accept this, provided that the terms of delegation are clear and specific. For example, in many authorities the principles under which the allocation of housing is to be made are laid down by the Housing Committee and the Housing Manager then operates the system within those principles under delegated powers. There are, however, other authorities where the members make the allocation on the principle that it would be undemocratic to leave the matter to an officer. This we believe generally to be inefficient, not in the sense that the members' decisions are wrong, but because the process will inevitably be slower and because the knowledge and skill of a trained officer are not being properly used. The democratic principle is, in our view, protected by the right of members to withdraw or amend the powers given to the officer.

. . . . . .

We do not believe that delegated authority, once given, requires a constant stream of reports back to the delegating committee. The officer's task is to get on with the job which he has been given to do and having given him the necessary powers the committee should allow him to exercise them according to his own judgement. He is, of course, accountable for the decisions which he takes, but such accountability in our view, should be checked by review and investigation techniques, where the decision as to the subject of review rests with the reviewing body and is not decided by what is, or is not, included in routine written reports.

An officer working under delegated powers needs, nevertheless, to keep in close touch with the committee responsible for the function which he is performing. We have deliberately avoided using the phrase 'his committee' despite its admirable brevity because we do not believe that such a phrase is compatible with the concept of a corporate approach; the officer is responsible to the Council for his actions, through the agency of the appropriate committee(s). It is in this area of informal contact between committee meetings that there is a need for a source of advice on the sensitive issues which inevitably arise in the course of day to day administration and which the officer must recognise as requiring member participation.

. . . . . .

A number of authorities and others submitting evidence to us have raised the question of advice from officers to party groups. This problem arises specifically when the central policy and resources committee, whatever its title, is a bi-partisan committee. In such circumstances the critical decisions are normally taken by the majority party group before the committee meets and their decisions are taken in the absence of and often without the benefit of advice from the officers. We believe that the advice of officers must be available wherever the effective decisions are taken and if it is the party group which makes these decisions then a way must be found of making officers' advice available. This might be done through a representative group of majority party members, who would themselves be responsible for briefing the group meeting. It follows, in our view, that similar facilities should be afforded to the opposition party(ies).

The Member's Role: organisational implications

. . . . . .

Perhaps the first point to establish is that a change in structure does not necessarily result in a change in management process, though it may well facilitate such a change. To illustrate the point, we have received evidence from a number of authorities who have established a central policy committee, though it may be called a management committee or some other title. We have also had the opportunity of discussing the work of such committees with members and officers in the authorities which we have visited. In a number of authorities we have found that the so-called policy committee is in fact not concerned with the central policy and strategic decisions at all. In some cases it has become what one member called 'the waste paper basket of the Council', operating as a low-key general purposes committee; in others it is responsible for any matter which comes up between meetings of other committees. What has happened in these authorities is that the structure has been changed, but the management process has not.

. . . . . .

The Policy and Resources Committee

As we have already said, the Council is the ultimate decision-making body of the authority, and the broad policy decisions which themselves determine the overall plan for the community should be taken by the Council. In order to take those

decisions the Council needs comprehensive and co-ordinated advice on the implications for the community and we believe that this function requires the creation
of a central policy committee. Such a committee will aid the Council in setting its
objectives and priorities and, once the major policy decisions have been taken, will
be instrumental in co-ordinating and controlling the implementation of those
decisions. It would have a particular role to play in the formulation of the structure plan for the area, either directly in a county or by way of consultation in a
district.

This 'Policy and Resources Committee' as we have chosen to call it, would, as its
name implies, have ultimate responsibility under the Council for the major resources
of the authority, finance, manpower and land (with which we include buildings).
The central control of finance has long been accepted and we believe that the dual
role of the policy and resources committee in advising the Council on future plans
and objectives and in co-ordinating the implementation of those plans, necessitates
overall control of the other major resources . . .

Resource sub-committees

In each of these areas of finance, manpower and land it is important that the policy
and resources committee should deal only with matters of major importance, not,
for example, with trivial questions of expenditure. The more routine matters
requiring member participation should be dealt with by three resource sub-
committees each dealing respectively with one of the three main resources.
. . . . . .
The membership of the three resource sub-committees should not be limited to
those who are members of the policy and resources committee. They will play a
substantial part in the corporate management processes of the authority and thus
provide an excellent opportunity for members to become familiar with and take
part in the management of the authority as a whole. The presence of 'back bench'
members will also go some way to counter any suggestion that all power is concentrated in the hands of the members of the policy and resources committee. For
these reasons we recommend that a substantial proportion of members of the sub-
committees should not be members of the parent committee. This form of organisation will enable members of operational committees to see and appreciate the
need for a corporate approach towards the policy and resources of the authority. It
is essential however, that the chairmen of the sub-committees should be members
of the main policy and resources committee.

If it is the responsibility of the policy and resources committee to control the
broad allocation of the various resources of the Council, it must also have the overall authority to create the management and review processes which are necessary to
ensure that those resources, once allocated, are properly used. For this purpose the
committee will need to keep the organisation structure and management processes
of the authority under continuous review and see that they keep pace with the
demands made upon them.

Monitoring and review — The Performance Review Sub-Committee

As far as the review processes are concerned, the regular monitoring and review of programmes against defined objectives is a responsibility which must rest primarily on the members of the particular programme committee. That committee should ensure that its reviews are systematic and thorough and should satisfy itself that necessary action is taken to deal with any variation in or from the approved programme. We believe, however, that some form of independent review process should also be considered. What we have in mind is a body of members within each authority rather like the Public Accounts Committee. We believe that a watchdog body of this sort, with the standing and formal authority to make detailed investigation into any project, department, or area of activity would provide an extremely useful service to management. In our view that standing and authority is most likely to be derived from a close link with the policy and resources committee. The role of such a body, as we see it, is very much complementary to those of the resource sub-committees which we have recommended earlier and we suggest that it should in fact be a fourth sub-committee of that committee. It would therefore be chaired by a member of the parent committee. Other members need not be members of the parent committee, but would be called upon according to the knowledge, skills or experience which they could bring to bear upon the area being examined. They would include representatives of the appropriate committee. Service upon such a body would provide an excellent opportunity for the development and involvement of some of the younger members. We envisage that the 'Performance Review Sub-Committee' would submit its report to the policy and resources committee and that the appropriate committee and department would have the opportunity to comment upon this report.

. . . . . .

Summary

1. The Council should not operate solely as a decision-making body. It should also have a role as a policy formulating and debating forum.
2. Each authority should establish a Policy and Resources Committee to provide co-ordinated advice to the Council in the setting of its plans, objectives and priorities. The Committee should also exercise overall control over the major resources of the authority and co-ordinate and control the implementation of the Council's programmes.
3. Resource sub-committees of the Policy and Resources Committee should exercise day to day control over staff, finance and land. A fourth sub-committee would operate as a performance review body with the power to investigate any project, department, or area of activity.
4. Membership of the Policy and Resources Committee should not be limited to the chairmen of other committees. The committee should include other members, including, wherever possible, members of the opposition party.

5. The committee structure of the authority should be linked to the objectives of the authority and the programmes necessary to achieve those objectives, rather than to the provision of particular services. Each programme committee should be serviced by the skills and experience of appropriate departments.

6. There appears to be little advantage from the management or administrative viewpoint, in the creation of area committees operating under delegated authority.

7. Committees should make a realistic and critical examination of alternatives before taking final decisions. As with the full Council, committees should be encouraged to hold debates and discussions without the need for formal decisions at the conclusion.

8. Chairmen of committees exercise great influence over the running of the authority and should be chosen with this in mind.

9. Within programme areas, working groups of members should be set up without the constraints of formal sub-committees, in order to provide members with the opportunity to identify themselves with areas of activity in which they have a particular interest and also to provide officers with an immediate point of reference to opinion of elected members.

Terms of reference for a Policy and Resources Committee

a. To guide the Council in the formulation of its corporate plan of objectives and priorities and for this purpose to recommend to the council such forward programmes and other steps as may be necessary to achieve those objectives, either in whole or in part, during specific time spans. For this purpose to consider the broad social and economic needs of the authority and matters of comprehensive importance to the area including the contents of structure plans. To advise the Council generally as to its financial and economic policies.

b. Without prejudice to the duties and responsibilities of the programme committees, to review the effectiveness of all the Council's work and the standards and levels of service provided. To identify the need for new services and to keep under review the necessity for existing ones.

c. To submit to the Council concurrent reports with the programme committees upon new policies or changes in policy formulated by such committees, particularly those which may have significant impact upon the corporate plan or the resources of the Council.

d. To be responsible for allocating and controlling the financial, manpower and land resources of the Council.

e. To ensure that the organisation and management processes of the council are designed to make the most effective contribution to the achievement of the Council's objectives. To keep them under review in the light of changing circumstances, making recommendations as necessary for change in either the committee or departmental structure, or the distribution of functions and responsibilities.

f. To be concerned together with the appropriate programme committee in the appointment of Heads of Departments and any Deputies.

. . . . . .

THE ORGANISATION AT OFFICER LEVEL

The Chief Executive

The Maud Committee recommended that there should be one person recognised as the head of the authority's paid service who should have authority over the principal officers so far as this is necessary for the efficient management and execution of the authority's functions. We subscribe to this view . . .

. . . . . .

    The range of issues and problems facing any local authority is too numerous and varied for the Chief Executive to grasp in detail and heads of departments must therefore retain the responsibility for the effective and efficient running of the service for which their departments are responsible. This means that the Chief Executive must act primarily as the leader of a team of Chief Officers and co-ordinator of activities. In that capacity he must ensure that the resources and organisation of the authority are utilised effectively towards the attainment of the authority's objectives. In addition he is the Council's principal adviser on matters of general policy and as first officer has a particular role to play as the Council's representative in contacts outside the authority.

. . . . . .

Summary

1. The officer structure of the new local authorities must be founded upon the existing professional base, not least because the best potential managers in the short and medium term are to be found already established in the professions of local government.
2. Each authority should appoint a Chief Executive to act as leader of the officers of the authority and principal adviser to the Council on matters of general policy.
3. The post of Chief Executive should be open to officers of any or no profession. The qualities of the man himself are more important than his profession or academic background.
4. In order to provide young officers of potential with the broad management experience needed for the development of future Chief Executives serious consideration should be given to 'horizontal' movement between departments at appropriate points in their careers.
5. The Chief Executive should be free of specific departmental responsibilities.
6. There should be no formal appointment of a full time Deputy Chief Executive.
7. Each authority should establish a Management Team of Principal Chief Officers whose corporate identity should be recognised formally within the management structure.
8. The Management Team should be responsible, under the Chief Executive's leader-

ship, for the preparation of plans and programmes in connection with the long-term objectives of the Council and for the general co-ordination of the implementation of those plans.

9. As officers reach more senior positions, advancement should depend progressively more upon general management ability. At Chief Officer level management skills are at least as important as professional skills and appointments should be made on that basis.

10. Chief Officers should be given an annual appraisal of their performance, possibly by the Performance Review sub-committee advised by the Chief Executive. The latter should be appraised annually by the Policy and Resources Committee.

11. The justification for a deputy for every Chief Officer is open to considerable doubt. Any such post should be kept under review to ensure that it is essential.

12. The departmental structure should continue to be based upon the services required by the Council in order to fulfil its plans and objectives. The traditional one department—one committee link should be broken, thus aiding the development of a corporate rather than departmental approach to management.

13. There appear to be substantial problems inherent in grouping departments together under 'directors', particularly if those directors exercise a co-ordinating role only.

14. There is little point in forcing efficiently run departments into illogical groupings merely to provide an even balance of work between one director and another. Some departments, particularly those with a 'staff' rather than a 'line' function, may well be more effective if left alone.

15. Multi-disciplinary working groups of officers should be set up to service the programme committees.

16. Area offices, operating under clearly defined delegated powers, will be required in many authorities. Wherever possible, area boundaries should coincide with boundaries of the new districts.

. . . . . .

Job specification for a Chief Executive

1. The Chief Executive is the head of the Council's paid service and shall have authority over all other officers so far as this is necessary for the efficient management and execution of the Council's functions.

2. He is the leader of the officers' management team and through the Policy and Resources Committee, the Council's principal adviser on matters of general policy. As such it is his responsibility to secure co-ordination of advice on the forward planning of objectives and services and to lead the management team in securing a corporate approach to the affairs of the authority generally.

3. Through his leadership of the officers' management team he is responsible for the efficient and effective implementation of the Council's programmes and policies and for securing that the resources of the authority are most effectively deployed towards those ends.

4. Similarly he shall keep under review the organisation and administration of the authority and shall make recommendations to the Council through the Policy and Resources Committee if he considers that major changes are required in the interests of effective management.

5. As head of the paid service it is his responsibility to ensure that effective and equitable manpower policies are developed and implemented throughout all departments of the authority in the interests of both the authority and the staff.

6. He is responsible for the maintenance of good internal and external relations.

THE NEW AUTHORITIES: FUNCTIONS AND POSSIBLE MANAGEMENT STRUCTURES

. . . . . .

It is not our intention to lay down one structure which all authorities should adopt, but everything that has gone before in this report leads inevitably to certain basic structural features which we recommend should be common to all authorities.

The first of these is the Policy and Resources Committee, supported by its four sub-committees, viz:

Finance — responsible for day to day finance matters.

Personnel — responsible for establishment and personnel activities.

Land — responsible for questions of land/building acquisition, utilisation and disposal.

Performance — responsible for the monitoring of results against objectives and
Review   appraisal of standards, calling committees and officials to account . . .

The other important common feature at member level does not appear in the structure diagrams which follow. We have referred on a number of occasions to informal groups of members being set up for particular purposes both within and between programme areas. By their very nature these groups are not part of the formal structure of the authority, but the structures which we suggest will provide ample opportunity for such groups to be created.

At officer level too there are similar common features. The Chief Executive, supported by his management team, is basic to our conception of the management process in the new authorities and appears, therefore, in each of our diagrams.

The framework within which we have designed our structure is depicted in outline in . . . diagrams 1(a) and 1(b).

. . . . . .

The non-metropolitan county

The first type of authority which we consider is the non-metropolitan county, and one possible committee structure is illustrated in diagram 2(a) . . .

. . . . . .

One possible departmental structure associated with the committee structure in diagram 2(a) is shown in diagram 2(b) . . .

In this structure, there are no 'directors' and the Principal Chief Officers do not have authority over other Chief Officers. The latter would have direct access to the appropriate committee(s) but on major matters would go through the management team. They would be called in to assist the management team on matters within their sphere of responsibility. The diagram in fact represents no more than an array of possible departments with an indication of which Chief Officers are likely to be members of the management team. It is not intended to carry any implications about the relative positions of the various Chief Officers shown, each of whom is directly responsible to the Chief Executive.

. . . . . .

In diagram 2(c) we illustrate an alternative departmental structure in which some departments are grouped together under directors . . .

. . . . . .

The Metropolitan County

The role of the metropolitan county is likely to be in many ways different from that of its non-metropolitan counterpart. On the one hand it has fewer statutory functions in its own right, and on the other it has a far more compact area with problems and needs which, generally speaking, are far more likely to be common right across the county.

The first of these factors means that the committee structure required for the exercise of the council's statutory functions is extremely simple, as diagram 3(a) indicates . . .

. . . . . .

Our comments about the Planning and Transportation Committee in the non-metropolitan county . . . apply equally to the metropolitan county. The Council is, of course, also the Passenger Transport Authority and we have therefore illustrated this role in our diagram.

In this structure we have excluded many of the functions exercisable concurrently with the metropolitan districts, particularly those falling within the broad amenity/recreation heading. We suggest that in metropolitan areas particularly such functions will be more appropriate to the district level . . .

At first sight, therefore, the metropolitan county would appear to have a limited range of tasks, particularly at member level, though of course the two committees referred to in the preceding paragraphs cover very important functions. We suggest, however, that . . . the metropolitan county is particularly well placed to promote and co-ordinate a total approach to the substantial urban problems of its area and that the county should as and when required set up groups of members to examine and report back on particular needs and problems. In the first place such groups would report back to the Policy and Resources Committee of the county, but their findings would clearly be fruitful subjects for discussion at the joint county/district policy committee.

A possible departmental structure would be that shown in diagram 3(b).

We do not show any alternative structure for the metropolitan county because the range of statutory functions does not in our view justify any grouping of departments under directors. We envisage, therefore, that the basic structure will be on the lines which we have illustrated.

. . . . . .

The Chief Executive of a strategic planning authority like the metropolitan county is perhaps more likely to have an engineering or planning background than in other authorities, but even if he is professionally qualified in one of these fields he should not have particular responsibility for those areas of the authority's affairs.

The Metropolitan District

In the metropolitan district, analysis of the statutory functions suggests that there would be six major areas of activity, viz:

> Development
> Housing
> Social Services
> Education
> Leisure
> Environmental Health

In districts where the substantial redevelopment and refurbishing of an outworn area is a major problem, it would be possible to argue that the development and housing functions are so interrelated that they should both be within the sphere of responsibility of one committee. Generally speaking, however, we would envisage separate committees and the structure illustrated in diagram 4(a) reflects this view.

. . . . . .

The departmental structure follows broadly the same pattern as that shown in earlier diagrams for the non-metropolitan county.

Diagram 4(b) illustrates the type of structure likely to be appropriate where there is no grouping of departments under directors and diagram 4(c) shows a 'directorate' structure . . .

We believe that the Chief Housing Officer (diagram 4b) and the Director of Housing (diagram 4c) should in each case be responsible for the total housing function, including management, assessment of need, improvement, slum clearance and any advisory service. In order to carry out these functions they would use the services of the appropriate specialist officers of other departments.

The Non-Metropolitan District

The allocation of functions of non-metropolitan districts suggests that there might be either three or four programme committees. In the ordinary way we can see a logical division into three programmes but the size and/or special characteristics of some districts suggest that four committees might be required. An additional committee may be required in those districts which will retain responsibility for existing passenger transport undertakings.

In diagram 5(a) we illustrate a possible committee structure containing three committees. In that structure the allocation of main functions between the committees is:

Housing Services	Housing Management	
	Maintenance	
	Improvement	
	Assessment of Future Need	
	Advisory Service	
	Slum Clearance	
	House Purchase Loans	
Development/	Local Plans and Development	
Leisure Services	Development Control	
	Land Use	Development
	Derelict Land	
	Building Regulations	
	Recreation and Tourism	
	Entertainments	Leisure & Recreation
	Museums	
	Commons	
Environmental	Highways	
Health and	Litter	
Control	Coast Protection	
	Land Drainage	Control/Protection
	Markets	
	Home Safety	
	Licensing & Registration	
	Food Safety & Hygiene	
	Refuse Collection	
	Local Sewers	
	Clean Air	
	Noise	
	Nuisances	Health
	Offensive Trades	
	Health Education	
	Pollution Control	
	Cemeteries & Mortuaries	
	Conveniences	

In this structure it is suggested that there might be established two working groups of members for each of the programme committees. The two areas of activity in the Housing Services Committee might, for example, be the public and private aspects of housing. In the other two committees the areas of activity are as shown in the list of functions in the preceding paragraph.

In the alternative structure in diagram 5(b) the major difference would be the creation of a separate Recreation and Amenities Committee and the allocation of the highways and litter control functions to the Development Services Committee.

At departmental level we feel that there are a number of possible permutations, because of the wide range in size and type of district. We are agreed that each district will require the following officers:

Chief Executive
Chief Housing Officer
Chief Environmental Health Officer
Treasurer (or Chief Financial Officer)
Secretary.

In addition districts will require some or all of the following skills:

Architecture
Engineering
Estates and Valuation
Law
Planning

and in some of the larger districts it may be necessary for each to be represented by a Chief Officer heading his own department. In others it may be that there will be scope for the dually-qualified man to head a department combining two skills and in yet others the requirement may depend upon the arrangements made between district and county for the discharge of particular functions. Some districts may find it convenient to use the services of private practitioners.

Such is the wide variety in the size and nature of districts that it may be necessary to appoint other Chief Officers, like Passenger Transport Manager or Chief Amenities and Recreation Officer. Diagram 5(c) represents the position in the largest district. In diagram 5(d) which might represent medium sized and smaller districts, the general structure is very similar, but a Chief Technical Officer heads a department in which all design and construction work and the management of the authority's labour force might be located, together with various other appropriate services.

Fig. 1(a) *Outline Committee Structure*

Fig. 1(b) *Outline Departmental Structure*

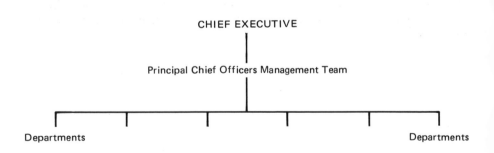

Fig. 2(a) *Committee Structure – Non-Metropolitan County*

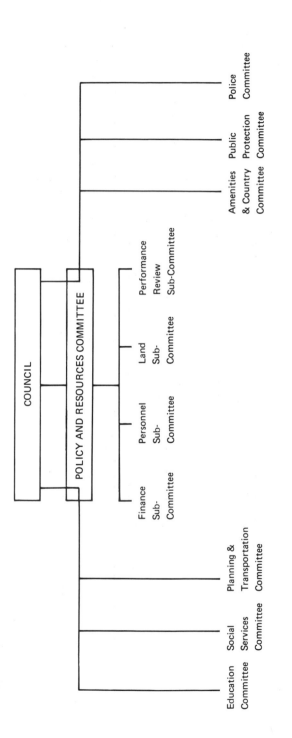

Notes: 1. A separate National Parks committee will be required in appropriate counties.
2. The Police committee is the policy authority, but by convention it is expected that it will use the same lines of communication as other committees. The diagram reflects this.

Fig. 2(b) *Departmental Structure A – Non-Metropolitan County*

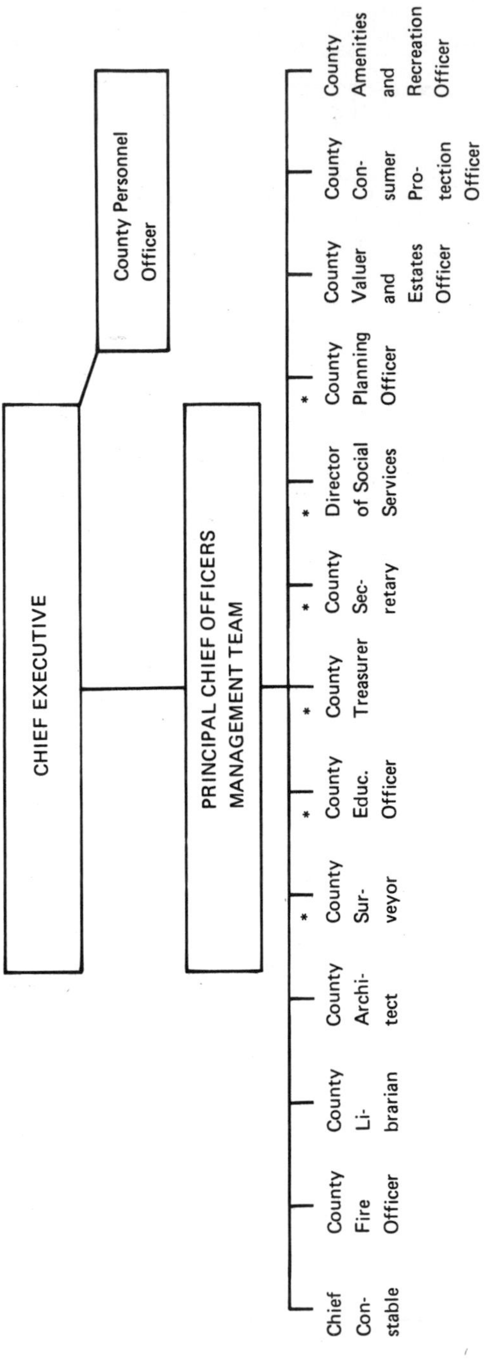

CHIEF EXECUTIVE

County Personnel Officer

PRINCIPAL CHIEF OFFICERS MANAGEMENT TEAM

Chief Con-stable

County Fire Officer

County Li-brarian

County Archi-tect

* County Sur-veyor

* County Educ. Officer

* County Treasurer

* County Sec-retary

* Director of Social Services

* County Planning Officer

County Valuer and Estates Officer

County Con-sumer Pro-tection Officer

County Amenities and Recreation Officer

*Members of management team.

Fig. 2(c) *Departmental Structure B – Non-Metropolitan County*

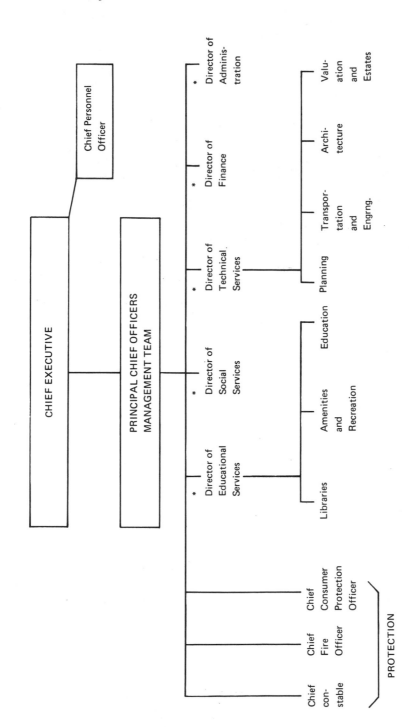

CHIEF EXECUTIVE

Chief Personnel Officer

PRINCIPAL CHIEF OFFICERS MANAGEMENT TEAM

Chief constable

Chief Fire Officer

Chief Consumer Protection Officer

PROTECTION

* Director of Educational Services

Libraries

* Director of Social Services

Amenities and Recreation

Education

* Director of Technical Services

Planning

Transportation and Engrng.

* Director of Finance

Architecture

* Director of Administration

Valuation and Estates

*Members of management team.

Fig. 3(a) *Committee Structure – Metropolitan County*

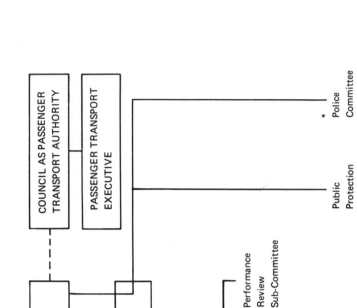

*See Note 2 to Diagram 2(a)

Fig. 3(b) *Departmental Structure – Metropolitan County*

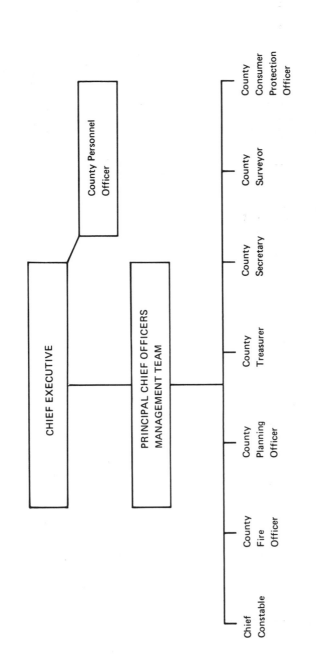

Note: Logically the members of the management team would be the Planning Officer, Treasurer, Secretary and Surveyor, but in view of the limited range of departments authorities may wish to include all the chief officers.

Fig. 4(a) *Committee Structure – Metropolitan District*

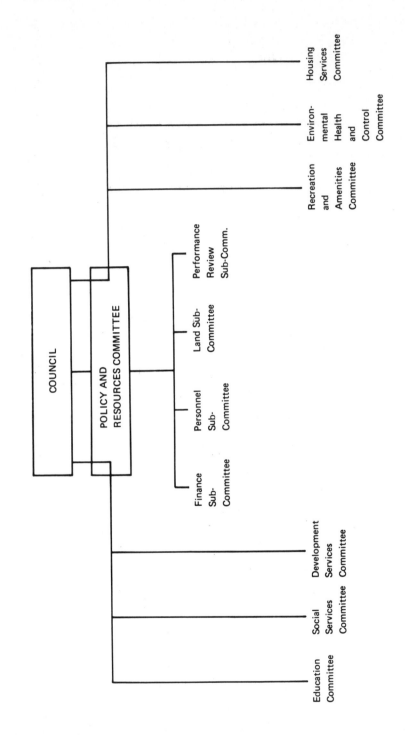

Fig. 4(b) *Departmental Structure A — Metropolitan District*

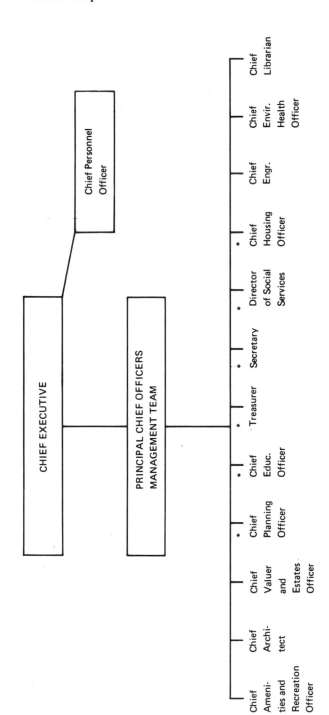

*Members of management team.

Fig. 4(c) *Departmental Structure B – Metropolitan District*

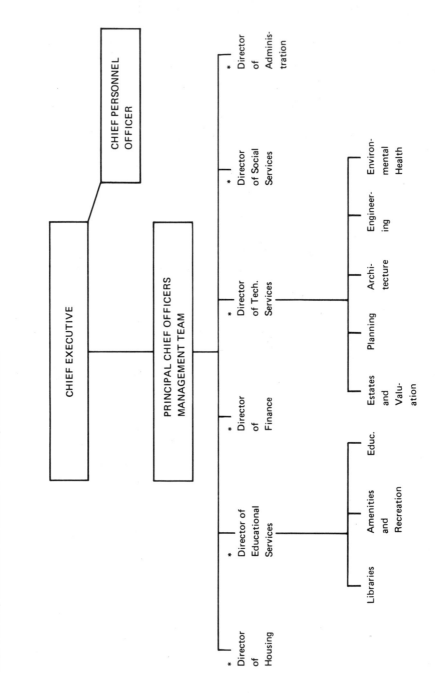

*Members of management team.

Fig. 5(a) *Committee Structure A – Non-Metropolitan District*

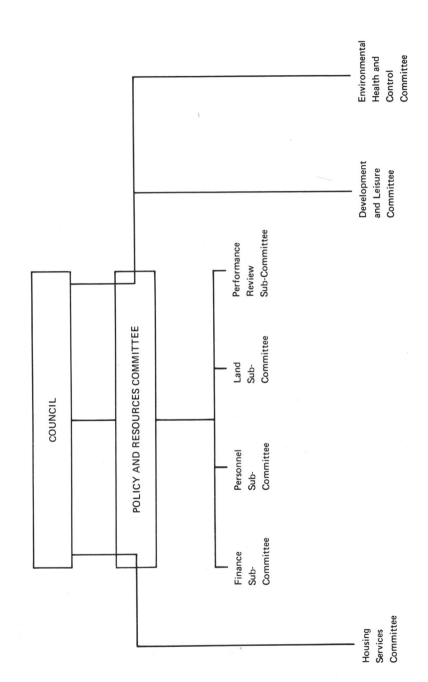

Fig. 5(b) *Committee Structure B – Non-Metropolitan District*

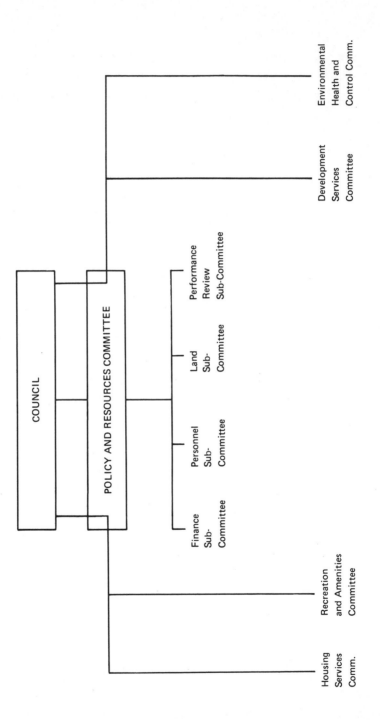

Fig. 5(c) *Departmental Structure – Larger Non-Metropolitan District*

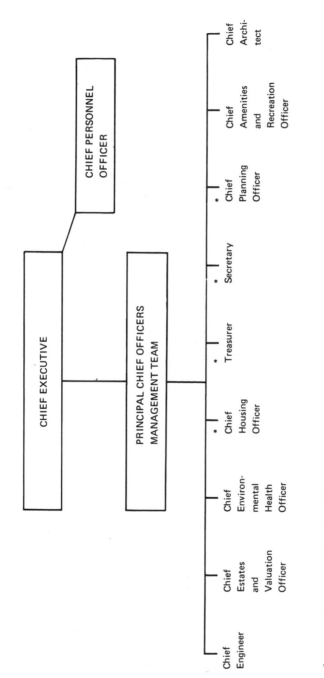

*Members of management team. Local circumstances may justify additional members.

Note: In appropriate authorities the Passenger Transport Manager may also be a chief officer.

Fig. 5(d) *Departmental Structure — Average Non-Metropolitan District*

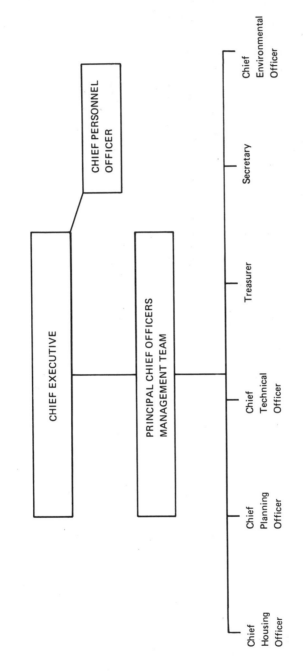

Note: In view of the relatively small number of departments, all chief officers will probably be members of the management team.

46 AREA MANAGEMENT

From *The Liverpool Inner Area Study: Proposals for Area Management* (Department of Environment, 1974); by permission of H.M.S.O.

11. A final, more precise definition of area management must await the results of the experiment. However, it would be closely concerned, in particular, with three questions posed by the present situation in the study area:

(i)   whether, by establishing an effective representation of departments at an area level, the sense of remoteness and alienation experienced by people living in inner areas could be reduced. This might be achieved by providing better information about Corporation activities in the area; by simplifying the processes through which an individual has to pass in order to have his or her problem effectively attended to; and by making the services by the Corporation physically and psychologically more accessible

(ii)   whether an effective corporate approach could be developed to the identification and solution of problems, and the implementation of policies, at the area level. This aspect would be concerned primarily with the measurement and allocation of resources for the area

(iii) whether the effectiveness of elected members of Council could be improved, through making available to them more detailed and authoritative information about the needs of the area in which their wards lay, and in developing an integrated approach to the provision of services and allocation of resources in the area.

......

... an empirical approach was used, in which practical requirements for the definition of an area were identified:

(i)   it should be sufficiently large to enable satisfactory planning and decision making to take place within the area without constant reference to adjoining areas; and to enable effective political representation to take place, and not to require a large number of senior administrative and professional staff appointments if the pilot area were extended into a District wide system of areas

(ii)   it should be sufficiently small to enable the area administration to be easily accessible to people living in the area; to be reasonably homogeneous, so that, for instance, scarce professional resources could be concentrated on specific, local problems; and to ensure that it would not acquire excessive political or administrative significance which might detract from the status of the District Council.

(iii) it should minimise unnecessary disturbance to existing social and community groups and to current well established arrangements for decentralisation within Corporation departments.

......

21. The first main field for area management would be the identification and definition of corporate planning objectives for the area based on an analysis of its needs from the perspective of individuals and communities in the area. The work would involve an evaluation and reconciliation of the short and long term policies being developed for each local authority service by each department, and an assessment of how they meet local needs and circumstances. The aim would be to recommend programmes for action by each department that would, in combination with each other, represent a coordinated and socially effective programme.

22. Initially, implementation of this function would take the form of participation in the annual budget cycle, by preparing evidence on the allocation and use of resources for the area as a whole, covering all District Council expenditure directly affecting the area, both revenue and capital. To this end, the budget proposals of each programme department should be scrutinised and reported on by area management before decisions are finally made on the next year's budget . . .

23. Later, this role could conceivably be considerably extended whilst still functioning within the framework of the District Council. Thus area management could become the authority with responsibility for preparing an annual budget for the area, local plans and other major policy statements for the development of the area and the operation of local authority services within it.

24. Secondly, area management would have the responsibility of making proposals for, and carrying out action based on, a special local budget allocation within the Corporation's annual budget. This special local budget would be apart from the normal budget allocations of programme departments acting within the area . . .

. . . . . .

27. Thirdly, area management should become a main source of advice and information services for the area to elected members; Corporation departments; other government departments and voluntary organisations; and local residents, businesses and other organisations in the area. However, the precise definition of this function requires further study, and positive proposals will be made at a later stage, either within area management itself or, if necessary, . . . as a further action project.

28. Each of these first three functions would be a new activity specifically brought about through the inception of area management. The fourth function is in the field of current activities already being carried out by the Corporation. Initially, the distinctive role of area management in this field of the implementation of departmental programmes and policies in the area would be advisory. Responsibility for the definition of policies and the delivery of services would remain with programme departments and committees, in particular with those officials who already have delegated powers within their own department for the use of resources in local areas. Area management, however, would have the responsibility for systematically reviewing this work and, if necessary, offering advice . . .

29. At a later stage, some executive functions now carried out by programme departments might usefully be transferred to area management, as part of the experiment.

FRAMEWORK

30. In order to carry out those functions, it will be necessary to establish an organisation or framework for area management which meets the following requirements:

   (i)   effective political and administrative control of area management, as an experiment being undertaken by the Liverpool District Council, with financial assistance from the Department of the Environment

   (ii)   adequate political accountability for the actions of area management, capable of functioning effectively from the outset, but with a capacity for later modifications during the course of the experiment should this be found to be desirable

   (iii) efficient administration of the functions of area management, with the capacity to provide a strong and distinctive perspective on the area's problems from the local point of view, and with flexibility to develop during the course of the experiment

   (iv) effective monitoring of the progress of the experiment.

31. In addition to the existing committees and departments of the Council, three new proposals are made for this experiment. Their character, functions and relationship to the existing structure are described below, and the three are:

   (i)   an Area Consultative Committee of elected members

   (ii)   an Area Executive or Manager, as chief officer for the area, with his or her own full time staff

   (iii) an Area Management Group of officers from other Corporation departments.

Political Control

32. The first requirement means that Liverpool District Council must retain overall control of the experiment through its Policy & Finance Committee who would receive reports on progress and recommendations for the future conduct of the experiment and its possible wider application . . .

Political accountability

33. The second requirement is to build effective political accountability into the framework for area management. This is essential if area management is to have functions which include budgetary powers or any executive function. Several possible alternative models could be constructed of the ways in which the experiment could be made accountable to elected members, or other groups.

. . . . . .

35. Two measures are necessary in this situation. Firstly, political accountability and community involvement in area management must be given a formal, political structure within which it can be properly examined. For this, an Area Consultative Committee should be established, recruited from the elected members for wards

contained wholly or partly in District D. A maximum of 21 members from seven wards would be involved. The Committee should have powers to coopt other members, including representatives of community groups in the area.

36. The main duty of this Committee would be to take consultations as it deems appropriate, and make recommendations within say six months, to the Policy & Finance Committee directly (that is, not to the special sub-committee noted in paragraph 38) on the powers, duties and responsibilities of elected members and other representatives of the area, in the area management . . .

38. Secondly, however, some form of political accountability must form part of the framework for area management from the outset, if it is to carry out those functions listed in the previous sections. This is best exercised directly through Policy & Finance Committee, if necessary acting through a special, interim sub-committee, until the Area Consultative Committee has reported and a decision made on its recommendations. The Committee or sub-committee which is accountable for the functions of area management would act on the advice of the Area Executive.

Administrative responsibility

39. The third principle requirement is for an efficient administrative system to carry out the functions of area management, comprising three elements: a full time Area Executive, to be responsible for the area administration; a small, full time staff working for the Area Executive; and an interdepartmental Area Management Group of technical officers from programme, and other departments.

40. The Area Executive would be a senior member of staff, directly responsible in the official hierarchy to the Chief Executive. His, or her duties would be:

   (i)   having considered the advice of the Area Management Group, to submit reports and make recommendations on the following subjects to the Chief Executive, and through him, to the Policy & Finance Committee or other committee responsible for the actions of area management:

   (a)   the implementation of departmental programmes and policies as they affect the area including, if necessary, recommendations for changes in the work of other departments as they affect the area. These would arise only if there was a conflict between the needs of the area and city wide policies for a particular programme, which could not be resolved within the Area Management Group

   (b)   corporate planning objectives for the area, and advice on the annual budget estimates prepared by programme departments, as they affect the area

   (c)   proposals for the contingency and special project budgets

   (d)   proposals for, and reports on, special services to be attached to area management, such as advice and information services, and executive functions.

   (ii)   acting in his or her own capacity, to administer and direct the work of area management, including:

  (a) acting as adviser to the Area Consultative Committee
  (b) acting as chairman of the Area Management Group
  (c) preparing technical reports on the work of area management at all
      levels and for all functions
  (d) making recommendations to the Chairman or Deputy Chairman of
      the Committee with political accountability for area management on
      items of expenditure from the contingency budget
  (e) administering the expenditure from the contingency and special proj-
      ect budgets
  (f) directing the work of special services attached to area management.

41. The Area Executive would thus be the key figure in the administrative structure of area management. He or she would coordinate all the functions of area
management and ensure that a corporate approach was achieved in problem definition and solving, as well as in the day to day administration of the Corporation's
area based services. As such, he or she would have to be able to identify with the
area, its people and their needs and aspirations, and would have to be able to work
effectively with the representatives of programme departments in the area who
would have the actual responsibility for providing executive services to the area.
. . . . . .

43. The Area Management Group should comprise a representative from each
programme and function department with a major responsibility for services to the
area, that is:
Education
Environmental Health
Housing
Planning
Recreation and Open Space
Social Services
Solicitor and Secretary (Community Development)
Transportation & Basic Services
Treasurer's
other staff would attend, by invitation, when necessary.
. . . . . .

46. The main initial function of the group would be to advise the Area Executive
on all matters relating to the area, and to acquire a corporate approach to the planning and development of local authority services for the area. Each member of the
Group would be the link between area management, in the person of the Area
Executive, and his or her own department.

Section IV
England: Finance

All reforming proposals in British local government have faltered at the obstacle presented by local government finance. Yet these critiques could scarcely avoid drawing attention to the overwhelming significance of two related financial issues: first, the contentious character of the system of local taxation, and secondly, local dependence upon centrally controlled financial resources.

The tax available to local authorities is a 'rate' on property, determined in relation to the assumed rental value of the property, and to the revenue requirement of the authority. After an upward property revaluation in 1963 which occasioned an outburst of public protest, the Government appointed a Committee of Enquiry (the Allen Committee). The Committee's Report, in 1965, demonstrated clearly that rates were an inequitable tax, bearing most heavily upon those taxpayers with least resources (47). Legislation in 1966 provided some relief to domestic rate-payers through a system of rate rebates, but these were attracted by only a small percentage of rate-payers. The Redcliffe-Maud report again drew attention to the issues, and Government undertook to review local government finances. The result was a consultation paper (1971), generally regarded as a disappointment in its failure to offer any radical solutions (48). It did contain a full analysis of the various proposals for alternative sources of local revenue, only to be forced back upon the conclusion that all alternatives had disadvantages at least as great as those of the existing system, for which some improvements were suggested. The whole issue was reopened in 1974, when another public outcry following heavy rate increases in many of the new authorities, brought yet another Committee – Layfield – this time to review the whole system of local government finance. This report proposed to retain rates (assessed on capital rather than rental values) and to supplement these by a local income tax (50).

Those anxious for reform in the field of local government finance could be little happier with the development of central–local financial relations. The developing significance of local government expenditure as a proportion of gross national product (and of national public expenditure: 27% in 1975–6) makes it inevitable that central government should exert control, through restraints on local borrowing for capital investment, and through the mechanism of the rate-support grant (which makes up the difference between local revenue for current expenditure, and the total current expenditure requirement). In both cases, central government have relaxed slightly the rigidity of their controls. Since 1971, the capital expenditure of local authorities has been divided into 'key' sectors and 'locally-determined' sectors. Borrowing for 'key' sector activities is subject to specific approval by central government. For the 'locally-determined' sector, a block loan sanction is arranged annually, leaving local authorities some freedom of choice between projects to which the block loan may be applied. But it should be noted that all major services fall in the 'key' sector.

As to grants, central government fixes the total amount of grant available to be distributed between individual authorities, and does this on the basis of estimated local authority expenditure and revenue. A percentage of the total figure, payable as 'rate-support grant' is then determined (for 1974–5, it was 60.5%). Central government is also responsible for determining the distribution of the rate support grant between individual local authorities. Grants have been increasingly allocated on a block basis rather than on the basis of earmarking specific grants for specific services (see **49** for a more detailed account of the grants system).

The need in 1975–6 for strict control of total public expenditure severely affected local government expenditure. In recognition of the need for close liaison and planning over this area, a new Consultative Council was set up, comprising Ministers, representatives of local authority associations, and senior officials from both central and local government. This might lead to a better understanding by central government of the financial problems of local government, and in particular of the close relationship between policy planning and resource allocation. The Layfield proposals **(50)** rested on the opposition of clear alternatives – either more central control or more local autonomy – though a note of reservation by Professor Alan Day rejected this analysis as misunderstanding the complexity of central–local relations. The only really innovatory proposal, a new local income tax, came at a time when the political climate was unfavourable to increases in public expenditure (which this proposal involved). The hope for any fundamental change will depend on the political response to Layfield, which was not known at the time of going to press.

47 THE ALLEN REPORT ON RATES

From *Committee of Inquiry into the Impact of Rates on Households, Report* (The Allen Report, Cmnd. 2582, 1965); by permission of H.M.S.O.

Characteristics of rates as a tax

43. Tax receipts are classified in the national income accounts under three main headings: (*a*) taxes on income; (*b*) taxes on capital; and (*c*) taxes on expenditure. Broadly speaking, taxes which add to costs of production and distribution are treated as taxes on expenditure, and rates are included in this category along with customs duties, excise taxes, purchase taxes, vehicle and other licence duties and stamp duties on the transfer of property. Since, as already explained, domestic

rates are levied on the rateable value of occupied real property, and are therefore a tax on the use of a particular good (i.e., accommodation), we find no difficulty in accepting rates as a tax on expenditure.

44. Taxes on expenditure can be further classified into, first, specific taxes, that is, taxes based on some physical attribute of the good, such as weight; and secondly, *ad valorem* taxes, that is, taxes based on the value of the good or service. Rates, like purchase tax, are an *ad valorem* tax: the tax base is the rateable value and the level of tax is the rate poundage. For a tax on expenditure, rates, however, have an unusual characteristic which affects their incidence. The level of poundage, unlike the level of purchase tax, differs from area to area. As a result the rates paid on a dwelling in one area may differ from those paid on a dwelling with the same rateable value in another area.

45. In the United Kingdom the liability for the payment of most taxes on expenditure, and therefore their immediate impact, falls on the manufacturer or seller of the goods in question and not on the final consumer. (This is why taxes on expenditure are often known as 'indirect taxes', as distinct from 'direct taxes' which are collected directly from individual persons, e.g., income taxes. We prefer not to use the terms direct and indirect because they sometimes have other meanings.) With rates, however, like licence fees and vehicle duties, the buyer of the commodity is liable for payment of the tax . . .

46. Two other characteristics of rates make them more obtrusive, and so more unpopular, than other forms of tax. First, if money incomes are rising and with them consumers' expenditure, the income tax and purchase tax base automatically expands. This gives the central government a great advantage because, without any increase in tax levels, extra revenue will be raised to finance increased expenditure. Local authorities, on the other hand, if they wish to increase expenditure to improve or expand services, or merely to cover rising prices and costs, do not have the same good fortune. The tax base for rates only expands substantially either when there is a general revaluation of property which, at best, takes place every five years, or when a substantial number of new properties are built. Increases in local expenditure falling wholly or partly on the rates therefore require an upward adjustment in the 'level of tax', that is, an increase in the rate poundage. Someone who pays more income tax because his income has gone up may do so without much complaint; but if required to pay more rates resulting from a higher rate poundage he may feel bitter resentment.

47. Secondly, even though the total purchase and excise taxes paid in a year may be substantial, the amount of tax paid at any one time by consumers (so far as retailers can pass on such taxes to consumers) is likely to be very small. It is one thing to pay £36 a year in taxes in amounts of less than 2s. a day, as does someone who smokes ten cigarettes a day, but another to pay it in half-yearly amounts of £18. The collection of income tax by weekly or monthly instalments under P.A.Y.E. similarly takes much of the sting out of increases in total income tax payments. Yet rates are commonly payable in half-yearly amounts.

Rates as a charge for services rendered

48. Evidence from the public repeatedly put before us the view that rates ought to have some relation to the services enjoyed by the individual ratepayer. Retired people without children of school age complain that the greater part of the rates they pay is spent on the education of other people's children; others protest that their rates go to subsidise the rents of local authority tenants who are often better off than themselves.

49. . . . . It is doubtful whether rates as now levied can be regarded even in part as a charge for services rendered. The essence of local government is that it provides services, such as law and order, the benefits of which are indivisible by their very nature. Any charge for those services must be arbitrary and also compulsory, that is, a tax. Although the benefits of many present-day local services, particularly the social services which have been developed so notably since the First World War, can be ascribed in a rough and ready way to particular groups and individuals, it is widely accepted that such services should be heavily subsidised. We have therefore no hesitation in rejecting the notion that rate payments are other than compulsory exactions, and in all subsequent discussion we treat them as a tax.

Rates in the national economy

50. The total amount paid in taxation (including rates) is obviously closely linked to the growth in current government expenditure, central and local. Since before the Second World War both central and local government current expenditure has increased substantially in money terms. The first is now a much higher proportion of national income and the second a rather higher proportion.

Table 50 Central and local government current expenditure, United Kingdom. Selected years 1938–1963

Year	Central Government Expenditure			Local Government Expenditure		
	£ million (1)	1938 = 100 (2)	% of National Product (3)	£ million (4)	1938 = 100 (5)	% of National Product (6)
1938	1,099	100	21.2	416	100	8.0
1952	4,515	411	32.3	874	210	6.3
1955	4,963	452	29.5	1,101	265	6.5
1960	6,629	603	29.3	1,731	416	7.6
1963	8,111	738	30.6	2,336	562	8.8

Source: *National Income and Expenditure 1964* (Tables 4 and 5).

51. Yet, despite the growth in local government expenditure, rates have fallen as a proportion of the total revenue of local authorities.

Table 51(a) Sources of finance of local government current expenditure, United Kingdom. Selected Years 1938–1963

Percentages

Year	Rates (1)	Other local income (2)	Central Government grants (3)
1938	43.2	27.9	28.9
1952	41.0	18.4	40.6
1955	39.2	20.3	40.5
1960	39.2	21.1	39.7
1963	39.3	20.8	39.9

Source: *National Income and Expenditure 1964* (Table 5).

. . . . . .

Rates and total taxes

56. Critics of the rating system may be surprised to find that (as Table 56 shows) rates constitute a relatively small proportion of total taxes. Rates are relatively less important as a source of revenue to the public sector than national insurance contributions. In 1938, rates amounted to almost twice the sum of unemployment and health contributions; but in 1963, rates totalled £1,014 million, while national insurance contributions reached £1,303 million. In recent years, however, rates, as a proportion of total taxes, have been increasing again.

Table 56 Rates as a proportion of total taxes on expenditure, United Kingdom. Selected years 1938–63

Year	Taxes on income	National insurance and health contri- butions	Taxes on expenditure		Total taxes	Rates as % of Col. (5)	Rates as % of Col. (3) + Col. (4)
			Rates	Other			
	£ million (1)	£ million (2)	£ million (3)	£ million (4)	£ million (5)	(6)	(7)
1938	386	109	212	410	1,117	19.0	34.1
1952	2,173	476	392	1,901	4,942	7.9	17.1
1955	2,319	594	475	2,179	5,567	8.5	17.9
1960	2,725	913	771	2,623	7,032	11.0	22.7
1963	3,385	1,303	1,014	3,034	8,736	11.6	25.0

Source: *National Income and Expenditure, 1964* (Tables 4 and 5).

The impact of domestic rates

. . . . . .

58. Since in most cases it is the occupiers of dwellings who are liable to pay the rates, it is often assumed that it is the occupiers who bear the burden. The answer to the question 'who bears the tax?' is however not so obvious as appears at first sight, but for the moment it can be accepted that at least the first impact of rates is felt by occupiers.

59. A number of private investigations in the past, and also more recently published official statistics, have confirmed that the impact of rates is regressive in relation to incomes: the lower the income, the higher the proportion that is taken in rates. The official statistics are of particular interest to our investigations because they were derived, like much of the material which we ourselves have analysed, from the Family Expenditure Survey carried out each year since 1957. In Table 59 we show the average rate payments as a percentage of income (after deducting direct taxes and adding social benefits) by family type. As comparisons with earlier years

Table 59 Average payments of rates and taxes on expenditure as a percentage of income (after direct taxes and benefits), United Kingdom. Average of 1961 and 1962

Range of income £s a year	1 adult (1)	2 adults (2)	2 adults 1 child (3)	2 adults 2 children (4)	2 adults 3 children (5)
Rates as a percentage of income					
216–382	5.0	4.0			
382–460	4.8	3.7			
460–559	4.3	3.1	2.4	2.2	
559–676	4.0	3.1	3.0	2.6	2.4
676–816	3.8	3.0	2.4	2.3	2.2
816–988	3.9	2.8	2.4	2.3	1.9
988–1,196	3.1	2.5	2.3	2.3	2.0
1,196–1,448		2.3	2.1	2.1	1.6
1,448–1,752		2.3	2.3	2.3	
1,752–2,122		2.3	2.1	2.0	
Total taxes on expenditure as a percentage of income					
216–382	14.8	18.4			
382–460	18.4	19.2			
460–559	17.1	17.1	18.2	21.6	
559–676	17.2	18.0	18.0	16.4	16.4
676–816	15.8	17.5	17.6	16.9	14.8
816–988	20.7	18.6	15.7	16.6	15.7
988–1,196	13.5	18.7	16.1	15.3	14.2
1,196–1,448		15.9	17.3	15.1	12.9
1,448–1,752		15.6	15.3	13.4	
1,752–2,122		14.3	14.4	10.4	

Source: *Economic Trends*, February 1964 (Tables 5 and 6 are merged according to the numbers given in Tables 1 and 2).

are difficult, we have confined the table to 1961 and 1962, but there is little to suggest any major changes in the general pattern at least since 1957.

60. For the larger families rates take a fairly uniform percentage of income whatever their income group, but rates are far more regressive for the 'one adult' and 'two adult' households who, as we found from our surveys, are predominantly retired people. In the case of the two lowest income groups rates also represent a large proportion of taxes on expenditure.

48 THE 1971 GREEN PAPER: RATES, AND THE ALTERNATIVES

From *The Future Shape of Local Government Finance* (Cmnd. 4741, 1971); by permission of H.M.S.O. This was a consultative document or 'Green Paper', but resulted in only minor changes.

Rates have considerable merits as a tax: their yield is large — exceeded only by taxes on income — they can be varied easily from place to place, are clearly related to the areas of local government, and are comparatively cheap to administer and collect.

But they have defects too. Their effect on individual ratepayers in some cases bears little relationship to ability to pay. The yield does not have the buoyancy required to keep pace with the growth of services.

GROWTH OF EXPENDITURE AND GROWTH OF RATES

Local government expenditure is absorbing an increasing share of national resources. Even though its rate of growth has been slightly reduced recently it is still greater than that of the economy as a whole. Not only is the share of resources taken by local authorities growing faster, but the cost of providing local authority services is increasing faster than costs in general. This is because wages and salaries form an exceptionally large part of the total cost of local authority services so that the effect of pay increases on local authority expenditure tends to be more marked than on prices in the economy as a whole.

The yield from rates, on the other hand, tends to grow more slowly. While the level of rates has over the last 25 years grown broadly at the same pace as earnings, the real growth of the values on which rates are levied — new construction and the improvement or replacement of existing property — has been much smaller than the growth in the standard and scope of services. The combined growth from these two factors — the rate in the pound and the growth in property — has been insufficient to finance a constant share of local expenditure and the central government has therefore had to make good the gap.

On present trends there will continue to be a gap between the amount required to finance a programme of development of local authority services and the yield of the local revenue on which the provision of such services largely depends. The problem is how to fill the gap.

One possibility would be to cut back still further the rate at which local authority expenditure is growing. But even without any improvement in standards some growth is clearly essential to cope with population growth and similar factors outside the control of local government. Any attempt to reduce the rate of growth must also deal with the inherent tendency to grow disproportionately fast because of the high proportion of pay mentioned previously. There remains the question how fast we can afford to improve standards.

Other possibilities would be to shift some of the burdens from local government to central government and to increase the income from charges for the provision of certain services. But the first of these runs contrary to the Government's objective of devolving power from central to local government, and the scope for the second is limited . . .

If local authority expenditure continues to grow in line with recent trends, there are three − and only three − possible ways of filling the gap referred to . . . either property occupiers must pay more, or the national taxpayer must bear an increasing proportion of local expenditure, or new and buoyant sources of local revenue must be found.

FILLING THE GAP

The first course would mean for the householder that rates would be increasing faster than his income. This would be widely resented by local electors and would make the financing of local services progressively more difficult for local authorities.

The second course would be to continue the gradual increase, year by year, in the proportion of local authority expenditure met by central government grants. The gap between revenue and expenditure could be met over the decade after reorganisation by increasing the overall grant percentage from its present level of 60 per cent to a level in 1985 of about 66 per cent.

There are fears that the higher the contribution of central government the less responsibility remains in the hands of the local people. A block grant system can be designed to overcome this difficulty. Indeed sensitivity to changes in expenditure can be increased, in that if an authority has a fixed grant from the Government, and it then decides to increase its own expenditure, the increase in that expenditure will be proportionately higher in relation to its own income the larger the original government grant.

The third course would be to find new local taxes. In discussion of various possibilities for different sources of local revenue no net addition to taxation is envisaged. To the extent that new sources of local revenue become available there will be a corresponding reduction in the need for national taxation.

There have been many proposals for abolishing rates and replacing them with some new form of local tax, and the subject has been studied exhaustively both inside government and elsewhere. Hitherto the almost universal conclusion — reached, for example, by the Royal Commission on Local Government in England — has been that a property tax such as rates must remain the principal source of local revenue, though it may be possible to reduce the extent to which local expenditure is dependent on the rates by providing other sources of revenue to supplement them.

There is a distinction between giving local authorities a share in the proceeds of a central tax as opposed to making them free to fix their own tax rates for their own areas. The former is in effect a government grant. It is the latter which really adds to local discretion.

. . . . . .

IMPROVING RATES

One of the main disadvantages of rates is that they tend to hit hardest those householders at the lower levels of income; in other words the lower the ratepayer's income the greater the proportion of it that is taken in rates. There is already in existence a scheme of rate rebates to help the poorer ratepayer. We could graduate the relief and extend its scope so that, as with rent rebates, even householders with incomes above the national average could be covered if they have large families and their rates are relatively high. In graduating the relief we could take account of personal circumstances in much the same way as personal allowances for taxes on income. Rates would thus become much more closely tied to ability to pay, certainly at those levels of income at which they at present cause hardship . . .

. . . . . .

APPENDIX 3 IMPROVEMENT OF THE RATING SYSTEM

The Rating Authority

In England and Wales the rating authorities at present are the county borough councils and the borough and district councils, the latter two levying rates to cover the net cost of the services performed both by themselves and by the county councils. The county councils obtain their share of the levy by precepting upon the borough and district councils, the amount of the precept being expressed in terms of a specified rate poundage in the area of the district authority. This arrangement, which is clearly set out in the combined rate demand, enables the ratepayer readily to identify how much of his rate bill is attributable to each authority.

In the new two-level system proposed by the Government the new counties and districts will be independent of one another, but it seems necessary to retain an arrangement whereby one authority collects the rates for both. Whether the county council or the district council is better fitted to do this is arguable, but the Government have already announced their decision that the present system under which the district councils are the rating authorities should be retained.

. . . . . .

The Advantages and Disadvantages of Rates

Despite the criticisms frequently levelled at them rates have many positive merits as a local tax. Their yield is substantial, certain, and predictable; and straightforward increases in poundages secure proportionate increases in yield. They are a tax on fixed property which is unambiguously related to one particular area and cannot be transferred to another area to take advantage of a lower level of taxation. Their burden falls, to a large extent, on local electors — though not all electors pay rates — and the need to raise poundages to finance increases in expenditure provides a direct link between what the local electorate demands in terms of local services and what it must pay to finance them. There is virtually no scope for evasion, and local variations present no difficulty. The cost of collection and administration including the cost of valuation — at less than 2 per cent of yield — is low by comparison with the costs that would be entailed in local operation of other possible taxes.

But rates also have disadvantages. For the domestic ratepayer at the lower income levels rates tend to be regressive — that is to say, the lower the householder's income the greater the proportion that will be taken by his rates — although at average income levels and above rates are no more regressive than the other main taxes on expenditure. Moreover rates are the largest tax which is demanded in substantial amounts from those of average means or less. In the commercial and industrial sectors, rates fall relatively heavily on those whose operations depend upon substantial investment in fixed property and plant — and anomalies in the rating of plant and machinery aggravate this effect. Periodic revaluations are needed to ensure that rateable values maintain their relationship with current rental values, and, between revaluations, poundage increases are necessary simply to offset the effects of inflation. In addition, valuation of dwellings has become increasingly difficult because there is at present a growing scarcity of evidence of open market rentals, on which rateable values are based, in large parts of the domestic sector.

The Scope for Improvement

Many of these disadvantages could, however, be moderated, if not cured, by improvements to the present rating system.

The regressiveness of rates at low income levels has already been mitigated by a rate rebate scheme . . . If an effective scheme reached up to about the average income, rates would cease to be regressive compared with most other taxes.

The proposal sometimes put forward that rates should be allowed as a deduction against income tax would if anything make the rating system more regressive, and would not allow fairly for variation in family income. Three factors bear on this:

first, those who paid no tax would get no relief; second, the larger reliefs would tend to go to taxpayers with the larger rate bills; and, third, the higher the marginal tax rates on the income of a ratepayer the greater would be the relief.

The impact of rate demands for large amounts at a time has already been lessened by the right accorded to domestic ratepayers in legislation introduced by the previous Government to pay rates in not less than ten monthly instalments. Payment by instalments in this manner could be further encouraged, and might indeed become recognised as the normal pattern of payment. It might be facilitated by having a tear-off strip on the demand note which would need only a bank address and a signature to become a standing order on a bank.

. . . . . .

Periodic revaluations of the present kind could be avoided only if the concept of open-market value were abandoned, but it is difficult to find an alternative basis which would be regarded as generally fair and which would not have more serious drawbacks. The disadvantages of this aspect of the rating system could perhaps best be minimised by ensuring that revaluations are not postponed beyond the statutory quinquennium.

The scarcity of evidence of open-market rental values in the domestic sector might be overcome by changing from rental to capital values, evidence of which is much more widely available. An appropriate conversion factor could then be used to convert these values to rateable values which would compare satisfactorily with those of sectors still based on rental values . . .

A New Scheme for Rate Rebates

The present rate rebate scheme was introduced in 1966, and provides for the remission of two-thirds of the rate bill above a minimum payment of £7.50 a year for householders whose income falls within specified limits. The present qualifying income limits are £12.25 a week for a married couple, and £10 a week for a single person, increased by £2 for each dependent child. Householders with incomes above these limits also qualify for some rebate, but the amount is tapered off sharply as income rises so as effectively to exclude altogether those with incomes above £20 a week or thereabouts.

About 900,000 householders received rebates in 1969–70, and there were, in addition, over 2 million households on supplementary benefit whose rates were fully taken into account in the allowances they received. This means that some 3 million households — about 18 per cent of the total in Britain — at present enjoy full or partial relief of rates on grounds of low income.

Experience of the present scheme has highlighted its main weakness. In the first place, it is limited in scope. The qualifying income limits are not far above the supplementary benefit level, and they are well short of the levels of income at which rates cease to be markedly regressive; moreover the sharp rate of taper means that, for those qualifying for other welfare benefits which also taper off as income rises, the combined rate of reduction can be unacceptably high. Secondly, all those whose income falls within the qualifying limits – whether only just or by a substantial margin – are entitled to the same degree of relief. Finally, the treatment of income from disablement pensions, and of additional members of a household such as housekeepers and relatives other than spouses, is anomalous and can cause hardship.

These weaknesses could not be eradicated merely by raising the income limits, since it would still be impossible to differentiate between different income levels within those limits, and thus to adjust the amount of rebate to the degree of need. In order to overcome them it appears that a new scheme is necessary, in which not only would entitlement to relief extend further up the income scale, but the amount of relief given would also be graduated in relation to income.

The main features of such a scheme might take the following form.

Entitlement to relief would be based not on gross but on net income. This would be arrived at by deducting up to, say, £2 a week for income from disablement pensions and other payments of a similar kind to the sick or handicapped, and deducting variable allowances – in much the same way as for income tax purposes – for the single person, the married couple, and dependent children. The problem of additional adults in the household could be dealt with by giving the householder an option between a proportionate reduction in the amount of rates reckonable for the calculation of rebate as in the present scheme, or aggregation of incomes within the household combined with a further personal allowance for each additional adult whose income was aggregated in this way.

The amount of relief might be two thirds of the amount by which rates exceeded a specified percentage of net income. So long as rates took less than that specified percentage of net income – which might be 6 per cent – the rate-payer would be required to meet them in full. The provisions for tapering off relief as incomes rose could be made as gradual or as sharp as seemed desirable, taking into account the arrangements for entitlement to other welfare benefits. To avoid excessive administrative cost it would doubtless be necessary to provide that no relief would be paid where the amount involved was less than a minimal sum.

The applicant would have to declare his gross income from all sources, and if entitlement to relief was based on income for the preceding tax year, then for those assessed by PAYE – the majority – the certificate of pay and tax deducted – Form P 60 – would provide most of the necessary evidence. However, to make the scheme more responsive to significant falls in income levels, provision might be included to enable rating authorities, where circumstances justified it, to base the calculation of rebate on current income in, say, a quarterly period. As in the present scheme, those in receipt of supplementary benefit including an allowance for payment of rates in full could be excluded.

With a scheme of this kind, extending the possibility of relief for those with a number of children and relatively high rate bills to householders with roughly the average national income, over 3 million ratepayers might qualify for rebate, and the loss of rate income might be of the order of £65 million a year as compared with £16 million for the present scheme. The greater part of this loss of income might be met by the Government through a high-percentage specific grant outside the rate support grant arrangements.

Assessments of Dwellings on Capital Values

. . . . . .

Such a change would not be quite as straightforward as it sounds. Sale prices sometimes reflect the personal preferences and needs of a particular purchaser — not to mention anticipated development value — rather than the value to any occupier, and are quite sensitive to state of decoration and repair. Capital values would need careful definition to take account of such factors. It would also be necessary to find an appropriate divisor for converting capital values to rateable values comparable to those of other sectors which would still be based on rental values.

Some of these problems could be lessened by the adoption of a system of 'broad-banding' of capital values for assessment purposes. Up to a capital value of £5,000 properties might be grouped together in successive bands of £250 value; between £5,000 and £10,000 in bands of £500; and thereafter in bands of £1,000. Rateable value might then be calculated on the lower limit of the band in which the property fell. It might also be provided that during the currency of each Valuation List no increase or decrease in assessment should be made unless the alteration in capital value amounted at least to the width of band in which the existing capital value of the property lay. This would avoid much of the criticism that arises now from increases in rateable value following minor improvements to houses, and incidentally would also save a lot of litigation.

. . . . . .

A change to capital values might result in some changes in relativities between the assessments of different types of domestic property. The 1973 revaluation in England and Wales, which will still be based on rental values but which will allow evidence about the value of any type of dwelling to be used in assessing that of any other, is in any case likely to produce some changes of this kind. The effect of a change to capital values might be to increase the assessments of houses — particularly modern ones, but also older houses to some extent — by comparison with assessments on purpose-built flats and maisonettes; while assessments would move in the opposite direction for near-slum houses and 'white elephants'.

. . . . . .

APPENDIX 2 ADDITIONAL SOURCES OF LOCAL REVENUE

General Considerations

. . . . . .

Local taxation in any form raises one general problem. In a country like the

United Kingdom any local tax is bound to have some effects which spread beyond the boundaries of the local authority determining the rate at which it is to be levied. The local authority's primary concern must inevitably be for finance to meet its own local needs; it must be governed by the views of the local electors, and decisions taken in this light may not coincide with the wider national interest.

With a single local tax it is possible for central government to judge with some accuracy what the impact of local taxation on the economy will be. But if there were a choice of local taxes, and local authorities were free to exercise that choice in a number of ways by reference to local conditions, the task of predicting the impact of local taxation for the purpose of managing the economy would become much more difficult. Moreover a local authority is not in a position to take account of the effect of its decisions on the national economy, whereas the central government is able to relate the levels of individual taxes to the need to preserve a balance of taxation appropriate to overall economic management. It will always be in a better position than any individual local authority to take account of the relative effects of various types of taxation on the economy as a whole. In some countries in order to meet this problem a limit is imposed on the rate at which a particular tax can be levied by local authorities, but this generally leads to authorities all levying up to the limit. The tax then ceases to be locally variable and becomes a variant of government grant.

. . . . . .

It may be convenient, when comparing possible sources of local revenue, to judge them by their ability to satisfy three main conditions. First is the practicability of genuinely local operation — how feasible would be local variations in the rate of tax. Second is the extent to which its effects fall on local electors — would they be sufficiently conscious of the tax for its impact to impose discipline on local expenditure decisions. Third is the effect on the national economy as a whole — what implications would the tax have on the cost of living or through industrial costs on the balance of payments and how readily could its economic effects be offset by adjustments of national taxes.

A Local Income Tax

One of the criticisms most frequently levelled against rates as the principal local tax is that they are insufficiently related to the local taxpayer's ability to pay; this would not be so, it is argued, with a local income tax.

Administration A local tax on incomes and profits could take one of two forms: a tax assessed and collected locally, on information supplied by the Inland Revenue, or a system under which only the tax rate is fixed by the local authority, with assessment and collection left in the hands of the Inland Revenue.

. . . . . .

To get the right amount of tax from individuals local authorities would need to know the total income of each resident. Tax offices hitherto have rarely been concerned with total income as such: most income of individuals is taxed at source, whether under PAYE or deducted at the standard rate from dividends and other annual payments, and a taxpayer's total income needs to be ascertained only for the purposes of surtax or in a comparatively few cases for certain personal allowances. While tax offices will become more concerned with total income under the Government's proposals for reforming personal taxation, in the great majority of cases – such as taxpayers not liable at rates above the basic rate – it will still not be necessary to compute total income exactly. This general difficulty might be reduced by excluding some forms of income, such as investment income up to a certain amount, but this would make for a more rough and ready scheme, giving rise to anomalies and inequities. Information about total income would not be available until well after the end of the tax year. Local tax would consequently have to be assessed and paid on all incomes on the basis of the income of the preceding year, which might be greater than that in the year when tax was payable.

If local authorities were responsible for assessment and collection they would have to set up their own machinery, thus duplicating to a considerable extent the existing central machinery. Since they would be collecting the tax directly from the taxpayer and not at the source of income they would be likely to need a relatively larger collection staff than the central government. The difficulties of collecting tax from people who are not householders, and who may have no distrainable effects, would also make their task more difficult than that of collecting rates. These problems would be avoided if assessment and collection were the responsibility of the Inland Revenue, but extra work would still be created.

To deal with income from employment it would be necessary to adapt the PAYE system. The PAYE codes used for national tax would not be suitable for local tax deductions because they take account of some factors which are, and would be, relevant only for national tax. Moreover, employers would have to make separate tax deductions for each local authority area, with adjustments when employees moved their homes from one area to another. Employers operating on a nation-wide scale would have to face particularly heavy extra burdens. An alternative would be to apply direct assessment – the system which would have to be adopted for dividends and similar payments – to PAYE income as well. This too would mean extra work for the assessing authority, on a larger scale than anything likely to arise from the Government's proposals for reforming the national tax system. A massive administrative effort would therefore be needed by the Inland Revenue, or the local authorities, or employers, or by some combination of all three, if the tax was to work satisfactorily.

. . . . . .

Suitability Demands on individuals would be more closely related to ability to pay than are rates, and local authorities would also draw a contribution to their revenues from the many individuals who are not, for rating purposes, the occupiers of property, and therefore do not pay rates directly. The yield could be substantial – an additional levy of about 3 percentage points on the standard rate of income tax would finance a reduction in grant from 60 per cent to below 50 per cent — and it would have a built-in buoyancy in a period of rising incomes at least as great as the national rate of increase of incomes. It is, however, less easy to envisage regular increases in the rate of a local tax on incomes, so that the real scope for local variation and matching the tax yield to local revenue requirements is rather less than might appear.

Economic Effects With a local income tax alongside the national tax, central and local government would be sharing between them the yield, and the built-in buoyancy, of taxes on incomes. Sharing any tax in this way brings its own difficulties to each party. On the one hand, the scope for independent local variation would be severely limited; on the other, the central government's scope for manoeuvre in raising or lowering national rates would inevitably be reduced. Moreover, the economic impact of a change in national tax rates could be blunted by conflicting changes in the local tax.

. . . . . .

Motor Fuel Duty

A significant proportion of local expenditure is devoted to catering for motor transport, and the control of traffic — particularly in urban areas — is becoming increasingly important. For this reason a tax related directly to the use of motor transport is a natural candidate for consideration; and the Royal Institute for Public Administration put forward in their evidence to the Royal Commission on Local Government in England a detailed scheme for providing local government with additional revenue out of the yield of the motor fuel duty.

Administration A simple transfer of the motor fuel duty would mean that local authorities would take over its collection completely, with power to impose different rates. As an alternative the central government might continue to collect the bulk of the duty and distribute the receipts among local authorities according to the quantities sold in their areas; authorities could then be empowered to levy an extra local duty and perhaps to grant a rebate if they chose.

If local authorities were made responsible for collecting any part of the duty on motor fuels, then operators of garages and petrol stations, oil distributors, and large industrial users who buy direct from the oil companies, would need to make regular returns of their sales or deliveries and to pay the appropriate local duty. Controls would have to be instituted to check the returns against records of purchases and sales, and against meter pump readings, stocks, and so on. Since there are nearly 40,000 retail outlets — without counting the large industrial users — which are not at present subject to revenue control, collection of the duty would be more expensive to administer and more susceptible of evasion than the existing arrangements under which HM Customs & Excise collect the duty from a relatively few refineries and bonded warehouses operated mainly by large companies.

The scope for evasion and abuse could be reduced if the central government continued to collect most of the duty and only a limited extra duty were collected by local authorities. But the administrative costs of supervising every garage and commercial depot would remain.

Suitability The rate of duty on motor fuel is currently 22½p per gallon, and the duty yielded just over £1,250 million in 1970–71. A transfer of about a third of the duty could compensate local authorities for a reduction in grant from 60 per cent to 50 per cent. Local collection would produce revenue related to the amount of fuel sold in the area, but its effects would not necessarily fall on local electors, since private motorists would not necessarily be residents and business users might well pass on the cost in prices.

Economic Effects The motor fuel duty provided over 8 per cent of central government revenue in 1970/71; it is also a major element in the effectiveness of the 'regulator', under which the Chancellor of the Exchequer can at any time impose a surcharge or allow a rebate of up to 10 per cent on Customs and Excise duties and purchase tax. Transfer of the whole, or a substantial part, of this revenue to local authorities would curtail the central government's scope for regulating the national economy – particularly in the short term. The smaller the part transferred, the less serious would be these effects; but, if local authorities were given discretion to vary the tax rates on their part of the revenue, partial transfers would involve the general difficulties that arise when a tax is shared between central and local government.

A scheme which involved different rates in adjoining areas would also tend to introduce distortions, since it would encourage both private drivers, and large users who purchase in bulk, to concentrate their purchases so far as they could in areas where the duty was lower. Moreover, since much of the burden of duty on motor fuel falls on commercial vehicles and on motor cars used in business, significant variations in duty rates between different local authorities would have important effects on local business and industrial costs, and thus lead to further economic distortion.

. . . . . .

Motor Vehicle Duties

The ownership of motor vehicles is another possible candidate for local taxation.

Administration The motor vehicle duties are at present collected by local authorities as agents of central government, but collection is being transferred to a central computer system. This involves a complex process of transfer from local authority collecting points to the centre, maintaining the existing arrangements as long as they are required, and should eventually bring staff savings, and make for easier enforcement. These are arguments against putting the process into reverse; and no significant further changes in the machinery could be introduced until centralisation, which will take several years, is complete. So if the receipts of the tax were to be transferred to local authorities, it would seem that the tax would need to be collected centrally and thereafter remitted by the collecting authority. It would not be practicable to give local authorities power to vary the rates of duty before 1980, but it would be possible before this — though probably not before 1977 — to start distributing the proceeds to local authorities while keeping responsibility for fixing the rates in the hands of central government.

Suitability The transfer of private motor vehicle duties at the present rate of duty would finance a reduction in central grants from 60 per cent to about 53 per cent. The duties on goods vehicles however do not seem to be suitable for transfer because of the ease with which the operational base of goods vehicles can be moved, the complicated structure of rates, and their importance for national transport policy. The private motor vehicle duties would have the advantage as a local tax that they would fall largely on local electors, although a significant proportion of private motor cars are used partly for business purposes or are provided by employers, and motorists are in any event less numerous than ratepayers. Against this, local variations would create administrative problems for centralised collection, and since owners would seek to register their vehicles in low-taxed areas, total yield might diminish, higher rated areas might lose revenue, and inaccurate records might create difficulties of enforcement. To overcome these problems extra staff would be needed.

As the rate of growth of car ownership now appears to be slowing down, the buoyancy of motor vehicle duties is likely to be comparatively low, and frequent increases could well be necessary if their yield was to keep pace with growth in local authority expenditure. But this would encourage vehicle owners to arrange the renewal of their licence immediately before the time when increases were expected leading to severe 'peaking' of the work of issuing licences, and thus, particularly after centralisation, increasing the cost and difficulty of administration.

Economic Effects Because of the number of private cars used for business purposes there would be some addition to industrial costs if local authorities increased the rates of duty more than central government. Otherwise the transfer of the motor vehicle duties would be unlikely to have undesirable economic effects.

49 THE 1971 GREEN PAPER: CENTRAL—LOCAL FINANCIAL RELATIONS

From *The Future Shape of Local Government Finance* (Cmnd. 4741, 1971); by permission of H.M.S.O. See also **Docs. 20, 21, 22** in Section II, for references to financial controls exerted by central government upon local government.

The Government wish to give greater freedom to local authorities, but they cannot evade their own responsibility for management of the national economy, nor can they evade their duty to ensure minimum standards for essential services throughout the country. The problem for central government is how to resolve this dilemma within these constraints.

So far as management of the economy is concerned, the central government are able to influence the decisions of local authorities on current expenditure through the block grant and in other ways at the same time leaving individual authorities free in the last resort to decide for themselves how much they wish to spend. The Government welcome this. In view of the close working relationship between central and local government, experience shows that the aggregate effect of all these individual decisions can be predicted with some accuracy.

Capital expenditure presents different problems. There is a much greater possibility that, without central government controls, aggregate expenditure could substantially exceed the tolerable level. The local democratic concern may be with the immediate impact – the relatively small interest charges – rather than with the massive capital expenditure itself.

The Government have already introduced new procedures in England and Wales. These have reduced detailed government control at the same time giving local authorities greater freedom in planning their capital expenditure, simplifying administrative procedures and improving the central government's ability to monitor the total level and main trends of expenditure.

Under the new system capital projects in the 'key sectors' – those where national considerations and the need for maintenance of minimum standards weigh heavily – are controlled through programmes agreed with the responsible departments. For other projects each authority or group of authorities is given a block allocation for each year to spend as it likes in the 'locally determined sector'.

As experience grows, particularly in the new authorities to be created by local government reorganisation, these arrangements could be extended and in Scotland it should be possible to introduce control of capital expenditure through a system of block allocations.

Under the new arrangements the emphasis of the control is directed to the expenditure itself and to its timing. The Government will wish to discuss whether the present statutory control on borrowing for individual projects – the loan sanction – is still appropriate or whether it might be replaced by a more general control over capital expenditure.

The Control of Borrowing Order of 1958 made under the Borrowing (Control and Guarantee) Act of 1946 gives the Treasury a separate control which in recent years has been used mainly to regulate the terms and timing of borrowing on marketable securities for the purpose of monetary and market management and also to impose limits on the proportion of temporary debt. The Government in exercising their responsibilities will need to retain some powers to regulate the borrowing of local authorities but will both review the nature of such controls and also seek to simplify and widen the borrowing powers of authorities. Thus all counties, or regions in Scotland, and district councils might be given a general power to borrow including the consolidation of those special powers, such as to borrow in foreign currency or by the issue of bills, which at present depend on local legislation.

To ensure a real and effective partnership between central and local government, ways must be found of enabling local government to influence the central government's decisions on the total of local government expenditure.

. . . . . .

APPENDIX 4 THE FUTURE SYSTEM OF CENTRAL GOVERNMENT GRANTS

Introduction

Whether or not additional sources of local revenue can be found, government grants must continue to provide a substantial part of local authorities' income. The system under which grant is paid will thus play a cardinal role in the relationship between central and local government. The opportunity offered by local government re-organisation for a radical re-examination of the grant system must not be lost. And this aspect of local government finance is one which, above all, demands close consultation with representatives of local government. The ideas set out below are put forward as a basis for such discussion.

Character of Grants

One of the first questions to be settled is the relative weight to be given to block grants and specific grants respectively. How much of the total grant should be distributed as a block grant to which entitlement is determined by objective formulae? And how much should be related to actual expenditure on particular services? Block grants in some form have existed for a very long time. The Local Government Manpower Committee, however, drew particular attention to the detailed controls and intervention in local affairs which specific grants entailed and this led to the introduction of general grant under the Local Government Acts of 1958. Since then block grants have become dominant among government grants.

General grant replaced 10 specific grants and, together with rate deficiency grant, accounted for about 75 per cent of the grants paid towards the current expenditure of local authorities. The shift towards block grants was taken further by the Local Government Acts of 1966, under which rate support grants account for 90 per cent of grants towards current expenditure. A return to specific grants would be inconsistent with the intention that local government reorganisation should bring to local government greater freedom from detailed controls by central government. It seems therefore that as much as possible of the central government assistance to local expenditure should be given in the form of block grants and the Government therefore wish to explore with local government how many of the remaining specific grants may be absorbed into the block grant.

Despite the changes made in 1958 and in 1966, 47 specific grants towards current or capital expenditure of local authorities still exist. In the current year it is estimated that if the police grant, £111 million, the highways capital grant, £123 million, and housing subsidies, £245 million, are excluded, these specific grants will amount in total to no more than £100 million — or about 1¼ per cent of local government expenditure. Under many of them the amounts paid are very small indeed, but they each involve, to some extent, a specific control by central government over local authority activities; and the need to account for each in detail involves both local and central government in more work than if the services came within the block grant arrangements.

There may be good reasons why some of these grants should continue. Some are not so much grants as payments made for a service provided by local authorities as agents for central government; and it is therefore appropriate that some or all of the cost should be borne by central government in the form of a directly related payment — and indeed that there should continue to be control. Certain civil defence expenditure falls into this category. Others are grants which are paid also to persons or bodies other than local authorities, and for which local authorities are eligible when acting in a similar capacity. It seems inconsistent to deprive local authorities of such payments. An example of such a grant is that paid to fishery harbours, only a minority of which are the responsibility of local authorities.

A specific grant may be justified also where the expenditure on a service is large in relation to the resources of individual authorities, and its incidence is so irregular that it could not be adequately reflected in the distribution formula of a block grant. Such circumstances should, after reorganisation, be found rarely — except perhaps, in the case of some district councils outside metropolitan areas.

. . . . . .

Determination of the Block Grant

For rate support grant — as for general grant before it — the legislation provides that grant shall be fixed for not less than 2 years ahead. This was intended to provide some stability — letting local authorities know in advance what grant they would receive, and thus giving them the maximum freedom to plan their own expenditure ahead. In practice grant has never been fixed for more than 2 years ahead, and both central and local government have, from time to time, felt that even biennial settlements were too inflexible. As an alternative to the present pattern of biennial settlements, the total expenditure to which grant relates and the figure of grant might be provisionally settled for a 3 year period, but confirmed in relation only to the first year. Settlements of grant would be annual, but combined with the best indication possible of the trends, for, say, 2 years beyond.

An annual system would inevitably impose an additional burden of negotiation on both sides, but this might be considered a reasonable price to pay for the advantages the changed system would bring. In particular, annual settlements could be more closely meshed in with the Government's annual surveys of public expenditure . . .

Annual grant settlements and forecasts could, as at present, be made in terms of prices and rates of pay known and settled at the time of the settlement — subsequent increases when appropriate being taken into account in increase orders at the time of the negotiation of the next grant settlement.

As mentioned earlier in this Paper although the Government are seeking to give local authorities as much discretion as possible, they must be concerned with the total demand on national resources arising from the decisions of individual authorities taken as a whole; and must seek to influence these decisions by the amount of grant provided to augment local revenues. In each grant settlement therefore the Government's primary interest will be the prospective total of local authorities' current expenditure; but they will also be concerned in the share to be borne by local taxes and what contribution should be made from national taxation by way of grants.

. . . . . .

Once the forecasts for the total expenditure have been settled, it will be for the Government to take a view on the contribution that government grants should make. On this basis the present arrangement by which specific grants are treated as essentially a special element in the distribution of government grant as a whole would continue to be appropriate. But the present arrangements under which certain grant-earning expenditure is excluded from the total of relevant expenditure . . . lead to anomalies, and it is suggested that all such expenditure, including the gross expenditure of the metropolitan police, should be taken into account.

Distribution of Grants

Under the present grant system, having determined the total amount of the government contribution the amount expected to be paid by way of specific grants towards current expenditure is deducted and the remainder is the amount distributed as rate support grants. Some of this is set aside as the 'domestic element' to make good the loss of income from the reduction imposed by the Government in the rates in the pound which are levied on domestic ratepayers. The remainder — the great majority of the grant — is distributed as 'needs element' and 'resources element' which have regard to the needs of an authority to incur expenditure and to the resources available for that purpose. Block grant systems for many years have dealt separately with needs and resources and it is convenient to consider them individually now.

Equalisation of Needs

The formula for the distribution of the present 'needs element' incorporates over a dozen factors which are related to the need for local authority expenditure. These are: total population, numbers of children under 5 years of age, persons over 65, primary and nursery schoolchildren, secondary schoolchildren, further education students, university awards, school meals served, low density in persons per mile of road, high density of persons per acre, long term decline of population, the mileage of non-trunk roads and principal roads, and a special factor for authorities in the metropolitan police districts. The weightings attributed to all these factors, however, do not provide for equalisation of the burden of meeting needs; and, since the distribution formulae were originally established by reference to specific grants paid towards actual expenditure on individual services, one would expect to find only partial equalisation. With the evolution in the weightings over time there are now considerable variations in the extent to which various needs are equalised.

The right objective would seem to be the distribution of grant in such a way that the cost for each local authority of providing a standard level of service should be a standard amount per head.

. . . . . .

But the cost of providing a standard level of service varies widely throughout the country, and indeed the provision of a standard level everywhere is impracticable . . . However, if the principle of equalisation to a standard cost per head is accepted, it ought to be possible to derive a formula which would get a great deal nearer to this ideal than the present needs element formula.

. . . . . .

Equalisation of Resources

The present resources element of rate support grant has the effect of bringing up to a standard level the resources of all authorities with rate products per head below that level. In England and Wales at present the standard level is the national average, but in Scotland it is somewhat higher. Since the object of the grant system is to distribute a fixed total of grant among all local authorities in relation to their true needs and resources, a more equitable result could be achieved if a resources grant were given in such a way as to put virtually all authorities on a par. This could be done by bringing them up to the level of one of the richer authorities.

Because the formula for distributing the present resources element is based on the rate product per head of population, it results in equal rate poundages as between authorities incurring a standard expenditure per head. Thus if, after deduction of the needs element and of all grants other than the resources element, the expenditure per head of the authorities which receive resources element were uniform, so would be their rate poundages.

But equalisation of rate poundages does not necessarily equalise the burden on ratepayers. The wide variations in the rental values of domestic properties through the country lead to similar variations in rateable values, with the result for example that the rateable value of a 3 bedroom Parker Morris house in a northern industrial town may be only half that of a similar house on the south coast. The range of comparable dwellings can be as much as 1 to 3, excluding central London whose high values would further extend the range. Thus, if rate poundages were equal, the occupant of the house in the north would be paying only half the rates paid by the occupant of the house in the south. It is true that there are also regional variations in the level of wages, but these are not by any means as great; the range of variations in average industrial earnings between regions is only about 14 per cent. Thus the occupier of a house in the south is likely to be paying a substantially higher proportion of his income in rates than the occupier of a similar house in the north of England. To take full account of these variations a revised system might attempt to equalise not rate poundages but rate payments by comparable domestic ratepayers, by bringing into the distribution formula not only rate products per head of population but also variations in the rateable value of standard council houses and variations of average industrial earnings in each county or region.

Regional variations in the rateable values of comparable non-domestic properties are far less significant. Thus, while a system which sought to equalise the rate burdens for comparable householders might be appropriate for domestic ratepayers, a system designed to equalise rate poundages throughout the country might be more equitable for non-domestic ratepayers. There is thus a problem; that the system of equalisation which suits the domestic ratepayer may not suit the non-domestic ratepayer, and vice versa.

This problem might be solved by differential rating – that is to say, levying a rate of one poundage on domestic ratepayers and of another on non-domestic ratepayers. Differential rating in itself would not be new, in that the domestic rate poundage is already less than that levied on non-domestic ratepayers, and at various times in the past there has been partial de-rating of particular categories of ratepayer. The novelty would be that the differential between domestic and non-domestic poundages would vary from authority to authority.

This variation need not, however, be at the discretion of the individual authority. A relatively simple formula, similar to that used at present to calculate for each area the percentage entitlement to resources element, could be used to calculate the percentage by which non-domestic rate poundages should be reduced below, or increased above, the poundage to be levied on domestic ratepayers in the various areas. The calculations could be made and the percentages prescribed by central government.

Differential rating on these lines would mean that some local authorities would get an increase in their rate income from non-domestic properties, others a reduction. These effects could be compensated for in the distribution of grant – in much the same way as the domestic element of rate support grant at present makes good the reduction in income resulting from the lower poundage levied on domestic ratepayers. Those authorities who lost income by 'under' rating would receive extra grant, while those who gained income by 'over' rating would receive correspondingly less.

50 THE LAYFIELD PROPOSALS

From *Local Government Finance: Report of the Committee of Enquiry* (The Layfield Report, Cmnd. 6453, 1976); by permission of H.M.S.O.

1. When he announced the setting up of our inquiry, the Secretary of State for the Environment made it clear that we would be concerned not with interim problems of local government finance but with the long-term issues. Our inquiry was commissioned following the outcry against the unprecedented increases in rate demands in England and Wales in 1974. Complaints about rate increases were accompanied by widespread concern about the growth of local government expenditure. The immediate crisis was caused by a combination of factors which together would have placed an immense strain on any financial system and exposed any weaknesses in it. What the crisis exposed, however, was not simply the weak points in an otherwise sound system, but a collection of financial arrangements whose objectives were not clear and which had never been properly related to each other. The measures we consider to be required, therefore, are not merely adjustments to the present arrangements and palliatives to meet particular complaints, but the construction of a financial system.

2. The system should be based on accountability: whoever is responsible for spending money should also be responsible for raising it so that the amount of expenditure is subject to democratic control. The results should be fair both between individuals and between local authority areas. The financial arrangements should bring home to those taking decisions the economic implications of the choice between consumption and investment. They should also promote efficiency in the provision of services. The arrangements should be stable, flexible and comprehensible. These requirements cannot all be equally satisfied, but they are criteria against which any financial system for local government must be judged. The Redcliffe-Maud and Wheatley Royal Commissions were not asked to examine local government finance and the form of local government reorganisation was decided without a comprehensive review of the scope that it offered for new financial arrangements. As a result, a variety of two-tier organisations was adopted with diverse and overlapping responsibilities which present serious obstacles to the creation of a financial system providing clear accountability.

3. The financial system should reflect the roles of the government and local authorities. The government is responsible for the overall management of the economy. It is concerned with the level of output and employment, the balance of payments, the level of wages and prices, and the distribution of income and welfare. It needs to be able to ensure that changes in public expenditure, including local government expenditure which accounts for over a third of it, do not prejudice its economic objectives. The government is also concerned with the services for which local authorities are responsible, but control over their individual development is not essential for the purposes of economic management. The government now uses instruments designed for one purpose to achieve other purposes as well. It often appears to be pursuing conflicting objectives. As a result there is no clear control over local government expenditure and there is confusion over who is responsible.

4. The role of local government is to enable decisions to be taken democratically to cater for local needs and preferences. It was one of the purposes of local government reorganisation to strengthen this role, but in practice it has continued to be

eroded. How effectively local authorities will be able to discharge it in future depends on how much responsibility governments are prepared to let them have.

5. A financial system is not an end in itself but a means of achieving social and political purposes which lie beyond the scope of our inquiry. There is no simple solution. Choices have to be made.

6. The present arrangements have grown up over a very long period. Most of them have their origins in the last century and some go back even further. In reaching our conclusions we have been greatly influenced by the events of the last three years. But we have tried to consider them in perspective. It is not our main task to solve the immediate problems that currently face the government and local authorities. The frequency of change, especially in the last decade, has itself contributed to the difficulties we have observed, falsifying expectations, increasing administrative costs and dislocating the planning of resources. Although we make some proposals for early implementation our proposals are mainly of a long-term nature. Our inquiry is the first comprehensive review since 1914. Fundamental changes are needed with the aim of creating a durable system based on arrangements which are suitable for their purposes and consistent with one another. Many of the difficulties are of long standing. They cannot be quickly or easily overcome.

SOURCES OF REVENUE

7. The total cost of local services which has to be met from taxation in 1975/76 is £11,500 million. There are two separate issues to be considered in deciding how this expenditure should be paid for. The first is the final incidence of taxation, that is the relative burden of taxation on different classes of taxpayer and different income groups. The second is how much of that taxation should be levied by the government through the national taxation system and how much by local authorities from local taxes. In the past the two issues have had to be considered together because local authorities have only one major source of taxation so the question of how much taxation should be raised by local authorities could not be divorced from the impact of the rating system.

8. Rating forms a major element in the total taxation system, with a yield of over £4,000 million in 1975/76. There is a good case in principle for a tax on property, which is particularly suitable as a local tax. But the overall effects of a tax on domestic property, matched by the payment of a similar amount from public funds in reliefs and subsidies for housing, need to be considered in the current review of housing finance in order to ensure that in future the totality of the measures forms part of a coherent and equitable strategy. We have examined the effects of rating compared with other taxes and we have come to the conclusion that the abolition of rating would not be justified in terms of improving the incidence of taxation. Moreover, it is necessary to retain rating as a local tax in order to provide all district councils with a tax of their own. We consider that it is necessary to retain the rating of non-domestic as well as domestic property in order

to preserve the financial link between local authorities and industry and commerce in their areas that recognises their complementary interests.

9. For about 4½ million households the inherent regressiveness and unevenness of domestic rating is mitigated by the rebate scheme and supplementary benefits which relate rate payments to income and family circumstances. It would be neither practicable nor consistent with the nature of the tax to go further in this direction, for example by relating rate payments to the number of income-earners in each household. Although non-domestic rating can be made more consistent in its application, the unevenness and uncertainty of its effects restrict the contribution it can make to local taxation. Generally, while rating can continue to provide a substantial source of local revenue, we cannot suggest changes in the rating system which would enable it to finance a much bigger share of local government expenditure.

10. It would be practicable to introduce a local income tax provided it were accompanied by some administrative changes in the system of national income tax. We have therefore concluded that there are now two main possibilities: to continue with the present combination of rating and grants or to introduce LIT* as an additional source of revenue for those authorities responsible for the services that account for the most expenditure. In either case it would be practicable to reduce the burden of rating, in the one case by increasing grants and in the other by substituting LIT for part of the yield of rating. The resulting change in the incidence of taxation would depend in the first case on how the government chose to raise the revenue to finance increased grants and in the second on the adjustments in the national tax system which would be required to accommodate LIT. In either case the changes would be determined by the government's overall taxation policy. There is therefore likely to be little to choose between the alternatives we have suggested in terms of the resulting overall incidence of taxation. Whether LIT should be introduced therefore depends on a decision as to how much of that taxation should be levied by the government and how much by local authorities. That decision in turn depends on their respective responsibilities for expenditure. Although the present crisis has been seen by many as a financing crisis, changing the sources of finance will not prevent similar crises from recurring in future unless the new arrangement is founded on a clear definition of responsibility for expenditure.

RESPONSIBILITY FOR EXPENDITURE

11. The need for accountability for local expenditure is fundamental. For this reason we do not favour suggestions that a prescribed share of national taxation should be assigned to local authorities. Assigned revenues have the same characteristics as grants. The government must be accountable to the electorate at large through Parliament for the amount of taxes it raises. It cannot provide local authorities with a preponderant share of their income, whether in the form of assigned revenue or grants, without sooner or later taking responsibility for their expenditure.

12. If local authorities are to exercise discretion over the way they carry out

*LIT = Local Income Tax

their functions and to determine the level and pattern of expenditure on them, they should be responsible for finding the money through local taxes for which they are accountable. But the government also plays a major part in determining the level and pattern of local government expenditure. Government departments told us that they saw the relationship between central and local government as a partnership, which recognised their shared responsibility. In practice, expenditure is incurred in response to a wide range of pressures from the public, professional opinion and special interest groups which affect both central and local government. At present it is virtually impossible to distinguish their respective responsibilities for expenditure and for this reason there is a lack of clear accountability. We therefore considered a number of ways in which the financial responsibility of central and local government might be separated, so that expenditure arising from the government's decisions could be financed from national taxation and expenditure incurred by local authorities at their own discretion could be separately identified and financed from local taxation.

13. We received many suggestions that services such as education are really national rather than local services and should be paid for out of national taxation. The recognition that part of local authorities' expenditure on services was national in character was one of the original reasons for government grants. But for the government to pay the whole cost of a service would imply that it was wholly national in character. We consider that a service should be financed wholly by the government only if it is considered that there should be no room for local discretion in providing it. Moreover, we think that it would be unsatisfactory for local authorities simultaneously to be responsible to the government for some of their major services and to their local electorate for others. Such a division of responsibility would impair the ability of local authorities to consider the best balance of provision within their areas as a whole and would introduce distortions in the allocation of resources. The same considerations apply to the suggestion that the whole cost of specific blocks of expenditure, such as teachers' salaries, should be met by the government.

14. We were more attracted to the alternative of drawing a distinction between the cost of meeting national minimum standards, which should be financed out of national taxation, and the provision of higher standards at local discretion, which should be paid for out of local taxation.

15. We took a good deal of evidence and commissioned studies to see whether such a distinction could be drawn in practice. We came to the conclusion that it is not possible at present. There would be major practical problems in any attempt to lay down minimum acceptable standards in future. For most services standards could be defined only in terms of the manpower required or other measures of cost. Defining standards in this way would not be in the interest of efficiency and would not overcome the difficulty of measuring the cost of meeting them in each area. Basing contributions from national taxation on the actual cost of providing services would differ very little from the existing grant system. To provide a satisfactory basis for distinguishing national from local responsibilities, standards would have to

be defined for all the major services in terms of the results to be achieved and the necessary cost of meeting them would need to be established in each local authority area. Efforts to measure the output of local services in this way have not so far been very successful. We consider that whatever arrangements are adopted these efforts should be pursued in any event in order to promote efficiency and to help determine the distribution of grant. But a major commitment of resources would be needed to devise such measures and it would be optimistic to expect early results for the bulk of local government expenditure.

16. If these practical difficulties could be overcome, it is difficult to foresee whether a substantial measure of local accountability would ensue. It would be necessary to revise the form of statutes governing local services, which are mostly couched in very general terms. Once minimum standards were statutorily defined, there would need to be some machinery for ensuring compliance with them. Much would depend on how high the minimum standards were set and how they changed over time. The process of defining and revising them would itself tend to focus pressure on the government for their improvement. It would need to be considered whether Ministers would be content to set standards below the current level of provision and keep them stable for long periods, leaving local authorities to determine the pace and direction of growth; or whether they might set the standards high and change them frequently as a means of directing the development of local services. If, as seems possible, the cost of meeting minimum standards were to account for a large proportion of local government expenditure, a division of financial responsibility on this basis would tend to place the major share of responsibility with the government.

17. In the absence of a clear dividing line between central and local responsibilities, the present confusion can be ended only if the main responsibility for local expenditure and taxation is expressly placed either upon the government or local authorities. The first course would mean accepting the present drift towards central responsibility as inevitable and requiring the government to be more explicitly and formally accountable. No new source of local revenue would be needed but there would have to be significant changes in the organisation and procedures of government departments. The second course would require the introduction of a local income tax to supplement rating as a source of local revenue. But a wider local tax base could not by itself ensure that the present confusion of responsibilities was ended. It would need to be accompanied by the political will to allow local authorities more freedom to decide how to carry out their functions . . .

. . . . . .

New Institutional Arrangements

20. There is a need for a new forum to keep the financial relationship between the government and local authorities under continuous review, to establish closer contact between those who are concerned with the use of resources at both levels of government, to ensure more realistic estimates of the cost of introducing new legis-

lation, and to ensure the availability of coherent and up-to-date information as a basis for decisions and for monitoring their effects. Its membership should include Ministers and local elected representatives under the chairmanship of a Treasury Minister and it should be served by an office independent of central and local government. It is too early to say how the Consultative Council as constituted at present might develop, but it may be that it could be adapted to fulfil this role.

Improving Financial Administration

21. It is of the greatest importance that there should be adequate safeguards against waste, extravagance and inefficiency. While hospitality, attendance allowances and other expenditure attributable to councillors in the exercise of their functions accounts for only a small fraction of local authorities' budgets, all concerned in local government should recognise their responsibility to ensure that there are adequate internal safeguards against abuse. It is important that local authorities should obtain the maximum value for the money they spend on all their activities. More emphasis in the auditing of local authority accounts should be placed on efficient financial administration and value for money. There should be more systematic studies of the comparative performance of local authorities and periodic major reviews of trends in the use of resources in local authority services. To this end the audit service in England and Wales should be headed by an independent official who, with the advice of an expert panel, should have sole responsibility for the appointment of auditors to local authorities and for the organisation of the audit service. He should make regular reports on issues of general interest or public concern relating to more than one local authority. These reports could be made to a Parliamentary Committee or the new forum we have proposed or to a representative local government body.

22. The Chief Financial Officer of each local authority should be under a statutory obligation to report regularly to the council on defined major financial issues.

Transfer of Financial Responsibility

23. The government should meet the full cost of mandatory student awards, magistrates courts, probation and after care (in England and Wales) and means-tested benefits over which local authorities have no discretion. A new basis for sharing the costs of advanced further education and teacher training should be developed which will provide a closer and more evident relationship between what each authority pays and the benefit it receives.

24. The government should meet the whole cost of the Metropolitan Police unless local authorities in London are enabled to exercise the same control over its expenditure as local authorities exercise over police expenditure elsewhere. We do not recommend that the police service outside London should be wholly financed by the government. Such a change would have constitutional implications which are not for us to consider.

Capital Finance

25. We do not support suggestions that the government should write off existing loan debt or take over responsibility for its servicing. Nor do we think there should be a major extension of capital grants. Local authorities should continue to be able to finance capital expenditure from borrowing. The proportions in which they borrow from the market and from the Public Works Loan Board should be adjusted according to circumstances. The scale of temporary and short-term borrowing and the consequent need for re-financing should be kept under review. The practice of pooling loans should continue. However, new accounting arrangements should be developed which identify the full cost of using all assets.

Fees and Charging

26. A radical change in the policies for financing local services which would involve charging people to a much greater extent for the individual benefits they enjoy from those services could only be undertaken as part of a deliberate national policy which would not be confined to local government services. But there may well be scope for increasing the proportion of local government revenue derived from charges without any radical change in social policies. There should therefore be a review of policy and practice in charging for local services, to be carried out jointly by the government and local authorities. We have indicated what the aims of such a review should be and some of the considerations which should be taken into account. We have suggested that the accounting arrangements should identify the amount of any subsidy and that the amount of expenditure financed from fees and charges should be made explicit in the grant settlement.

Rating

27. For domestic property in England and Wales the rating system can be maintained only on the basis of capital value. Preparations for a revaluation on this basis should be put in hand as soon as possible. At the next revaluation the residential parts of business premises with living accommodation should be assessed so that those parts do not bear a heavier burden than other comparable domestic property. In Scotland the proposed revaluation should proceed in 1978 as planned and the basis of valuation should be reviewed thereafter.

28. The relative rate burdens of domestic and commercial and industrial properties should be determined by the government, having regard to the burden of rates on both sectors. The relative burden should not be changed between revaluations and that relationship should not be open to change as part of the grant settlement. Rating should be applied to the widest possible range of properties. These should include agricultural land and buildings. The method of assessment of public utilities should be in the hands of an independent body. Crown property should be assessed in the same way as other similar property, except where there are compelling

reasons against. We do not recommend any change in the rating of charities. Where assessments are made on the basis of rental values they should be made direct to net annual value instead of gross value.

29. Frequent and regular revaluations are essential. We propose modifications of the arrangements for appeals against assessments, designed to protect the interests of ratepayers while improving the prospect of regular revaluations. Rate bills should normally be payable by instalments by all ratepayers.

Grants

30. Block grants should remain the principal means of grant aid. Police grants should be included in the block grant and all transport expenditure should in due course be assisted in this way.

31. The distribution of grants should continue to take into account variations between areas in both their spending needs and their tax-raising capacities. Aggregate personal incomes are likely to be a more satisfactory measure of the ability of local authorities to raise money from domestic taxpayers in their area than domestic values. London should as far as practicable be included in the general system of distribution.

32. There should not be marked variations in the distribution of grants to individual authorities from one year to the next. The basis of distribution should be settled at least a year ahead of the current year. Adjustments for changes in pay and prices should not affect this basis.

33. There could be advantage in combining the needs and resources element of the block grant into a unitary grant, instead of treating them separately.

The Two-Tier System

34. Local taxation should be collected in a way which makes it clearer how much each authority is collecting and for what purposes. All local authorities should receive their own allocation of grant related to their expenditure needs and tax-raising capacity and should be responsible for their own taxation in England and Wales as in Scotland. An appropriate allocation of grant should therefore be made separately to metropolitan counties and non-metropolitan districts. The special problems of grant distribution within London should be considered with the London authorities.

. . . . . .

ALTERNATIVE SYSTEMS

39. We now describe arrangements which would be appropriate to the assumption, by the government or by local authorities, of the main responsibility for local government finance. In either case it is feasible to devise a system which could meet the main requirements we set out in earlier chapters of our report.

Central Responsibility

40. If the government assumed the main responsibility for local government expenditure, it would set the totals for local spending within fairly narrow limits. It would have to determine how much each authority was to spend and for what purpose. There would still be some scope for discretionary expenditure and a local tax would still be needed to finance it. The rates would be quite adequate for this purpose. The balance between rates and grants would be decided by the government on the basis of its judgement of what level of property tax would be desirable in the context of the total taxation system. There would still be some room for local authorities to vary their rate poundage to pay for discretionary expenditure. But the government would decide what rate poundages it expected local authorities to levy and any departure from these poundages would be clearly identifiable as the responsibility of the local authority.

. . . . . .

42. Control of expenditure would effectively be secured through the allocation of grant and, if necessary, limiting discretionary expenditure. To exercise control in this way would, however, probably require the submission of local authority budgets for scrutiny and approval. Where necessary it might mean adjusting either the grant or the approved items of expenditure in order to ensure that the grant and the yield of the standard proportion of local taxable resources were sufficient to finance the approved expenditure. Control would need to apply to both capital and current expenditure and there would need to be an associated control over borrowing.

43. The method of allocating grant and controlling expenditure would give the government a decisive voice in the policies and priorities of individual services. We have indicated, however, that there are a number of functions which local authorities could exercise with little government intervention, and there would be scope for local discretion in the management of the major services. Local authorities would also be able to influence central government policies through their collective voice in the forum we have recommended and individually through the closer contacts which would be needed with departments responsible for each service. But it would be difficult to reconcile the responsibility of councillors to their electorates for meeting the needs of their areas with their responsibility to the government to implement its policies. There could be particularly difficult problems where the political allegiance of the council was different from that of the government and there was strong disagreement about the policies to be pursued . . .

Local Responsibility

44. If the main responsibility for the level and pattern of expenditure on local services were to be placed on local authorities they would need to be able to raise a much bigger proportion of their own revenue from local taxation than at present. A local income tax would therefore have to be introduced to supplement the

revenue raised by the rating system. It would make for clear accountability and understanding if the major spending authorities levied only LIT and other authorities only rates. But because of the diverse allocation of functions and the other limitations on tax and grant levels such arrangements would mean high rates of LIT and the loss of a considerable part of the potential yield of rating. We therefore propose that all authorities should continue to levy both domestic and non-domestic rates and that the major spending authority in each area should also levy LIT. The government might feel the need to exercise some influence or control over the relationship between the two taxes and they might wish therefore to prescribe the limits within which the authorities with access to both taxes could vary the proportion of revenue raised from each of the sources.

45. The percentage of expenditure financed by grant would be much lower than at present, but there would be considerable room for judgement about the precise balance between grant and local taxation. It would be particularly important that the size of the grant should be determined earlier than now and its distribution stabilised. Because grant would need to be a smaller and more stable element in each authority's finances, grant negotiations would cease to dominate the discussions between the government and local authorities.

46. A unitary grant in this context would have the advantage over the present grant structure of enabling any desired degree of redistribution to be achieved with a lower rate of grant. But the grant would need to be expressed in a form which plainly did not imply that the government was seeking to determine what individual authorities ought to spend and what tax rates they ought to levy. The actual pattern of expenditure would continue to be accepted as the best representation of local expenditure needs. Serious efforts to improve the current methods of measuring local expenditure needs would therefore need to continue. The calculation of expenditure needs would however be used only to determine, in conjunction with the measure of taxable capacity, each authority's rate of grant. The grant would then be paid at that rate on whatever level of expenditure each local authority incurred. There should, however, be some limitation on the amount of grant in order to maintain adequate discipline over local government expenditure and to avoid an open-ended commitment by the government. For this purpose a level of expenditure would have to be specified for each authority, related to its assessed needs, above which the rate of grant would be reduced. This limitation should be settled at the same time as the grant itself so that authorities would know in advance how much grant they would receive in relation to any given level of expenditure.

47. The government must be able to influence the rate of growth of local expenditure for the purpose of economic management. We have emphasised that the exercise of such influence need not and, if there is to be local responsibility, should not be concerned with the allocation of expenditure between services. The existing detailed methods of control through loan sanction and the level of grant would therefore be inappropriate. If the grant is organised as we have recommended, local accountability, coupled with a much better understanding between the government

and local authorities, should provide a stronger discipline than at present over local government expenditure and should contribute to economic stability. Nevertheless, we propose that the government should have at its disposal instruments designed to exert a powerful influence over the growth of expenditure and its allocation between capital investment and current expenditure. The precise form of any new powers would depend on the financial structure within which they would operate but any proposal to change the degree of restraint being exerted should be subject to affirmative resolution of Parliament. Possible powers include requiring local authorities to raise additional taxation to finance increases in expenditure beyond a prescribed margin and prescribing the proportion of capital expenditure to be financed from revenue. We believe that instruments of this kind could provide a flexible means of influencing the growth of expenditure which could if necessary be applied severely when the economic situation required it without at the same time undermining local accountability.

48. The government will also have its own views about the development of individual services and their priority for expenditure. But it should seek to achieve its objectives by achieving a close understanding with local government rather than by detailed intervention and administrative control. Ministers with responsibilities for services which are administered by local authorities would have to be prepared to accept a less dominant role. An act of political will would be required to allow local authorities greater freedom to decide their own priorities and act accordingly. Where necessary specific legislation should be introduced to promote or alter policies when the government considers that to be essential.

Implementation

49. More explicit central control could be introduced fairly quickly. There has been a drift towards increasing government intervention for many years and many of the means of control are already available. The main new requirements would be to assess the expenditure plans of each authority and to provide that grant would be based on a prescribed figure. Some redeployment and perhaps some increase in staff would be needed.

50. A move to more local responsibility, on the other hand, would depend on the introduction of local income tax, which could not be achieved in less than five years . . . The amount that a given rate of tax would yield in each area, the new level of rating and the amount of grant to be paid would have to be worked out so that local authorities could decide what tax rates would be required to finance their expenditure and the government could decide what adjustments were necessary in its own taxation. The amount of money at stake would be very large and any miscalculation could have serious consequences.

51. In the meantime, it would be necessary to improve local accountability and some short-term measures would need to be taken to that end. The first requirement is that the grant should as far as possible be stabilised. We welcome the decision taken in making the grant settlement for 1976/77 to phase changes in dis-

tribution over a period of three years and to give advance notice of the level of expenditure on which the grant would be based. The grant should be fixed as far ahead as possible and in order to enable individual local authorities to plan their expenditure they should be given advance notice of the basis of distribution for later periods. Additional grants of a temporary kind should be introduced to compensate local authorities for unforeseen additional expenditure arising from new policies or newly-recognised special needs. In future Public Expenditure White Papers the implications for local government expenditure should be made clear.

52. Local authorities should be given more discretion over the way in which money is allocated between services and over the purpose for which loan sanctions are applied. The level of expenditure qualifying for grant will be based on the government's policies for local services, which will be set out in Public Expenditure White Papers. Nevertheless the government should refrain from issuing circulars and statements thereafter giving local authorities detailed guidance on how much money has been allowed for each service and how it should be spent.

53. These short-term arrangements would mean that the level of local expenditure would be determined by the accountability of local authorities to their electorates for the amount of rates they levied. Changes in grant distribution or the rating system that would obscure the relationship between spending and rate burdens should be avoided.

. . . . . .

MAKING THE CHOICE

58. We have suggested that the main responsibility for local expenditure and taxation should be placed either upon the government or upon local authorities. Each of the alternatives we have posed would provide a flexible basis for financing whatever level of local expenditure is considered desirable in future. Each would enable a fair and acceptable incidence of taxation to be achieved. In each case the responsibility for expenditure and taxation would be clear. The choice between them turns on what importance is attached to a few decisive administrative, economic and political issues.

59. First, introducing LIT is a necessary condition of greater local responsibility. The total public and private costs may well amount to about £100 million a year. The Inland Revenue would need to employ over 12,000 more staff. Such an increase in cost is not the most obvious way of setting out to achieve better value for money in public administration. But this cost has to be considered in the context of local government expenditure of some £13,000 million a year and the employment of nearly 3 million staff. The large and measurable cost of LIT has to be weighed against a judgement of the intangible but possibly greater gains which might be achieved in the use of these great resources.

60. Additional costs might also be involved if the government assumed greater responsibility. The preparation, scrutiny and co-ordination of budget proposals might involve some increase in staff for both government departments and local

authorities. More important, however, is whether more central control would lead to more burdensome administration at both levels of government. With an explicit chain of responsibility it is probable that much of the effort which at present goes into argument and persuasion could be reduced. But there would inevitably be a danger that, whatever the initial intentions, more detailed involvement by government departments would both increase the cost of administration and reduce its efficiency. There would also be a diversion of the energy and resources of Ministers and their departments from the tasks which only the government can perform.

61. The second main issue is the implications for economic management. If the government assumed responsibility it would effectively set the level of local government expenditure and would be able to ensure that it was not exceeded. But in doing so it would have to reconcile local needs and circumstances with the resources to be made available. The government would be subject to all prevailing pressures for increased expenditure. Local authorities would be making competitive bids for expenditure. Although they would still be concerned to make the best use of the resources available to them, they would be likely to pay more attention to obtaining more grant than making difficult choices about their own priorities. The Ministers responsible for individual services would be subject to even more pressure and we believe it might be difficult for the Treasury to hold the growth of local expenditure to a level consistent with other economic objectives.

62. If local authorities had the main responsibility the control of expenditure would depend greatly on the perceptibility of increases in LIT and the effectiveness of accountability to local taxpayers reinforced by the management of the grant. As compared with the situation described in the last paragraph, much would depend on whether local authorities would find it easier to persuade the government to pay more grant or their taxpayers to pay more tax. Much would also depend on how well local authorities would respond to the government's view of national requirements. Government powers to limit the expenditure which could be financed from increased local taxation would provide a powerful restraint on local authorities. These powers could be exercised solely on considerations of economic management without the Treasury being subject to pressure from spending departments for specific expenditure proposals.

63. The third, and perhaps the most important, issue is whether all important governmental decisions affecting people's lives and livelihood should be taken in one place on the basis of national policies; or whether many of the decisions could not as well, or better, be taken in different places, by people of diverse experience, associations, background and political persuasion. Local authorities are able to consider the needs and circumstances of their areas as a whole and respond to the preferences of people living there. There has been a growing demand for decisions to be taken closer to the people who are affected by them. We have pointed to the essential role of local authorities in enabling people to take part in decisions about the services and amenities in their areas, in promoting democracy, in acting as a counter-weight to the uniformity inherent in government decisions, and in providing a vehicle for formulating new policies and pioneering new ideas.

64. Governments on the other hand are elected with a programme to carry out national policies which may cut across local preferences. There are powerful pressures in society for more uniformity of provision, stimulated and expressed by well-organised and informed bodies of professional and other interests. From the point of view of organisations concerned with the welfare of the aged, the disabled or the homeless, variations in standards between one area and another are seen not as the legitimate outcome of local choice but as anomalies in the provision of services which happen to be administered by local authorities. Ministers who are subject to these pressures and who are anxious to implement their electoral commitments are also impatient of local choices which do not accord with their policies.

65. The pressures for uniformity are felt by local authorities also. While local responsibility would allow scope for the provision of services in some areas to advance faster than in others, it would not necessarily lead to wide disparities. But the standard or extent of local services and the level of local taxation would be determined to a much greater extent than now by the decisions of individual local authorities and could vary more widely between areas of differing social composition and political control.

66. Much turns on the value which is placed on local democracy itself. Central responsibility would tend to undermine the role of the local councillor. Most of the contact between government departments and local authorities would probably be between officials. Local government officers would therefore tend to regard themselves as increasingly answerable to government departments rather than council committees. In such circumstances it would be difficult to predict what the full consequences of adopting explicit central accountability would be upon local government that has been developed from an historical basis of local accountability by locally elected members. But it is likely that the main role of councillors would be to press the government for more grants to meet the needs of their areas. Shortcomings in local services could be blamed on the inadequacy of the grant, as they are increasingly at present. Ministers and their officials would become answerable to Parliament for local services. While local authorities might still retain a measure of discretion in the provision of services, their role would be a delegated form of local administration for which political responsibility clearly rested at the centre.

67. The choice we have posed is a difficult one. It is not for us to make it. It will have to be made by the government on a careful assessment of a wide range of administrative, economic and political issues many of which go beyond the scope of our Report. There is a strongly held view amongst us that the only way to sustain a vital local democracy is to enlarge the share of local taxation in total local revenue and thereby make councillors more directly accountable to local electorates for their expenditure and taxation decisions. On balance, we consider that the administrative cost involved in introducing a local income tax for this purpose would be justified. After many decades of uncertainty in the realm of local government finance the time has come for a choice on the issue of responsibility.

APPENDIX A. FINANCIAL STATISTICS

Source: Tables from The Layfield Report on Local Government Finance (Cmnd. 6453, 1976).

(i) Relevant Expenditure of Local Authorities. Division Between Types of Authority and Between Tiers. Great Britain 1975–76

Area of Great Britain	Number of Authorities	Division of Expenditure by Percentage Between types of authority	Between tiers
		%	%	%
Non-metropolitan areas			
Counties	47	42½	85
Districts	333	7½	15
Isles of Scilly	1	—	—
Total authorities in non-metropolitan areas	381	50	100
Metropolitan areas			
Counties	6	4	20
Districts	36	16	80
Total authorities in metropolitan areas	42	20	100
Greater London Area			
Greater London Council	1	9	45
Inner London	13	3	15
Outer London	20	8	40
Total authorities in London area	34	20	100
Scotland			
Regions	9	8½	85
Districts	53	1½	15
Islands	3	—	—
Total authorities in Scotland	65	10	
			100
Authorities in Great Britain	522	100	

(ii) Sources of Finance for Relevant Expenditure. Variations Between Types of Authority and Between Tiers. Great Britain 1975/76. (Percentage of Total Income from Rates and Grants)

	Non-metropolitan areas		Metropolitan areas		London		All Authorities England & Wales	Scotland		All Authorities Scotland
	Districts	Counties	Districts	Counties	Boroughs	GLC		Districts	Regions	
	%	%	%	%	%	%	%	%	%	%
Grants:										
Needs	–	39	43	–	50	–	34	19	55	49
Resources	30	15	19	26	3	2	16	25	10	12
Domestic	11	7	5	7	6	7	8	6	2	3
Specific	6	7	1	23	3	16	9	3	5	5
Total Grant	47	68	68	56	62	25	67	53	72	69
Rates:										
Domestic	24	14	13	18	11	22	13	21	12	14
Non-Domestic	29	18	19	26	27	53	20	26	16	17
Total Rates	53	32	32	44	38	75	33	47	28	31
Total Income	100	100	100	100	100	100	100	100	100	100

Sources: Return of Rates and Rating Review (published by Chartered Institute of Public Finance and Accountancy). Rate Support Grant Orders.

Notes

(1) Resources element in this table is assumed to be paid directly to the counties in England and Wales rather than through precepting arrangements. The figures used here for the resources element percentage going separately to the districts and counties have been provided by the Department of the Environment.

(2) The domestic element is assumed to be paid to both tiers of authority throughout Great Britain rather than to the rating authorities alone. The division of this element between the two tiers has been calculated in proportion to the average rate poundage levied by the two tiers.

(3) The figures for the GLC include income to the Inner London Education Authority and the Metropolitan Police Authority.

(iii) Growth in Expenditure by Local Authorities. Great Britain, 1949/50–1973/4

	£ million (current prices) Current Expenditure				Capital Expenditure			
Year	England	Wales	Scotland	Great Britain	England	Wales	Scotland	Great Britain
1949/50	849	—	100	949	331	—	45	376
1950/51	887	—	108	995	369	—	47	416
1951/52	988	—	123	1,111	426	—	58	485
1952/53	1,062	—	134	1,196	498	—	69	567
1953/54	1,127	—	142	1,269	544	—	74	620
1954/55	1,225	—	157	1,382	526	—	73	599
1955/56	1,331	—	171	1,502	541	—	72	613
1956/57	1,411	86	195	1,692	524	31	71	626
1957/58	1,537	93	202	1,832	499	29	71	600
1958/59	1,631	100	213	1,944	483	29	71	583
1959/60	1,759	106	221	2,086	539	33	72	644
1960/61	1,904	115	242	2,261	584	37	78	699
1961/62	2,102	130	264	2,496	697	45	91	832
1962/63	2,307	140	282	2,729	745	49	100	893
1963/64	2,515	153	308	2,976	921	58	130	1,110
1964/65	2,736	167	333	3,236	1,159	66	147	1,373
1965/66	3,118	189	366	3,673	1,225	64	155	1,444
1966/67	3,416	206	407	4,029	1,339	73	187	1,599
1967/68	3,761	227	445	4,433	1,486	77	228	1,791
1968/69	4,080	242	491	4,813	1,513	84	262	1,859
1969/70	5,112	293	555	5,960	1,613	94	251	1,959
1970/71	5,841	344	641	6,826	1,942	108	251	2,301
1971/72	6,691	389	722	7,802	2,108	123	261	2,492
1972/73	7,563	442	842	8,847	2,631	164	304	3,098
1973/74	9,189	543	1,001	10,733	3,510	228	397	4,136

(iv) Current Expenditure by Local Authorities 1973/74. Analysis by Service, Great Britain. Analysis by Type of Expenditure, England and Wales

(1)	Scotland	England and Wales					
			Salaries & Wages		Loan Charges		
	Total Expenditure	Total Expenditure	Expenditure	as percentage of total in col. (3)	Expenditure	as percentage of total in col. (3)	Other Expenditure
(1)	(2)	(3)	(4)	(5)	(6)	(7)	(8)
	£ million	£ million	£ million	%	£ million	%	£ million
Rate Fund Services:							
Education	353	3,357	1,828	55	302	9	1,227
Health & Personal Social Services	69	716	411	57	41	6	264
Police & Fire	68	658	513	78	24	4	121
Highways	65	560	185	33	89	16	286
Housing	26	283	10	3	184	65	89
Environmental	71	1,011	400	40	228	23	383
Other	88	1,133	656	58	38	3	439
Total Rate Fund Services	740	7,718	4,003	52	906	12	2,809
Housing Revenue Account	197	1,208	200	17	826	68	182
Other Trading	61	471	183	39	111	23	177
Total expenditure on Services	998	9,397	4,386	47	1,843	20	3,168
Superannuation & Special Funds	3	335	—		—		335
TOTAL	1,001	9,732	4,386	45	1,843	19	3,503

(v) Capital Expenditure by Local Authorities 1973/74. Analysis by Service, Great Britain. Analysis by Type of Expenditure, England and Wales

(1)	Scotland	England and Wales					
			New Construction		Land & Existing Buildings		
	Total Expenditure	Total Expenditure	Expenditure	as percentage of total in col. (3)	Expenditure	as percentage of total in col. (3)	Other Expenditure
	(2)	(3)	(4)	(5)	(6)	(7)	(8)
	£ million	£ million	£ million	%	£ million	%	£ million
Rate Fund Services:							
Education	58	479	325	68	74	15	80
Housing	38	774	10	1	40	5	724
Highways	44	329	257	78	56	17	16
Sewerage	29	286	251	88	2	–	33
Environmental	34	257	146	57	85	33	26
Other	24	305	210	69	30	10	65
Total Rate Fund Services	227	2,430	1,199	49	287	12	944
Housing	147	1,118	822	74	256	23	40
Other Trading	23	292	193	66	38	13	61
TOTAL	397	3,840	2,214	58	581	15	1,045

(vi) Sources of Income for Relevant Expenditure by Local Authorities. Great Britain, 1964/65–1975/76

Year	Government Grants	Rates	Total	Percentage of Total	
				Grants	Rates
	£ million	£ million	£ million	%	%
1964/65	1,156	1,107	2,263	51.1	48.9
1965/66	1,321	1,258	2,579	51.2	48.8
1966/67	1,457	1,415	2,872	50.7	49.3
1967/68	1,667	1,474	3,141	53.1	46.9
1968/69	1,784	1,561	3,345	53.3	46.7
1969/70	2,030	1,692	3,722	54.5	45.5
1970/71	2,377	1,839	4,216	56.4	43.6
1971/72	2,762	2,139	4,901	56.4	43.6
1972/73	3,303	2,420	5,723	57.7	42.3
1973/74	4,095	2,682	6,777	60.4	39.6
1974/75	5,023	3,100	8,123	61.9	38.1
1975/76	7,316	3,562	10,878	67.3	32.7
1976/77	–	–	–	66.4	33.6

Section V
The government of London

When the Local Government Commission for England was set up under the 1958 Act, London was excluded from its purview, and became the subject of a Royal Commission (established in 1957, under the chairmanship of Sir Edwin Herbert). The Herbert Report (**51**) in 1960, found local government in the national capital to be extremely fragmented, with no single authority able to exercise responsibilities over the whole metropolitan area. The Report proposed radical changes: a two-tier system, with a Council for Greater London, and 52 Greater London Boroughs. Despite considerable opposition, notably from the Parliamentary Labour Party, this solution was accepted by the government, and implemented by the London Government Act, 1963, with three chief modifications: first, a reduction from 52 to 32 second-tier authorities; second, the adoption of a minimum population size for these authorities of 20,000, instead of the 100,000 advocated by the Herbert Report; and third, the transfer of education from the first to the second tier, except for the area of the old London County Council, for which a special authority (the Inner London Education Authority) was created (**52**).

The decision on the required population size of authorities is significant, because the general figure in mind for the London Boroughs was an average of 250,000, later to be selected by the Redcliffe-Maud Report as a minimum population size for the provision of major services. Redcliffe-Maud was able to draw on the lessons of the London experience, as analysed by the Greater London Group (**53**), and must have been particularly impressed by the Group's judgement that 'the new London boroughs are of a size and have the resources for an efficient performance of their task'. And the 1963 reorganisation of London government can be seen to fore-shadow the metropolitan principle enumerated by Redcliffe-Maud and implemented by the 1972 Act. It is significant that the 1972 reorganisation produced relatively few changes in the London system (**54**); this suggests that the system created by the 1963 Act has worked reasonably well.

51 THE HERBERT REPORT

From *Royal Commission on Local Government in Greater London, Report* (The Herbert Report, Cmnd. 1164, 1960); by permission of H.M.S.O.

70. It is natural that after reviewing the history of inquiries into local government in the Review Area we should speculate on the causes of the setting up of our Com-

305

mission. These seem to us to be as follows, and we do not set them out in any order of merit.

(1) The spread of Greater London across the existing administrative boundaries and the creation thereby of new problems of local government. This is the continuation of a historic process.

(2) The wide discrepancy in size and resources of the authorities in the Review Area. This is, of course, not confined to the Review Area but is very marked in it.

(3) The influence of the history of local government in the Review Area, which has led in particular to two different systems, i.e. that within the Administrative County of London and that pertaining outside. The difference lies in the distribution of powers and in the existence of concurrent powers in important functions within the Administrative County.

(4) The demand by large boroughs and districts outside the Administrative County for county borough status and the consequent effect on county government. This has been present certainly for sixty years and is still strong. It is not of course confined to the Review Area, but the special circumstances of Greater London make it in a sense a different and particularly acute problem.

(5) The unsettling effect of the situation which has prevailed, with varying degrees of intensity, since 1945. The need for reorganisation has been in the air throughout this period.

. . . . . .

141. We have set out what we know to be a scanty summary of the story of local government in Greater London, and we now turn to the impressions which it leaves on our minds.

(1) First, there have been created within Greater London 'top-tier' authorities of a purely 'metropolitan' character, London County Council and Middlesex County Council, divided by a boundary explicable only in terms of history. These are both administratively strong authorities, but the London County Council's tradition is stronger and firmer than that of Middlesex. They possess two different forms of two-tier government, neither of them in substance like anything found elsewhere in England, even though the legal form in Middlesex is similar to that in other counties.

(2) The powers of both tiers of authorities and the distribution of powers between them differ as between London and the other counties.

(3) The authorities differ in other respects; some are very populous, some quite small; some are enormously rich in rateable value, others relatively poor; some have long traditions of unity within existing boundaries, others have been pieced together by more recent amalgamations.

. . . . . .

Party Politics

243. We do not conceive it to be any part of our duty to have regard to consider-

ations of party politics. We accept it as inevitable that whatever recommendations we make will be scrutinised in the light of possible electoral advantage or disadvantage. The control of the local government of a capital city is a prize on which party machines are bound to cast covetous eyes. We have already noticed how some of the evidence we received is coloured by considerations of this kind, and have recorded our view that this colouration is legitimate so long as its source is recognised. Indeed, it seems to us that under present day conditions party politics are a necessary part of the democratic process in local government, at any rate in a great city.

244. In almost all the local authorities in the Review Area the majority and minority parties are organised on party political lines, though the tightness of party discipline seems to differ somewhat as between one party and another. In most authorities major issues of policy, and even some minor ones, are settled in party meetings, so that the results of debates in council, and often in committee, are determined in advance; and indeed, as we mentioned in the previous section, one of the councillor's main functions is liaison between party and council . . .

. . . . . .

246. The rigidity of the system seems to decrease from the centre as one moves outward. It is strongest in the London County Council, where everything moves on party lines and where the distinction between representation and party membership seems to be a little blurred. We also noticed that a great many appointments made by the London County Council for unpaid service are made on a party basis, nowadays even down to school governors and managers, but we have not noticed the slightest inclination to allow politics to influence the appointment of officers.

. . . . . .

250. Accepting, therefore, as we do, the fact of party politics in a greater or lesser degree throughout the Review Area, we have rejected all suggestions made to us that we should consider the political consequences of one form of organisation or another. We have rejected the idea of some special form of suffrage (e.g. the single transferable vote) for London. We have also rejected any suggestion that we should recommend revised boundaries of local authorities so as to secure that political power is more balanced and that, as far as possible, long continued monopoly of power by one party or another is made less likely. We do not consider that this should be our business; it is a matter not peculiar to London, and in any event any such attempt would be speculative in its results. Whatever the form of government, political parties will adapt their organisations as the struggle for power requires.

. . . . . .

The Necessity for Overhaul

695. . . . . Where things are working well our inclination is to leave them alone. We do not believe that London's problems can be solved merely by improving the machinery of government. Our inclination is to recommend changes only where they appear to be essential.

696. In spite of these predilections the facts we have found to exist and the inferences we feel bound to draw from them drive us to the conclusion that, judged by the twin tests of administrative efficiency and the health of representative government, the present structure of local government in the Review Area is inadequate and needs overhaul.

697. We have made clear our belief that administration on the one hand and effective public participation on the other are integral parts of the one whole and that each deeply affects the other. We believe that anyone who reads what we have written up to this point will see that this is not merely a matter of theory but comes out constantly in practice. As we turn now to examine what changes in the structure of local government we should recommend, we hope that it will be equally clear that we have throughout tried to hold simultaneously in mind these two organically connected elements in the situation.

698. We start this examination from the premise that a number of the vital functions of local government within the Review Area require a broader treatment than can be given to them under the present system.

. . . . . .

Four Types of Solution in the Evidence

701. In so far as common problems are recognised to exist, four broad lines of approach have been explicitly suggested to us or are implicit in the evidence produced before us.

702. The first group of witnesses believes that for some purposes action can only be taken by central government.

703. The second group suggests the formation of *ad hoc* authorities for certain purposes.

704. The third group believes that these problems can be dealt with by consultation, more or less systematised, between local authorities and between their officers, or by the institution of joint boards or committees.

705. The fourth group believes that some form of local authority with a wider area than any existing is needed.

706. The first and second of these groups say, in effect, that local government machinery is essentially incapable of handling these matters and that it could not, by reason of their nature, be made adequate. The third and fourth groups of witnesses believe that a solution can be found within local government. This broad division of opinion is the first crucial thing for us to consider.

. . . . . .

. . . Now, having completed our task, we are convinced that the choice before local government in Greater London is, in truth, to abdicate in favour of central government, or to reform so as to be equipped to deal with present-day problems. There are great and growing problems to be solved and the present machinery of local government is inadequate to solve them. Unless this machinery is made adequate, the problems are so great and obtrude themselves so obviously on public attention that they will be taken out of the hands of local government.

. . . . . .

743. Our general conclusions are as follows:

(1) The primary unit of local government in the Greater London Area should be the borough, and the borough should perform all local authority functions except those which can only be effectively performed over the wider area of Greater London or which could be better performed over that wider area.

(2) The boroughs should have the style and title of 'Greater London Boroughs'.

(3) An authority covering the wider area of Greater London should be established with the style and title of 'the Council for Greater London'.

(4) The functions to be performed by each type of authority should be as far as possible self-contained without overlapping or duplication and without the necessity for delegation from one to another.

(5) The conception of an upper and lower tier of authorities should be replaced by the conception of the Greater London Borough as the primary unit of local government, performing all functions which can be performed within its own limited area, and of the Council for Greater London as a unit of local government performing functions which can only be or can be better performed over a wider area.

(6) The major functions of local government discussed in preceding chapters should be distributed between the Council for Greater London and the Greater London Boroughs in the manner recommended.

(7) The remaining functions of local government should be distributed between the Council for Greater London and the Greater London Boroughs in the manner recommended.

(8) The Council for Greater London should be elected by direct election on the basis of one member for each Parliamentary division and the voting should be in single member constituencies on the normal system. We can see no special circumstances in London which would justify us in recommending any special form of voting.

. . . . . .

(11) The appropriate range of population for a Greater London Borough should be between 100,000 and 250,000 and in constructing such Boroughs the following factors should be taken into account:

(*a*) As far as possible existing boroughs and county districts should be retained or amalgamated without change of boundaries.

(*b*) In shaping a new Borough, lines of communication should be taken into account.

(*c*) Regard should be had to the existing service centres.

(*d*) There should not be too many Boroughs.

(*e*) There is room for a little elasticity at each end of the population scale.

(*f*) There should be no county boroughs in the Review Area.

(12) The Greater London Boroughs should be delimited on the basis recommended . . .

. . . . . .

BASIS OF REORGANISATION

General Observations

745. We begin this chapter with some general observations upon the functions as we see them of the Greater London Boroughs and the Council for Greater London, and the relationship that should exist between them. We have no doubt that the Greater London Borough should be treated as the primary unit of local government in Greater London. In a tightly knit and largely built up area such as Greater London some functions of government which could in a large town, surrounded by country and isolated from other building development, be performed by a county borough cannot in the nature of things be dealt with by any of the Greater London Boroughs separately. But there is no reason why the greater part of the range of local government functions should not be performed by the Greater London Boroughs. The fact that the Greater London Boroughs are all part of a built-up area does not in principle differentiate them in this respect from boroughs of comparable size and resources elsewhere. It is necessary for certain functions to be performed by the Council for Greater London which outside London would be performed by a county borough, and therefore it is not practicable for the Greater London Boroughs to be county boroughs, since by definition the term 'county borough' excludes the exercise by any other local authority of functions within the borough boundaries. Nevertheless, we see no reason why the Greater London Boroughs should not perform most of the functions performed by county boroughs elsewhere.

746. Moreover, we believe that many of the functions at present performed by the counties, or divided as to their performance in Greater London between counties and county districts, could be better performed by the Greater London Boroughs. While we have had to treat with caution the terms 'remoteness' or 'nearness', those terms do stand for an important element in local government. Other things being equal, we see substantial advantages in having as many services as possible concentrated in the Town Hall, where they are administered by officers responsible to councillors representing a population of reasonable size. Our preference is in favour of making the size of the Borough as small as possible, having regard to the following limiting factors:

(1) that the scale of operations must be big enough to attract first rate people to the service of the Borough, both as councillors and officials;

(2) that the resources of the Borough must be sufficient to support the full range of Borough services, including both what we have termed compulsory and what we have termed voluntary services;

(3) that the size and population of the Borough must be large enough to make the administration of each of the various services reasonably efficient; and

(4) that the relationships between the Council for Greater London and the Greater London Boroughs might be more difficult to manage if there were too many Boroughs.

747. Lastly, and perhaps most important of all, we believe that the health of local government requires the rehabilitation of the metropolitan boroughs and county districts. We have already shown how their powers have been gradually eroded, not as a matter of policy but incidentally in the pursuit of national policies in relation to planning, education, personal health and other services . . . We believe that there is a serious danger that unless local government can be rehabilitated in the way we suggest there will be a drift towards some form of regional administration, with a good deal of intervention by the central government.

. . . . . .

CONSTITUTION OF THE NEW AUTHORITIES

Council for Greater London

. . . . . .

851. Those who have recommended the creation of such an authority have been divided on one main issue; should it be directly elected or should it be nominated by the other local authorities? We have come to the conclusion that it should be a directly elected body. The functions it will perform, if our recommendations are adopted, touch the lives of Londoners at many points. The planning of the siting of offices, factories, shops and houses, the management of traffic with its inevitable interference with individual liberty, the planning and construction of highways, the provision of a great deal of housing, the planning of primary and secondary education and the management of important sections of further education are matters upon which Londoners are entitled to make their opinions felt through the medium of the ballot.

852. Moreover, what is needed is a body representing Greater London to deal with the problems of Greater London. Its members ought not to be delegates from the Greater London Boroughs, whose functions are of great importance but limited in geographical scope. There ought to be ample scope in the work of the Council to arouse the interest of the electorate, especially as in our belief the creation of the Council would open the way to deal with some problems about which the public have become almost as fatalistic as they are about the English weather.

853. The Council will have a number of important functions to discharge in many respects wider than any entrusted to any county, borough or district council at present, but we hope also that it will be relieved of a great deal of the detailed routine which at present tends to clog the wheels of the county machinery. Allowing for the formation of the necessary number of committees, we conclude that a Council of about one hundred would be adequate. This being so, we think that the simplest course would be for one member to be elected for each Parliamentary constituency in the Greater London Area.

854. We think that all the members should be elected for a term of three years, and that all should go out of office simultaneously but be eligible for re-election. We are aware that there are arguments in favour of only a proportion of members retiring at any one time. To some extent this provides for continuity of experience. We believe, however, that the balance of advantage lies in requiring the Council as a whole to give an account of its stewardship to its constituents every three years in the form of a general election.

. . . . . .

856. At present the practice is that the electors vote on a Parliamentary constituency basis for three members of the London County Council and for one member of other county councils in county electoral divisions which do not correspond to Parliamentary constituencies. We believe it would be possible, and if so we think it very desirable, that elections for the Council and elections for the Greater London Borough Councils should be held simultaneously, so that at one and the same polling booth at one and the same time an elector votes on a Parliamentary constituency basis for one member of the Council for Greater London, and on a ward basis for his own Borough councillors as at present. It seems to us that this would bring about a very desirable measure of simplification and would help Londoners to understand better the types of council for which they are voting and the functions of the councils to which the candidates are seeking election.

. . . . . .

THE GREATER LONDON BOROUGHS

. . . . . .

924. The evidence reflected two differing points of view. Some witnesses put forward their ideas as to the size of boroughs appropriate for the Greater London area, making their own assumptions as to the functions which they would discharge; others based their evidence on the size of authorities best fitted for the discharge of individual services and generally on the assumption that the authority to be responsible would be responsible for the whole of that service. There has naturally therefore been a considerable variation in the range of population recommended for our consideration. A minority of our witnesses have favoured large boroughs with a population of 400,000–500,000, but the great majority of those who favoured a change from the present situation have recommended figures ranging between 100,000 and 250,000.

925. We are aware that as a matter of national policy the Local Government Act, 1958, assumes that a borough with a population of 100,000 is *prima facie* entitled to claim the status of a county borough and thus become responsible for the whole of the local government services. There is therefore not complete accord between the figures of population assumed by Parliament to be generally adequate for the discharge of all local government services and the evidence which we have received as to the appropriate size for boroughs in Greater London or as to the size which

would be most appropriate for the effective discharge of a number of individual services.

926. We have come to the conclusion that none of the various criteria of size expressed in terms of population which have been presented to us can be regarded as scientific, and all are subject to variation according to circumstances. There is no special virtue in any one figure; and although a population of 200,000 has probably been mentioned more frequently than any other, we think it well to remember that a borough of 200,000 is a large authority by the standards of this country and that there are authorities of half that size which no-one could characterise as being inadequate for their responsibilities.

927. After consideration of all the evidence submitted to us and in the light of our own experience, we have come to the conclusion that there is no particular figure at which we should be justified in claiming as a scientific figure, but that there is a reasonably wide range of population (100,000 to 250,000) within which the functions which we propose for the Greater London Boroughs can be effectively discharged.

928. We have given elsewhere our reasons for thinking that what we have described as the central area calls for exceptional treatment, and we do not think that the criterion of population should be the determining factor in the constitution of Boroughs in this area. The financial resources of this area are exceptionally high and the requirements of services such as personal health and welfare, in the organisation of which the case load is an important factor, can be met, when necessary, by combination or co-operation.

929. Outside this area two considerations have weighed with us in the application of a range of population. Where amalgamations are necessary — and we are satisfied that a substantial amount of amalgamation is required to produce Boroughs of the necessary size and resources — we think it desirable to amalgamate two or more existing units as a whole rather than, except when unavoidable or to a minor degree, to divide and regroup.

930. We are also of opinion that there is generally a strong case for creating Boroughs of greater population in the inner areas, where the population is closer together, than on the periphery, where an equivalent population would mean that many of the citizens would be remote from their centre of government. There are also a few areas where, owing to an exceptional concentration of open spaces, to adhere strictly to the lower limit would produce too scattered an authority.

. . . . . .

933. Our recommendation produces fifty-two new Boroughs. We do not consider that this number would prove unwieldy as regards relations either among themselves or between them and the Council for Greater London or between them and government departments.

The City of London

934. It will be seen that we propose that the City of London should remain as a

separate entity within its present limits. This is an anomaly but we recommend that this anomaly should continue . . .

. . . . . .

CHAPTER XX SUMMARY OF RECOMMENDATIONS

The Greater London Area

1000. The Greater London area should be as contained in our terms of reference, with the exclusion of the Boroughs of Dartford and Watford, the Urban Districts of Bushey, Chorleywood, Potters Bar, Rickmansworth and Waltham Holy Cross, the Rural District of Elstree, the Parishes of Aldenham and Watford Rural in the Rural District of Watford, and the Parish of Northaw in the Rural District of Hatfield.

Structure

1001. For local government purposes in this area there should be constituted a number of Greater London Boroughs and a Council for Greater London.

The Greater London Boroughs

1002. The Boroughs should be the primary units of local government and should perform all functions except those which can only be effectively performed over the wider area of Greater London. The needs of the wider area will make it necessary for concurrent or supplementary powers to be conferred on the Council for Greater London in relation to some aspects of environmental health and housing. Subject to this, the Boroughs should be responsible for:

Housing

Personal Health, Welfare and Children's Service (other than Ambulances)

Environmental Health (other than Refuse Disposal)

Roads (other than Main Roads)

Libraries

and they should have important functions in regard to education and planning.

They should have the status and constitution of municipal boroughs.

They should as a rule be within the population range of 100,000 to 250,000, and the necessary amalgamations should be broadly on the lines indicated in our Report.

The City of London

1003. The City of London should be treated exceptionally. It should be a Greater London Borough and should receive the additional functions proposed for these. Its relationship with the Council for Greater London should be generally the same as that of other Boroughs, although a number of matters, as for instance the Thames bridges, will require special consideration. In other respects the position of the City should remain unaltered.

The Greater London Council

1004. The Greater London Council should be the education and planning authority: statutory provision should be made for a distribution of functions between the Council and the Boroughs in the administrative discharge of these responsibilities. The Council should also be the authority for traffic, main roads, refuse disposal, and the fire and ambulance services. It should also have certain concurrent or supplementary powers for housing, the provision of parks and open spaces and of entertainments, main sewerage and sewage disposal, and land drainage.

The Council should set up an Intelligence Department to collect, collate and disseminate information relevant to the performance of local government functions in Greater London.

The Council should be directly elected with a member for each Parliamentary constituency in Greater London. Elections for this purpose should be held every three years, and at the same time and place as the election for that year of members of the Borough Councils.

Finance

1005. The existing London Rate Equalisation Scheme should be abolished and replaced by another of a different nature.

The County Councils of Essex, Kent and Surry should for a transitional period receive a payment from the Boroughs formerly in their Counties in order to reduce the rate burden falling upon them as a result of the change.

South-West Hertfordshire

1006. The proposal for a county borough of south-west Hertfordshire should not be accepted. There is in principle a case for the extension of the Borough of Watford, and such an extension is likely to increase the population to over 100,000. The decision about county borough status for Watford raises important questions of principle affecting the granting of county borough status to authorities adjoining Greater London and in the rest of the Home Counties. This is a matter appropriate to be dealt with by the Local Government Commission for England.

52 PROPOSALS FOR REORGANISATION

From *London Government: Proposals for Reorganisation* (Cmnd. 1562, 1961); by permission of H.M.S.O.

The Royal Commission

1. The Royal Commission on Local Government in Greater London was set up in December, 1957 —

> 'to examine the present system and working of local government in the Greater London area; to recommend whether any, and if so what changes in the local government structure and the distribution of local authority functions in the area, or in any part of it, would better secure effective and convenient local government; and to regard, for these purposes, local government as not including the administration of police, or of water, and the Greater London area as comprising the Metropolitan Police District together with the City of London, the Boroughs of Dartford, Romford and Watford, the Urban Districts of Caterham and Warlingham, Chorley Wood, Hornchurch, Rickmansworth, and Walton and Weybridge, and the Parish of Watford Rural in the Watford Rural District.' . . .

2. After an exhaustive consideration of the administration of the main local government services, and of the general functioning of local government in the areas, the Royal Commission summed up their conclusions in these words (paragraphs 695, 696) —

> 'Where things are working well our inclination is to leave them alone. We do not believe that London's problems can be solved merely by improving the machinery of government. Our inclination is to recommend changes only where they appear to be essential.
>
> In spite of these predilections the facts we have found to exist and the inferences we feel bound to draw from them drive us to the conclusion that, judged by the twin tests of administrative efficiency and the health of representative government, the present structure of local government in the Review Area is inadequate and needs overhaul.'

3. The Commission's criticisms of the present system fall under two main heads. First, they found that a number of vital functions — notably town planning, traffic, roads and overspill — which at present are the concern of many different authorities, require a broader treatment than can be given to them under the present system. Second, they found that for a variety of reasons the status and responsibilities of boroughs and urban districts have seriously declined; and they expressed the belief that the health of local government required the rehabilitation of these authorities.

4. The Commission's main recommendations, which were unanimous may be summarised thus:

(1) The conception of an upper and lower tier of authorities should be replaced by the conception of the Greater London borough as the primary unit of local government, performing all functions which can be performed within its own limited area; and a directly elected Council for Greater London as a unit of local government performing functions which can only be or can better be performed over the wider area of Greater London.

(2) The appropriate range of population for a Greater London borough should be 100,000 to 250,000 and, wherever practicable, existing boroughs and

county districts should be retained or amalgamated without change of boundaries.

5. The Commission recommended that the principle to be followed in assigning functions was that those to be performed by each type of authority should be as far as possible self-contained without overlapping or duplication. Their report contains detailed proposals for distributing functions. They considered that the boroughs' responsibilities should include housing, the Greater London Council having some concurrent and supplementary powers: personal health, welfare and children's services: environmental health, other than refuse disposal: roads, other than main roads: and libraries. They should also have an important part in the administrative discharge of education and planning functions. The Council for Greater London should be the education and planning authority, with some functions in these fields undertaken by the boroughs on lines to be laid down by statute, and the authority for traffic, main roads, refuse disposal, fire and ambulance services. They should also have concurrent or supplementary powers in respect of housing, parks, open spaces, entertainments, main sewerage and sewage disposal, and land drainage.

6. The report suggests the broad lines on which amalgamation of boroughs should take place, but the Commission made it clear that they had taken no evidence specifically on this, and that their recommendations were provisional.

Government's Main Conclusions

7. The Government have carefully studied the Royal Commission's report, and the views of the 100 and more local authorities and others who have commented on it.

8. The Government's main conclusion is that the Commission were justified in their criticism of the present structure of local government in Greater London, and that their broad design should be adopted as the basis for improving it. In particular the Government endorse the view that the boroughs ought to become the primary unit of local government; and that a new, directly elected, authority should be set up to administer functions which require to be dealt with over the whole of Greater London.

9. This conclusion is subject to two important qualifications of the Commission's plan. One is that the boroughs ought to be larger, and therefore fewer, than the Commission proposed. The other is that the structure recommended by the Commission for education is not considered to be satisfactory. On education the Government do not agree that the two-tier system proposed would be likely to work well. They think that, given larger boroughs, education could and should, over the greater part of the area, become a borough service. In the heart of London, however, the Government consider that the best arrangement would be to have a large education authority for an area comprising several boroughs. The Government's conclusions on education are set out in more detail . . . below.

10. Coming back to the broad design, the Government entirely agree with the Commission that Greater London has a recognisable civic unity and shape, largely

because it has grown outwards from a single centre. But its local government structure, inherited from the days when London was much smaller, in no way reflects that unity. The major services are administered by six county councils and three county borough councils, and three systems of local government exist side by side. They are: single-tier government in the county boroughs, two-tier government of the normal pattern outside the present administrative county of London, and a unique two-tier system within the administrative county, in which most of the important local government functions vest in the county council.

11. London has clearly outgrown the system of local government devised to meet the vastly different physical and social conditions of the last century. This great town now faces immense problems of congestion, of traffic, of land shortages, and of major redevelopment. All of its citizens are 'Londoners', not only those who live within the City and the 28 metropolitan boroughs. Greater London is their city and all are involved in what happens to it.

12. The Royal Commission were convinced that, unless some method could be found within the framework of local government to tackle the pressing problems of Greater London, the central Government would increasingly supersede the local authorities. They thought that that would be disastrous for local government, and they were right. That is the answer to those who say that a system of local government which recognises Greater London as a unit for some purposes is not local government at all. In the Government's opinion it is the only way to enable Greater London to enjoy an adequate measure of responsible self-government.

. . . . . .

15. The feature which attracted the greatest support was the conception of the borough as the primary unit of local government. The Government are sure that this is the right principle. It is a serious defect in the present organisation that many of the boroughs, and especially the metropolitan boroughs, have no real responsibility for the running of the local and personal services. The system proposed by the Commission would place personal preventive and environmental health services, welfare and children's services and housing, in the hands of one authority, local enough in character to enable local knowledge of the area and of its living and working conditions to be brought to bear. This would not only greatly enlarge the scope of the borough councillor, but would also make for more effective administration of these closely linked social services. The Government regard this as a key feature of the Commission's plan, and one well designed to attract into local government more men and women of real ability, by making sure that there are worthwhile jobs for them to do. If any re-organisation of local government does not secure this it will fail of its purpose.

. . . . . .

18. The Government recognise that the abolition of the present county pattern in the London area will present formidable problems of organisation. Their concern is to get the best administrative structure for local government. When that is settled they will give consideration to such related matters as the arrangements for the administration of justice, for the lieutenancies and for sheriffs. In general they wish

to emphasise that they propose to make only changes which are needed to achieve their main purpose and matters consequential to it. These proposals should not affect any existing cultural, social, sporting or other associations or loyalties which may be based on the traditional counties. They are, however, convinced that London needs a form of local government organisation to match its present physical shape and state. They are convinced, too, that this organisation must be one which recognises the unity and cohesion of the area, and which would combine ability to handle those issues that demand a comprehensive view of the whole area with the capacity to grapple effectively with the many and complex local problems. The Government believe that, provided these conditions are met, the new structure will provide fuller opportunities for really worthwhile local government service.

The Boroughs

19. The Royal Commission suggested that the boroughs should fall within the population range 100,000 to 250,000, and provisionally proposed a pattern comprising 52 new boroughs (including the City). The Local Government Act, 1958, provides that, in so far as the constitution of a new county borough outside the metropolitan area is affected by considerations of population, the Minister should presume that a population of 100,000 is sufficient to support the discharge of the function of a county borough council. This does not mean, however, that larger units would not be better if they could be set up without loss of convenience. Larger units would mean more work for each authority in all the personal services, and so make specialisation in staff and institutions more efficient and economical. In addition, larger units would be stronger in resources and so better able to secure the major redevelopments which many boroughs now need. They would be better able to maintain and improve the standard of their services and to undertake their development as circumstances may require. Moreover the very nature of London – continuously built-up at high densities, with a comprehensive system of transport and a population which in many of its daily activities pays little regard to local boundaries – distinguishes it from the typical county borough. Hitherto, London has suffered in its local administration from too great a proliferation of not very strong authorities. The aim now should be to create units which, while retaining their local character, are well equipped to provide a fully adequate standard of local services. In a closely-knit area such as London, the Government believe that this object can best be assured by aiming at a larger minimum population and rather fewer boroughs than suggested by the Commission. They consider that this will make not only for higher standards, but also for greater economy in administration.

20. The Government's general conclusion about the size of the boroughs is that it would be desirable to aim at a minimum population of around 200,000 wherever possible. Some boroughs might be substantially larger than this. They propose shortly to circulate, as a basis for consultation with the local authorities, an illustration of how larger boroughs might work out.

. . . . . .

22. The Government agree with the Royal Commission in thinking that the boundaries and status of the City of London should remain unchanged, and that it should receive the additional powers given to boroughs in the London area.

The Greater London Council

23. The Government agree that the Greater London Council should be directly elected. They propose to adopt the Commission's plan that its members should serve for three years and retire together.

. . . . . .

25. The Government agree generally with the principles applied by the Commission in deciding which areas they should recommend for inclusion in the Greater London administrative area. When consultation takes place with the local authorities about the borough pattern, there will be opportunity for any peripheral authority to make known its views about its inclusion in or exclusion from the London area. The districts left out of the London area will be brought within the ambit of the Local Government Commission, who will then of course be able to consider, among other things, Watford's claims for county borough status.

Functions

26. The following paragraphs set out the Government's broad proposals with regard to the administration of particular functions; many matters of detail will naturally require further consideration.

Personal Health and Welfare Services and Children's Services 27. There was no doubt in the Commission's mind that these services, with the exception of the ambulance service, should all be organised on as local a basis as possible; they recommend that they should become a borough responsibility. The Government agree with this conclusion. They concur also in the belief that positive advantages will follow from the concentration of responsibility for these services, and other associated ones such as housing and environmental health, in the hands of the same authorities.

Housing 28. The Government accept the Royal Commission's main conclusion that housing is essentially a borough service. New boroughs ranging upwards from around 200,000 population should be able to handle all aspects of their housing problems (including slum clearance) which can be solved within their own boundaries.

29. The Government think, however, that it would be right to confer reserve housing powers on the Greater London Council. That body should be solely responsible for arrangements for overspill outside the area. They should be empowered to build within the area if and only if that is necessary to help a borough unable to solve its own problems, or to secure development in accordance with the development plan. The Council should not build within the area except with the

consent of the council of the borough in question, or of the Minister if the two councils are unable to agree.

30. The Government concur in the Commission's proposal that houses in Greater London at present owned by the London County Council should pass initially to the Greater London Council. They also consider — a point not touched on by the Royal Commission — that in the first instance the houses owned by the London County Council outside Greater London would have to be transferred to the new Council. But in time all these houses ought, in the Government's opinion, to be transferred to local ownership and management.

Town and Country Planning 31. The Commission's main proposals were that the Greater London Council should be responsible for the preparation and periodic review of the development plan for the whole area, although, subject to some qualifications, the borough councils should be responsible for dealing with individual planning applications. The Government agree that this general scheme of working is right.

32. The need to have one plan for the whole of Greater London was the point on which there was the most complete agreement among the authorities in their comments on the Commission's report. The alternative proposals put forward by the county councils envisaged a master plan prepared by a joint planning board — a set of general principles, within the framework of which the present planning authorities would prepare their own development plans. The Government do not believe that this scheme would prove effective. It is true that the county councils who sponsored the joint board scheme also urged the need to look at a much wider area than that adopted in the Royal Commission's proposals; and it is true, too, that the influence of London spreads far beyond the continuous built-up area. There is however a clear distinction between the nature of the planning problems in the main built-up area — which clearly must be looked at as an entity for planning purposes — and those in the areas beyond. The two react on each other, but they can be handled separately.

33. A number of detailed matters connected with the part which the borough councils should play in planning, both in the build-up of the overall plan and in the handling of individual planning applications, need further consideration, and on these the Government have yet to reach final conclusions. In particular, further examination will be given to the proposition that it may be desirable to define special areas and within those areas to specify the kinds of development calling for reference to the overall authority.

34. The planning powers so far considered are those dealing with overspill, the development plan and the control of land use. Planning authorities also have powers to carry out comprehensive redevelopment, and that raises the question whether the Greater London Council should have any function in this field. Clearly the borough councils can be left to deal with most of such development entirely within their own boundaries — certainly in so far as it is of a fairly normal character, such as the clearance and fresh layout of obsolete development and minor improvement

to the road pattern. But where major schemes are concerned, entailing perhaps exceptionally heavy expenditure, on occasion traversing borough boundaries and usually involving major road improvements and affecting traffic conditions over a wide area, it may be necessary for the Greater London Council to carry out the work. In the Government's view they should have powers to do so, but (as in the case of housing) exercisable only with the consent of the borough councils concerned or, if there is no agreement, of the Minister.

Traffic and Highways 35. As with planning, there was widespread agreement that traffic management and the construction of main highways raised urgent problems which could be solved only in the context of Greater London as a whole. The essential recommendations of the Royal Commission in this field were that one authority should be responsible for traffic management throughout Greater London, and that the same authority should be responsible for the construction, improvement, maintenance and lighting of all main roads.

36. The Government accept both these recommendations in principle. A number of detailed matters will require consideration, especially the question of the complementary functions of borough councils, but in the Government's view there is no doubt that ultimate responsibility for traffic management and main roads should be placed on the Greater London Council.

37. The Commission differentiate between 'main roads' (by which they mean those chiefly used by through traffic) and other roads, and recommend that within Greater London this distinction should replace the existing road classification. All main road work should then rank for grant. The Government intends to give further study to these proposals, and also to the extent to which main roads in the Greater London area should or should not be designated as trunk roads under the direct responsibility of the Ministry of Transport.

Education 38. The proposal of the Royal Commission was that education functions should be divided between the Greater London Council and the boroughs. The Government appreciate the considerations which led the Commission to this proposal: that it is most important to give to the London boroughs an effective role in education; but that to divide the whole metropolitan area up into 50 or so self-contained units would result in a too fragmented system, especially in the heart of the area, where schools and institutions have been provided without regard to borough boundaries, and where the free movement of pupils across these boundaries has been one of the strengths of London's educational system.

39. The Government do not feel able to accept the division of the services between the two different types of authority. This is a system that can be made to work, but, as the Royal Commission themselves pointed out, it has not always worked very satisfactorily, and the Government believe that it would be wrong when reorganising the local government system in Greater London deliberately to legislate for a divided responsibility in the educational field.

40. As already indicated, the Government's view is that there should be assigned

to the boroughs services which can be effectively provided at the local level, and to the Greater London Council those functions which require to be planned and co-ordinated over the whole built-up area. Following this principle, they are satisfied that it would be wrong to entrust to the Greater London Council the function of carrying out the whole education services for Greater London; the area is far too large to form a single education unit. Moreover, their proposals to organise the area in larger and fewer boroughs than the Commission envisaged makes a big difference. The Government believe that, given larger boroughs, it would be satisfactory that over the greater part of the area education should become a borough service.

41. They do not think, however, that this would be right in the centre of London, where the absence of administrative boundaries and the consequent complete freedom for choice for pupils and students, is of special value. Here they would wish to see one education authority for an area much larger than can be envisaged for the individual boroughs. It might well be that a central area with a population of the order of 2 million would be appropriate.

. . . . . .

Environmental Health Services 46. The Government agree with the Royal Commission's conclusion that, subject to certain exceptions, the environmental health services should be the responsibility of the borough councils. In the Government's view there is a clear case for making the Greater London Council responsible for refuse disposal (as distinct from collection), and they agree with the Commission's proposal on this point. Further thought needs to be given to the allocation of responsibilities for main sewerage and sewage disposal, for land drainage and for certain major parks and open spaces.

Ambulance Service 47. The Government agree with the Commission's recommendation that the Greater London Council should be responsible for the ambulance service; the area for the efficient operation of the ambulance service is very much larger than that appropriate to the other health and welfare services.

Fire Service 48. The Government also agree that this service can more effectively be organised over a wider area, and should be the responsibility of the Greater London Council.

. . . . . .

Intelligence Department 50. The Commission recommended that the Greater London Council should set up a first-class intelligence department for continuous research into the many interlinked problems of Greater London as a whole, a department which should serve not only the authority itself but also the borough councils, the central Government and the public. In the Government's view there is a clear need for such an intelligence department, and they fully endorse the Commission's proposal.

Finance

51. Obviously the financial implications of any reorganisation of local government must be carefully considered. In the Government's view the financial arrangements should follow consequently on changes which are necessary for other reasons. It would be premature at this stage to set out detailed proposals on finance. There are many factors which make a reliable estimate of the financial consequences of reorganisation impossible at the present time. The probable effect on rate resources of the general revaluation for 1963 will not be known until 1962. The future cost of services when they fall to be carried out by altered or enlarged local authorities cannot be very closely estimated. For these reasons the Government have not yet reached a final conclusion on the Commission's proposal that the counties of Essex, Hertfordshire, Kent and Surrey should, for a limited period, be granted financial relief in respect of the severance of parts of those counties.

52. The Government appreciate that the reorganisation proposed would involve considerable reduction in the resources of Surrey, Essex and Kent, but they see no reason to dissent from the Commission's view that each of these counties would remain financially viable. Compensation for added burdens resulting from boundary adjustments has caused considerable difficulty and friction in the past, and the statutory provision for it was repealed by the Local Government Act, 1948. The Government would be reluctant to revive the principle of compensation for added burdens, though they will consider when further figures are available whether an exception should be made for the counties affected by the reorganisation of London Government.

53. The Commission noted that the average rate resources per head of population were higher in Greater London than in the rest of the country. But they recommend that a scheme of rate equalisation should be introduced to reduce the disparity between rates in the central area and those which may have to be levied by some of the other boroughs in Greater London. The Government agree that a scheme is needed.

53 AN ASSESSMENT OF THE LONDON REFORMS

From *Redcliffe-Maud, Research Study No. 2: The Lessons of the London Reforms* (1968); by permission of H.M.S.O. This report was the work of the Greater London Group, a study group at the London School of Economics and Political Science. Since the new London system came into effect only in 1965, the study is based on a relatively brief period of practical operation. For a more detailed account, see G. Rhodes and S. K. Ruck: *The Government of Greater London* (Allen & Unwin, 1970).

The general consensus of opinion among those most closely concerned with their implementation is that the London Government reforms are proving a success, though it must still be some time before their full potentialities are realised.

In the first place there is now one authority responsible for the strategic planning of London, or at least of the greater part of its built-up area. Clearly the influence of the Metropolis extends far beyond the present Greater London boundary, but there is no agreement as to the limits of this extent. In these circumstances it is logical to regard the continuous built-up area as the minimum overall administrative unit, and the confines of this area are roughly defined by the inside of the Green Belt. Precise limits, having regard to existing administrative units, were laid down by the Herbert Commission after prolonged consideration of the problem. On the whole, their recommendations were adopted, but owing to political considerations considerable areas were omitted, mainly in the South West. If the Greater London boundaries were revised, it would seem desirable to take the continuous built-up area as the criterion, and to consider again the proposals of the Herbert Commission.

Secondly, the most-purpose authorities, the new London Boroughs are of a size and have the resources for an efficient performance of their task.

Thirdly, there has been a remarkable degree of co-operation and mutual understanding between the GLC and the Boroughs. There have of course been differences between the two tiers, but these have nearly all been amicably resolved, sometimes in favour of the GLC, sometimes of the Boroughs, but by no means always one way.

When the situation is examined in more detail, there have been disadvantages and difficulties as well as advantages in the change, but the majority of the former seem capable of being overcome in the course of time. A contributory factor in some of the difficulties has been certain defects in the framing of the London Government Act.

(a) Advantages

(i) The Greater London Council *Highways* and *Traffic Management* are intimately related, and the responsible committee of the GLC is concerned with both.

With regard to *Highways*, the effects of its decisions are as yet hardly visible to the public, since those schemes which are completed or in progress were in the pipeline before the advent of the GLC. But plans are now being completed for the situation in London in 1981 and after, when, it is estimated, the traffic will be nearly twice what it is today. They include the provision of the motorway box round Central London at a cost in the neighbourhood of £400 millions, improved North and South Circular Roads and a new outer ring road. Only an authority with the resources and status of the GLC could hope to implement projects of this magnitude. Meanwhile a great number of smaller improvement schemes are being carried out throughout the Greater London area.

Responsibility for *Traffic Management* was taken over by the GLC from the London Traffic Management Unit of the Ministry of Transport. No Londoner will be in any doubt as to the amount of activity which has taken place in this sphere, but again many of the schemes which have come into operation since 1965 were in the pipeline before that date. Nevertheless traffic management orders made by the GLC have increased in number from 92 in 1965 to 255 in 1967, which is some indication of the effort the GLC is putting into its task . . .

It is not easy as yet to pronounce on the success of these efforts.

All that can be safely said is that traffic conditions have not worsened since 1964, despite a large increase in the number of registered vehicles, and may have slightly improved.

In the sphere of *Housing* the GLC is not only dealing with the problem of over-spill by the organisation of emigration to New Towns and elsewhere on an even greater scale than the London County Council but it is also doing what the LCC was not in a position to do, that is, enlisting the co-operation of the Outer Boroughs in relieving the overwhelming difficulties of those near the centre. It can also play a strategic role in the 'rippling out' process — i.e. in assisting those who while unwilling to live outside Greater London, are prepared to move from the Inner to the Outer Boroughs.

In *Planning* the advantages of the strategic powers are not yet fully apparent since the Greater London Development Plan is not to be presented until the end of 1968, and the published interim plan was somewhat disappointing. But there is promise in the thoroughgoing nature of the work being undertaken in preparation of the plan, more particularly in respect of the land use, employment and housing surveys.

. . . . . .

(ii) The London Boroughs Foremost among the advantages of the new Boroughs are the increased resources at their disposal. This gives them the possibility of attracting higher grade staff and more specialists, to pursue positive training and recruitment policies and to offer better career prospects. They can undertake projects beyond the scope of their predecessors. Centralised supply service both within the boroughs and with the wider use of the GLC Supplies department, has effected economies. The larger and more diversified areas covered by the new boroughs facilitate greater flexibility in the use of resources, more particularly in the way of specialised equipment.

Their increased responsibilities and heavier load of work has encouraged them to take a close look at their administrative procedures in order to speed the despatch of business. Some have already cut down the number of committees, have introduced methods of achieving better overall control and co-ordination, and have recognised the need for more delegation to Committee Chairmen and officers.

Initiative and innovation have been fostered, not only in administration, with a greater concentration on organisation and methods, work study and the use of computers, but also in such fields as public relations, social studies and shopping surveys.

The allocation to the Boroughs of most of those functions which most nearly concern the individual citizen has brought local government closer to him and should in time make it a more comprehensible entity, and the efforts now being made to improve their public relations should enhance this effect.

With regard to the functions previously administered by the constituent authorities for which the new boroughs are now responsible, the effect has been a general levelling up to the best standards in force at the time of the take over . . .

. . . . . .

Of the functions newly undertaken by the boroughs, by far the most important are the *Welfare Services* (Children's, Personal Health and Welfare Departments). By general consent this is leading to an all round improvement, not only in the individual services, but in their co-ordination, and in particular in their co-ordination with Housing. In some boroughs it has already been found possible to house them together under one roof. The smaller size of the authorities has kindled informed enthusiasm among a larger number of members and the services have become more accessible to the public (the marked increase in the number of Registered handicapped is an indication of this) . . .

In the 20 Outer London Boroughs now responsible for *Education* there is a general feeling that the change has effected improvements, certainly in the field of primary and secondary education, less certainly in further and specialist education. Policy is now made by those who have personal knowledge of the area, and is less of a Procrustes bed where the need for conformity may disregard the claims of the outlying parts. This it is considered combines efficiency with improved democratic control. Members and officers are nearer to pupils, teachers, parents and employees: in particular, there are closer relationships between Chief Officers and head teachers.

. . . . . .

(*b*) Disadvantages and Difficulties

. . . . . .

(i) **Those Affecting both GLC and Boroughs** Curiously little attention was given either by the Herbert Commission or in the discussions which preceded the Act to the results of the reforms on the manning of the new authorities, or on their financial effects . . .

With regard to *staff*, it is true that the Act established a Staff Commission but the main objective of this was to safeguard the position of serving officers, and it was little concerned with the manpower efficiency in the new authorities. One borough has gone so far as to say that its operations were a hindrance rather than a help.

. . . the increase in the total number of specialist departments, notably in the fields of the welfare services and planning, disclosed a serious shortage of trained and experienced officers in those fields. As a result, competitive bidding began among the boroughs to fill thin establishments (and in the case of planning with the GLC also) and positions were upgraded in order to attract candidates. To meet this situation, the London Boroughs set up organisations for the training of social workers and planners, and are endeavouring to ensure that those trained shall remain with the training authority. To combat competitive bidding through the upgrading of posts, the London Boroughs Association in association with the GLC, the Whitley Council, and the London Boroughs' Training Committee is shortly to study the stabilisation of grading through methods of job evaluation. Meanwhile the shortages, which are nation wide, continue and inhibit progress in various directions.

The two main defects of the London Government Act were first that a joint responsibility was given to the GLC and the Boroughs for certain functions (notably Planning, Housing and Highways and Traffic) without sufficiently clear definition as to what their respective responsibilities were. Secondly, the permanent administrative structure in Greater London in respect of Education and Parks was left undecided.

To grapple with the problems involved in *Planning* an Officers' (GLC and LBA) Joint Working Party was established early in 1965 with which technical officers from the Ministry of Housing and Local Government have from time to time been associated. It is a measure of the complexity of these problems, and the assiduity with which their resolution has been pursued, that this body had produced its twelfth report by November 1966. As a result of its efforts, a firm understanding has been reached as to the role to be played by each of the two tiers, and in consequence planning applications are now being dealt with expeditiously (apart from the few cases of peculiar complexity which arise) and the means have been agreed of obtaining the basic data from which the Greater London Development Plan can be framed.

The Group considers that further defects in the present planning set-up are
  (i) that the GLC has been given no specific power to plan in detail London's vital central area nor to exercise planning control in that area;
  (ii) that the Ministry of Housing and Local Government, and not the GLC, is responsible for the decisions of appeal against the London Borough planning decisions. This has imposed a burden on the Ministry resulting in intolerable delays and it is moreover a function which should properly belong to the planning authority for Greater London . . .

In the field of *Housing* a somewhat similar role to that of the Officers' Working Party on planning is played by the Standing Working Party on London Housing. This was set up in 1965 as a result of the initiative of the Joint Parliamentary Secretary of the Ministry of Housing and Local Government, and comprises three members from the Ministry, five from the London Boroughs Association and four from the GLC, with an officer from the Ministry as Secretary. This produced its first report in January 1967 called 'The Housing Role of the Greater London Council within London', which goes some way towards defining responsibilities, but does not resolve the question left open in the London Government Act as to how long the GLC shall continue to exercise concurrent powers with the Boroughs and when the former L.C.C. housing estates, and which of them, shall be handed over to the Boroughs (Sections 21(5) and 23(4)). In this the GLC maintain, and are supported in their attitude in the Report mentioned above, that they must have a large pool of accommodation throughout London for persons displaced by reasons of their operations in their other functions (highways redevelopment, education). The Boroughs on the other hand stress the anomalies and extravagance of having two systems of management and two rent structures operating side by side in the Boroughs. Here it is of interest that the Inner London Housing Divisions of the GLC do not coincide with the Inner London Boroughs . . .

On the whole the problems in relation to Planning and Housing are on the way to a solution, with the display of mutual respect and with a sense of responsibility on both sides. This is not the case with regard to Highways, where no working party is in existence such as those mentioned above. One of the major difficulties here is that the Act gives the GLC control of metropolitan roads but nowhere clearly defines what these are, merely giving a list of them, amounting to 550 miles in all, in a Schedule. The GLC wants more of them, contending they play a vital part in the strategic planning of a highway system. Most of the Boroughs want the GLC to have fewer, largely because the GLC under Regulations has planning control over areas 200 feet on each side of a metropolitan road, and they do not wish to lose these powers. There is the further factor that the GLC, as the strategic authority, is primarily concerned with efficiency, while the Boroughs are more responsive to strong local feelings on such matters as amenity. There is no present indication that these conflicts are being resolved. A clear definition of what constitutes a metropolitan road would help, with a decision as to whether the criterion for its determination should be its use as a main through route, or the weight of traffic carried (irrespective of destination) or both.

While the question of metropolitan roads is one factor which complicates the issue of *traffic management* in Greater London the root of the trouble here lies deeper. Although the GLC is designated as traffic authority for the area as recommended by the Herbert Commission, it in fact shares this function with the Ministry of Transport, the Police and the Boroughs. Thus while the operation and maintenance of signal systems and traffic signs is the responsibility of the GLC on metropolitan roads, it is that of the Ministry on trunk roads, and of the Boroughs on the remainder . . . No single authority has responsibility for co-ordinating off-street parking, and there is no single focus for liaison with motoring, pedestrian and other organisations. There is an obvious need for much greater integration in this field, and it is to be hoped that we may before long see legislation dealing with the whole question of the status of the GLC in relation to London's transportation and traffic problems.

In respect of *Education* for Inner London, and of *Parks* for Greater London as a whole, the Act laid down provisions which were to be subject to revision in 1970. The inevitable result of this was to create uncertainty, especially among staff, and to encourage an attitude of intransigence on the part of those with vested interests.

In the case of *Education*, the Government has put an end to the uncertainty by making the ILEA permanent . . .

Finally, the London Government Act gave little recognition to the fact that it was a new pattern of local government, for which the existing Local Government legislation might not be appropriate. It assumed throughout that the Greater London Council should have the constitution and administrative nature of a County Council, and the new boroughs that of existing boroughs up and down the country. Almost the only major innovations, apart from the reallocation of functions and redrawing of boundaries, were the reduction in the Outer London boroughs of the proportion of aldermen to councillors from a third to a sixth, the obligation on the boroughs to appoint architects, and the requirement of the GLC to institute a research and information unit.

The resultant situation is forcefully described in the evidence of the London Boroughs Association to the Seebohm Committee:

'Parliament's efforts hitherto in the direction of governing the internal organis- ation of local authorities have been piecemeal and on each occasion directed to limited objectives. The result is a patchwork quilt of statutory requirements which lacks logic, encourages excessive compartmentalism, and severely restricts the scope for local authorities to experiment with new forms of committee and staff structures.

Thus, for example, London Boroughs are required to appoint Health, Children's, Welfare and even, in some cases, Allotments Committees (though Welfare may be combined with some other Committee with the Minister's consent) and Outer London Boroughs must appoint Education Committees. Oddly enough, although housing is one of the most important services, there is no statutory provision requiring the appointment of a Housing Committee. Nor are London Boroughs required to appoint Finance Committees (though County Councils are required to do so).

The patchwork quilt requires London Boroughs to appoint a clerk, a treasurer, a medical officer of health, a surveyor, a children's officer, an architect (by 1968) and, in the case of Outer London Boroughs, a chief education officer. They are not, however, required to appoint a planning officer, housing manager, librarian or welfare officer. Statute spells out in some detail the duties of some of these officers, such as the medical officer of health and the children's officer; in the case of some of the other officers, such as the clerk and the surveyor, the statutory duties are very limited in comparison with the functions they in fact perform: in the case of the architect the statute merely provides that one must be appointed but assigns no duties to the post. Another vagary allows the authorities, if so minded, to spend unlimited sums of money without any report from the treasurer. Anomalies of this nature abound.'

The conclusion is drawn that the internal organisation of local authorities as a whole needs to be examined in the light of the great growth of services since the basic statutory framework was established in the nineteenth century.

Some mention has been made above of the efforts of some London boroughs to effect a rationalisation of their administrative procedures, but obviously such efforts must be inhibited by the legislative limits within which they must at present be confined.

(ii) Those Affecting the Boroughs The difficulties in welding two or three or more existing authorities into one new borough have not proved as formidable as at one time appeared probable. The sort of situation which seemed likely to give trouble was where two authorities of differing political complexion were united, or two county boroughs, each with its own traditions and methods, but in practice such differences seem to have been effectively reconciled. Perhaps the greatest difficulty has been caused where the union resulted in an almost even balance of political power, as in Havering, where Council meetings of marathon length have resulted.

There is however little evidence as yet of the existence of any degree of community feeling in the new boroughs . . .

Members have further to travel to reach their Town Halls, though their scope is wider when they get there. But in those boroughs which are rationalising their administration by reducing the number of committees and increasing delegation to officers, it is said to be becoming more difficult to find the larger number of members a sufficient amount of work to provide them with responsibility and interest. Here there seems scope for greater emphasis on the 'Ombudsman' function of local councillors, and on the part which questions can play in council proceedings. On the other hand, because of the wider functions of both tiers of government, it has now become virtually impossible for a member to hold office both in the GLC and a new borough, as once used to happen fairly frequently with the LCC and the Metropolitan Boroughs.

Chief Officers and Senior Officers have to spend much of their time serving on working parties and advisory bodies set up to co-ordinate policy and practice as is shown from much that has been said above. This perhaps can be reckoned as an advantage as well as a disadvantage, and in any case these demands are likely to lessen as conditions become more stabilised . . .

. . . . . .

EMERGENCE OF A NEW TYPE OF TWO-TIER SYSTEM

Perhaps the most significant feature of the London Government Act 1963 from the angle of Local Government reform was that it introduced two entirely new types of authority into the country's administrative structure in the form of the Greater London Council and the London Borough councils. These new types of authority together constitute a new two-tier system, but one differing fundamentally from the existing two-tier system of County and County Districts.

I. Features of the existing system in the country generally in contrast with that now operating in London may be distinguished as follows:

(*a*) In the County–County District system, nearly all the most important functions are operated by the County.

(*b*) There has been a steady reduction in the number of functions performed by the second tier authorities. A number of functions can be delegated to them by the counties, but the latter exercise control over finance and policy, and this can lead to friction and frustration.

(*c*) There are wide variations in the size and resources of all types of authority . . .

(*d*) The County Borough system has obvious merits in the concentration of responsibility for all local government functions in one authority. But the existence of two-tier and one-tier authorities side by side can and often does lead to friction. County Boroughs find their surrounding areas of interest and natural expansion under the control of the counties, while the larger non-county boroughs and urban districts may be ambitious for county borough status and so become progressively unwilling to accept County Council authority . . .

II. (*a*) In the Greater London set-up, the division of functions between the two tiers is not between the more important and the less important functions, but between those of a strategic nature which can only be effectively administered over a large area and those which intimately concern smaller local communities. In the words of the Herbert Commission, 'the boroughs should be the primary units of local government and should perform all functions except those which can only be effectively performed over the wider area of Greater London'.

(*b*) In most functions responsibility attaches exclusively either to the GLC or to the London Boroughs. In three fields, however, Planning, Highways and Traffic Control and Housing, and also in Parks, there is some overlap. More is said of this later.

(*c*) Excluding the City the Boroughs do not vary greatly in size and wealth. Averaging 250,000 in population, 21 of them are within the 200–300,000 range, 6 are over 300,000 (the largest 340,000) and 5 under 200,000 (the smallest 146,000). The product of 1d. rate of 28 of them is between £35,000 and £90,000 and of four over £90,000, the average being £74,000.

(*d*) The London Boroughs are of a size with the larger county boroughs, and in fact only Birmingham, Liverpool, Manchester, Leeds, Sheffield and Bristol in England and Wales are larger than the largest of them. Westminster has a higher rateable value than any of these six, and Camden than any except Birmingham. Sutton, the borough with the lowest rateable value, is comparable in that respect with Hull and Bradford, while the rateable values per head of population are strikingly higher in London. It is thus not only their population but also their financial resources which make them viable units for the responsibilities with which they are charged . . .

. . . . . .

HOW THE SYSTEM WORKS

(*a*) The Machinery

An essential requirement of the new model of local government now operating in London is that there should be a co-ordination of effort between the elements comprising it and a notable feature of its performance is the degree of co-operation which has been achieved, both between the Greater London Council and the Boroughs and among the Boroughs themselves.

A leading part in this achievement has been played by the London Boroughs Association. Originally called the London Boroughs Committee (the name was changed in 1966 to what was considered a more appropriate title), its inaugural meeting was held in Guildhall on 24 June, 1964 and its constitution (under general local government powers) laid down in September 1964, its objects being

(*a*) To protect and advance the powers, interests, rights and privileges of the constituent Councils and to watch over those powers, interests, rights and privileges as they may be affected by legislation, or proposed legislation.

(*b*) To discuss questions of London government and to advise and assist the constituent Councils in the administration of their powers and duties.

(*c*) To express the views of the association and to consult with appropriate bodies or persons whenever deemed advisable. Provided that the Association shall not have power to bind or commit a constituent authority.

The work of the Association is at present carried out through four Committees – General Purposes, Works, Social Services and Education. Each Council has one representative, on each of the first three committees (a total of 99) and these Borough members constitute the Association: Town Clerks are the Honorary Secretaries of each committee and also of the Association.

The Education Committee comprises one representative of each of the twenty Outer London Boroughs. These are not full members of the Association unless they happen to be on one of the other Committees . . . in its two years of existence the LBA has attained a wide sphere of influence and has become an integral part of local government in London.

While the London Boroughs Association, as might be expected, is the chief agency for co-operation among the Boroughs, there are two other bodies, the London Boroughs Management Services Committee and the London Boroughs Training Committee, which also play important roles in serving the common needs of large groups of boroughs . . .

. . . . . .

The three organisations mentioned have all been constituted under Local Government Acts, but co-operation between the authorities concerned is also empowered by the Local Government Act 1963, which, in Section 5(3) says that the GLC, the boroughs and the Common Council may agree with any one or more of themselves or with any contiguous authority for the undertaking by one party for another, of any administrative, clerical, professional, scientific or technical services, on such terms as they may agree.

Whether or not inspired by this Section of the Act, boroughs have combined for a wide variety of purposes outside the scope of the LBA and the two committees mentioned above.

(*c*) Co-operation between the Boroughs and the GLC

(i) through the LBA The foregoing pages give some indication of the part that has been and is being played by the LBA in fostering among the boroughs a sense of common interest in developing at the second tier a new system of government which shall meet the needs of London as a whole, and not merely those of the individual authorities. This consciousness on the part of the boroughs of a London role as well as an individual role (in addition to the offices of the LBA as a negotiating body), has certainly contributed to the development of a happier relationship between the boroughs and the GLC than might have been feared. For there are obvious elements of likely friction between them.

First a disparity in size such as exists between the individual boroughs and the GLC is liable to lead to accusations of paternalism or of abuse of power being levelled against the larger body. The GLC has been personified as 'Big Brother' by certain outer boroughs and by their local Press, when disputes have arisen.

Secondly, political control may be exercised by different parties in the GLC and the boroughs. Up to April 1967, Labour held the GLC and most of the boroughs. Now Labour still holds most of the boroughs, with a Conservative majority at the GLC. What will be the outcome of this remains to be seen, and the borough elections in 1968 may change the situation again. But up to the present the issues between the two tiers have not generally speaking been party political issues, and as has already been mentioned, representation of the boroughs on the LBA is not wholly on party political lines.

Thirdly, there are wide social and other differences between the built up inner boroughs and the outer boroughs, some of which still have considerable tracts of open country within their boundaries.

The main areas of conflict are, as might be expected, those where there is an overlap of functions, viz. Housing, Town Planning and Highways. In the first two many difficulties have been resolved, but this is hardly the case with Highways and Traffic Control . . .

54 THE 1972 ACT

From *The Local Government Act, 1972* (Department of Environment Circular 121/72, 1972); by permission of H.M.S.O. This extract describes the application of the 1972 Act to London government.

Application of the new Act to Greater London

64. The basic structure of London government, the existing London authorities and the allocation of functions between them are untouched. But in a number of matters affecting the constitution, election and procedure of local authorities, the new Act also applies to Greater London.

65. The constitutional and electoral provisions relating to the Greater London Council and London borough councils are reproduced in Schedule 2 to the Act, and provision is made for these to be brought into line with the rest of the country as regards the cessation of the offices of Greater London Council alderman in 1976

and London borough alderman in 1977, with a power in both cases for the Secretary of State to fix another year by order. The Secretary of State is also empowered to make orders regarding the term of office of councillors and the timing of elections. Consultations on these matters will be initiated with the London authorities in the very near future.

66. Greater London is brought within the terms of reference of the Local Government Boundary Commission for England as regards future boundary changes and the regular review of areas.

67. The provisions of the Act relating to the procedure and general powers of local authorities apply to the London authorities as well as to the rest of the country, as do the provisions affecting, for example, allowances to members (except those of the Greater London Council), admission to meetings, arrangements for the discharge of functions and the general power of expenditure. Finally it should be noted that while the allocation of functions between the London authorities is unchanged, they are affected by some of the changes made by the Act to the legislation relating to particular functions.

APPENDIX A. THE LONDON BOROUGHS

Population, area, and density, of London boroughs

Borough	Estimated population		Total area 1975 (land and inland water only) hectares	Population density – Persons per residential hectare
	1961 thousands (1)	1975* thousands (2)	(3)	(4)
City of London	5	5	274	771
Camden	246	193	2,171	248
Greenwich	230	210	4,744	132
Hackney	257	206	1,949	274
Hammersmith	222	172	1,617	302
Islington	261	174	1,489	275
Kensington and Chelsea	219	162	1,195	327
Lambeth	342	297	2,727	228
Lewisham	290	247	3,473	145
Southwark	313	236	2,880	222
Tower Hamlets	206	150	1,973	325
Wandsworth	335	288	3,492	208
Westminster, City of	272	214	2,158	408
Total Inner London	3,198	2,554	30,142	227

Population, area, and density of London boroughs

Borough	Estimated population		Total area 1975 (land and inland water only) hectares (7)	Population density — Persons per residential hectare (8)
	1961 thousands (5)	1975* thousands (6)		
Barking	177	154	3,419	142
Barnet	318	303	8,953	91
Bexley	210	217	6,064	96
Brent	296	263	4,421	134
Bromley	293	295	15,180	67
Croydon	324	325	8,658	88
Ealing	302	298	5,547	145
Enfield	274	262	8,118	108
Haringey	259	233	3,031	189
Harrow	209	201	5,081	85
Havering	246	237	11,780	85
Hillingdon	228	232	11,034	85
Hounslow	209	203	5,853	121
Kingston upon Thames	146	136	3,755	90
Merton	189	173	3,796	119
Newham	265	233	3,637	239
Redbridge	250	231	5,647	109
Richmond upon Thames	181	168	5,525	109
Sutton	169	166	4,342	85
Waltham Forest	249	228	3,967	159
Total Outer London	4,794	4,558	127,808	106
Greater London	**7,992**	**7,112**	**157,950**	**131**

1 hectare = 2.4711 acres approx.
1 acre = 0.4047 hectares approx.

*Provisional figures

Source: *London Facts and Figures*, Greater London Council, 1976; reprinted with permission.

Income of London boroughs, 1975– 76 *

Borough	Rates paid per domestic hereditament £ (1)	Total rate call**		Domestic rate call as percentage of total (4)	Rate Support Grant† as percentage of total (including precept) expenditure (5)
		Domestic £ thousands (2)	Non-domestic £ thousands (3)		
City of London	209	456	155,358	−††	−††
Camden	193	12,618	56,901	18	28
Greenwich	102	7,792	9,459	45	65
Hackney	101	7,020	11,368	38	60
Hammersmith	114	6,668	11,971	36	54
Islington	140	7,928	23,488	25	47
Kensington and Chelsea	196	12,163	19,000	39	44
Lambeth	113	10,938	20,858	34	52
Lewisham	105	9,673	6,954	58	70
Southwark	107	9,786	21,286	31	53
Tower Hamlets	134	7,687	20,283	27	47
Wandsworth	102	10,098	9,565	51	72
Westminster, City of	225	19,810	160,404	11	16
Total Inner London	134	122,636	526,894	19	36

Income of London boroughs, 1975–76*

Borough	Rates paid per domestic hereditament £ (6)	Total rate call**		Domestic rate call as percentage of total (9)	Rate Support Grant† as percentage of total (including precept) expenditure (10)
		Domestic £ thousands (7)	Non-domestic £ thousands (8)		
Barking	122	7,034	10,914	39	49
Barnet	143	15,025	10,703	58	51
Bexley	124	9,568	7,847	55	53
Brent	165	14,652	18,927	44	47
Bromley	164	17,491	11,167	61	49
Croydon	166	18,485	24,123	43	43
Ealing	165	15,860	21,790	42	41
Enfield	142	13,307	15,213	47	46
Haringey	149	11,199	11,876	49	51
Harrow	172	12,261	8,689	59	49
Havering	137	11,399	9,941	53	58
Hillingdon	157	12,431	25,090	33	33
Hounslow	149	10,442	21,711	32	39
Kingston upon Thames	141	7,077	8,835	44	43
Merton	151	9,711	8,998	52	44
Newham	131	10,203	16,643	38	49
Redbridge	145	11,757	8,755	57	50
Richmond upon Thames	151	9,606	7,955	55	44
Sutton	148	8,954	7,022	56	49
Waltham Forest	138	11,403	9,463	55	59
Total Outer London	149	237,866	265,663	47	47
Greater London	**143**	**360,502**	**792,557**	**31**	**42**

*Provisional figures
**Excludes losses in collection and the domestic rate rebates grant
†Needs, resources, and domestic elements
††Less than 0.5%

Source: *London Facts and Figures*, Greater London Council, 1976; reprinted with permission

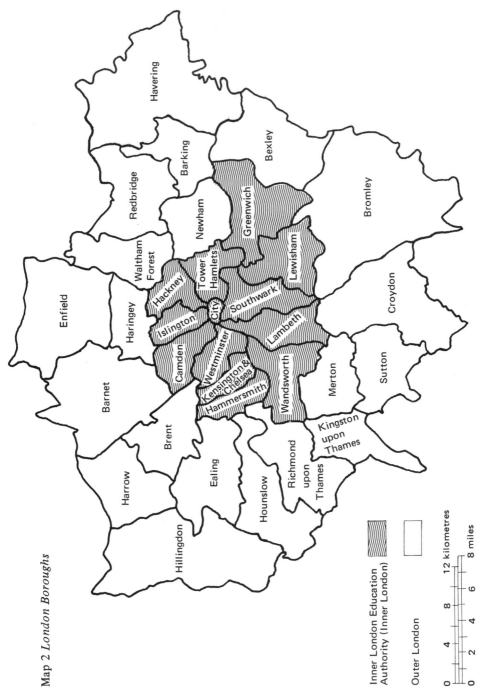

Map 2 *London Boroughs*

Inner London Education
Authority (Inner London)

Outer London

0   4   8   12 kilometres

0   2   4   6   8 miles

Source: *London Facts and Figures, 1976*; reprinted with permission.

Map 3 *Greater London Councillors, by Constituency and Party, at 31 January 1976*

Based on the election of 12 April 1973

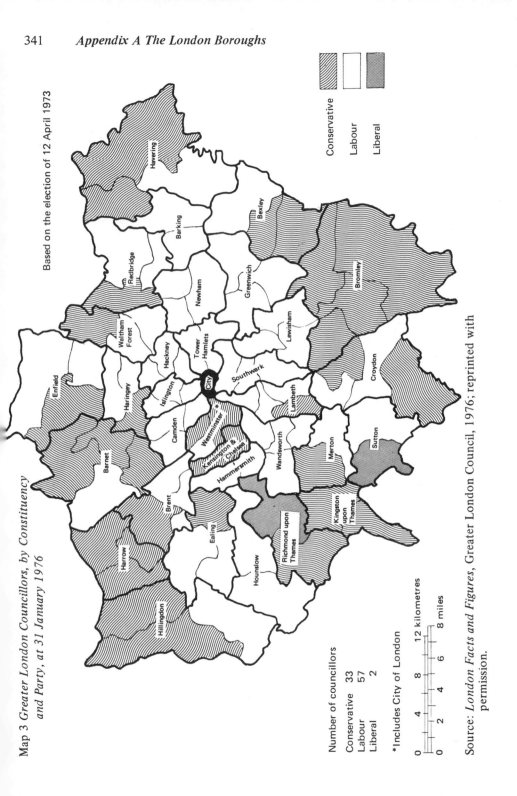

Conservative

Labour

Liberal

Number of councillors

Conservative 33
Labour 57
Liberal 2

*Includes City of London

0   2   4   6   8   12 kilometres
0   2   4   6   8 miles

Source: *London Facts and Figures*, Greater London Council, 1976; reprinted with permission.

Local government in Scotland

The historical evolution of units of local government in Scotland produced, by the end of the nineteenth century, three types of authority: 200 boroughs, 33 counties, and 869 parishes. The first attempt at integrated reform took place in 1929, with the abolition or consolidation of many small units of local administration, the division of the boroughs into two classes — large and small — and the creation of some county districts. This system endured more or less unchanged up to 1972 (55). Apart from the basic local government structure, there were other functional bodies — for example, water boards, fire authorities, police authorities — which were made up of representatives from several local authorities. There were also various special agencies, set up by central initiative, operating in the field of economic and industrial planning. These agencies often depended on co-operation with local authorities, and the Scottish Office (the central government department responsible for Scottish affairs) took the lead in initiating the reform of local government, partly because of its perception of the need for a local government system which could more effectively share in the planning and promotion of economic development. It was the Scottish Office which produced the 1963 White Paper (56); but the change of government in 1964 had the effect of shelving the 1963 proposals, and ultimately produced an investigation by Royal Commission. The ensuing Wheatley Report (57) followed the 1963 White Paper in recommending a two-tier system, but on a very different geographical basis. The two tiers were to be 7 regions and 37 districts, with major functions allocated to the regional tier. The Wheatley proposals appeared to be dominated by criteria of efficiency rather than democracy, with one authority containing a population of 2½ millions — almost half the entire population of Scotland. On this, and other grounds, the proposals were attacked both by existing local authorities, and from various points in the political spectrum. In consequence, although Government's response to Wheatley was favourable, significant changes were made, notably the creation of a class of 'islands' authorities to meet the special needs of Orkney, Shetland, and (subsequently) the Western Isles; the creation of 8 rather than 7 regional authorities, with some redrawing of Wheatley's regional boundaries; and the creation of 49 rather than 37 district authorities, to meet the argument that Wheatley's district authorities would be too remote from their electorates. Another change was the transfer of certain functions, notably housing, from the regional to the district tier. In short, the 1971 White Paper involved considerable restructuring of Wheatley's geo-political map, while accepting the general principles upon which that map was based (58).

    The White Paper was translated into practice by the Local Government (Scotland)

Act of 1973, and the new system came into being in April 1975 (59). The final proposals again extended the number of authorities (from 8 to 9 regions, and from 49 to 53 districts). The distribution of functions is similar to the distribution between non-metropolitan counties and districts in England and Wales, but the 'islands' authorities have been described as 'most-purpose' authorities. A controversial feature remains the size of the Strathclyde region; it has been pointed out that some citizens and councillors would have to travel a hundred miles to their regional centre.

There are three other significant areas of change. First, following the precedent of England and Wales, Scottish local government has been given an Ombudsman (60). The legislative provisions generally reflect the English legislation; publicity is to be the principal weapon of censure in proven cases of maladministration; and care is taken to avoid duplication of the work of the Parliamentary Commissioner for Administration, and the Health Service Commissioner for Scotland.

Secondly, in parallel with the Bains Report in relation to England and Wales, a working group set out guidelines for the new Scottish local authorities to consider when setting up their organisational and management structures (61). The main recommendations of the Paterson Report (1973) are a carbon copy of Bains — a corporate management approach; co-ordination through a new Policy and Resources Committee; and a single chief executive, leading a management team of chief officers. It is expected that many Scottish local authorities will adopt these principles.

The future of local government in Scotland may be considerably complicated by the new proposals for legislative devolution to an elected Scottish Assembly of a range of subjects which include local government. These arrangements provide not only that the new executive responsible to the Assembly would exercise over local government the range of central controls now operated by the Scottish Office; but that the Assembly could reorganise the local government system yet again, either wholly or in part. Since the recent reorganisation has been more radical than in England and Wales, and correspondingly more traumatic, this is in practice unlikely, but much will depend on the political composition of the new Assembly.

55 THE UNREFORMED STRUCTURE

From *Royal Commission on Local Government in Scotland, 1966–69, Report:* (The Wheatley Report, Cmnd. 4150, 1969); by permission of H.M.S.O. This extract from the Wheatley Report describes the system which endured more or less unchanged from 1929 to 1973.

1. THE NEED FOR REFORM

(a) The Present System

48. The structure remains very much as set out in the Local Government (Scotland)

Act, 1929. There are the following five kinds of authority, each with its elected council:

Counties of cities	(4)
Large burghs	(21)
Small burghs	(176)
Counties	(33)
Districts	(196)

Each of these is entitled to exercise the functions assigned to it by statute, together with, in the case of the districts and small burghs, any functions that may be delegated to it by the county council. Thus while there are only 35 education authorities (the counties and the four cities), there are 56 health authorities (the counties, the cities and the large burghs) and 234 housing authorities (the counties, the cities and all the burghs).

49. In distributing responsibilities in such varied ways parliament has obviously meant to secure that functions are conferred on authorities according to their capacity to discharge them. But such is the range of size within each type of authority that anomalies abound. A small burgh with a few hundred inhabitants may have far greater responsibilities than a district council with a population of 60,000. A county council with a population as small as 13,000 has a complete range of local government functions; a large burgh seven times as populous has a more restricted range of functions . . . Some functions — education, health, planning and housing, for example — are exercised directly and individually by the authorities on which the functions are conferred by the statute. Quite often, however, authorities are reckoned too small to carry out their statutory functions effectively. When this happens, they may choose (or be compelled) to form joint committees with neighbouring authorities. Accordingly, against a total of 56 police and fire authorities in Scotland, there are at present only 20 police forces and 11 fire brigades . . .
. . . . . .

Structure

76. One witness conveniently summarises the views of a number of others:
'A basic defect is the separate and independent existence of a relatively large number of local authorities (many of them having jurisdiction over very small areas, serving small populations or carrying out limited functions, and with boundaries which have little relevance to modern needs), which tends to arouse, foster and institutionalise conflicts of interest between members from different areas and their authorities, and so to place unnecessary and obviously undesirable obstacles in the way of the efficient and expeditious discharge of the work of local government.'
. . . . . .

Functions

78. The general complaint is that the scale on which functions are discharged is not

appropriate: the areas are too small. Thus either the service is a poor or narrowly conceived one, or it is wasteful of resources and staff. In a small authority proper arrangements for internal management and career structure are difficult to achieve, and it is not easy to find chief officers of the right calibre. Joint arrangements between authorities, it is submitted, do not provide the right answer to the problem of the inadequate authority. The joint committee responsible for a particular function will either tend to work in isolation from the constituent authorities, or it may be dominated by the parochial interests of the councillors who compose it, to the detriment of the service provided.

79. The criticism is also made that the system separates functions which ought to be discharged together. Small burghs, for example, are responsible for housing but not for health and welfare, with which housing is closely connected.

. . . . . .

Finance

81. We are told that the fragmented character of the local government structure makes for a very unequal spread of rateable resources. Too many authorities have to be bolstered by some form of equalisation grant. This is only one facet of the excessive dependence of local government on Exchequer aid. It is said that this dependence stems from the inadequacy of the rating system, and results in the twin evils of subservience to the central Government and the lack of a responsible attitude to finance within local government.

82. Many witnesses complain that methods of allocating the cost of services which involve more than one authority are inequitable, for example when one authority takes overspill population from another, or provides services like roads and sewerage within the area of a new town. And there is a hearty dislike of the system of requisitioning, on the ground that it separates to an unacceptable degree the responsibility for spending money from the responsibility for raising it . . .

Membership and internal organisation

83. A persistent refrain in the evidence presented to us is the low standing of local government at the present time. Few people, we were told, know or care what their local council does, and they are quite unconscious of any responsibility on their part for the efficiency of the services the council provides — as evidenced by the small numbers in which they turn out to the polls. It is claimed that it is becoming more and more difficult to find good candidates to stand for local government elections.

84. Local authorities themselves are said not to be organised in a way that encourages good people to serve on or under them. Confined within an archaic statutory framework, the committee system does not match up to the needs of the present day. The procedure focuses attention on detail and does not allow a wider

perspective. As a result local authority business is alleged to be transacted in a cumbersome, time-wasting, uninteresting and inefficient manner.

Relationship with central Government

85. Whether as a consequence of the weaknesses outlined above, or because of the deliberate policy of the central Government, it is widely believed by witnesses that the balance of power and responsibility between local and central government has gone wrong. As one witness put it: 'Whatever may have been the origins and history of local authorities, today they are the agents of Central Government.' In support of these assertions, witnesses point to the removal of functions from local government to ad hoc agencies, the enforced reorganisation of other functions, constant administrative interference with the work of local government and arbitrary manipulation of local authorities' capital programmes without regard to the authorities' own assessment of priorities . . .

. . . . . .

87. In the first place, the Community Survey shows that there is no popular clamour for a change in the structure of local government. The public are, on the whole, satisfied with the services provided by local authorities. However, they are not well-informed as to what these services are, and they do not seem to have a clear idea of what their elected representatives do, or ought to do, on their behalf.

88. Secondly, from our Intelligence Unit's study of percentage polls and contested seats, it appears that in 1967, which was the last year in which elections took place in every different kind of local authority in Scotland, 63 per cent of the seats were uncontested. Where there were contests, only 47 per cent of the electorate on average registered their votes.

89. Thirdly, the Intelligence Unit, in the course of their studies on communities drew our attention to repeated examples of local government areas which do not correspond with patterns of settlement and communication, especially in central Scotland.

90. Fourthly, the survey of local government manpower carried out by the Intelligence Unit reveals serious shortages of skilled staff, particularly architects, engineers, planners and social workers . . .

56 THE 1963 REFORM PROPOSALS

From *The Modernisation of Local Government in Scotland* (Cmnd. 2067, 1963); by permission of H.M.S.O. These proposals were produced by the Scottish Office, the central department of British government responsible for Scottish affairs.

17. In order to build a modern structure on the foundations of the present system, it would appear necessary both to regroup areas and to reallocate functions. The

areas of existing authorities could be enlarged, by combination as necessary, to enable them to administer their services more effectively. First, the counties could be regrouped so that their councils could exercise certain major functions through-out a wider area. Secondly, within the enlarged counties, new authorities could be created to be responsible for areas formed by combining existing burghs with neighbouring landward areas.

18. The amalgamation of the burghs with the landward areas centred on them — which would be a new feature of local government — would recognise their common interest. It would also take account of improvements in communications and changes in the habits of life of communities. In some cases the area surrounding a burgh can form a coherent unit with the burgh itself; in others the new authority might comprise several (usually small) burghs with the contiguous landward area; and in relatively few instances a landward area might itself, for particular reasons, provide the basis of a new authority.

19. The result of the regrouping would be a simple two-tier system under which the new county councils would be responsible for major services throughout the enlarged area of their jurisdiction. The new authorities formed by the combination of burghs and surrounding landward areas would be responsible for essentially local services. The clear division of functions between the two kinds of authority should produce a more business like system. It should also make a more direct appeal to candidates for election who are particularly interested in the type of work to be discharged by either authority. The fact that counties could in future concentrate on a restricted range of major services and the new authorities on functions appli-cable to their immediate areas would also reduce the time which councillors have to spend in council or committee meetings. The effect of these various factors should, in sum, be to strengthen interest in local government and attract candidates from a wider field.

Counties 20. These authorities, if regrouped as suggested above, would in future be responsible only for the major services which are not readily susceptible to local lines of demarcation. The need for joint committees (except to meet the special cases of water supplies and river purification) would largely disappear. The growth of joint committees (which frequently involve burghs as well as neighbouring counties) has in the past led to complications — the combined area being different for different purposes. These difficulties could be removed under the new system.

21. The new county councils could with advantage be directly elected in order to provide a more direct link between the authority and the electorate . . .

22. Where there were greater resources represented by a larger area of jurisdiction, the new county council would be better able to employ fully expert and highly qualified staff and to make use of the latest technical equipment . . .

Burgh and Rural Councils 23. The regrouping could logically extend to provide for the reorganised counties to comprise a number of enclaves formed, as a rule, by the amalgamation of burghs and landward areas. A new authority would be responsible for each enclave and could administer throughout its area a defined range of services where local control is the prime essential. It could in fact undertake services which are at present discharged by three different authorities, *i.e.*, the town council, the county council (as regards the landward area) and the district council. A title would have to be found for the new authorities. They might appropriately be designated 'burgh councils' or 'rural councils' depending on the circumstances of each area. There would, however, be no distinction between the powers and functions of burgh councils and rural councils.

24. It is suggested that the area of the new councils might appropriately have a population of at least 40,000. But there is nothing sacrosanct in this figure. The population in certain urban and industrial areas, which have a strong local identity, would in many cases be appreciably larger, with the accompanying advantage that the number of local authority boundaries in conurbations would be substantially reduced. Any new structure must be sufficiently flexible to allow for the problems of remote areas where, because of sparsity and difficulties of communication, the council area might have an appreciably smaller population.

. . . . . .

28. The new enlarged counties could be responsible for the following services:

Child Care	Local Health and Welfare Services
Civil Defence Corps and other Civil Defence matters	Major Town and Country Planning
	Police
Education	Remand Homes
Fire	River Purification
Food and Drugs Regulations	Roads (except unclassified roads)
Food and Milk Administration	Valuation
Libraries	Water Supply and Sewerage

29. The functions to be reserved to the new burgh and rural councils could include the following:

Allotments	Public Parks
Burial and Cremation	Public Regulations
Cinema Licensing	Public Ways and Footpaths
Civil Defence (except as allocated to counties)	Registration of Births, Deaths and Marriages
Clean Air	Scavenging
Coast Protection	Slaughterhouses
Entertainments	Taxicab Licensing
Factory Regulations	Town and Country Planning
Flood Prevention	(day-to-day administration)
Housing	Unclassified Roads
Physical Training and Recreation	Weights and Measures

30. As regards Town and Country Planning, the county council could be responsible for determining the main framework of the development plan, particularly as regards such functions as the communications patterns, the scheduling of land for industrial development, population growth and movement, etc. The burgh and rural

councils could handle individual applications for planning permission, subject to a power enabling the Secretary of State to define cases of development, either on a specified scale or in specified areas, where applications would be dealt with by the county. A broad division on these lines appears practicable but the detailed implications would require close examination.

. . . . . .

Rating 35. Under a new two-tier system both types of authority would be directly elected and could exercise entirely separate functions. This suggests that both county, and burgh and rural councils, as regards their respective services, should be rating authorities in their own right. As a matter of convenience, however, the burgh and rural councils should collect the county rates on an agency basis at the same time as they collected their own rates. The rate demand should make clear the services and the authority for whom the rate payment is required.

57 THE 1969 WHEATLEY REPORT

From *Scotland: Local Government Reform* (a short version of the Wheatley Report, Cmnd. 4150–I, 1969); by permission of H.M.S.O. The Royal Commission on Scottish local government was appointed in the same year (1966) as the English Royal Commission, and reported in the same year (1969); it was chaired by Sir Andrew Wheatley, a member of the 1967 Maud Committee on Management in Local Government.

BASIC OBJECTIVES

What kind of qualities should be built in to a new structure? We decided that there were four main objectives to be kept in view:

Power   Local government ought to play a more important part in the running of the country. It should be able to take on more responsibilities, and be less dependent on central Government. This involves accepting a greater share of the financial burden (leaving less to be contributed by the taxpayer). It should be capable of pulling together as a whole.

Effectiveness   Every local government service should operate on a scale which allows it to function properly, providing high standards of service, good value for money, flexibility to cope with future changes, and co-ordination of services that affect one another.

Local democracy   There should be an elected local council genuinely in charge of the local situation, and answerable to local people for its handling of it.

Local involvement People ought to be brought as much as possible into the process of reaching decisions. There should always be means of expressing the local point of view. It is not good enough to rely on long range administration by officials at headquarters.

. . . . . .

THE METHOD OF APPROACH

There are three basic factors to be considered when devising a structure of local government:

Local government exists to provide services or exercise *functions*.

The functions have to be exercised over suitable *areas*.

The functions and the areas have to be brought together to form *authorities*.

Functions

We looked at the main groups of functions — not every function, because some had no direct bearing on structure.

Planning is a big and growing task so far as local government is concerned. Authorities must plan how our towns and cities are to be redeveloped, where new communities are to be built up, where industry should be located, where new highways ought to run, which areas ought to be set apart and developed for recreation. In a sense planning is the widest of all local government functions, because it determines how the total resources of the authority are to be used, and so it has a bearing on all other functions.

Such planning obviously needs to be done on a broad scale — far broader than is possible within the present local government structure. And the areas for planning have to be drawn carefully, so as to expose the natural regional pattern of Scotland and allow it to be developed properly.

That is what we call 'strategic' planning. Local plans have to be drawn up as well — for cities, towns, even villages. Development has to be controlled in accordance with these plans. All this is planning too, but of a different kind, and on a different scale, from the strategic variety.

The personal social services. By this we mean education, social work and health. These are costly services, needing large professional staffs and expensive equipment and premises. At the moment far too many authorities are trying to run them with quite inadequate resources. To help to cure this, it has been suggested that education should be taken away from local authorities, or that the cost of education should be borne by the Government. We are convinced that this would not be in the best interests either of local government or of the public. Education should continue to be provided by local authorities — but by much larger authorities than at present, with a minimum population of about 200,000.

Education, social work and health should be kept together under the same authorities. People who need help from one of the social service departments will often need help from the others, and so the departments must be able to work together as closely as possible.

Housing. Bad housing is the greatest scourge of 20th century Scotland. It cannot be properly tackled so long as there are 234 separate housing authorities..

There are many different sides to housing — assessing the total housing situation in an area; building new houses and letting and managing them; improving the existing housing stock; and helping private house-owners, tenants and housing associations in various ways. Some of these tasks can be carried out more locally than others. But the main tasks of reviewing housing need and planning, building and management all go together, and should be carried out by very big authorities. Housing is closely linked, too, with major planning and with the personal social services.

Police and fire also need wide areas, as is generally recognised nowadays.

Environmental services, which cover an extensive range from street cleansing to food hygiene, do not call for anything like the same scale of operation as planning, education, housing and police. A population of 50,000 seems to be a good guide to the minimum size.

Amenity services like museums, community centres and parks, can again be much more local.

Summing up our findings so far — that is looking at local government functions alone — we might say that a strong case has been made out for certain services to be provided over very wide areas, much bigger than anything we have in Scotland at the moment. Other services would not fit into such a pattern, and ought to be more locally administered.

The services seem to fall naturally into groups. Planning goes along with certain 'impersonal' services like roads, water and industrial development. The personal services form another group. The problem is to find the right area not for each function considered on its own, but rather for each group of functions.

Areas

It is vital that local government services should be provided over areas that correspond with genuine communities — that is natural groupings of population with interests and allegiances in common. The boundary lines should not be drawn arbitrarily, like many local authority boundaries at the present day.

We discovered that, generally speaking, a community could best be defined in terms of an area focusing on a town which forms its main centre and to which the inhabitants of the area travel for business, shopping and recreation. In this concept of community the distinction between town and country cannot be maintained.

Communities exist in different sizes and levels. We can talk about a regional community, and on the other hand we can talk about a locality. Within a region there might be scores of localities.

In Scotland we found that there were four different levels of community. We call them the parish, the locality, the shire, and the region. We regarded these levels of community as the most likely bases for creating local government units and assigning functions.

Authorities

A local authority is not just a body supplying services over a certain area. It is part of a system of local democracy. This means that a local authority has to have certain special features.

It should be *independent*. For that purpose, it seems important that all the members of an authority should be directly elected, not nominated; that each authority should be able to raise finance for itself; and that each should exercise a suitable range of functions in its own right.

An authority should be *viable*. We took this to mean two things. Firstly, it must be strong enough, administratively and financially, to do its job well. Secondly, it must attract good candidates to stand for election, and induce people to turn out to vote at elections.

An authority should be *community-based*. Unless its area corresponds with a genuine community, people will not think of it as *their* authority.

. . . . . .

BUILDING UP THE STRUCTURE

A local government structure must be reasonably *compact and concentrated*. Responsibility should not be spread over too many levels of authority, because then some levels would have too little to do. As we noted earlier, local government services fall into a limited number of groups which ought to be administered together, and this again points to a limit on the number of levels of authorities.

Furthermore the structure should be much more *logical and consistent* than the present one. Local government has to form a coherent system, and this will not happen if there are too many different kinds of authorities, related to one another in complicated ways.

In our final approach to a solution, we considered the following:

A system of 'all-purpose' authorities, each handling all local government services within its area. This has many advantages. It is the simplest of all to understand and to operate. But it does not fit the geographical and social facts of Scotland. Any all-purpose system for Scotland would be bound to fall between two stools. Authorities would either be too small for the large-scale services, or too big for the local services. So we ruled out that particular solution.

A 'tier' system. This means that there are two or more levels of authorities. One level, consisting of a few large authorities, handles the biggest scale of services, and there is another level, or levels, of smaller authorities to deal with the more local services. This is not quite so straightforward as the all-purpose system, but it is more flexible. Most of the evidence was in favour of a tier system, with not more than two tiers. We too thought this the most promising line of approach.

An all-Scotland authority. Could the upper of the tiers be the whole of Scotland? This was suggested in the evidence, but we were not attracted by the idea of a single unit of local government functioning in parallel with the Secretary of State. In any case the whole of Scotland seemed to us far too wide an area for administering most of the major functions of local government.

Regional authorities. We prefer the idea of basing the upper tier on the 'regional' level of community we have identified. This appears to fit all the large-scale services very well. It is possible that the personal social services could be quite well administered over rather smaller areas than the regions, but we have not been able to find smaller areas that form communities and at the same time suit the personal services. Besides, we see a great deal to be gained by giving all these major services — that is the personal services as well as strategic planning, the impersonal services and housing — to the same level of authorities, which means, in our view, keeping them all at the regional level.

The second tier. The other services, though not on such a large scale, are nevertheless very important for the ordinary citizen. They include local planning and redevelopment, housing improvement, libraries, environmental and amenity services, as well as various regulative duties.

The choice for a second tier of local government lies between what we have called the 'shire' level of communities (37 units for the whole of Scotland) and the 'locality' (with about 100 units for the whole of Scotland). We rule out the 'parish' level as being generally far too small to carry local government functions.

Most of us prefer the 'shire' level. We think that all the services just mentioned could be handled very well at that level, and that a strong second tier would result . . .

Conclusion. The position is that we are in favour of a two-tier system, with regional authorities constituting the first tier and looking after major services. In the view of the majority, the second tier should consist of authorities at the 'shire' level (from now on we call them 'district' authorities), responsible for a wide range of local services. More locally still, there should be community councils.

THE STRUCTURE WE RECOMMEND

Regional authorities There should be seven regional authorities for Scotland:

> *Highlands*
> *North East*
> *East*
> *South East*
> *Central*
> *West*
> *South West.*

. . .

Regional authorities should exercise the following main functions:
Major planning and related services (industrial development, transportation and roads, water, sewerage etc., redevelopment, new towns, control of the countryside and tourism)
Personal social services (education, social work, health)

Housing
Protective services (police, fire, civil defence)
Weights and measures and consumer protection
Refuse disposal
Coast protection
Parks and recreation
Museums and art galleries
Registration of births, deaths and marriages
Registration of electors.

District authorities There should be 37 district authorities.

. . .

The main functions recommended for district authorities are as follows:
Local planning and related services (assistance to industry, redevelopment, con-
    trol of the countryside)
Building control
Housing improvement
Ancillary housing functions
Civil defence (local aspects)
Parks and recreation
Community centres
Museums and art galleries
Libraries
Environmental functions (refuse collection, food and drugs, clean air, etc.)
Regulation and licensing
Licensing courts
Administration of justice.
The two levels of authorities should be independently elected, have their own
means of raising finance, and carry out in their own right the functions listed above.
In many spheres, however – particularly intelligence, certain aspects of planning,
housing, redevelopment, and the provision of parks and recreational facilities –
they will have to work closely together.

Community councils There should also be provision for community councils
throughout Scotland. These would not be local authorities, nor would they be
created by act of Parliament. It would be for local communities to decide whether
they wanted community councils or not. A council would be able to give expression
to local opinion, to improve the amenity of its area, to run certain services or
facilities locally by arrangement with the district authority or the regional auth-
ority, and to maintain traditional and ceremonial functions.

The structure as a whole How does this structure appear when it is fitted together?
It provides seven very strong regional authorities, capable of running the large-scale
expensive services. These authorities should be able to take on new services – even

the National Health Service, if it were to be decided that it should become part of local government. The more local services operate under the 37 district authorities — big enough to tackle the local problems confidently, but more accessible than the regional authorities, with most parts of their areas within relatively easy reach of the headquarters. At the most local level of all, where it would be a mistake to try to operate local government services, there is still the opportunity of expressing the local voice and promoting local amenity through community councils.

INSIDE THE SYSTEM

So far the structure built up is no more than a framework. To make it a vital organism something more is needed. In particular, we have to consider the *people* in local government and the way in which their work is to be organised.

Management

The elected councillor is the key person in local government. His job, both as a policy-maker and as a local representative, must be so arranged that he can be effectively in charge of affairs and also effectively in touch with his constituents. We make various recommendations designed to secure this result. Elections should be held only at four-yearly intervals, so as to give councils time to work out their policies and put them into effect. There should be one councillor for each electoral division, so that a constituent is in no doubt who is his elected representative. A balance should be struck between a manageable size of constituency and a manageable size of council. Accordingly, a maximum of 75 should be set for the membership of an authority: in most cases the number could be much less.

We think that councillors should be paid. But we are not anxious to see them spending more time in the council chambers. On the contrary, we think that they should spend less time and delegate much more of their work.

We do not lay down any particular scheme for the organisation of council business. Each council must decide that for itself. We do, however, suggest some principles. We see the first need as **unified management**. Within each council there has to be some group of members responsible for co-ordinating policy and its execution. On the departmental side, too, there must be co-ordination under a chief officer with real responsibility.

Secondly, **devolution**. Both elected members and officials must learn to delegate matters to the lowest and most local level consistent with the nature of the problem involved. More work should be off-loaded from the council and its committees on to officials or, in suitable cases, special agencies set up to look after particular services. Local committees, consisting of elected members of both tiers of authorities as well as other local people, could be set up to allow certain aspects of administration to be dealt with locally. Local officers should be trusted with more responsibility, so that normally a member of the public can get an authoritative answer to his problem without having to refer back to headquarters.

Thirdly, **communication**. The convenience of the public needs to be more carefully studied. Offices should be sited as locally as circumstances permit. Local government staff should take pains to get on the same wavelength as those with whom they are dealing, and to avoid technical jargon.

It should be made clear to people how their complaints or representations can be further considered if they do not think they have had a fair hearing locally. We do not think that an ombudsman for local government should be appointed right away, but the need for such an appointment should be reviewed once the new system has had a chance to settle down.

. . . . . .

Local and central government

Local government must have a new relationship with central Government. On the local government side, it would help towards this end if there was a strong association of all local authorities. On the central Government side, there should be a branch of the Secretary of State's departments with an oversight of all departmental arrangements affecting local government.

These, however, are simply pieces of administrative machinery. Something much more fundamental is needed as well. The whole attitude of Government towards local authorities must change if local government is to take its proper share in the running of the country. We propose the following reforms:

(1) The statutes should be rewritten to give local authorities a broader range of powers and duties. Authorities should also have 'general competence' powers to do things not specifically covered by statute.

(2) Administrative rules and supervision by Government departments should be less strict and detailed.

(3) Local finance should be entirely reviewed. The present arrangement, by which local authorities get more money from central Government sources than from local rates, is not good for the standing of local government. Although the partnership between central and local government should be maintained, local authorities should be much less dependent on Exchequer finance.

(4) The central Departments should not control local government spending as they do now. Subject to overall limits which must be set in the interests of the nation's economy, local authorities should have much greater freedom to decide what are the real local priorities.

All this can happen only in a structure of local government in which authorities are able to be strong, disciplined and well placed to give value for money. It is this that our recommendations are designed to secure.

Map 4 *Scotland: the Wheatley Proposals*

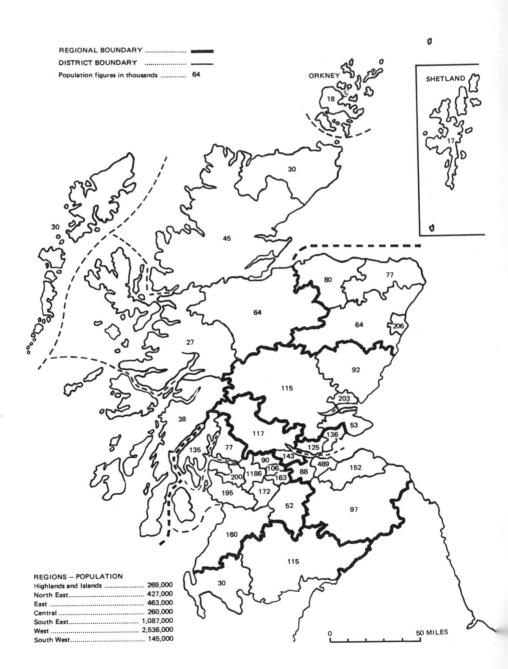

REGIONAL BOUNDARY ....
DISTRICT BOUNDARY ....
Population figures in thousands **64**

ORKNEY

SHETLAND

REGIONS — POPULATION
Highlands and Islands 269,000
North East 427,000
East 463,000
Central 260,000
South East 1,087,000
West 2,536,000
South West 145,000

0   50 MILES

Wheatley's Recommended Local Authorities. Populations, Areas and Rateable Values.

Regional Authorities

Region	Population 1968 mid-year estimate	Population 1980 estimate	Area 1968 (to nearest hundred square miles)	Population per square mile (to nearest whole number)	Rateable Value 1967-68 £ million
Highlands and Islands	269,000	279,000	14,100	19	5.2
North East	427,000	441,000	3,100	138	10.9
East	463,000	540,000	3,300	141	12.8
South-East	1,087,000	1,260,000	2,600	424	32.5
Central	260,000	288,000	1,000	257	8.2
West	2,536,000	2,615,000	3,200	789	72.9
South West	145,000	159,000	2,600	57	3.3
SCOTLAND	5,187,000		29,900	174	145.8

District Authorities

District	Population 1968 mid-year estimate	Area 1968 (to nearest ten square miles)	Population per square mile	Rateable Value 1967-68
Highlands and Islands Region				£
1. Shetland	17,000	550	31	151,000
2. Orkney	18,000	380	47	208,000
3. Western Isles	30,000	1,120	27	316,000
4. Caithness	30,000	1,220	25	491,000
5. Ross-Sutherland	45,000	3,670	12	876,000
6. Inverness and Nairn	64,000	2,260	28	1,556,000
7. Lochaber and Skye	27,000	2,690	10	677,000
8. Argyll	38,000	2,180	18	847,000
North East Region				
9. Moray-Banff	80,000	770	103	1,964,000
10. Banff-Buchan	77,000	710	109	1,475,000
11. Dee, Don and North Kincardine	64,000	1,530	42	1,117,000
12. Aberdeen	206,000	100	2,168	6,306,000
East Region				
13. Angus and South Kincardine	92,000	920	100	2,080,000
14. Perth and Kinross	115,000	1,980	58	3,136,000
15. Dundee	203,000	110	1,884	6,064,000
16. North Fife	53,000	270	191	1,547,000
South East Region				
17. Kirkcaldy	136,000	80	1,624	3,663,000
18. Dumfermline	125,000	120	1,025	2,974,000
19. Edinburgh	489,000	110	4,658	17,835,000

District	Population 1968 mid-year estimate	Area 1968 (to nearest ten square miles)	Population per square mile	Rateable Value 1967-68
20. West Lothian	88,000	140	617	1,998,000
21. Mid and East Lothian	152,000	440	345	3,649,000
22. Borders	97,000	1,670	58	2,347,000
Central Region				
23. Falkirk-Grangemouth	143,000	120	1,201	4,894,000
24. Stirling-Clackmannan	117,000	890	131	3,339,000
West Region				
25. Dumbarton	77,000	240	319	2,134,000
26. Glasgow	1,186,000	150	7,956	38,035,000
27. Kirkintilloch-Cumbernauld	90,000	100	907	1,831,000
28. Coatbridge-Airdrie	106,000	40	2,405	3,048,000
29. Motherwell	163,000	90	1,898	4,997,000
30. Hamilton-East Kilbride	172,000	180	956	3,806,000
31. Lanark	52,000	510	102	1,245,000
32. Paisley	200,000	120	1,677	5,524,000
33. Greenock, Cowal and Bute	135,000	480	281	3,183,000
34. North Ayrshire	195,000	480	405	4,734,000
35. South Ayrshire	160,000	820	195	3,914,000
South West Region				
36. Dumfries-Kirkcudbright	115,000	1,900	60	2,718,000
37. Wigtown	30,000	660	46	626,000

Source: Cmnd. 4150, 1969 (The Wheatley Report)

58 THE 1971 WHITE PAPER

From *Reform of Local Government in Scotland* (Cmnd. 4583, 1971); by permission of H.M.S.O.

THE STRUCTURE FOR THE FUTURE

The Need for Reform

. . . . . .

9. The Government accept the Commission's conclusion that the structure of local government is no longer adequate to cope with present day needs. Many boundaries are out of date, often dividing centres of population from hinterlands with which they have close connections, and sometimes even splitting continuous urban areas. Many authorities are too small and, however commendable their endeavours, they do not have the staff and financial resources to discharge all their responsibilities effectively. Anomalies in the allocation of functions between the various types of local authorities cause fragmentation and friction in the provision

of services. The consequences are evident: the elector is confused about who is responsible for what; local services do not achieve the highest standards; *ad hoc* or joint administrative arrangements prove necessary, and as a result responsibility to the ratepayer is eroded; local government has become too dependent on central government, with an inevitable loss of local control over local affairs.

The Structure Required

. . . . . .

11. As the Royal Commission noted, the demands on local government will increase, and the new authorities must have sufficient resources to achieve the rising standards of service which the public is likely to expect over the years ahead. This means inevitably that local authorities will have to be larger. With larger authorities however, there must be concern lest local government becomes remote from the individual.

12. The key to resolving this difficulty lies partly in the right choice of structure, and partly in ensuring that each authority enjoys independent status and is directly accountable to the electorate for its actions and the conduct of its business. Local interest and attention will then be engaged, and the citizen will know that he has a stake in an authority which is concerned about his needs . . . The Government are convinced that the Royal Commission was right to conclude that the particular needs and circumstances of Scotland require a two-tier structure. Nevertheless, within Scotland there is such a wide variation in the character of areas, and in the nature of problems, that considerable flexibility is necessary.

The Regional Level

. . . . . .

16. The Government are satisfied that within the new structure larger regional authorities should be created — appointed by, and directly responsible to, the electorate — with the power and resources to provide the larger scale services on their own account. As the Royal Commission pointed out, there is no necessary connection between size and efficiency; but a close examination of the present situation leaves no doubt that regional authorities will enjoy substantial advantages through economies of scale. Many of the problems which now face local government do not relate to any single local authority area, and many are incapable of solution by the separate efforts of the authorities directly involved. Problems which are regional by nature must be dealt with on a regional basis; the solutions ought not to be hampered by unsuitable local authority boundaries.

17. In defining the regions the Government accept the approach adopted by the Commission: local authorities' areas must be delineated by boundaries drawn to accord with travel-to-work, shopping and education patterns, recreational and leisure movements, and lines of communication. All these reflect the interdependence of centres of population and the surrounding areas. These social and economic

ties will become even stronger as mobility increases, and it is important that the new local government structure should acknowledge these natural links and not cut across them. Throughout Scotland a regional coherence can be traced around the main centres of population, and it is by reference to this identifiable community of interest that the regional authorities should be defined . . .

The District Level

18. The Government believe that a second level of authorities is also needed. These district authorities will not be subsidiary to the regional authorities but will be complementary to them. Each type of authority will be independent of the other, and, while consultation and co-operation between them will be essential, their statutory functions can be quite distinct, the regions dealing with the services which require management over a wide area and the districts with the more local services. In this way effective administration of all local government services will be secured, and at the same time there will be ample scope for the expression of local opinion in the processes of government at both regional and district level.

19. The areas of the district authorities must also be worked out on the principle of community interest. The Government have studied carefully the various types of community — 'shire', 'locality', and 'parish' — described by the Commission. In reaching their own conclusions they have also taken account of the widespread opinion that in the structure advocated by the Commission the proposed district authorities are too remote from the electorate, while their functions are too limited. The Government have sought to ensure that the district authorities correspond with genuine local communities, and that they have important functions to discharge, with resources to match them.

20. The Government therefore accept the main principles stated by the Royal Commission, but they consider that a number of modifications and improvements will ensure that the Commission's aims can be more successfully achieved.

21. The detailed changes proposed are discussed in the ensuing chapters. The main alterations are that there should be one more region (the Borders); both Orkney and Shetland should be given separate status, with independent control over almost all local government services; the number of districts should be increased by 14 to 49; and additional functions, notably in relation to housing, should be conferred on the district authorities.

LOCAL GOVERNMENT FUNCTIONS

22. In allocating functions to the two levels of authorities the Government recognise three requirements: that responsibility for any particular function must be assigned to the authority which will do the job most effectively, given the character of the function and the resources which its provision requires; that account must be taken of the interconnections between individual services and groups of services; and that each level of authority must have substantial and satisfying tasks. The

division of responsibilities should be clear-cut: where powers are delegated by one authority to another there is an erosion of the principle that local authorities should be independent and directly accountable to their own electorates, and confusion or friction is apt to result.

Regions

23. The Government consider that the functions appropriate to the regional authorities fall into two categories which are not entirely distinct from each other. First there are the strategic services which need to be co-ordinated over a wide area. Secondly, there are a number of major services which only an authority with considerable resources will be able to provide fully and effectively. In all these services regional authorities must have more than a supervisory or planning role. They must have executive powers, and the necessary resources to decide regional priorities, budgets and investment plans for all the services under their control.

24. *Strategic services*. The Government endorse the Commission's view that strategic planning will be fundamental to all the regional authorities' activities. This will not be merely land-use planning in the accepted sense, but will involve the formulation of an economic strategy for the region relating to patterns of settlement, the development of communications and centres of population, and the use of resources, particularly land and finance. Regional authorities should therefore also have responsibilities for transportation and roads, industrial development, and the services ancillary to major planning.

25. *Roads*. The Government have examined the possibility of dividing responsibility for highways so that regional authorities would plan, build and maintain the principal roads and district authorities the local roads. However, they consider that the entire road network must be planned as a whole, and also that the creation of two separate levels of highway authorities would produce an inefficient use of resources, particularly scarce professional staff. A link between local roads and the planning responsibilities of district councils can be effectively kept through consultations undertaken when the district councils formulate their local plans on the basis of the regional strategy for their area, including the road network.

26. *Police and fire services*. The second category of regional services is less directly related to the planning and development of the infrastructure, but these functions involve heavy expenditure and offer opportunities for economies of scale. They also demand specialist staff and technical equipment, and highly specialised facilities. Because of such requirements the police and fire services should be administered by the regional authorities, although in a few areas joint arrangements similar to those now existing may have to continue.

27. *Education and social work* also fall into this category and the Government have reached the conclusion that these too should be regional responsibilities. The Government share the Royal Commission's views that these interconnected services must be the responsibility of a directly elected authority and that a substantial population is needed to support an acceptable standard of service.

28. The Government have considered whether, in view of the large concentration of population and the many important centres in the west of Scotland, any special arrangements should be made there in order to ensure that the education and social work authority should not appear too remote from the individual citizens with whom it is so intimately concerned. They have come to the conclusion that there is no practicable alternative to placing education and social work at the regional level. To divide this region into several smaller regions would frustrate the overall planning which this part of Scotland pre-eminently requires; and to interpose directly elected, and financially responsible, education and social work authorities of intermediate size between the region and the districts would cause confusion and administrative fragmentation. The Government consider that the risk that the authority might seem remote can be overcome through administrative decentralisation, which the regional authority can best arrange.

Districts

29. The Government intend, as the Commission suggested, that the role of district authority should be very different from that of the region: the regional authority will formulate and carry out a broad strategy, and will administer large-scale services; the district authority will concentrate on caring for and improving the local environment. With a coherent set of functions related to the essentially local matters, the district authorities will have a task that is constructive, absorbing and important for their local communities.

30. *Local planning.* The Government agree with the Commission that the regional authorities should determine the strategic planning policy and should be required to prepare structure plans, within the terms of the Town and Country Planning (Scotland) Act 1969, for the whole or part of their areas: and also that within this framework the district authorities should deal with day to day development control, and should prepare local plans under the same Act dealing with details of land use and specific action areas for redevelopment. This division of responsibility assigns to each type of authority the aspect of planning particularly appropriate to its own capacity and interest. Policy decisions will be taken at both levels, and there will be ample scope for direct local participation. The Government consider, however, that these arrangements should not be applied throughout the whole of Scotland, as the Commission proposed. This would require the creation, in the remoter parts of the country, of unduly extensive district authorities merely in order to support the minimum planning staffs. A more flexible approach is preferable, and the Government intend that the regional authority should be responsible for all planning in the outlying areas (the Highlands, the Borders, and the South-West).

31. *Housing.* The Commission suggested that district authorities should have responsibility for housing improvement because it is closely linked with their other local environmental functions. The Government agree, but consider that the building, management and improvement of houses are interdependent. Existing auth-

orities have become increasingly aware of the importance of a complete housing policy, for example relating replacement to improvement, and the finance of building to rent policies. To divide the housing function in the way indicated by the Commission would risk a serious dislocation of responsibilities.

32. The Government, having studied all the evidence available, agree with the substantial body of opinion that housing should be a district function. Local interest in housing is understandably intense, and the housing service should be responsive to this interest. The Government are satisfied that all the new district authorities will have sufficient resources – of finance and professional skill – to discharge their housing responsibilities well. With the main responsibilities for housing, local planning, amenity and the environment, district authorities will be able to maintain and improve the quality of house-building for local needs, to formulate sound policies for allocation and other aspects of house management, and to devote the necessary effort to the improvement of old property and the encouragement of private house-building.

33. Housing also has wider implications, as a component of the regional strategy, particularly in relation to overspill and industrial development. The regional authority must be able to take the initiative in arranging for the building by the district authorities or other agencies (for example the Scottish Special Housing Association) of houses for these purposes. It is not necessary that regional authorities should themselves build houses, but they will be given the power to ensure that housing for major redeployment of population, or to support substantial industrial development, is provided where and when it is required. This need not result in any interference with the practical responsibility by the district authorities (or other agencies) for the construction and management of the houses.

34. *Local health and amenity*. The environmental functions related to local health and amenity will clearly be an important part of the district authorities' group of responsibilities. There are, however, a few modifications of the Commission's proposals which the Government consider desirable: for instance, they believe that refuse disposal, as well as collection, should be a district function; on the other hand the law on food standards and labelling (because of its connection with weights and measures and the other consumer protection services), and on animal health (which involves the police), should be administered by the regional authorities.

. . . . . .

THE NEW LOCAL AUTHORITY AREAS

41. The Government have examined with great care the areas proposed by the Royal Commission for the regional and district authorities. They accept the Commission's general approach, but have decided that some modifications of the pattern of authorities are necessary in order to produce a structure flexible enough to suit the requirements of different parts of the country.

Highlands Region

42. The Government recognise the force of the criticisms which have been made of the extent of the proposed Highlands region, covering almost half the area of Scotland. They have looked closely at suggestions that it might be divided into two or even three separate regions. They have concluded, however, that any such division would entail an arbitrary fragmentation of the growing community of interest in the Highlands. Nevertheless some adjustment must be made to reduce the practical difficulties which would confront a regional authority responsible for such a widely spread region.

43. First, Orkney and Shetland, because of their separate identity and remoteness from the mainland, should become virtually all-purpose authorities, with complete statutory responsibility for almost the whole range of local government functions. It will, however, be necessary to retain for the police and fire services arrangements, similar to those at present in force, for administration over a wider area. The Orkney and Shetland authorities will also have to continue to rely on the mainland for assistance in the more specialised aspects of education and social work.

44. Secondly, the Government consider that the major part of Argyll has stronger links, evident particularly in existing lines of communication, with Glasgow than with the rest of the Highlands region, and should be transferred to the West region. Ardnamurchan and the Glencoe district in the present county of Argyll will remain in the Highlands region.

45. Thirdly, it is proposed that the number of districts within the revised Highlands region should be increased from five to ten, so as to bring the local government organisation nearer to the people in areas where the population is widely dispersed. The resulting pattern follows fairly closely that outlined in a note of reservation to the Wheatley report. The Government accept, so far as the Highlands are concerned, the view expressed in the note that district authorities of the size proposed should not exercise planning functions . . .

. . . . . .

North-East Region

47. The region outlined by the Commission is acceptable, except for the proposal that the county of Kincardine should be split between the North-East and East regions. The whole of the county looks to Aberdeen as its regional centre, and should therefore be included in the North-East region. The district authorities, the number of which should be increased from four to five, will have responsibility for local planning along with the other local services.

East Region

48. Subject to the removal of the southern part of Kincardineshire to the North-East region, the Government accept the region proposed by the Commission . . .

49. At the district level the Government consider that no increase is necessary in the four district authorities recommended by the Commission.

South-East Region and Borders

. . . . . .

51. The second question is whether the four Border counties should be given separate regional status. The Commission concluded that, because of the strong existing links between the Borders and Edinburgh, and because of doubt about the adequacy of the resources of the Borders to meet regional responsibilities, a separate region should not be created. However, the Commission themselves recognised that the Borders have a special character and distinctive problems. The Government believe that, with the evidence that now exists of local determination to solve problems by joint effort, the further development which the area so urgently needs will best be achieved by a Borders regional authority. Although the population of the region falls below the levels suggested by the Commission for the provision of major services, these levels, as the Commission themselves accepted, were only a general guide, and population is not the only, nor always the most important, factor. Operational considerations will make special arrangements necessary for the joint administration of the police and fire services over the South-East and Borders regions. The region may also be dependent on the neighbouring South-East region for the more specialised educational and social work services, but otherwise the Borders authority will discharge the entire range of regional functions.

52. In the South-East region, comprising Edinburgh, the Lothians, and south Fife, the Government propose that there should be six district authorities, each carrying the full range of district functions. In the Borders region there will be four district authorities. Responsibility in the Borders for local planning, building control and libraries will rest with the regional authority, not the districts, for the same reasons as apply in the Highlands.

. . . . . .

West Region

54. There has been a good deal of criticism of the very large West region proposed by the Royal Commission, and the Government have examined closely the scope for dividing the region or limiting its size. They have concluded that there is no alternative to a single regional authority for the west of Scotland. Despite all the difficulties to which the Commission's proposal gives rise there is considerable agreement that the crucial planning and other related problems of the West need to be approached on a very wide basis. Only a regional authority covering the whole of the area will have the broad perspective and the essential resources of finance, manpower and land to cope with them effectively. Moreover, the evidence shows that the interdependence and community of interest between Glasgow and the rest of the entire proposed region are as strong as between any Scottish city and its

hinterland. Thus any solution which did not provide a single regional authority would be a denial of the Government's approach, and would in the long run damage the interests of every part of the area.

55. The West region proposed by the Government will have a population of about 2,562,000; the transfer of Argyll from the Highlands to the West region will be counter-balanced to some extent by the removal from the West region of the Girvan district council area of Ayrshire (with a population of about 11,000), which appears to have closer links with the South-West region than with the West.

. . . . . .

57. The number of district authorities will be increased from 11 to 13 by the addition of Argyll and by the division of the Hamilton—East Kilbride district into two.

South-West Region

58. The Government accept the region suggested by the Royal Commission, subject to the inclusion of the Girvan area, transferred from the West region, which will raise the population of the region to about 156,000. As in the case of the Borders, although the population of the South-West does not fully meet the criteria established by the Commission, the region has a homogeneous character and sufficient resources for the successful discharge of its responsibilities. However, as in the Borders, it may have to depend to some extent on the neighbouring region for specialised assistance in some aspects of education and social work.

59. It is intended that the number of districts within the enlarged region should be increased from two to four: and that the regional authority, like those of the Highlands and the Borders, should deal with all aspects of planning, with building control, and with libraries.

. . . . . .

COMMUNITY COUNCILS

61. The Royal Commission suggested that each district authority should be required to prepare a scheme for the formation of community councils within its area; and that community councils should not be part of the formal local government structure, with statutory functions to perform. But they should be able to express local opinion, to improve the amenity of their areas, and to run certain local services or facilities, as agents for the district or regional authorities. They should have no right to raise money by rates, local tax or requisition, but could receive grants from district or regional authorities, as well as private donations, and could devise their own finance-raising methods.

62. . . . . The Government intend to consult all the interests concerned about the Commission's detailed recommendations for the scope of activity, financing and composition of community councils; but they incline to the view that any community which wishes to set up such a council should be enabled to do so.

63. The Government agree with the Commission that community councils should not have statutory functions: this is the corollary of the proposal that their formation should be optional, depending on local wishes. These councils will not be local authorities in the familiar sense; they will be outside the local government system. The Government do not consider that community councils should, as the Commission suggested, administer services on behalf of the regional or district authorities: this agency arrangement would run counter to the principle that authorities should be accountable to their electorates, and experience shows that such an arrangement seldom works well. However, in expressing and representing local opinion on issues which affect the local community, and in safeguarding and improving local amenity, community councils could find a worthwhile and interesting role. In their further consultations the Government will be concentrating in greater detail on how the community councils' activities in these fields would work in practice.

64. The Government's provisional opinion is that the areas of community councils should, except perhaps where the population is sparsely scattered, be slightly larger than the 'parishes' identified by the Commission. In order to ensure that the councils reflect a true cross-section of local opinion and activities, consideration might be given to the possibility of providing for the representation on the councils, alongside individuals chosen by popular local election, of appropriate local organisations. The Government do not consider that community councils will take over from, or remove the need for, amenity associations, village hall committees, or voluntary organisations working in specialised fields; and because a continuing function is foreseen for such local bodies they should probably be represented, in a minority, on the community council.

THE STATUS OF LOCAL GOVERNMENT

. . . . . .

Relations with Central Government

68. The Commission concluded that central control over the work and organisation of local authorities was excessive, and that within the reorganised structure a new form of relationship between local and central government should be created. The Government agree: they regard it as essential to the success of the new system that the authorities should be, and should be seen to be, the partners and not the dependants of central government. The new authorities proposed in the earlier part of this White Paper will have sufficient professional skill and technical advice at their disposal to make it possible to reduce the degree of central intervention in the management of local affairs.

69. There are two main areas in which central control can be eased. The first is the financial field. It is essential for the proper management of the national economy that some central regulation of local authorities' financial activities should

continue. More financial responsibility should be devolved to local authorities, however, and the Government will be discussing possibilities with the local authority associations.

70. The Government believe that some administrative and technical controls which central departments operate over particular local government services could also be relaxed. There is still supervision in some areas where it has ceased to be relevant to present day circumstances. The Government and the local authority associations are already studying the possibility of ending certain controls . . .

71. The Government intend to remove many of the existing restraints and to operate flexibly those which remain. This should ensure that central departments concentrate on broad national policy, and local authorities on the management of local affairs and on regional and district problems.

. . . . . .

Management

75. The Government endorse the Commission's view that good management is vital to the effective operation of local authorities and that as much responsibility as possible should be delegated to officials, while councillors decide policy. These questions of internal organisation, however, are mainly matters for each local authority. Imposed solutions would not be satisfactory. Local authorities will no doubt wish to make a further study of these matters and the principles of management involved, and the associations will be invited, in advance of reorganisation, to reconstitute a working party on management topics.

Complaints Machinery

76. The Commission thought that there might be a case for a commissioner to deal with complaints against local authorities, but that no decision should be taken as to the need for such an appointment until after the new structure had settled down. The Government agree that new machinery is needed but consider that there would be advantages if it were introduced at the same time as local government reorganisation becomes effective. They intend to examine the matter in consultation with the local authority associations.

. . . . . .

Review Body

87. The Government accept the case made out by the Commission for a thorough and continuous review of local government machinery in the future: and they agree that this can be carried out most effectively by a single standing body specially constituted for the purpose . . .

59 THE NEW SYSTEM

From *Brief on Local Government Reform* (Scottish Office, 1974); by permission of
H.M.S.O.

THE NEW STRUCTURE

The objective of re-organised local government is to give a better service to the
public. The new structure which will be established on May 16, 1975 under the
terms of the Local Government (Scotland) Act 1973 provides, to this end, for nine
regional councils and 53 district councils, with 'most-purpose' status for three new
islands councils for Orkney, Shetland and the Western Isles. The new authorities
will replace the present structure of four cities, 21 large burghs, 176 small burghs,
33 counties and 196 districts.

The recommendations of the Royal Commission on Local Government in
Scotland (1966—69) were substantially accepted by the Government, and the basis
for change was set out in a White Paper published in February, 1971. The main
departures represented by the structure in the Act from the recommendations of
the Royal Commission are an increase in the number of regions from seven to nine
(the Borders and Fife), separate status for Orkney, Shetland and the Western Isles,
and an increase in the number of districts from 27 to 53. In addition, most of
Argyllshire will be included in the Strathclyde region in a separate Argyll district
rather than in the Highland region; and Kincardineshire will be in the Grampian
region rather than being divided between Tayside and Grampian regions.

Under the new legislation, the four cities cease to be all-purpose authorities and,
with their surrounding areas, will constitute district authorities within the regions
in which they are situated. The difficulties of creating a new structure are reflected
in the large, sparsely-populated area to be covered by the Highland region (a population of 175,000 in an area between John O'Groats and Ardnamurchan) in contrast
to the population of 2,500,000 in Strathclyde region (nearly half of Scotland's
total). This imbalance of size has been a natural target for criticism, but the boundaries of the Strathclyde region correspond broadly to a distinctive area with regional
characteristics and large-scale problems. Any sub-division would have meant a
weakening of administrative cohesion and an impairment of strategic opportunities.

At both levels within the new system strong authorities are being created which
will be attractive bodies for public service by elected representatives and full-time
officials.

Boundaries

It has been necessary to define the new local authorities by reference to existing
administrative boundaries of one sort or another. The Government are aware of

some anomalies which have been created because of the need to keep to these boundaries; and such cases will be referred for early consideration by the new Local Government Boundary Commission which is being set up under the Act. The Commission will hold an initial review of the administrative and electoral boundaries of the new authorities and thereafter will have a continuing responsibility in relation to local government and electoral boundaries, with a duty to make comprehensive reports in 10–15 year cycles.

Community councils

Under the new legislation, any community which so wishes will be able to form a community council (which will not have statutory functions) to express local views and to take action on behalf of the community. Responsibility for drawing up schemes for community councils lies with district and islands councils who before May 16, 1976 (or a later date agreed by the Secretary of State) must carry out full public consultations, prepare plans showing proposed community areas, and draw up codes of procedure and arrangements for elections. These schemes must be approved by the Secretary of State, who may hold a public inquiry into any objections or representations and amend the scheme if he sees fit. After that stage, it will be for the inhabitants of each community area to petition the district or islands council to put into operation the machinery for holding an election and setting up a council. The aim is not to set up an executive third tier of local government, but to create a type of organisation quite different from the regional, islands and district councils which can turn its attention to anything of concern to the local community without being limited to performing tasks laid down by statute.

Community councils are free to raise funds for their work by their own efforts, to receive grants related to particular projects they undertake, and to receive help in money, staff or facilities from regional, islands or district councils. The size of a 'community' will depend entirely on local circumstances and needs. In some cases a community area will virtually define itself – a village or small town with its surrounding area. In other cases, such as larger urban areas, definition may be rather harder; but in general the aim is that the size of the area should be such as to provide a ready base for the gathering of views and decisions on action in local interests.
. . . . . .

Allowances for councillors

Taxable attendance allowances payable as of right will be given to councillors to replace the present system of loss of earnings allowances. While the old system mitigated the actual loss suffered by councillors who could prove loss, professional and self-employed people found it difficult to prove that any actual financial loss had in fact been incurred in respect of individual attendances at meetings.
. . . . . .

Admission of Press and public to meetings

The new legislation widens the existing law in the Public Bodies (Admission to Meetings) Act 1960, so that committees of local authorities shall admit Press and public to their meetings with certain exceptions where for good reason (such as staff business or approval of contracts) they take a resolution to exclude the public. This will take effect from May 16, 1975. Under the present system there is no obligation on committees (unless they are composed of the whole authority) to admit the Press and public.

ELECTIONS

Tuesday, May 7, 1974 — that was the date when voters in Scotland were able to cast their first votes for councillors on the new regional, islands and district councils set up under the Local Government (Scotland) Act 1973. One vote could be cast for representatives on regional or islands councils and (except in the islands council areas) one vote in addition for councillors on the district councils.

Every region and every islands area was divided into electoral divisions, and every district into wards. Each division and each ward returned one councillor. The newly-elected councils will work in 'shadow' form on matters of internal management and preparatory tasks alongside the old authorities until May 16, 1975 when they take over and the existing councils no longer function.

Terms of office for councillors will normally be of four years; but since elections will take place every second year for the regions and district councils alternately some adjustment is necessary in the early years. Elections for the islands councils will coincide with those for the regional councils. To bring the elections into an alternate region/district two-year cycle, the first two terms of office for district councillors will be of three years each.

Thus the timetable of elections for the new authorities in the early years is:

May 7, 1974 — Elections for regional/islands and district councils
May 16, 1975 — Old authorities cease to exist, new councils take over
        1977 — Elections for district councils
        1978 — Elections for regional/islands authorities
        1980 — Elections for district councils
        1982 — Elections for regional/islands authorities
        1984 — Elections for district councils

RELAXATION OF CENTRAL GOVERNMENT CONTROLS

Over the years, successive Acts of Parliament have given the Government a very far-reaching system of controls over local authority activities. These controls range from matters of basic importance — such as the protection of individuals' rights or surveillance over very large sums of capital investment — down to what may be quite trivial powers to intervene in the minor day-to-day activities of local authorities.

Some of these controls may well be irksome to local authorities in that they restrict their freedom of activity, but others may be needed to ensure common standards throughout the country or to provide for settling disputes between authorities.

In 1973 the then Secretary of State for Scotland completed work on a comprehensive review of statutory controls exercised by his Departments over local government in pursuance of the undertaking, stated in the Government's White Paper on the Reform of Local Government in Scotland, to reduce central controls. As a result of this review, the Government in June, 1973 put forward amendments to the Bill (as it was then) adding to the substantial number of relaxations already provided for in the legislation.

The Government also introduced a provision giving the Secretary of State the power to make statutory orders to modify or revoke Government controls over local authorities contained in existing legislation, without having to introduce an amending Act of Parliament. This means that procedure for future relaxations will be simpler.

Examples of the types of controls already relaxed in the Act are:

Transport: The great majority of Ministerial controls over passenger transport authorities cease with local government reorganisation. The only important exceptions are the powers to make orders designating a passenger transport area, to transfer existing municipal bus undertakings to a passenger transport executive and to bring into force certain provisions of the Transport Act 1968 which give a passenger transport executive responsibility for bus licensing and the control of local rail services. All controls exercised over a passenger transport executive will now become the responsibility of the regional authority.

Financial Controls: Borrowing: Control of capital expenditure on a 'programme' basis will be substituted for the old system of controls over individual borrowing applications. A number of minor controls in the borrowing field have also been abolished.

Payments for purposes not otherwise authorised: Under previous legislation — Section 339 of the Local Government (Scotland) Act 1947 — a local authority could, **with the consent of the Secretary of State**, spend money up to a limit in the interests of the area or its inhabitants, or for certain charitable and other purposes. The 1973 Act removes the need for the Secretary of State's consent, and at the same time raises the limit on these payments from the equivalent of a rate of .8p in the £ to 2p.

. . . . . .

FINANCE

The main purpose of Part VII of the Act and the related Schedules 8, 9 and (in part)

29 is to provide a framework for the financial administration and functioning of the new authorities.

All the authorities are required to have a general fund, to make arrangements for the proper administration of their financial affairs and to maintain accounts, which are to be subject to audit. Approval by the Secretary of State of capital expenses, which may be given on a programme basis, will replace the present requirement to obtain the consent of the appropriate Minister for every exercise of borrowing powers, project by project.

New arrangements are made regarding local government audit. Most of the Secretary of State's responsibilities are transferred to a body to be called the Commission for Local Authority Accounts in Scotland. It will arrange for the audit of all local authority accounts, either by accountants in professional practice or by auditors in its own employment, will consider reports on the audits, will investigate matters raised and will make recommendations to the Secretary of State and the authorities concerned. These arrangements are designed to enhance the public accountability of local authorities and to reduce the part played in audit matters by the Secretary of State. In cases where the Commission recommends recovery of any amount, the Secretary of State will be concerned only with the Commission's recommendation and any representations made by persons affected, before deciding whether the recovery should be made in full, in part, or not at all. As regards rating, the Act does more than adapt the present arrangements: it makes a fundamental change. Rates are at present determined and levied by one authority only in each rating area (ie by each county, in respect of the landward area, and each burgh). Authorities providing services other than the rating authority requisition for a share of the cost on the rating authority — and the county requisition for major services usually accounts for the larger part of the burgh rate. The Act divides the rating function: under its provisions every new authority will determine a rate for its own services, but the collection of rates and the administration of rating are made the responsibility of regional and islands councils. Except in the case of joint committees and the like, and in a few cases where a region's water supply area extends beyond the region, the present system of requisitions will disappear.

New Local Government Areas in Scotland. Regions and Districts

Region	Districts	No. of Districts	1971 Population
HIGHLAND	Caithness Sutherland Ross and Cromarty Skye and Lochalsh Lochaber Inverness Badenoch and Strathspey Nairn	8	175,000

Region	Districts	No. of Districts	1971 Population
GRAMPIAN	Moray Banff and Buchan Gordon City of Aberdeen Kincardine and Deeside	5	437,000
TAYSIDE	Angus City of Dundee Perth and Kinross	3	397,000
FIFE	Kirkcaldy North East Fife Dumfermline	3	328,000
LOTHIAN	West Lothian City of Edinburgh Midlothian East Lothian	4	742,000
CENTRAL	Clackmannan Stirling Falkirk	3	263,000
BORDERS	Tweeddale Ettrick and Lauderdale Roxburgh Berwickshire	4	99,000
STRATHCLYDE	Argyll Dumbarton City of Glasgow Clydebank Bearsden and Milngarie Bishopbriggs and Kirkintilloch Cumbernauld Monklands Motherwell Hamilton East Kilbride Eastwood Lanark Renfrew Inverclyde Cunninghame Kilmarnock and Loudon Kyle and Carrick Cumnock and Doon Valley	19	2,578,000
DUMFRIES AND GALLOWAY	Merrick Stewartry Nithsdale Annandale and Eskdale	4	144,000

No. of Regions – 9   *No. of Districts* – 53
ISLANDS AREAS:
ORKNEY
SHETLAND
WESTERN ISLES
No. of Island Areas – 3

Distribution of Functions

REGIONAL AND ISLANDS AUTHORITIES *Exercised concurrently by regional and district authorities.	DISTRICT AND ISLANDS AUTHORITIES †Except in Highland, Dumfries and Galloway and Borders regions where the function will be regional.
Education	Local planning†
Youth Employment	Development control†
Social Work	Comprehensive† urban redevelopment
Police	Listed buildings†
Fire	Conservation areas†
Strategic Planning	Industrial Development*
Derelict Land*	Derelict Land*
Industrial Development*	Housing
Water	Building control†
Flood Prevention	Tourism*
Sewerage	Countryside*
Coast Protection	Caravan sites
Roads	Recreation*
Public Transport	Parks*
Road Safety	Museums*
Airports	Libraries†
Ferries	Community Centres*
Harbours	Art galleries*
Tourism*	Environmental health
Countryside*	Cleansing
Parks*	Refuse collection and disposal
Recreation*	Public conveniences
Museums*	Burial and cremation
Art Galleries*	Markets and slaughter-houses
Community Centres*	Food hygiene
Consumer Protection	Clean air
Weights and Measures	Inspection of shops, offices and factories
Food standards and labelling	Licensing:
Registration of births, deaths and marriages	Dogs
Electoral registration	Theatres and cinemas
Valuation	Liquor
	Betting and gaming

Map 5 *Scotland: the New System*

Source: Scottish Office Brief on Local Government Reform

Map 6 Scotland: Strathclyde Region

Source: Scottish Office Brief on Local Government Reform

60 THE SCOTTISH LOCAL GOVERNMENT OMBUDSMAN

From *Local Government (Scotland) Act, 1975*; by permission of H.M.S.O.

PART II LOCAL ADMINISTRATION

21. (1) For the purpose of conducting investigations in relation to any authority to which this Part of this Act applies there shall be a commissioner to be known as the Commissioner for Local Administration in Scotland.

(2) Appointments to the office of Commissioner shall be made by Her Majesty on the recommendation of the Secretary of State after consultation with such bodies representing local authorities as appear appropriate to the Secretary of State, and a person so appointed shall, subject to subsection (3) below, hold office during good behaviour.

(3) A person appointed to be the Commissioner may be relieved of office by Her Majesty at his own request or may be removed from office by Her Majesty on grounds of incapacity or misbehaviour, and shall in any case vacate office on completing the year of service in which he attains the age of sixty-five years.

(4) For each year, the Commissioner —

(a) shall submit a general report on the discharge of his functions to the designated body, and

(b) shall review the operation of the provisions of this Part of this Act about the investigation of complaints, and shall have power to convey to local authorities or to government departments any recommendations or conclusions reached in the course of his review.

. . . . . .

23. (1) This Part of this Act applies to the following authorities —

(a) any local authority;

(b) any committee, joint committee or joint board the members of which, other than ex officio members, are appointed by one or more local authorities;

(c) any education committee, joint committee of education authorities, and any person or body which discharges the functions of an education authority by virtue of an arrangement made under Schedule 10 to the Act of 1973;

(d) any water development board within the meaning of the Water (Scotland) Act 1967;

(e) any river purification board within the meaning of section 135 of the Act of 1973;

(f) any person or body which by virtue of section 56(1) of the Act of 1973 discharges any of the functions of a local authority.

(2) Without prejudice to subsection (1)(f) above, this Part of this Act applies to—

(*a*) any joint committee constituted by an administration scheme under section 36 of the Fire Services Act 1947;

(*b*) any joint police committee constituted by an amalgamation scheme made or approved under the Police (Scotland) Act 1967;

(*c*) any social work committee established under section 2 of the Social Work (Scotland) Act 1968;

(*d*) any Children's Panel Advisory Committee formed under paragraph 3 of Schedule 3 to the said Act of 1968;

(*e*) any joint committee, for the administration of superannuation schemes for persons employed in local government service or teachers, established by regulations under section 7 or 9 of the Superannuation Act 1972 respectively.

24. (1) Subject to the provisions of this Part of this Act, where a written complaint is made by or on behalf of a member of the public who claims to have sustained injustice in consequence of maladministration in connection with action taken by or on behalf of an authority to which this Part of this Act applies, being action taken in the exercise of administrative functions of that authority, the Commissioner may investigate that complaint.

(2) A complaint shall not be entertained under this Part of this Act unless –

(*a*) it is made in writing to a member of the authority, or of any other authority concerned, specifying the action alleged to constitute maladministration, and

(*b*) it is referred to the Commissioner, with the consent of the persons aggrieved, or of a person acting on his behalf, by that member, or by any other person who is a member of any authority concerned, with a request to investigate the complaint.

(3) If the Commissioner is satisfied that any member of any authority concerned has been requested to refer the complaint to the Commissioner, and has not done so, the Commissioner may, if he thinks fit, dispense with the requirements in subsection (2)(*b*) above.

(4) A complaint shall not be entertained unless it was made to a member of any authority concerned within twelve months from the day on which the person aggrieved first had notice of the matters alleged in the complaint, but the Commissioner may conduct an investigation pursuant to a complaint not made within that period if he considers that there are special circumstances which make it proper to do so.

(5) Before proceeding to investigate a complaint, the Commissioner shall satisfy himself that the complaint has been brought, by or on behalf of the person aggrieved, to the notice of the authority to which the complaint relates and that that authority has been afforded a reasonable opportunity to investigate, and reply to, the complaint.

(6) The Commissioner shall not conduct an investigation under this Part of this Act in respect of any of the following matters, that is to say –

(*a*) any action in respect of which the person aggrieved has or had a right of appeal, reference or review to or before a tribunal constituted by or under any enactment;

(*b*) any action in respect of which the person aggrieved has or had a right of appeal to a Minister of the Crown; or

(*c*) any action in respect of which the person aggrieved has or had a remedy by way of proceedings in any court of law:

Provided that the Commissioner may conduct an investigation notwithstanding the existence of such a right or remedy if satisfied that in the particular circumstances it is not reasonable to expect the person aggrieved to resort or have resorted to it.

(7) The Commissioner shall not conduct an investigation in respect of any action which in his opinion affects all or most of the inhabitants of the area of the authority concerned.

26. (1) Where the Commissioner proposes to conduct an investigation pursuant to a complaint, he shall afford to the authority concerned, and to any person who is alleged in the complaint to have taken or authorised the action complained of, an opportunity to comment on any allegations contained in the complaint.

(2) Every such investigation shall be conducted in private, but except as aforesaid the procedure for conducting an investigation shall be such as the Commissioner considers appropriate in the circumstances of the case; and, without prejudice to the generality of the preceding provision, the Commissioner may obtain information from such persons and in such manner, and make such inquiries, as he thinks fit, and may determine whether any person may be represented (by counsel or solicitor or otherwise) in the investigation.

27. (1) For the purposes of an investigation under this Part of this Act the Commissioner may require any member or officer of the authority concerned, or any other person who in his opinion is able to furnish information or produce documents relevant to the investigation, to furnish any such information or produce any such documents.

(2) For the purposes of any such investigation the Commissioner shall have the same powers as the Court of Session in respect of the attendance and examination of witnesses, and in respect of the production of documents.

(3) The Commissioner may, under subsection (1) above, require any person to furnish information concerning communications between the authority concerned and any Government department, or to produce any correspondence or other documents forming part of any such written communications.

(4) No obligation to maintain secrecy or other restriction upon the disclosure of information obtained by or furnished to persons in Her Majesty's service, whether imposed by any enactment or by any rule of law, shall apply to the disclosure of information in accordance with subsection (3) above; and where that subsection applies the Crown shall not be entitled to any such privilege in respect of the production of documents or the giving of evidence as is allowed by law in legal proceedings.

28. (1) In any case where the Commissioner conducts an investigation, or decides not to conduct an investigation, he shall send a report of the results of the investi-

gation, or as the case may be a statement of his reasons for not conducting an investigation —

(a) to the person, if any, who referred the complaint to the Commissioner in accordance with section 24(2) of this Act, and

(b) to the complainant, and

(c) to the authority concerned, and to any other authority or person who is alleged in the complaint to have taken or authorised the action complained of.

(2) Where the complaint was referred by a person who was a member of an authority but who has since ceased to be a member of that authority, the report or statement shall be sent to the chairman of that authority.

(3) Apart from identifying the authority or authorities concerned, the report shall not —

(a) mention the name of any person, or

(b) contain any particulars which, in the opinion of the Commissioner, are likely to identify any person and can be omitted without impairing the effectiveness of the report,

unless, after taking into account the public interest as well as the interests of the complainant and of persons other than the complainant, the Commissioner considers it necessary to mention the name of that person or to include in the report any such particulars.

(4) Subject to the provisions of subsection (7) below, the authority concerned shall for a period of three weeks make copies of the report available for inspection by the public without charge at all reasonable hours at one or more of their offices; and any person shall be entitled to take copies of, or extracts from the report when so made available.

(5) Not later than one week after the report is received by the authority concerned, the proper officer of the authority shall give public notice, by advertisement in newspapers and such other ways as appear to him appropriate, that the report will be available for inspection as provided by subsection (4) above, and shall specify the date, being a date after the giving of the public notice, from which the period of three weeks will begin.

(6) If a person having the custody of a report made available for inspection as provided by subsection (4) above obstructs any person seeking to inspect the report, or to make a copy of, or extract from, the report, he shall be liable on summary conviction to a fine not exceeding £50.

(7) The Commissioner may, if he thinks fit after taking into account the public interest as well as the interests of the complainant and of persons other than the complainant, direct that a report specified in the direction shall not be subject to the provisions of subsections (4) and (5) above about its publication.

29. (1) If in the opinion of the Commissioner, as set out in the report, injustice has been caused to the person aggrieved in consequence of maladministration, the report shall be laid before the authority concerned, and it shall be the duty of that

authority to consider the report, and to notify the Commissioner of the action which the authority have taken, or propose to take.

(2) If the Commissioner –

(*a*) does not receive any such notification within a reasonable time; or

(*b*) is not satisfied with the action which the authority concerned have taken; or

(*c*) does not within a reasonable time receive confirmation from the authority concerned that they have taken action, as proposed, to the satisfaction of the Commissioner,

he shall make a further report setting out those facts; and section 28 of this Act shall apply, with any necessary modifications, to that further report.

. . . . . .

31. (1) If, at any stage in the course of conducting an investigation under this Part of this Act, the Commissioner forms the opinion that the complaint relates partly to a matter which could be the subject of an investigation –

(*a*) by the Parliamentary Commissioner, in accordance with section 5 of the Act of 1967, or

(*b*) by the Health Service Commissioner for Scotland in accordance with section 45 of the Act of 1972,

he shall consult with the appropriate Commissioner about the complaint and, if he considers it necessary, inform the person initiating the complaint under this Part of this Act of the steps necessary to initiate a complaint under the Act of 1967 or under Part VII of the Act of 1972, as the case may be.

(2) Where, by virtue of subsection (1) above, the Commissioner consults the Parliamentary Commissioner or the Health Service Commissioner in relation to a complaint under this Part of this Act, he may consult that Commissioner about any matter relating to the complaint, including –

(*a*) the conduct of any investigation into the complaint, and

(*b*) the form, content and publication of any report of the results of such an investigation.

(3) If, at any stage in the course of conducting an investigation, under –

(*a*) the Act of 1967, or

(*b*) Part VII of the Act of 1972,

the Parliamentary Commissioner or the Health Service Commissioner conducting the investigation forms the opinion that the complaint relates partly to a matter which could be the subject of an investigation under this Part of this Act, he shall consult with the Commissioner about the complaint and, if he considers it necessary, inform the person initiating the complaint under the Act of 1967 or Part VII of the Act of 1972, as the case may be, of the steps necessary to initiate a complaint under this Part of this Act.

. . . . . .

32. (1) In this Part of this Act, unless the context otherwise requires –

'action' includes failure to act, and other expressions connoting action shall be construed accordingly;

. . .

(2) It is hereby declared that nothing in this Part of this Act authorises or requires the Commissioner to question the merits of a decision taken without maladministration by an authority in the exercise of a discretion vested in that authority.

61 INTERNAL ORGANISATION AND MANAGEMENT

From *The New Scottish Local Authorities: organisation and management structures* (The Paterson Report, 1973); by permission of H.M.S.O.

The terms of reference agreed by the Steering Committee were to:
(1) set out the considerations which should be borne in mind by local authorities in determining their structures of management at elected member and officer levels including internal arrangements bearing on efficiency in the employment of manpower;
(2) advise on the formulation of patterns of organisation most likely to be suitable for various types of authority to be established in 1974/75;

. . . . . .

The basic pattern

3.1 With certain significant exceptions, which we examine in the next section of this chapter, the structure found in most Scottish authorities is still largely traditional. Historically, as obligations have been placed on local authorities to provide particular services, new committees and departments have been grafted on to the existing structure. As a result, a high degree of specialisation or departmentalism is found . . .

3.2 The number of standing committees in the four cities ranged from 13 to 22. The number most frequently found in counties and also in large burghs was 10, with a range from 7 to 15, although one county in fact has 25 standing committees. In the small burghs the most frequent number was 6, with a range from 4 to 15.

3.3 In all types of authority the most usual size of committee was between 30 per cent and 40 per cent of the full council membership. Conveners' and provosts' committees, because of their particular functions, tended to have a lower membership, usually between 10 per cent and 20 per cent of the full council. On the other hand four large burghs indicated that all or most of their committees consisted of the full, or almost the full, council. Nine small burghs which replied also said that they followed this practice although all had a total council membership of 12 or fewer.

3.4 Notwithstanding the co-ordinating role performed by clerks and chief financial officers, the general picture of the structure at officer level is that of a number of independent departments whose heads are directly responsible to a committee or group of committees. Within counties and large burghs the usual number of departments is around 14 or 15, and in the cities from 22 to over 30. At the other end of the scale, most small burghs, with their limited range of functions, have between 2 and 4 departments.

3.5 In general, the process of formulating policies and devising plans to implement these policies is carried out independently within the various service committees and their respective departments, each making separate recommendations to the full council. Although there is now widespread recognition that the activities of any one committee or department interact to a substantial degree with those of other parts of the organisation, particularly in terms of their effect on the public, there is still very little in the way of formal co-ordination across the whole range of an authority's activities.

3.6 At committee level, such co-ordination as does exist usually takes place in the finance committee which, in the absence of any other committee charged with co-ordination of policy, attempts to fill the gap. However, while the finance committee does exert some overall influence, the effectiveness of this is limited because:

(1) its members are in no position to assess whether the sum total of the various departmental spending proposals really represents a cohesive programme geared to achieve the authority's objectives (which in most cases have never been defined specifically)

(2) they lack guidelines to assist them in reconciling the competing claims of the various services for finance

(3) they are concerned only with the financial implications of the departmental programmes and not with the deployment of other important elements of resource necessary for the implementation of the programmes.

. . . . . .

3.9 In many authorities, particularly in the more industrialised and urban areas, organised political groups have a significant influence on the decision-making process. While decisions are still taken formally within the authority's committees, the decision-making process in relation to major and politically sensitive issues takes place outwith the council chamber at meetings of the majority party group and its executive. Like Wheatley, we have found no real evidence that the group system militates against effectiveness. On the contrary, it has been suggested to us that the existence of a strong group produces benefits in terms of coherence and consistency of approach . . .

At this point we would merely endorse the Wheatley Commission's opinion: 'Whatever view may be taken on this issue, party politics must be accepted as a fact of life. They can neither be legislated for, nor legislated out of existence; and it is a mistake to allow feelings on the matter to influence the choice of a management structure.'

. . . . . .

CONCLUSIONS

3.10 Our review of the existing scene has confirmed our previous belief that most Scottish local authorities are still organised on the traditional departmental basis . . .

. . . . . .

3.20 What is required for the new authorities is a form of organisation which will at the same time:

(1) provide the means of achieving a unified approach to the formulation and implementation of policies and plans to meet the real needs of the community,

(2) preserve the strengths of the expert professional approach which will still be required for the effective discharge of the local authority's functions,

(3) ensure a challenging and worthwhile role for elected members and officers, and

(4) be sufficiently flexible to adapt and respond quickly to change.

. . . . . .

The corporate structure in outline

4.12 We have referred . . . to the need in all but the smallest authorities for a body of members responsible for the preparation of advice to the council on major policy, priorities and allocation of financial, manpower and land resources; within this task we would also include reviewing the effectiveness of the action taken to implement the policy decided upon by the council. Our consultations revealed that the vast majority of members and officers in Scottish local government agree with this basic need.

4.13 Although many different forms have been suggested for this central co-ordinating body, essentially they fall into three basic types:

cabinet

management board

policy committee

. . . . . .

4.14 In the cabinet system there would be a leader and several 'ministers' each directly responsible for a particular service; any committee other than the cabinet itself would be advisory only; chief officers would be answerable to their ministers and subject to only general co-ordination by the chief executive officer. In the management board system committees would be deliberative and representative, not executive; chief officers would take instructions from the council and the management board through the chief executive officer.

4.15 Among the advantages claimed for the cabinet and management board systems are that they would:

1. provide for the quick and efficient despatch of business, and

2. provide a clear avenue of approach and answerability by chief officers.

4.16 In our view, however, these claimed advantages are outweighed by the restrictions which such systems would place on participation by all members in the affairs of the authority . . . we reject any form of organisation based on either of these systems.

4.17 It seems to us that the best balance between the conflicting demands of effectiveness and democracy is struck by the policy committee type of approach. Because it is, in our view, impracticable to consider policy in the abstract without reference to the resources needed for implementation, we prefer the title of policy and resources committee, as advocated by Bains and others.

The policy and resources committee

4.18 The functions of the policy and resources committee are well described in the observations made to us by the Joint Advisory Committee of the Strathclyde Region. 'The Policy and Resources Committee should have more than a co-ordinating role. It should be responsible for identifying and setting out for consideration by the whole council the fundamental objectives which the council should be aiming to achieve, charting the broad course to be followed and setting the policy guidelines. It should also be charged with responsibility for co-ordinating the activities of other committees and for recommending how disputes between such committees might be resolved. It should have a free-ranging remit enabling it to monitor and review the performance of service committees and departments towards the attainment of the Council's objectives.' . . .

4.19 We consider it important to underline the relationship between the policy and resources committee and the service committees. We have already indicated our belief that the strengths of the specialist approach should be preserved in whatever new forms of organisation are finally implemented by the new authorities. We think it essential therefore that, within the framework of the overall policy plan, the service committees continue to be responsible for policy formulation and implementation within their own particular spheres of interest . . .

4.20 On the question of resources a distinction can be made between:
1. the major policy area concerned with overall deployment of resources in line with assessed priorities, and
2. the on-going task of detailed allocation and management of the individual resource elements of finance, manpower and land.

The former must clearly be the province of the policy and resources committee. The latter task would also be undertaken by the policy and resources committee in the smaller authorities . . .

4.21 The monitoring and review of performance against the authority's agreed objectives is a vital task — so vital in fact that we see this as a major function of the policy and resources committee itself and as an integral part of the continuing cyclical process. Therefore we would not envisage this task being allocated to a performance review sub-committee as suggested by Bains.

. . . . . .

4.25 Regarding the composition of the policy and resources committee, possible alternatives are:

1. to have the policy and resources committee consist solely of the majority party with suitable provision for keeping minority parties adequately informed.
2. to have minority party representation on the main committee but to set up a sub-committee consisting of majority party representatives only.
3. to have a multi-party committee and to set up suitable procedures for briefing the party groups.

. . . . . .

4.27 In practice, in many authorities with highly organised political parties, the single party approach will be adopted by the majority party and accepted, and perhaps even tacitly endorsed, by the minority. Whatever approach is adopted we stress the need to make effective arrangements for the provision of officer advice to the party groups prior to decisions being taken . . .

4.28 To be properly effective we consider that the size of the policy and resources committee must be kept to reasonable proportions consistent with an adequate level of representation. Our view is that the minimum membership should be around 8 and the maximum between 12 and 15, depending on the size of the council.

The chief executive and the management team

4.29 The need for corporate arrangements at the officer level is so widely accepted that we believe we can now take as read the necessity for a cohesive team of officers with an acknowledged leader working to a common set of objectives.

4.30 In all the evidence which we received from members and officers alike there was almost unanimous support for the appointment of an officer recognised as the head of the authority's paid service, accountable to the council for the provision of co-ordinated advice and the effective implementation of agreed policies and plans, and with direct authority over and responsibility for all other officers where they are carrying out statutory duties or are exercising their professional judgement.

. . . . . .

4.33 The role of the officers' management team is to act as the focal point for the preparation and presentation to the council, via the policy and resources committee and the service committees, of co-ordinated advice on policies and major programmes of work. This implies a commitment on the part of all members of the team to act with the wider objectives of the whole authority in mind, not being concerned solely with the activities and interests of their own particular departments. We consider that this is a realistic and indeed essential aim. It is consistent with good management theory and practice and we can see no reason why it should not be applicable within local government.

. . . . . .

RECOMMENDED STRUCTURES FOR THE NEW AUTHORITIES

The basic structure

The executive office 8.4 We have already indicated that the chief executive should not have direct responsibility for a major department except in the smaller authorities; at the same time, however, it is vital to ensure that he does not become isolated but has at his disposal all the necessary facilities to keep himself fully informed and, in particular, to carry out his co-ordinative role in policy planning. His support will clearly come in large measure from the heads of the service departments and the central support services and from the policy planning unit where it exists.

8.5 In the larger authorities, however, the immense demands which will be made on the chief executive require a more formalised arrangement for his support. We favour the concept of the 'executive office' whereby the chief executive is assisted, in his tasks of co-ordinating policy planning, monitoring the effectiveness of the authority's programmes and managing the central services, by two or three officials of chief officer status. These would be a director of finance, a director of administration and, in the largest authorities of all, a director of policy planning. These officers could be designated as deputy chief executives.

. . . . . .

Regions

Service committee structure 8.10 We consider that all regions will require at least seven service committees as set out below:

Education
education services
Social Work
social work services
Transportation and Basic Services
roads; lighting; traffic management and road safety; special engineering services; passenger transport, harbour services, airports
sewerage and sewage treatment; flood prevention and arterial drainage; coast protection
water
Leisure and Recreation
recreation and parks, including recreational use of countryside; museums and art galleries; theatres and halls; community centres
Consumer Protection
trading standards and food standards and labelling
public analyst
diseases of animals
Police and Fire

police
fire
General Purposes
law and procedure; parliamentary and court work
ceremonial, hospitality
registration of births, deaths and marriages
home defence
miscellaneous
. . . . . .

Resource committee structure 8.15 All regions will require standing committees or sub-committees with responsibility for:
finance
manpower
planning and development.
We have already stressed the cardinal importance of effective allocation of resources which is a key role of the policy and resources committee. We therefore re-emphasise the necessity for a strong element of linked membership between these committees and the policy and resources committee. Alternatively resource sub-committees of the policy and resources committee could be created.
. . . . . .

8.17 Because of the reduction in the number of councillors it seems inevitable that members will require to specialise to some extent in order to facilitate the effective despatch of business, and that the size of the service committees and the resource committees will require to be limited, consistent with the need for adequate representation. We therefore consider that no committee should consist of more than one third of the members of the full council. In Borders, however, with a council membership of only 23, this limit might have to be exceeded.
. . . . . .

Officer structure 8.21 In the basic officer structure we envisage the following separate departments:
education
social work
engineering and technical services
leisure and recreation
consumer protection
physical planning
architecture
. . . . . .

Districts

Service committee structure 8.30 We consider that all districts except the very smallest will require four service committees as follows:

Housing
assessment of need
design, construction and improvement
housing management
Environmental Health
sanitary services
cleansing
burial grounds and crematoria
markets and slaughterhouses
Leisure and Recreation
assessment of need
provision and management of recreational facilities, including parks, swimming
baths, sports centres, community centres, halls and theatres
provision and management of libraries and museums (except districts in Highland,
Borders, and Dumfries and Galloway)
General Purposes
regulation and licensing
law and procedure, parliamentary and court work
ceremonial, hospitality
miscellaneous.

. . . . . .

Resource committee structure 8.33 In the large urban districts, as in the regions, we
consider that there will be the same requirement for three resource committees or
sub-committees:
finance
manpower
planning and development
with the same strong links with the policy and resources committee as already
described.

8.34 In the smaller districts we consider that the oversight of the main elements
of resources could be the responsibility of the policy and resources committee itself
and that separate resource committees or sub-committees would not be needed . . .

. . . . . .

Officer structure 8.40 We consider that all districts should appoint a chief executive.
In the largest districts we believe that the executive office arrangement will also be
necessary. In the smaller districts, the reduced scale and complexity of activities
together with economic considerations would make it necessary and practicable
that the chief executive should assume direct responsibility himself for a main
department.

8.41 Subject to possible groupings discussed below the basic officer structure
would contain the following units:
housing

physical planning and building control (except in general planning authority areas)
cleansing
sanitary services
libraries (except in general planning authority areas)
museums
swimming pools and sports centres
parks and other recreational facilities

together with finance, legal and administration, and architectural services . . .

. . . . . .

TERMS OF REFERENCE FOR THE POLICY AND RESOURCES COMMITTEE

1 To guide the council in the formulation of its policy objectives and priorities, and for this purpose to recommend to the council such forward programmes and other steps as may be necessary to achieve those objectives, either in whole or in part, during specific time spans. For this purpose to consider the broad social and economic needs of the authority and matters of comprehensive importance to the area, including the contents of structure and local plans. To advise the council generally as to its financial and economic policies.

2 Without prejudice to the duties and responsibilities of the service committees, to review the effectiveness of all the council's work and the standards and levels of service provided. To identify the need for new services and to keep under review the necessity for existing ones.

3 To submit to the council concurrent reports with the service committees upon new policies or changes in policy formulated by such committees, particularly those which may have significant impact upon the policy plan or the resources of the council.

4 To advise the council on the allocation and control of its financial, manpower and land resources.

5 To ensure that the organisation and management processes of the council are designed to make the most effective contribution to the achievement of the council's objectives. To keep them under review in the light of changing circumstances, making recommendations as necessary for change in either the committee or departmental structure, or the distribution of functions and responsibilities.

6 To be concerned, together with the appropriate other committees, in the appointment of heads of departments and any deputies.

. . . . . .

TERMS OF REFERENCE FOR THE CHIEF EXECUTIVE

1 The chief executive is the head of the council's paid service and shall have authority over all other officers so far as this is necessary for the efficient management and execution of the council's functions, except where:

principal officers are exercising responsibilities imposed on them by statute.

the professional discretion or judgement of the principal officers is involved.

2 He is the leader of the officers' management team and, through the policy and resources committee, the council's principal adviser on matters of general policy. As such it is his responsibility to secure co-ordination of advice on the forward planning of objectives and services and to lead the management team in securing a corporate approach to the affairs of the authority generally.

3 Through his leadership of the officers' management team he is responsible for the efficient and effective implementation of the council's programmes and policies and for securing that the resources of the authority are most effectively deployed towards those ends.

4 Similarly, he shall keep under review the organisation and administration of the authority and shall make recommendations to the council through the policy and resources committee if he considers that major changes are required in the interests of effective management.

5 As head of the paid service it is his responsibility to ensure that effective and equitable manpower policies are developed and implemented throughout all departments of the authority in the interests both of the authority and the staff.

6 He is responsible for the maintenance of good internal and external relations.

Proposed Executive Office

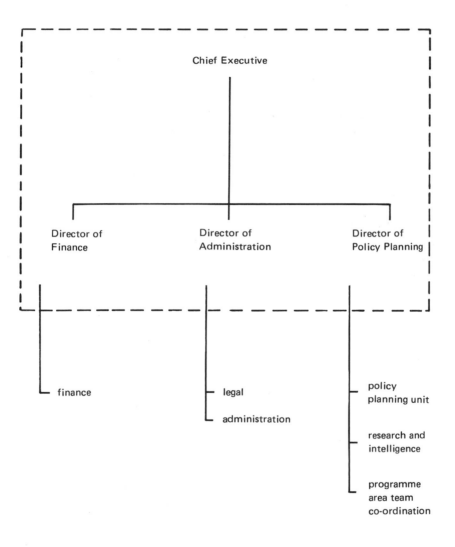

Proposed Committee Structure

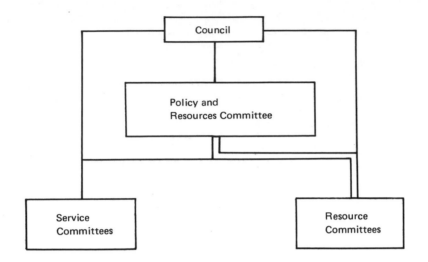

Officer structure

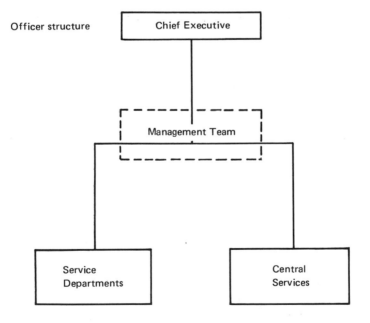

Fig. 1 *Regional Committee Structure*

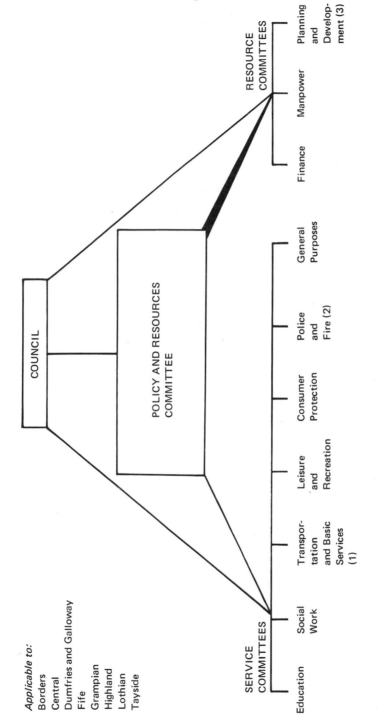

Applicable to:
Borders
Central
Dumfries and Galloway
Fife
Grampian
Highland
Lothian
Tayside

[1] Except in Lothian, Grampian and Tayside which would have separate committees or sub-committees for roads, for sewerage and water and for public transport.
[2] Except in Highland, Borders and Lothian where there will be joint committees.
[3] Highland, Borders, and Dumfries and Galloway would also require sub-committees for planning and building applications.

Fig. 2 *Regional Committee Structure*

Applicable to Strathclyde

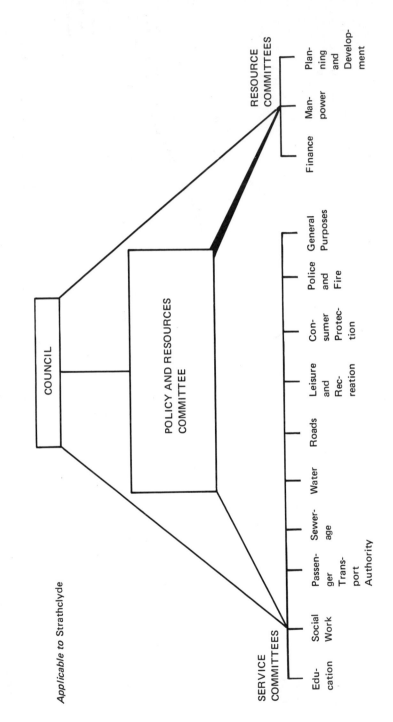

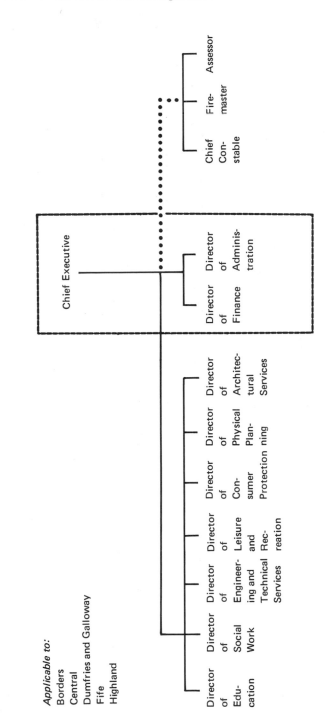

Fig. 3 *Regional Officer Structure*

Applicable to:
Borders
Central
Dumfries and Galloway
Fife
Highland

Chief Executive

Director of Finance

Director of Administration

Chief Constable

Fire-master

Assessor

Director of Education

Director of Social Work

Director of Engineering and Technical Services

Director of Leisure and Recreation

Director of Consumer Protection

Director of Physical Planning

Director of Architectural Services

━━━━━ the Executive Office

Fig. 4 *Regional Officer Structure*

Applicable to:
Grampian
Lothian
Tayside

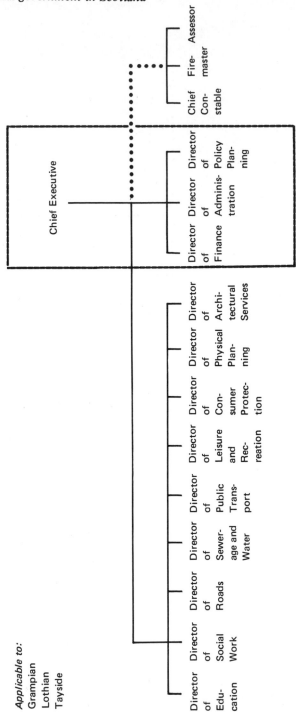

——— the Executive Office

Fig. 5 *Regional Officer Structure*

Applicable to Strathclyde

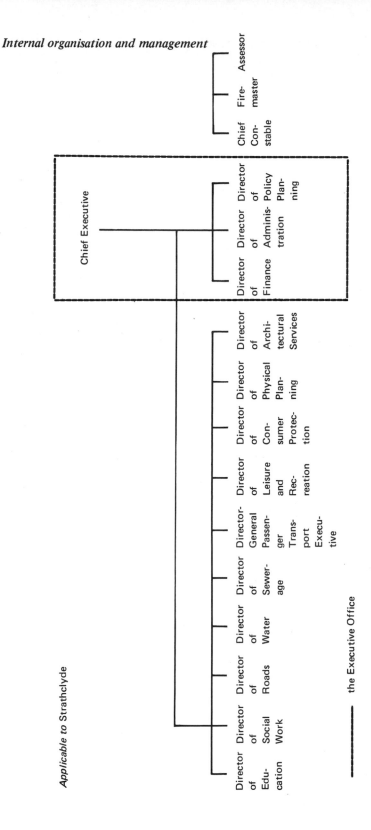

Fig. 6 *District Committee Structure*

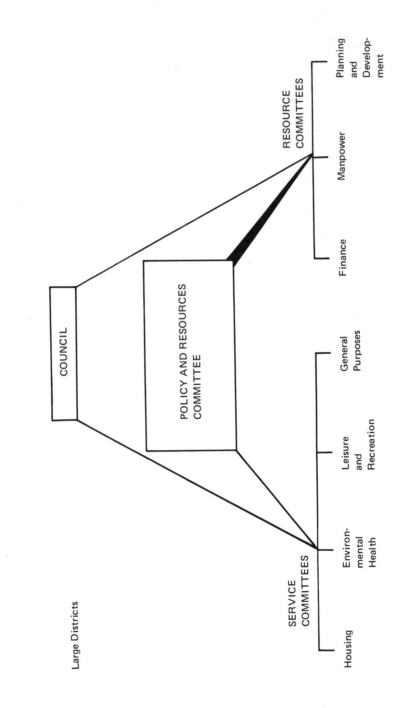

Fig. 7 *District Committee Structure*

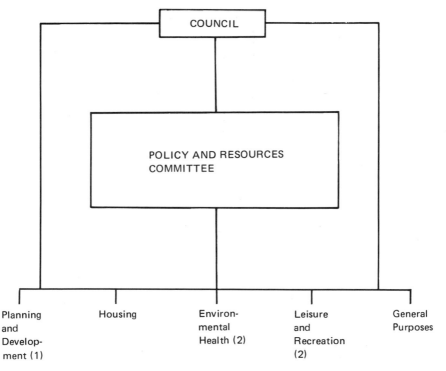

¹ Except in districts within general planning authorities.
² In the smallest districts Environmental Health and Leisure and Recreation could be combined.

Fig. 8 *District Officer Structure*

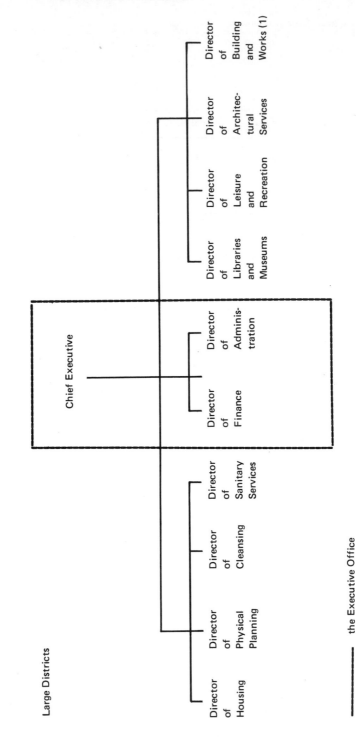

Large Districts

————— the Executive Office

[1] Dependent on existence and scale of direct works departments.

Fig. 9 *District Officer Structure*

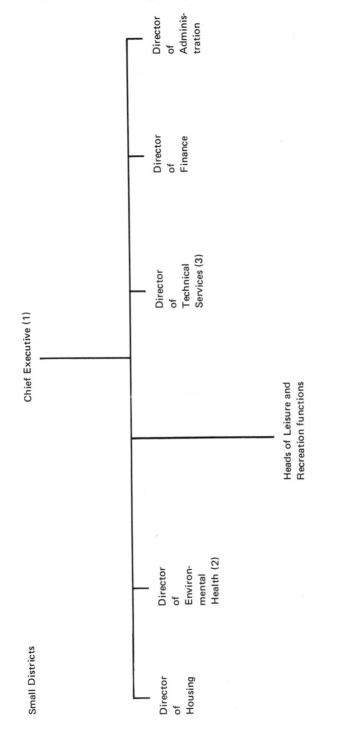

Small Districts

Chief Executive (1)

Director of Housing

Director of Environmental Health (2)

Heads of Leisure and Recreation functions

Director of Technical Services (3)

Director of Finance

Director of Administration

[1] Will probably have direct responsibility as a director of one of the main departments.
[2] Responsible for cleansing and sanitary services.
[3] Responsible for architecture, direct works and, where applicable, physical planning and building control.

Section VII
Local government in Wales

Wales has invariably been treated as part of England for local government purposes, and the pre-1972 structure derived from the nineteenth century legislation which established the English system: two-tier administrative counties and county districts, and a number of all-purpose county boroughs. The first proposals for structural change came from the Local Government Commission for Wales established under the 1958 Act. Their final proposals (*Report and Proposals for Wales*, 1962) based on a smaller number of authorities created by amalgamation (7 instead of 13) were strongly opposed by existing local authorities. The Commission's recommendations were not accepted, and a further review was mounted in 1965, by an Inter-Departmental Working Party (principally consisting of central government officials). Their report (1967, **62**) demonstrated a cautious approach to reorganisation, though their working principles were similar to those of the rejected Local Government Commission. The Government accepted the 1967 proposals, with modifications, but this exercise was overtaken by the publication in 1969 of the English and Scottish reports. Influenced by these reports, the Government instituted a further review of the counties of Glamorgan and Monmouthshire, with the object of establishing a more satisfactory pattern of local government in areas of urban concentration. The resulting White Paper (1970) proposed three unitary authorities, based respectively on Swansea, Cardiff and Newport. This proposal was hotly opposed, since district councils in these areas would disappear.

This rather confused situation was resolved by the 1970 change of government; the new Conservative administration reviewed all previous proposals and presented a set of revised recommendations in a 1971 Consultative Document (**63**). This document provided the basis for the provisions of the 1972 Act which had application to Wales. These provisions (**64**) reflect a uniform approach to the reorganisation of local government in England and Wales, except that there is no application of the 'metropolitan' principle. The new system has 8 counties and 37 districts (as against 7 counties and 36 districts proposed in the 1971 paper); population ranges diverge from the Redcliffe-Maud criteria to a greater extent than those established for the English authorities: the range for the top tier is 99,000 (Powys) to 536,000 (mid Glamorgan), and for the second tier 187,000 (Radnor) to 286,000 (Cardiff). There is to be a third level of community councils comparable to the parish level in England. The provisions for elections, finance and boundary review are much the same as for England. But geographical changes in Wales are quite considerable, with amalgamation of all existing counties, and the splitting up of Glamorgan into three different areas.

407

The future of Welsh local government is complicated by the 1975 proposals to give Wales an elected Assembly with executive powers and very limited legislative power over devolved subjects, one of which is local government. The Welsh Assembly will have no powers to change the local government system, but will be able to exercise the powers of control and regulation normally the province of the Department of the Environment. The detailed implications of these arrangements are by no means clear.

62 THE 1967 PROPOSALS

From *Local Government in Wales* (Cmnd. 3340, 1967); by permission of H.M.S.O.

61. Because of the urgency of the need in Wales and because, as a result of the work of the Local Government Commission for Wales and subsequent work, reorganisation proposals were well advanced, the Government decided to proceed with a reorganisation of local government in the Principality instead of waiting until that in England and Scotland could be carried out following the Royal Commissions' reports.

62. The main defects in the present Welsh organisation are that most of the local authorities are too small and weak to discharge their responsibilities effectively. It is considered that the immediate action appropriate to remedy this defect should consist of extensive amalgamations of existing authorities within the present tier structure together with such changes in functions and finance as would be involved by these amalgamations. Further adjustments might need to be made if experience of the working of the new system in Wales and of the changes decided on for England and Scotland showed them to be needed.

63. The proposals put forward are:

County boroughs (1) Merthyr Tydfil should cease to be a county borough. Cardiff, Newport and Swansea should retain this status with the revised boundaries already approved by the Secretary of State.

Counties (2) The following five new administrative counties should replace the present 13 —
  Gwynedd — an amalgamation of Anglesey, Caernarvonshire, Denbighshire, Flintshire and Merioneth;
  Powys — an amalgamation of Montgomeryshire, Radnorshire and Breconshire;
  Dyfed — an amalgamation of Cardiganshire, Carmarthenshire and Pembrokeshire;
  Glamorgan — the existing county except the Rhymney Valley;
  Gwent — the existing county and the Rhymney Valley.

Districts (3) 36 new districts, preserving where possible the identities of existing counties which are to be amalgamated, should be created in place of the present

164 non-county boroughs, urban districts and rural districts and the county borough of Merthyr Tydfil.

Common Councils (4) The present parishes should be reorganised by the new counties so as to strengthen their ability to carry out their functions.

(5) Councils, on similar lines to existing parish councils, should be set up in urban areas where the inhabitants so wish. These, and their rural equivalents in the parishes, might be known as 'common councils'.

Dignities and privileges of boroughs (6) Arrangements should be made for the continuance of the dignities and privileges of boroughs.

Further adjustments of boundaries (7) Provision should be made for making further adjustments in boundaries after the new authorities have been set up.

County functions (8) The new county councils should have responsibility for the same functions as the present county councils, notably, education, personal health and welfare, child care, civil defence, town and country planning, roads, traffic management and road safety, weights and measures, animal health, composition and description of food and drugs, small-holdings, and the registration of vehicles, births and deaths.

County borough functions (9) The county borough should continue to have the functions both of county and of district councils.

District functions (10) The new district councils should be empowered to exercise uniformly throughout their districts the general powers which existing legislation gives to non-county borough, urban district and rural district councils. Their main responsibilities would be for housing, control of communicable disease, environmental health, hygiene and sanitary arrangements for food (including meat and milk), coast protection, markets, car parks, physical training and recreation, and the Shops Acts.

. . . . . .

Other functions for which responsibilities are allocated between different classes of authority (12) The responsibility for weights and measures, animal diseases, and the enforcement of provisions relating to the composition of food and drugs should be carried out by the new county and county borough councils and, at least for the interim period referred to at (11) above, by those of the new district councils which both satisfy the population requirements of the existing legislation and include existing authorities which already discharge the responsibility.

The functions of common councils (13) The limit of expenditure for purposes not otherwise authorised should be raised.

Further adjustment of functions (14) The reorganisation legislation should enable further minor adjustments of functions to be made by statutory orders.

. . . . . .

Finance (15) Until more fundamental changes are made in the local government financial system for England and Wales as a whole, the existing rate support grant arrangements should be retained for Wales. But the counties should become the rating authorities and the districts and common councils should precept on them.

. . . . . .

Staff Commission (17) A Welsh Staff Commission should be set up to consider and keep under review arrangements for the recruitment and transfer of all local government employees, to consider such staffing problems arising from the reorganisation as might be referred to them by the Secretary of State, and to advise the Secretary of State of steps needed to safeguard the interests of staff affected by the reorganisation.

A new Welsh Council (18) As an evolution of the Welsh Economic Council and of certain organisations peculiar to Wales (particularly the previous Council for Wales, the Welsh Arts Council, the Development Corporation for Wales and the Wales Tourist Board) early action should be taken to set up a new Welsh Council which would initially have the following advisory and promotional functions:

To provide a forum for the interchange of views and information on developments in the economic and cultural fields and to advise on the implications for Wales of national policies.

To formulate development proposals for Wales having regard to the best use of its resources and to advise the Secretary of State for Wales on major land use and economic planning matters.

To advise the Minister of Transport and the Secretary of State on transport policy and planning in Wales.

To give advice on the national parks and countryside.

To advise on the arts in Wales particularly where arrangements need to be made on an all-Wales basis.

To keep under review and help to promote the publicity and similar work for encouraging industrial and tourist development in Wales done by the Development Corporation, the Tourist Board and other bodies.

To encourage co-operation between the local authorities, through schemes which would first require the approval of the appropriate Ministers.

. . . . . .

(20) The Council should initially consist of some 40 members drawn mainly from the local authorities, industry, the trades unions, the Universities and the principal promotional bodies. Appointments to the Council would be made by the Secretary of State, who should also be consulted about the composition and terms of reference of its committees. The Council would elect its own Chairman and its reports would be published. The Secretary of State would appoint a small number

Distribution of Welsh local authorities by size of population
A. Existing Authorities

Size of population	Parishes	Rural districts	Urban districts	Non-county boroughs	County boroughs	Counties
0–500	531	–	–	–	–	–
501–1,000	175	–	4	1	–	–
1,001–2,500	126	3	14	6	–	–
2,501–5,000	43	11	13	5	–	–
5,001–10,000	15	20	14	8	–	–
10,001–20,000	4	11	13	5	–	1
20,001–40,000	1	10	15	4	–	1
40,001–100,000	–	4	–	3	1	5
100,001–250,000	–	–	–	–	2	4
250,001–500,000	–	–	–	–	1	1
500,001 and over	–	–	–	–	–	1
Total number of authorities	895	59	73	32	4	13
Total population	803,620	803,620	793,010	474,220	630,360	2,070,850
Average population per authority	898	13,621	10,863	14,819	157,590	159,296

B. Proposed New Authorities (Excluding the New Common Councils)

Size of population	Districts	County boroughs	Counties
0–500	–	–	–
501–1,000	–	–	–
1,001–2,500	–	–	–
2,501–5,000	–	–	–
5,001–10,000	–	–	–
10,001–20,000	1	–	–
20,001–40,000	7	–	–
40,001–100,000	24	–	–
100,001–250,000	4	2	1
250,001–500,000	–	1	2
500,001 and over	–	–	2
Total number of authorities	36	3	5
Total population	2,128,290	572,920	2,128,290
Average population per authority	59,119	190,973	425,658

Notes
    (1) The population figures all relate to June 1966 except those for the parishes, which are from the 1961 census.
    (2) Under the proposals in this White Paper the reorganisation of the parishes will be for the new counties to undertake and the number of common councils to be created will depend on local demand for them.

of Government officials to act as assessors to the Council and its committees and provide for civil servants to be seconded for work on the Council's secretariat. Local authorities might also second members of their staff for work with the Council.

. . . . . .

63 THE 1971 CONSULTATIVE DOCUMENT

From *The Reform of Local Government in Wales: a Consultative Document* (Welsh Office, 1971); by permission of H.M.S.O.

The Welsh people have the right to the kind of local government which meets the needs of Wales in the second half of the twentieth century and in which they can participate effectively and to the full. Existing local authorities − 181 county, borough and district councils and over 600 parish councils − have done their work well. Most of these authorities, however, serve small populations and have scanty resources. This means that they must inevitably look to the Welsh Office and other government departments to establish priorities and take decisions in matters which local democratic bodies should properly settle for themselves.

2. The Government are determined that local government should be powerful enough to take its own decisions, establish its priorities and allocate the resources available to it. They want reformed local government to be free from detailed control by central government. The purpose of this document is to set out the Government's proposals to this end.

. . . . . .

4. The Government have reviewed the proposals of the last administration. These treated Glamoragn and Monmouthshire separately from the rest of Wales, an approach which received very little support and which the Government think wrong. For the rest of Wales a sound foundation was laid in the 1967 White Paper. The Government, however, put their present proposals forward in their own right, as a scheme which they think is well suited to the needs of Wales.

The principles of reform 5. Many important services are most effectively organised on a large scale. This permits the recruitment of specialised staff and makes for economy in operation. Further, people expect a general uniformity in the standard of service provided by local authorities, wherever they may live. These considerations point to having strong authorities, serving sizeable populations and covering substantial areas of the country. It is necessary to take into account also geographical considerations, historical associations and the strength of community feeling. Some services, however, can be dealt with quite adequately on a more local scale; and the Government consider that there is every justification for district councils with clear cut executive responsibilities to run these services. They are firmly opposed to monolithic authorities, which moreover would deny opportunities of local public service to all save a few.

6. The Government therefore propose that there should be throughout Wales a uniform system of local government with responsibility for services divided between a small number of county councils and a larger number of district councils . . . The district councils would be autonomous within their own areas of responsibility. Additionally, community councils should be created, with limited but real responsibilities, at the level of rural parishes, and if the local residents desire it, in urban areas . . .

7. The Government consider that the existing county boroughs should be brought within the uniform system proposed. The division between county boroughs and administrative counties is one of the main defects of the present system. This division must be ended. Only thus will it be possible for large towns and the areas which surround them to be properly planned and properly served. The Government wish to ensure the healthy development of the four county boroughs; in their view this can best be done by integrating them fully into the wider communities of which they are part.

II. BASIC STRUCTURE: THE ALLOCATION OF FUNCTIONS

Allocation of the More Important Functions

8. Given that the main executive functions of local government should be divided between two sets of local authorities, the new structure will depend primarily on how these functions are allocated. The principle of these proposals is that the new county councils and the new district councils must each have a range of important responsibilities which they can perform economically and efficiently, which will provide satisfying work for elected members, and which will together form a balanced and coherent set of functions for each council as a whole and for their officers working as a team . . . Essentially, the new county councils will be made responsible for those functions for which large areas or large populations, or both are required: examples are the strategic aspects of town and country planning, the planning, construction and maintenance of roads, traffic management, the education service, the personal social services, the fire service. The new district councils will be responsible for those functions which can be satisfactorily administered on a more local scale: examples are housing, the more detailed aspects of town and country planning, refuse collection and public cleansing.

The personal health services 9. The Government have announced their intention to unify the administration of the National Health Service, which will be administered by health authorities outside local government. Responsibility for the personal health services at present provided by county councils and county borough councils will be transferred to the new health authorities.

Police authorities 10. Four joint police authorities have been established in Wales, covering respectively the five North Wales counties, the six counties in Mid and

West Wales, the geographical county of Glamorgan and the geographical county of Monmouthshire. It is intended that these police authorities should continue and the necessary administrative adjustments for this purpose should be brought about.

Functions of the New County Councils

11. Following the publication of the White Paper of July 1967 there were discussions with the local authority associations during which opposing arguments were deployed on the extent to which district councils should be involved in the discharge of a number of functions for which the primary responsibility rests at present with county councils and county borough councils: the functions discussed were education, the personal health services, welfare services, children's services, town and country planning, highways and traffic management, libraries, weights and measures, trade descriptions, the composition and description of food and drugs, smallholdings and animal diseases. For all of these functions except smallholdings and children's services, there is provision under the existing law for some non-county borough and district councils, either as of right or by decision of the appropriate Minister, to exercise responsibilities which are otherwise discharged by county councils. The detailed provisions vary with each service. In general the Government accept the criticisms of these provisions implied in the Report of the Royal Commission on Local Government in England, which mentioned their complexity and their effect in producing a pock-marked pattern of county administration. In all these services the Government are clear that the main responsibility must remain with the county councils.

Education and the personal social services 12. In education and the personal social services the compulsory delegation of responsibilities to district councils and the provisions requiring the setting up of divisional executives should be ended. In education, the Borough of Rhondda is at present an excepted district, and four county councils operate divisional administration over parts of their areas. These forms of administration can seriously impair the effectiveness of the education service and increase the risks of friction between county and district councils without substantial compensating advantages. The existing schemes of divisional administration will not therefore be replaced when they lapse on the disappearance of the existing authorities, and there will be no statutory provision for making new ones. Similarly, excepted districts will have no place in the new local government structure. As for the social services, the Borough Council of Rhondda exercise claimed delegated health and welfare (but not children) functions under the Local Government Act 1958. Action is being taken under section 10 of the Local Authority Social Services Act 1970 to revoke Rhondda's delegation scheme in so far as it relates to social services functions, and none of the new district councils will have any delegated social services functions.

Development plans 13. The general principle of the new proposals for town and country planning is that the new county councils should have the undivided responsibility for preparing development plans, including both the structure plans and the local plans which are the main elements in the new procedures laid down in the Town and Country Planning Act 1968 . . . But the district councils would have the right to be consulted during the preparation of plans, and would have major responsibilities for securing their implementation through their development control powers and their powers for the acquisition, development and redevelopment of land.

Development control 14. The new district councils will be given direct responsibility, in their own right and not by delegation from the county councils, for deciding most planning applications in their areas. All planning applications will be made to the district councils. To ensure that planning control is exercised in harmony with plan making, the advice of the planning officers of the county councils must be readily available to the district councils when they are taking decisions on planning applications. The planning officers must of course be familiar with local considerations. The county councils will be involved in deciding planning applications only where these involve major matters of policy or where they are in limited categories — for example, mineral working — specifically reserved for their decisions. This will mean that by far the larger proportion of planning applications will be determined by the district councils.

Highways and traffic management 15. All the direct responsibilities for highways and traffic management will be allocated to the new county councils. This will mean changes in the existing law under which all borough and urban district councils are responsible for unclassified roads in their areas, and borough and urban district councils with populations of 20,000 or more may claim to undertake the improvement and maintenance of county roads in their areas, approved expenditure being met by the county councils. These existing provisions are confusing and inefficient, particularly in that the claiming arrangements involve work on plans and estimates being duplicated in the county and district council's highway departments . . . Ways will have to be found by which the interests of district councils can be adequately expressed. However, a basic condition of any arrangement must be that professional highways and traffic management staff should be employed as one body by the county council.

Libraries, weights and measures, trade descriptions and food and drugs 16. In these services, the Government think it right to allow for the possibility that where a district council has a sufficiently large population to provide them economically and efficiently and their provision by the district council would not substantially damage the service in the remainder of the county, the district council should be allowed to provide the service . . .

Functions of the New District Councils

17. These will consist essentially of the functions most closely and directly con-

nected with the physical fabric of individual towns and villages and the countryside; namely housing, including slum clearance, house and area improvement, house-building and housing management; building regulations; development control; acquisition and disposal of land for planning purposes; development and redevelopment; provision of land and other assistance to industry and clearance of derelict land; along with clean air, the control of nuisances, food hygiene, refuse collection and disposal, coast protection, the provision of parks, playing fields, museums, art galleries, public baths, public washhouses, public conveniences, markets and slaughterhouses and burials and cremations.

. . . . . .

Powers of Community Councils

21. The powers of community councils in the new structure need to be considered in relation to the powers of district councils, since most of them are bound to be exercised concurrently. As far as executive functions are concerned, the Government are clear that community councils ought to have, substantially, the powers of the existing parish councils.

III. THE NEW ADMINISTRATIVE MAP OF WALES

22. The proposals of the previous administration for the areas of the new authorities have been carefully considered, in the light of the known views of the existing authorities. In carrying out this review one crucial factor has been the minimum sizes of population necessary to support economically the responsibilities to be assigned to the new county and district councils. These figures are not capable of mathematical proof. They must be matters of informed judgement. The Government's view is that for authorities responsible for education and the personal social services one should aim at a population of at least 250,000. It must be emphasised that this figure is put forward as the desirable minimum. It does not imply that much larger figures are not entirely acceptable where there are good reasons for them: for example, reasons based on the social and geographic characteristics of an area or on the need to avoid as far as possible the division of existing strong administrative units. On the other hand, it may be necessary for other geographic reasons to accept population figures below the desirable minimum in some instances. The figure of 250,000 has the support of the conclusions of the Royal Commission on Local Government in England, which were to a large extent confirmed, in relation to very different kinds of areas, by the conclusions of the Royal Commission on Local Government in Scotland.

23. For county councils and district councils alike it is necessary to consider not only the needs of the individual services for which they will be responsible but also the desirability of devising areas which will be large enough, populous enough, and varied enough to provide a sufficient flow of interesting and rewarding work for elected members and a strong team of officers. All the new district councils must

have sufficient work and resources to provide a satisfying career to those who work for them. The ability of the new district councils to meet these requirements will not depend only on the range of functions which are assigned to them; equally important are the size of the area and its population, which will together determine the volume of work and the range of problems on which the officers will have to advise. The present proposals are based on the proposition that a population of 40,000 is a desirable minimum to be aimed at in working out a pattern of districts.

24. However, these suggested minimum populations for the new counties and the new districts have to be considered along with two other important factors — the sparsity of population over much of Wales, and the need to have regard as far as practicable to the loyalties within existing administrative areas. It follows that there must continue to be wide variations in the population sizes of the new Welsh counties and districts.

Wales Outside Glamorgan and Monmouthshire

25. . . . In general, the Government accept the proposals made by the previous administration for counties and districts outside Glamorgan and Monmouthshire. It is intended to continue with the proposals to create two counties in North Wales rather than one, and to leave the boundary between the counties of Glamorgan and Dyfed as the present boundary in the Amman Valley. It is proposed, however, to alter the proposals of the previous administration in three areas; the Conway Valley, the southern edge of Breconshire, and the present county of Pembrokeshire.

The Conway Valley 26. The present boundary between Caernarvonshire and Denbighshire follows the River Conway for the greater part of its course. But there are two substantial areas — the Creuddyn peninsula (which includes Llandudno) and the parish of Maenan — lying to the east of the river which are in Caernarvonshire and not Denbighshire. The line has, with some slight modifications, formed the boundary since 1284. The Local Government Commission for Wales considered that the boundary was unsatisfactory in that it divided communities having common interests, that the whole of the Conway Valley should be in one county, and that this should be a north-western rather than a north-eastern county. Several local authorities in the area have also suggested that the boundary is unsatisfactory.

27. It is considered that this is an area where the advantages of unifying the administration of the valley outweigh the objections to dividing an existing county and existing districts . . .

The southern edge of Breconshire 28. The small towns and villages of Breconshire, south of the watershed of the Brecon Beacons, are closely linked economically and socially with the neighbouring areas in Glamorgan and Monmouthshire. The Local Government Commission recommended that this southern part of Breconshire should be united for administrative purposes with Glamorgan and Monmouthshire. The majority of the local authorities directly concerned support such a change on the grounds that it would strengthen the administration of the area, and be much more convenient from the point of view of access to the likely centres of district and county administration.

. . . . . .

Pembrokeshire 30. Under the original proposals of the previous administration the present county of Pembrokeshire would have been divided between three districts within the new county of Dyfed. As part of the revised proposals which were announced in November 1968, the county was instead to be divided into two districts.

31. The Pembrokeshire County Council and most of the borough and district councils in the county agree that the county should remain a unit of local government. There are, however, sharp differences of opinion on how this should be achieved. The County Council have proposed that the present county, perhaps with boundary adjustments, should form a unitary authority, responsible for all the major local government services. This suggestion is opposed by most of the borough and district councils, who want the county to be divided into at least two districts, though there is strong feeling among most of them in favour of maintaining Pembrokeshire as an administrative county.

32. As has already been made clear, the Government are not prepared to accept that any part of Wales should form a unitary authority. They are satisfied also that the proposal for a new county of Dyfed must stand and that the population of Pembrokeshire is not large enough to allow it to remain as a separate administrative county. The choice then is between having two districts in Pembrokeshire on the lines proposed by the previous administration or making the whole of the present county one new district.

33. The main arguments in favour of having two districts are that these will be sufficiently large in population to be effective units, that Milford Haven and the Cleddau estuary together make up a considerable physical barrier within the county, and that the existence of two district councils instead of one will provide substantially greater opportunities for holding elected public office. On the other hand, it is argued that to make Pembrokeshire one district will accord with the wishes of the inhabitants, who would much prefer the county to remain an administrative unit of some kind. Further, it is suggested that industrial development on either side of Milford Haven and the construction of a bridge across the estuary will bring the different parts of the county together and indeed make it undesirable to separate them for the purpose of district council functions, including in particular development control and functions relating to industrial development. The Government accept the arguments for maintaining the unity of Pembrokeshire and have concluded that the right answer is to make the present county one district.

Glamorgan and Monmouthshire

34. The previous administration proposed that Glamorgan and Monmouthshire

should be treated differently from the rest of Wales. They proposed that there should be three unitary areas incorporating the present administrative counties and four county boroughs. There would be no executive second tier. These proposals aroused widespread opposition. In the Government's view they are not the right answer, and they must be put aside.

35. This area contains half the population of Wales. It is one of the greatest concentrations of industry in the United Kingdom, and it has a proud tradition of democratic local government. The Government's objective has been to devise proposals which will safeguard this tradition and enable South East Wales to develop to the full its potential for economic growth. At the same time the pattern of administration in South East Wales should be of a kind with that in the rest of the Principality so that Wales as a whole has a uniform system of local government well suited to the nation's needs.

36. The Government propose that South East Wales should be organised as three strong counties and seventeen districts, with community councils in the rural areas and in urban areas as well where public opinion calls for them.

37. There is good evidence that socially, economically and geographically South East Wales falls into three well defined areas. In the west there is the region which looks naturally to Swansea and to the industrially important areas of Neath and Port Talbot. East of a line running roughly north—south from Hirwaun to Porthcawl, the mining valleys and the Vale focus on Cardiff. Newport, in spite of its relative proximity to Cardiff, is the natural focus of the Monmouthshire valleys.

38. The Government's proposals mean that Swansea, Cardiff and Newport would be integrated with the areas for which they are the service and commercial centres, and from which as industrial areas in their own right they draw workers.

39. The three counties now proposed would be the three most powerful local government units in Wales. East Glamorgan, including the present county boroughs of Cardiff and Merthyr Tydfil would have a larger population (by some 24%) than the present administrative county. Its services would be integrated with those at present provided by Cardiff and Merthyr Tydfil; there is general agreement that such integration is desirable.

40. The Government accept that the administration of the Rhymney Valley should be unified within an authority looking to Cardiff rather than to Newport, and that the boundary should run along the watershed to the east of the Rhymney river as far as possible . . .

41. The new county including most of Monmouthshire and the county borough of Newport would be the second largest of the new Welsh counties in terms of population, and West Glamorgan, including the present county borough of Swansea, would be the third in terms of population.

42. The Government have given anxious thought to the only alternatives which in their view are worth considering. The first would leave undivided the present administrative county of Glamorgan, while including within it the three county boroughs of Cardiff, Swansea and Merthyr Tydfil. (Most of the administrative county of Monmouthshire together with Newport would constitute a new county

as in the proposals already described.) This would not divide the administration of the present county of Glamorgan, which operates large scale services in keeping with the size of its population, on which the new county's services could build. There are, however, serious disadvantages. The new county would have nearly twice the population of the present administrative county and nearly half the population of Wales. The county would be pulled apart by the competing interests of two major cities forty miles from each other. The opportunities for public service as members of the county council would be greatly reduced as compared with the present councils of the administrative county and the three county boroughs. The arguments clearly point in favour of recognising the effective line of division between East and West Glamorgan and creating two powerful administrative bodies which will rank with any in the United Kingdom.

43. The second alternative would be to divide the present administrative county of Glamorgan and the three county boroughs into three or more counties. There are again strong objections to this. First, it would further divide the existing county administration. Secondly, to divide the proposed county of East Glamorgan would inevitably mean the separation of areas which ought to be administered together for the purposes of town and country planning and transportation. Thirdly to separate Cardiff and its neighbouring areas from either Mid-Glamorgan, or the north-eastern Glamorgan valleys, or from both, would mean the creation of at least one authority which was comparatively weak in terms of rateable resources, and was handicapped by lack of resources and lack of suitable land in seeking solutions to its problems.

The Detailed Proposals for the New Counties

44. Details of the counties now proposed follow. It is proposed to adopt the names Clwyd, Dyfed, Gwent, Gwynedd and Powys, which have found a fair amount of acceptance. The names of East Glamorgan and West Glamorgan are adopted provisionally.

(a) Clwyd:

(Population: 354,000; Acreage: 599,000; Rateable Value: £13.9 million.)
This would be an amalgamation of Denbighshire (except for the area to be included in Gwynedd), Flintshire and Edeyrnion Rural District.

(b) Dyfed:

(Population: 319,000; Acreage: 1,425,000; Rateable Value: £10.5 million.)
This would be an amalgamation of Cardiganshire, Carmarthenshire and Pembrokeshire.

(c) East Glamorgan:

(Population: 928,000; Acreage: 359,000; Rateable Value: £32.1 million.)
This would be an amalgamation of Cardiff and Merthyr Tydfil County Boroughs, that part of the County of Glamorgan not included in West Glamorgan, the parishes of Penderyn and Vaynor (Vaynor and Penderyn Rural District), the Urban Districts of Bedwas and Machen and Rhymney, the wards of Aberbargoed, Cwmsyfiog, New Tredegar and Phillipstown in Bedwellty Urban District and the parishes of Marshfield,

Michaelstone-y-Vedw, Peterstone Wentlooge and St. Mellons (Magor and St. Mellons Rural District).

(d) West Glamorgan:

(Population: 371,000; Acreage: 201,000; Rateable Value: £17 million.)

This would be an amalgamation of Swansea County Borough and the Boroughs of Neath and Port Talbot, the Urban Districts of Glyncorrwg and Llwchwr and the Rural Districts of Gower, Pontardawe and Neath (except the parish of Rhigos) in Glamorgan.

(e) Gwent:

(Population: 442,000; Acreage: 335,000; Rateable Value: £16.4 million.)

This would be an amalgamation of Newport County Borough, the County of Monmouthshire except those parts to be included in the East Glamorgan County, the Urban District of Brynmawr and the parish of Llanelly (Crickhowell Rural District).

(f) Gwynedd:

(Population: 221,000; Acreage: 956,000; Rateable Value: £6.7 million.)

This would be an amalgamation of Anglesey, Caernarvonshire and Merioneth, except for Edeyrnion Rural District, together with Llanrwst Urban District and the parishes of Llansantffraid Glan Conway (in Aled Rural District), Eglwysbach, Llanddoget, Llanrwst Rural and Tir Ifan (in Hiraethog Rural District) which are at present in Denbighshire.

(g) Powys:

(Population: 100,000; Acreage: 1,255,000; Rateable Value: £2.6 million.)

This would be an amalgamation of Breconshire (except for Brynmawr Urban District and the parishes of Llanelly (Crickhowell Rural District), Penderyn and Vaynor (Vaynor and Penderyn Rural District), Montgomeryshire and Radnorshire.

The New Districts in Glamorgan and Monmouthshire

45. A further study has been made of Glamorgan and Monmouthshire in the light of the decision to incorporate all the county boroughs into the district structure . . . Considerations affecting the proposals for the three new South Wales counties are also mentioned briefly below:

West Glamorgan:

(a) In view of the economic and social links between Gower and Swansea, Swansea is linked with Gower Rural District, except for the parish of Llanrhidian Higher, which is linked with Llwchwr Urban District and Pontardawe Rural District.

East Glamorgan:

(b) The City of Cardiff forms one new district, with the addition of Penarth Urban District and the bordering parishes of Lisvane, Llanedeyrn, Marshfield, Michaelstone-y-Vedw, Peterstone Wentlooge, Radyr, St. Fagans, St. Mellons and Tongwynlais, all of which have strong ties with the City.

(c) The district structure in the Pontypridd/Llantrisant area has been recast to take account of the emergence of Llantrisant as a major growth centre and the former Pontypridd district has been expanded to include the whole of Llantrisant and Llantwit Fardre Rural District together with some of the adjoining parishes of Cardiff and Cowbridge Rural Districts. It should be noted that this proposal does not assume any particular decision with regard to the proposed new town at Llantrisant. It is based on the evidence of continued growth in the area, quite apart from the new town proposal.

(d) The Cynon Valley district now includes the parish of Rhigos from Neath Rural District and the parish of Penderyn from Vaynor and Penderyn Rural District.

(e) The Merthyr Tydfil district includes the parish of Vaynor.

(f) The Rhymney Valley district will now be in East Glamorgan.

Gwent:

(g) Newport forms one new district, with the addition of Caerleon Urban District and the whole of Magor and St. Mellons Rural District except for the four parishes to be included in East Glamorgan and the parish of Henllys which would be included with the Eastern Valley district. The administration of the coastal area needs to be unified, and this can best be done by the district now proposed.

. . . . . .

The Capital of Wales

47. The proposals for counties and districts will not affect Cardiff's position as the capital of Wales. The distinguishing marks of a capital city will remain. The people of Wales will continue to regard Cardiff as their capital. The Welsh Office is in Cardiff, and with the transfer to the Secretary of State for Wales of responsibility for primary and secondary education and for the children's services in Wales, more of the important decisions affecting Wales will be taken in Cardiff. The city status of Cardiff, as of Swansea, will be maintained, and enhanced by extensions of boundaries.

48. Cardiff is not only the capital of Wales but it will be the only new district with a population exceeding a quarter of a million and will therefore have a far greater concentration of population than any other new district. For this reason it will have planning problems which will be unique in Wales and which will require massive and continuous efforts by the City Council as redevelopment authority if they are to be solved. It is therefore proposed that there should be special arrangements whereby the new Cardiff City Council will have power to prepare the local plan or plans for their area under section 6 of the Town and Country Planning Act 1968. The plans would have to conform with the structure plans prepared by the County Council for East Glamorgan but they would set out in detail how the structure plans were to be implemented in the City.

IV. THE COMMUNITIES

49. It is proposed . . . that the new community councils should have essentially the same executive powers as the present parish councils. The community councils

would be able to express local wishes and needs, and they would be set up wherever there was an evident local desire to have such bodies.

50. The present rural parishes would not be a satisfactory basis for a system of community councils, partly because many of the parishes are too small to support effective councils and partly because many urban areas, where there might well be a demand for community councils in the new structure, are not within the pattern of rural parishes. It is intended therefore to proceed with the suggestion made in the White Paper of 1967 that there should be a review as soon as possible after the appointed day to produce a new pattern of communities and community councils, the latter to be set up in urban areas as well as in what are now rural districts wherever there was an evident demand for them.

51. Under the previous administration it was proposed that these reviews should be carried out by the new county councils. In view of the urgency and importance of the task, and the likelihood that the new county councils will be heavily engaged with other matters in the period immediately after the appointed day, consideration is being given to the possibility that the reviews might be undertaken by a commission, which would also be responsible for reviewing the detailed boundaries of the main authorities . . .

. . . . . .

X. CONCLUSION

66. Briefly, the Government propose that the whole of Wales should be reorganised as a two tier structure of main authorities, with seven county councils and thirty six district councils. Most of the county councils would have populations in the range 200,000–430,000, though there would be one very thinly populated one – Powys – with just 100,000 population in about 1.3 million acres – and one heavily populated one – East Glamorgan, with over 900,000. Most of the district councils would have populations in the range 40,000–100,000, though there would be a few below 40,000 and one very large one based on the existing City of Cardiff with a population of 316,000. The main functions of the new county councils would be highways and traffic management, education, and the personal social services. The main functions of the new district councils would be housing, refuse collection and public cleansing, clean air, and the prevention of nuisances. Responsibility for town and country planning would be shared between county and district councils.

. . . . . .

ALLOCATION OF MAIN LOCAL AUTHORITY FUNCTIONS BETWEEN NEW WELSH COUNTY COUNCILS, DISTRICT COUNCILS AND COMMUNITY COUNCILS

County Councils

Education

Personal social services

Town and country planning:

Plan making (subject to special arrangements by which the new Cardiff City Council would make plans for the city)

Development control – special cases only

Acquisition and disposal of land for planning purposes, development and redevelopment (concurrently with district councils)

Provision of land and other assistance for industry (concurrently with district councils)

Clearance of derelict land (concurrently with district councils)

Highways and traffic management

Car parks (concurrently with district councils)

Libraries (subject to a limited number of the stronger district councils exercising these functions)

Weights and measures, trade descriptions, Fabrics (Misdescription) Act 1913 and Consumer Protection Act 1961 (subject to the possibility of a few district councils exercising these functions)

Composition and description of food and drugs (subject to the possibility of a few district councils exercising these functions)

Smallholdings

Animal diseases

Museums and art galleries (concurrently with district and community councils)

Physical training and recreation (concurrently with district and community councils)

Explosives and fireworks

District Councils

Housing (including slum clearance, house and area improvement, house-building, housing management)

Building regulations

Town and country planning:

Development control – most planning applications

Acquisition and disposal of land for planning purposes, development and redevelopment (concurrently with district councils)

Provision of land and other assistance for industry (concurrently with county councils)

Clearance of derelict land (concurrently with county councils)

Car parks (concurrently with county councils and subject to their approval)

Clean air

Refuse collection and disposal

Coast protection

Control of communicable disease

Food safety and hygiene

Markets

Public conveniences

Slaughterhouses

Parks and playing fields (concurrently with community councils)

Museums and art galleries (concurrently with county councils and community councils)

Allotments (community councils will also have powers)

Cemeteries, burial grounds and crematoria (community councils will also have powers)

Public baths, swimming baths and wash houses (concurrently with community councils)

Shops Acts

Offices, Shops and Railway Premises Act

Community Councils

(Powers will also generally be held by district councils, and sometimes by county councils)

Parks and playing fields

Museums and art galleries

Allotments

Burial grounds and crematoria

Public baths and wash houses

Bus shelters

Clocks

Community centres and halls

Cycle parking places

Footpaths and bridleways, repair and maintenance

Footpath lighting

War memorials

64 THE NEW SYSTEM

From *Cymru 1972: Annual Report* (Welsh Office, 1973); by permission of H.M.S.O.

The Local Government Act 1972 received the Royal Assent on October 26, 1972. On April 1, 1974 the existing 13 counties, 4 county boroughs, 32 non-county boroughs, 73 urban districts and 59 rural districts will be replaced by 8 new counties and 37 new districts. The districts will contain about 1,000 communities, generally the areas of existing parishes, boroughs and urban districts.

The councils of the new counties and districts will be known as county and district councils respectively, but the latter will have the right to petition for the grant of a Royal Charter which would give the district the status of a borough. Such a charter would make the district council a borough council and the chairman and vice-chairman would have the style of mayor and deputy mayor respectively.

Urban district councils and all save six of the existing borough councils could apply to the Secretary of State for a direction that there should be a council for the community from April 1, 1974. Parishes which have a council immediately before April 1, 1971 will have a community council on that day.

. . . . . .

In section 269 of the Act, Wales is defined as meaning the area consisting of the new counties established by section 20; this includes the present administrative county of Monmouthshire and the present county borough of Newport. The definition operates for almost all the provisions of the 1972 Act and for every Act and instrument passed or made on or after April 1, 1974.

The areas, boundaries and electoral arrangements of the new local government areas will be kept under review by the Local Government Boundary Commission for Wales which is to be set up under the Act.

Basically the new county councils will be responsible for the functions requiring large populations — notably education, the strategic aspects of town and country planning, the personal social services, the fire service and the planning, construction and (except for minor roads) the maintenance of highways. The new district councils will be concerned with services such as housing, the more detailed aspects of town and country planning, refuse collection and disposal, parks, playing fields, public baths, public conveniences, burial and cremation, and markets. Community councils will, broadly speaking, have the same functional responsibilities as parish councils now have and will have a right to be consulted about planning applications affecting land in their areas.

New Counties and Districts

Counties	Districts
Clwyd	Colwyn
	Rhuddlan
	Delyn
	Alyn-Dee
	Glyndŵr
	Wrexham Maelor
Dyfed	Ceredigion
	Preseli
	South Pembrokeshire
	Carmarthen
	Llanelli
	Dinefwr
Gwent	Newport
	Islwyn
	Blaenau Gwent
	Torfaen

	Monmouth
Gwynedd	Ynys Môn – Isle of Anglesey
	Dwyfor
	Arfon
	Aberconwy
	Meirionnydd
Mid Glamorgan	Ogwr
	Rhondda
	Cynon Valley
	Merthyr Tydfil
	Rhymney Valley
	Taff-Ely
Powys	Montgomery
	Radnor
	Brecknock
South Glamorgan	Cardiff
	Vale of Glamorgan
West Glamorgan	Swansea
	Lliw Valley
	Neath
	Afan

APPENDIX A. SIZE OF LOCAL AUTHORITIES

From P. G. Richards, *The Reformed Local Government System* (2nd revised edn, Allen & Unwin, 1975); by permission of the publisher.

(i) Counties

Name of county	1971 Census population (thousands)	Rateable value at April 1971 (£000s)
Clwyd	358	14,345
Dyfed	314	10,848
Gwent	439	17,001
Gwynedd	219	6,828
Mid Glamorgan	530	13,937
Powys	98	2,659
South Glamorgan	389	18,652
West Glamorgan	371	17,260

(ii) Districts

County	Number of districts	Population range (000s)	Rateable value at April 1971 range (£000s)
Clwyd	6	38−104	1,223− 3,571
Dyfed	6	36− 76	820− 2,718
Gwent	5	64−136	1,479− 8,051
Gwynedd	5	26− 59	750− 1,846
Mid Glamorgan	6	63−123	1,522− 3,610
Powys	3	18− 42	600− 1,030
South Glamorgan	2	103−286	4,006−14,646
West Glamorgan	4	56−188	1,822− 8,198

Section VIII
Local government in Northern Ireland

Until reformed in 1972, the system of local government in Northern Ireland reflected the English system, and was similarly based on nineteenth century legislation. The movement towards reform originated in the recognition of the deficiencies of the system in relation to modern responsibilities, and the early reform proposals (1967, 1969) concentrated on the question of the type of structure most appropriate for the provision of services to the public (65), and produced a scheme for 17 single-tier authorities. But political developments in Northern Ireland from 1968 onwards altered the whole context of local government reform. The civic rights campaign of this period drew attention to the deep distrust felt by the Catholic minority community towards local authorities dominated by the Protestant majority. Views about how to attack discriminatory practices by local authorities focussed on two alternatives: either to remove significant (or sensitive) functions from the control of local authorities, or to ensure that local authorities were responsive, and accountable to all their electors.

The Macrory Report (1970) stemmed from the need for an urgent response to the criticisms of local government, and recommended drastic changes in the local government system (66). All existing authorities were to be abolished, 26 new districts were to be created; and their functions were to be restricted, in the main, to local environmental matters, with major services transferred to central control (though on the basis of decentralisation to administrative units which would include local authority representation). These proposals were given effect by the Local Government Act (Northern Ireland) 1972 (67).

Local government has now lost most major functions. Functions relating to education and libraries, and youth services, are to be exercised by five area boards. Health and social services will be managed by four area boards on behalf of the Department of Health and Social Services. Housing will be the responsibility of the Northern Ireland Housing Executive. Fire services come under a Fire Authority for Northern Ireland; electricity services under the Northern Ireland Electricity Service. Most of the bodies have a membership partly nominated by central departments and partly provided by the new district authorities. The Housing Executive has a local office in the area of each district. These arrangements flowed directly from Macrory's clear preference for administrative decentralisation of centrally controlled services rather than the local administration of locally controlled services, and represented a vote of no confidence in the existing system of local government in Northern Ireland.

When the Macrory Report was debated at Stormont (Northern Ireland's legislat-

429

ive assembly) in October 1970, opposition members argued that the system of election to the new authorities should be on the basis of proportional representation, to
safeguard minority interests and reduce the possibilities for electoral malpractices.
The 1972 legislation nonetheless provided for conventional elections in single-
member wards. But on 30 March 1972, as violence in Northern Ireland escalated,
the British Government instituted direct rule. One of the early policy decisions was
that the first elections for the new district councils should be conducted, as an
experiment, on the basis of proportional representation, each elector having a single
transferable vote. The election took place on 30 May 1973; Doc. **69** analyses the
effects of the new electoral arrangements. It is worth noting that while under the
old system, it was usual for many seats to be uncontested, in 1973 all 526 seats
were contested.

Another way to safeguard the local elector is to give him a means of redressing
grievances against local administration, and the creation of a Commissioner of Complaints in 1969 was intended to provide such a means **(68)**. In respect of central
departments there is a Northern Ireland Parliamentary Commissioner for Administration, and both posts are currently held by the same man, Mr Stephen McGonagle.
It is interesting to compare the Northern Ireland local ombudsman (for that is what
the Commissioner for Complaints is) with the English and Scottish versions **(34, 35,
60)**. The courts are used to give teeth to what is elsewhere a relatively toothless
institution, perhaps reflecting a concern that Northern Ireland local authorities
might not respond impartially to complaints from all their electors, and the jurisdiction extends to a number of public bodies which are not local authorities, but do
not fall wholly within the scope of central government.

In the last decade, local government in Northern Ireland has seen more radical
changes than in any other part of Britain. This is part of the attempt, compelled by
the circumstances of political conflict in Northern Ireland, to create new political
institutions which would command the support of all communities there; but it
also reflects the ability of central government to remove power and responsibility
from a local government system incapable of acting either democratically or
efficiently. And here we see central government acting in defence of democratic
practice against a local government system guilty of abuse of that practice: a notable
reversal of the essential philosophy of British local government.

65 THE 1967 WHITE PAPER: STATEMENT OF AIMS

From *The Reshaping of Local Government: Statement of Aims* (Cmnd. 517,
Belfast, 1967); by permission of H.M.S.O.

7. The present local government system stems from the nineteenth century and
while it met the needs of the country well for several generations and has been
served by devoted people, it is now, by common consent, in need of overhaul . . .
    8. Seventy-three separate, directly elected local authorities, with twenty-four

statutory committees specially constituted and exercising special powers, and with a further thirty joint authorities or specialized bodies financed basically from the rates; twenty-seven of those seventy-three main authorities having a population of under 10,000; forty-six having a rateable valuation on which one penny in the pound produces less than £500; a two-tier system in the county areas involving county council administration as well as Borough, Urban and Rural District Council administration; a total of about fourteen hundred Aldermen and Councillors devoting a great deal of time and energy to public affairs; a complex administrative system and a financial system which as the result of attempts over generations to achieve the many aims of responsible public finance has become exceedingly complex; rapidly changing times which result in the lessening of distances and in services outgrowing the administrations originally created for them; and throughout all, a growing critical awareness and popular demand for better services and for more uniform standards: these represent some of the features of local government which are widely recognized — both inside and outside local authorities — as calling for re-shaping if local government is to play a still greater part in the social progress of the country . . .

. . . . . .

15. One of the starting points now adopted by Government in setting in train the re-shaping of future local government under the constitution of Northern Ireland as compared with the nineteenth century arrangements under the Parliament of Westminster, is . . . the desirability of asking Parliament to strengthen local government and at the same time to co-ordinate local government closely with the Executive and other branches of the State and Society.

16. The second starting point is to suggest that the three tests of successful local government might be: efficiency, economy and the effective representation of local aspirations, all in harmony with public policy as a whole.

17. Thirdly, it is idle to try to establish such concepts as 'the proper sphere of local government' or 'a clear dividing line between local authority functions and the functions of central government or other public bodies'. A complex and growing service like Education can quite properly fall partly to local authorities, partly to a statutory agency like the Youth Employment Service, partly to voluntary managers and Boards of Governors and partly to the Ministry of Education. Again, no matter how sharply defined the Planning responsibilities of local authorities may be, Parliament will always expect Government Departments to take a most active part in Planning. Furthermore, the needs of society change; growing national services such as Hospitals, Cash Relief and Medical Services have long since moved out of the field of local government but their place has been taken by Slum Clearance and Re-development, Clean Air, Private Streets, Physical Training and Recreation and many other powers and duties. A static local government would soon decline; changing responsibilities to meet the needs of changing times stimulate fresh approaches.

18. The fourth starting point is to remind the public at large of the difficulty of carrying out public business under the local government system, and to ask for more sympathetic understanding and greater support for the work of those engaged

in local government, involving as it does a multiplicity of duties, discharged through the Committee system, under constant publicity and unending criticism.

19. The fifth requirement is to bear in mind throughout these discussions the need to attract more candidates for election, of the standard of the best Councillors now serving on Councils.

66 THE MACRORY REPORT, 1970

From *Report of the Review Body on Local Government in Northern Ireland* (The Macrory Report, Cmnd. 546, Belfast, 1970); by permission of H.M.S.O.

In view of the decision to set up a central housing authority, announced in the Communiqué of 10th October, 1969 (Cmd. 4178), the Review Body are asked:

1. To review existing published Government proposals for reshaping local government in Northern Ireland.

2. To examine any further proposals which may be made to the Review Body.

3. To examine the consequences of the decision on housing.

4. To consider any implications of that decision for the health, welfare, child care, education and public library services at present discharged by local government.

5. To advise on the most efficient distribution under the Parliament and Government of Northern Ireland — whether under local government or otherwise — of the functions dealt with in proposals 1 or 2 above.

6. To bear in mind the implications for elected local government of any courses of action which the Review Body may deem advisable.

7. To recommend how local opinion can best be brought to bear on administration.

8. To advise on the number of local government areas; and to submit interim reports if they think fit . . .

EXISTING PROPOSALS REVIEWED

22. The Terms of Reference required us to review existing published Government proposals for re-shaping local government in Northern Ireland. These are mainly contained in the Statement of Aims and Further Proposals; and in the Green Paper of 1969 on the Administrative Structure of the Health and Personal Social Services in Northern Ireland, hereafter, for the sake of brevity, simply called 'the Green Paper'.

. . . . . .

24. Further Proposals suggests that local government should take the form of a single tier of 17 area councils providing the local physical and environmental services. This was an imaginative concept and a major step forward. But since we

believe, as we explain later, that some of the major local government services require
to be treated in the first instance on a regional ràther than a local scale (and by a
regional scale we mean one covering the entire province), this has made it possible
for us to modify the proposal by increasing the number of councils, thus giving
them closer contact with the views and wishes of the citizens.

The Green Paper

. . . . . .

26. The basic proposal of the Green Paper is that the tripartite structure
described above should be replaced by an integrated system under which, in any
given area, a single authority would be responsible for the provision of comprehensive health services. The arguments in favour of this course are summarised in the
Green Paper as follows:

'(a) the present structure is tripartite while the individual's needs for services
should be seen as a continuum;

(b) the separate branches of the health services are increasingly interdependent
in treatment and care, and the administrative structure should be designed
to secure fully co-ordinated planning as well as joint action;

(c) a single authority for each area could more easily secure the most effective
use of the financial and human resources available;

(d) advances in knowledge and the emergence of new needs make it desirable
that resources can be quickly and effectively deployed to meet new
situations;

(e) the different financial basis of the local authority services has presented
obstacles to the balanced development of community care;

(f) the three-tier management structure in the hospital service leads to duplication of effort and difficulties in communication.'

27. Accordingly, the Green Paper has suggested that the Hospitals Authority,
the Hospital Management Committees and the General Health Services Board should
be replaced by *area authorities*, which as agents of the Government would be
responsible for the planning and provision of a single co-ordinated health service for
their area and take over many of the functions of local health authorities. To the
authors of the Green Paper it did not seem that either the existing county councils
or the proposed area councils would provide adequate areas for the administration
of the services. They therefore proposed a minimum of three and a maximum of
five areas, each with its area board responsible directly to the Government for the
provision of services but with the local authorities having a voice in their administration through representation on the board. Appointments to the area boards
would be made by the Minister concerned, after consultation with a wide range of
interests, and the choice of chairman and vice-chairman would also rest with the
Minister.

. . . . . .

The Joint Communiqués

35. We have taken note of the Joint Communiqué of the Westminster and Stormont Governments of 29th August 1969, and the Joint Communiqué issued following the discussions between the British Home Secretary and the Northern Ireland Government on 9/10th October 1969. Both are of far-reaching importance so far as local government is concerned, particularly the latter, which announced the following:

(*a*) the intention to establish a Commissioner for Complaints to deal with complaints of maladministration, including religious discrimination, by local authorities or public bodies;

(*b*) the intention to introduce an approved code of employment procedure applicable to all public bodies, including local authorities;

(*c*) the intention to establish a permanent statutory Local Government Staff Commission with strong advisory powers to assist local authorities in the selection of candidates for senior and designated appointments and a continuing duty of reviewing appointment procedures;

(*d*) the intention to create a 'single-purpose, efficient and streamlined central housing authority', with the corollary that this authority must be able to rely upon 'the assured provision of water and sewerage and their organisation on a scale and in step with house-building; road programmes to suit; and above all the prompt release of land for housing estates, redevelopment and attendant social and recreational services';

(*e*) the recognition that one result of the decision to establish a central housing authority was the need to re-assess the consequent shape, size and staffing of local councils without housing functions, together with the implications for the social services at present discharged by local government – health, welfare, child care, education and libraries.

. . . . . .

In favour of elected local government

39. The case for a continued reliance on elected local government for the discharge of the widest possible range of local functions has been pressed by many and perhaps most strongly by the three main Local Authority Associations and the Belfast City Council. As presented, it was a reasoned and impressive case. At the risk of doing some injustice to the argument by compressing it, we would attempt to summarise it as follows:

(*a*) local government is not just a purely functionsl method of administration for the provision of services, it is something that enables people to play a part in the process of government and as such assists in political education; it is not enough to relegate local authorities to a purely advisory and consultative role for local involvement means more than the right to discuss what someone else has the power to decide; there can be no participation, nor can there be effective representation of local aspirations without responsibility, and responsibility means that functions must be exercised as of right, within the framework of an independent budget; and given that for these reasons local authorities are worth preserving, they must be allotted as wide a range of functions as possible or they will cease to be viable;

(*b*)   anticipating the possibility of the suggestion that the major local government services might be transferred to Stormont, the argument contends that 52 Stormont Members could not properly supervise the administration of these functions as well as carry out their primary legislative and deliberative duties and that such a course would therefore require a considerable enlargement of the House of Commons; but the argument then proceeds to assert, in the trenchant words of the Association of Local Authorities of Northern Ireland, that 'the concept of a semi-sovereign Parliament adopting the additional mantle of a sort of super county council to administer its own laws is quite unacceptable'; in short, it is said, provincial Government is no substitute for local government and the civil service, with little or no experience of direct administration, cannot be regarded as equipped to take over local government;

(*c*)   the possible alternative of a series of *ad hoc* specialised boards for the major services is condemned on a number of grounds, for example, the inability of the citizen to fix responsibility for what he dislikes and to express his dislike to someone readily accessible and ultimately answerable to him; the difficulty of securing co-operation between the different boards; the tendency of Ministers and their advisers, in making appointments to the boards, to nominate amenable and 'safe' men to the exclusion of the rebel, the unorthodox and the young; the insulation of boards from public opinion and the absence of direct accountability to the electorate; the tendency of the concentration of power at the centre to produce a passive acceptance of what is provided by authority and uninformed complaint when personal interests are touched; such a system, it is argued, runs counter to what is advanced as a basic and essential principle, namely that local services should be provided by authorities governed by elected representatives answerable to the electorate for their stewardship not only in the quality of the services but also for the price paid for those services; such, in résumé, are the arguments against the *ad hoc* board system and they are of formidable weight.

. . . . . .

42. Some of those who favoured in principle the continuance of the major services in the hands of elected local authorities made it a condition of their support that election should be by proportional representation, though without specifying which of the various forms of proportional representation they had in mind. As we have said earlier, we were not asked by our Terms of Reference to examine the electoral system or to study the advantages and disadvantages of proportional representation voting for local government . . .

43. . . . . because proportional representation was strongly supported in more than

one of the submissions that we received, we did in fact give it some consideration and we put the suggestion to a number of other witnesses. Very few were prepared to condemn it out of hand and some thought that the system, which was indeed in force in Northern Ireland for a short time some fifty years ago and which aims in particular to give numerical representation to minority parties in accordance with their voting strength, might well be appropriate to the particular conditions of the province. We would go so far as to say that the classic arguments that are marshalled against the proportional representation system for national elections do not seem to have the same force when applied to local government elections . . .

44. In all, then, there was a strong body of opinion which held that the full range of present local government functions should remain in the hands of elected local authorities, including housing despite the decision that had already been taken by the Government to transfer the housing function from local authorities to a central housing authority. It is undeniable that nearly all who subscribed to the school of thought outlined in the foregoing paragraphs believed that this decision was wrong in principle and they resented it . . .

In favour of centralisation of major services

. . . . . .

46. The main reasons put forward for some form of centralisation of the major services can be summarised as follows:

(a) the need for co-ordination of housing with the other environmental services;
(b) the need to reduce duplication and waste and to bring together people with expert knowledge of the respective functions;
(c) the relative smallness of Northern Ireland, both in area and population, coupled with the facts that many of the services are largely financed from central funds and that in many cases the operational functions and policies are the direct result of Government legislation;
(d) the need to eliminate the indecision, delay and duplication that are said to result from the present division of responsibilities among a whole series of Government departments, local councils, boards and other statutory bodies;
(e) the alleged failure of local government to attract sufficient number of elected representatives of the right calibre.

We should add that many though not all, of the witnesses in this category would give local authorities some degree of representation on the central authorities that they proposed, or on the area sub-authorities through which they envisaged those central authorities operating.

THE PROBLEM OF THE MAJOR SERVICES

. . . . . .

58. As we see it we are concerned primarily with making recommendations as to how the whole range of functions at present vested in local authorities can best be

administered. Unlike, however, the Redcliffe-Maud or Wheatley Commissions our Terms of Reference do not confine us to the present local government functions; we can also take account of those performed by the Ministries and by other public authorities. In considering the best system of administration we have applied the three tests suggested in the Statement of Aims — efficiency, economy and the effective representation of local aspirations, all in harmony with public policy as a whole. We accept these as yardsticks by which to measure any proposals that we might put forward and it is therefore right that at the outset we should explain our interpretation of these terms.

59. *Efficiency* we take to mean broadly, in this context, the provision of the services that the public wants, where and when they are needed, without undue delay, unnecessary complication or evasive procrastination. Efficiency need not be and should not be, 'soulless', and if it were, it would almost certainly run counter to the third test, the effective representation of local aspirations. It must therefore be responsive to people's wants; Oliver Cromwell was a highly efficient adminis-trator, but his belief that the people should have 'not what they want but what is good for them' has never been much favoured by the public.

60. By *economy* we understand that the services should be provided without waste of men, money or materials; they should be provided, that is to say, at the lowest cost consistent with their being of the highest quality and the cost should be one which the citizen who uses and pays for them considers reasonable in relation to the standard of service provided.

61. The *effective representation of local aspirations* seems to us to have more than one facet. It is closely tied in with local involvement and this, in the simplest sense, means that every citizen should be sufficiently interested in the affairs of local government at least to exercise his or her vote. But it means too that for those citizens who are ready and willing to take an active part in public affairs there should be scope for the fulfilment of the civic ambition . . . we have considered the range of functions for which local authorities at present are responsible and we have had little difficulty in arriving at the conclusion that in today's conditions many of these functions need to be based upon larger administrative units than any of the local authorities that exist today in Northern Ireland, with the possible single exception of the County Borough of Belfast . . .

. . . . . .

The alternative systems

69. There are two main alternative systems for the administration of services which are normally regarded as falling within the local government sphere: the unitary authority and the two-tier division. In the former system all the services in each area are provided by a single authority, as is more or less the case at the moment in the County Borough of Belfast. It has one great advantage: responsibility is clearly vested in one authority, not shared, and this enables the whole of the services in the area to be planned and co-ordinated by a single body. This was the system recom-

mended by the Maud Commission, except for certain large urban agglomerations. It is particularly appropriate for a country with a substantial number of large towns which with their surrounding countrysides can form units large enough to administer a wide range of services. It is not a system readily applicable to Northern Ireland, which is mainly rural and has few large towns.

70. The two-tier system is based on the well accepted understanding that the optimum management unit is by no means the same for each service. Some require large units and some can be perfectly efficiently administered by small ones. Without any suggestion whatever that any particular service is more 'important' or more 'valuable' than any other, the two broad categories can be seen to take on the character of wide-area or regional services and of small-area, local or district services. From this point on we propose to use the terms 'regional' and 'district' to designate these two categories of function.

. . . . . .

74. It has already been decided by the Government of Northern Ireland that housing should be treated as a regional service. We consider that in Northern Ireland the following services or functions at present provided wholly or partly by local authorities should also be treated as regional —

Education
Public Libraries
Personal health, welfare and child care
Planning
Roads and traffic management
Water
Major sewerage systems
Food composition, standards, labelling
Tourism
Electoral arrangements
Motor taxation
Criminal injuries compensation
Major harbours
Gas
Electricity
Public road passenger transport
Fire.

It seems to us that for the regional services (excluding the trading undertakings) the choice can only lie between:

(*a*) creating not less than three, nor more than five, large local authorities, leaving Stormont with general powers of supervision, control and stimulus.
(*b*) investing Stormont (itself an elected authority) with prime executive responsibility for the regional functions.

. . . . . .

79. Let us first consider course (*a*). The difficulty here is that local authorities large enough to be effective units for all the major services would be too large to be

close enough to the people in the small towns, villages and rural areas. There would thus need to be another level of local authorities, closer to the people — as indeed was recognized in some of the major papers put to us. But, when we bear in mind the size, population and resources of the country it seems to us clear that Northern Ireland cannot afford two levels of local authorities below Stormont without running the risk of still being as seriously over-administered as we consider it now to be.

. . . . . .

81. We therefore favour course (*b*) and our main recommendation is that Stormont itself should be responsible for the regional services and that, as we explain later in more detail, the district services should be the responsibility of not more than 26 district or borough councils, each based on a town or other centre.

. . . . . .

83. It seems to us that the individual main functions could appropriately be vested in Ministries as follows:

Education and public libraries in the Ministry of Education;

Personal health, welfare and child care, food composition, standards and labelling in the Ministry of Health and Social Services;

Planning, roads, traffic management, water, main sewerage systems in the Ministry of Development;

Electoral arrangements, criminal injuries compensation in the Ministry of Home Affairs;

Tourism in the Ministry of Commerce;

Motor taxation in the Ministry of Finance.

Implications for Stormont

84. We fully recognise that this recommendation has important implications for Ministers and their departments and for Parliament. At present Stormont, subject to certain exceptions, is primarily concerned with major issues of policy, whether or not involving legislation and with the general oversight of a large number of functions for which primary responsibility is vested in locally elected councils. Our recommendations would make Stormont directly responsible for a number of important executive functions and for their effective provision and performance over the whole of the country. Stormont would thus be a Parliament in the ordinary sense of the term and also a metropolitan or regional authority in the local government sense.

85. Since Ministers will have to answer in Parliament for the effective provision of regional services and the performance of regional functions over the whole country, the Ministries clearly must concern themselves directly with policy, finance, law and standards, as well as programmes and priorities within the regional, economic and physical plan; and it will not be possible for them to divest themselves of that responsibility.

86. It does not necessarily, and in all cases, follow that the Ministries must themselves deal with the detailed carrying out of those policies, the actual employment

of all the professional, technical and operative staff, the handling of transactions in land, buildings and machinery, day-to-day supervision and quick short-term decisions on the ground — all that is conveniently covered by the term 'management', which we use in that sense from now on.

Administrative machinery

87. We do not think it would be right for us to try to dictate in advance in any detail the administrative machinery by which the Ministries will discharge their duties of management. Each ministry will need to make its own assessment. But . . . there will plainly have to be some degree of decentralisation and delegation . . .
. . . . . .

DISTRICT COUNCILS

113. We now consider the question of locally elected councils, their number, size and character, and the services which we recommend should be vested in them. As we have made clear earlier, functions and size are interrelated. In our view locally elected bodies in Northern Ireland should satisfy three criteria:

- (*a*) their areas of administration should be small and cohesive enough to provide close local contacts yet be large enough and have sufficient functions to enable them to employ adequate senior staff;
- (*b*) they should provide all who wish with an opportunity to partake in the discussion and settlement of local policy, an opportunity not dependent on Ministerial wishes or powers;
- (*c*) they should be based on the main centres of population and provide a close link between town and country.

The councils we recommend

114. In the present system we have been impressed by the standard reached by many of the borough and district councils in the administration of local services and we concluded that areas of that size are very suitable for the running of local functions. We are satisfied that these functions could effectively and efficiently be administered in Northern Ireland by a number of district councils on the present model by integrating town and country; and this indeed is the model of the district authorities recommended for Scotland by the Wheatley Commission. In considering the number of district councils there should be, we have taken account of the great deal of work carried out in drawing up the proposal for a total of 17 area councils which is put forward in Further Proposals. There are a number of arguments which can be advanced in favour of this or even a smaller number of councils, say 12–15. For example, the smaller the number, the larger the council areas would be and the greater the likelihood of a sufficient load of work to employ qualified professional and technical staff. Another advantage would be that there would be fewer bodies

to be consulted and fewer concerned with the carrying out of the public services; it could be said that with such factors as increased mobility, greater ease of communications and more expensive technical equipment all tending towards larger units, this makes sense. On the other hand, although the concept of 17 local councils was a useful starting point for us, it has lost much of its force because of the Government's decision on housing and our decision on the administration of the regional services. As an alternative we considered making every existing borough and urban district the centre for a new district; this would have given a total of 35 districts. But on closer examination, we found that some of the towns concerned were not main centres of district activity, for instance Warrenpoint, Dromore, Donaghee and Tandragee. We therefore concentrated on those places which we considered were main centres and this brought the total down to a maximum of 26 districts in all. It seems to us that district councils based on that number of districts would meet the tests which we set out in paragraph 113 above.

. . . . . .

115. Accordingly we recommended that not more than 26 borough or district councils be established, the precise number and their boundaries to be determined by a Local Government Boundary Commission.

. . . . . .

The county councils

117. There would be no place for the county councils in the structure that we are recommending, for their functions would be taken over either by Stormont or by the district councils. We realise how unwelcome this will be to the county councils who have discharged the burden of major services over many years and whose members and officers have given devoted and efficient service to the work. It may however, come as no great shock for it was explicitly foreseen in Further Proposals that for the county councils there might be no place in whatever new local government system might emerge.

The county borough councils

118. Our proposals also mean the transfer of major functions from the two county boroughs of Belfast and Londonderry to Stormont.

Functions of the district councils

119. Until the precise boundaries of the new district councils are fixed, it is not possible to give an exact forecast of their size, but so far as we can see, there will be few with a population less than 30,000 and many will be considerably larger. Under our proposals in place of the present 73 local authorities there will be not more than 26. It is important to remember that these new authorities will be operating under the new electoral law of one man one vote at age eighteen, and that their

wards will be determined by an independent commission. The functions of these district councils will be of four kinds: executive, representative, consultative and ceremonial.

Executive functions

120. These will arise in two distinct ways. There will be those which the councils operate in their own right by virtue of the powers vested in them by Parliament, and those which they may carry out as agents of one or other of the Stormont Ministries. The vested functions should be:

Environmental health, including
   Food hygiene
   safety, health and welfare in offices and shops
   port health
   clean air
   environmental health education
   abatement of nuisances
Cleansing, including
   refuse collection and disposal
   control of dumping
   streets
   litter, car bodies
Urban drainage
Harbours
   other than major harbours
Sewerage
   other than major systems
Public conveniences
Cemeteries and crematoria
Bye-law control of building
Recreation, including
   parks
   open spaces
   swimming pools
   caravan sites
   youth welfare
Entertainment and culture, including
   promotion, direct or indirect, of drama, music, painting, sculpture
   museums and art galleries
Protective services, including
   safety in the home
   water safety
   road safety

Regulatory services, including
   licensing of cinemas, dance halls
   street trading
   explosives and fireworks
   dangerous buildings
   licensing of pleasure boats
Bye-laws, including
   good rule, vandalism, noise
Markets and abattoirs
Civic improvement schemes.

121. We were attracted by the recommendation of the Redcliffe-Maud Commission that local authorities should have a general power to spend money for the benefit of their areas and inhabitants. The present interpretation of ultra vires can restrict worth-while local experiments. We think therefore that consideration should be given to empowering the new district councils to spend up to say a 6d. rate for the benefit of their areas and inhabitants.

. . . . . .

Implications for elected local government

127. Our Terms of Reference ask us to bear in mind the implications for elected local government of any courses of action which we may deem advisable. The implications of the course that we are here recommending are, we suggest, almost wholly favourable for elected local government which, in this context, means the district councils that we have proposed. The main characteristic of most of the functions that we have recommended should be vested in them as of right is that they are essentially local, and the principal role of a district council, in our view, will be to concern itself with local matters — with local conditions, local amenities, local cultural facilities, local recreational facilities, youth welfare, children's play centres, local problems of vandalism and the like. But from what we have already said it will be clear that this is not the only part that we see district councils playing in the structure that we are recommending. We have indicated that there are a number of ways in which functions could usefully be delegated to them as agents for the central administration. They will be the bodies that will send forward some of their number, elected councillors, to serve on area boards for those regional services for which this system is adopted. They will act as 'consumer councils' for the services provided for their citizens, which will mean close consultation between the district councils and central administration. The role that we see them playing in the structure as a whole is not just an important one, it is essential.

128. The district councils will be firmly in control of the management of their own local affairs, firmly in control of their local rates. They will be bigger and stronger than the majority of existing urban borough and rural district councils. The distinction between urban and rural will disappear, yet the areas will not be so

large as either to risk loss of local contact between the electors and the elected or to make such demands upon the travelling time of councillors as to make it difficult to hold meetings in the evening.

Community groups

129. With the districts themselves there will, we think, be a place for community groups by which we mean bodies who seek to represent views of a neighbourhood but who are not publicly elected and who do not have statutory functions. We welcome the suggestion made to us by more than one witness that bodies of this kind could play a wider part in the life of the province . . .

. . . . . .

FINANCE

. . . the course that we recommend, which seems to us to have the merits of efficiency, simplicity, fairness in operation and the preservation of the independence of the district councils, is as follows:

(*a*) as a contribution towards the cost of the regional services transferred to central government one uniform rate for the whole of Northern Ireland should be struck centrally; this rate revenue would then be pooled with all other Northern Ireland revenues out of the total of which the cost of the regional services and other Government services would be financed. A solution on these lines was foreshadowed in paragraph 46 of Further Proposals and there seems to us to be a clear case for adopting this course to provide for the rate share of the cost of services whose standard is determined by central government and which should be at a uniform level throughout Northern Ireland; under these arrangements the cost of the regional services would appear in the estimates and accounts of the Government departments concerned and be subject to annual Parliamentary approval;

(*b*) in addition each district council should strike for its district such rate as it considers necessary for the district services for which it is responsible; we regard it as essential for the independence of the district councils that the decision on this rate should be a matter for them, and for them alone;

(*c*) the collection of both rates, the uniform provincial rate and the district rate, should be a combined operation carried out centrally; for this purpose there might well be established a Central Revenue Office, which would also be responsible for the collection of all other Northern Ireland revenues, such as estate duty, stamp duties and motor taxes. The Central Revenue Office would then hand over to each district council the amount for which it had precepted. It would of course be possible to carry out the collection of rates the other way round, that is to say, to give responsibility for the collection of both rates to the district councils. We have recommended the first course not only because on balance we believe that it will work more efficiently, but because, as we have said, local councils have an understandable dislike of incurring unpopularity as the collectors of rates for the major part of which they are not responsible;

(*d*) the transfer of regional services to Stormont will substantially reduce the imbalance of rate money to Exchequer money in district council finances ... If however all district councils are to provide an acceptable standard of district services, it will still be necessary in the new system to help the councils who have inadequate rateable resources either by an equalisation scheme between the councils themselves or by means of a general Exchequer grant. We think that the form and calculation of this assistance can best be left to the normal processes of negotiation.

. . . . . .

Local opinion

. . . . . .

160. Under the system that we are recommending local opinion will in the first instance be brought to bear through:

(*a*) the Members of the House of Commons acting not only in the normal way on behalf of constituents but also in holding a watching brief over the Ministries' general performance of the regional services;

(*b*) the Members of the Senate, all of whom also have local affiliations;

(*c*) the district councillors, of whom, given 26 councils with an average of around 20 members each, there will be over 500 in all. These councillors will not only be responsible for the administration of their own local affairs but, through service on such area boards as may be set up and their right to be consulted by other administrative bodies, will be able to bring local opinion to bear upon the administration of the regional services.

161. We endorse the proposal in paragraph 76 of the Statement of Aims that the function should be given to local authorities of keeping the citizens informed of 'the plans and proposals of the council, of the reasons for decisions and of the recurring question of where the money comes from and where it goes to'. We were impressed by an excellent gazette that is produced by one borough council. We understand that it is widely circulated and read, and it must plainly do much to inspire interest and a sense of civic pride.

162. The Local Authority Associations representing as they do a vast repository of knowledge and experience, can do much to bring local opinion to bear upon administration. Their weight would be even more effective if there were fewer of them, and we found general agreement among their representatives that there is at present too great a proliferation. The course that we are recommending can pave the way to an amalgamation that would produce a single powerful association of great value.

The councillor

163. Turning to the reflection of local opinion inside local government itself, there are two people who matter a great deal. One is the councillor. In the words of the Wheatley Report, 'the elected councillor is the key person in local government. His job, both as a policy-maker and as a local representative, must be so arranged that he can be effectively in charge of affairs and also effectively in touch with his constituents'. We believe that our recommendations for district councils will secure this result.

The citizen

164. Perhaps more important even than the councillor is the citizen, the ordinary man (or woman – or child– for whose benefit the whole structure of local government ultimately exists . . . So how will our system look to the ordinary householder – whether in Belfast, Londonderry, Dungannon or the Glens of Antrim? Will he feel that he can make his wishes and aspirations readily known and have his complaints sympathetically listened to?

165. First of all at the elective level, he will have three opportunities of casting his vote; a vote to elect a councillor to his district or borough council; a vote to elect a Member of Parliament to Stormont; and a vote to elect a Member of Parliament to Westminster. He will vote in each case on the franchise of 'one man, one vote'; and in local government on the basis of new single-seat wards which will be drawn by an Independent Wards Commission.

166. Secondly, within the public services of Northern Ireland he will recognise to all intents and purposes much the same centres of activity as he has known and been accustomed to. There will be the district council to which he will look for his local services and local amenities, matters such as refuse collection, clean streets, swimming pools and parks. There will be, in all probability the area board for health or education which to him should most easily and naturally take the place of his former county borough or county council for the area offices will be in familiar buildings in towns that he knows well. And there will be Stormont.

. . . . . .

THE SYSTEM IN BRIEF

  I. Two levels of executive responsibility:
    A. the elected regional Government responsible to Parliament and working through Ministries;
    B. up to 26 elected district councils working as local authorities responsible to their electorates.
  II. Ministries responsible for regional (or wide-area) services;
    District councils responsible for the district (or local) services.
  III. Ministries to decentralise to provincial towns the day-to-day management of

regional services under flexible arrangements appropriate to the particular service e.g.

Health, welfare, child care, education and public libraries to agent boards in
four areas;

Other services to local offices or delegated to district councils.

IV. District councils responsible for district functions in five categories:

    (i)   executive functions directly conferred on them by law.

    (ii)   agency functions delegated by Ministries.

    (iii) representative role on area boards and other agencies.

    (iv) consultative role as consumer councils.

    (v)   ceremonial.

V. Rate to be struck in two parts: regional and district.

VI. Community groups for small localities where desired.

67 THE NEW SYSTEM

From *Ulster Yearbook* (1974); by permission of H.M.S.O.

On 1 October 1973 the former two-tier structure of county, district, and borough
councils and the all-purpose county borough councils gave way to a new system of
single-tier district councils. This reorganisation, which followed the passing of the
Local Government (Boundaries) Act (N.I.) 1971 and the Local Government Act
(N.I.) 1972, formed an important part of the total re-organisation of services which,
beginning with the transfer of housing functions from the former local authorities
to the Northern Ireland Housing Executive, was completed on that date.

Functions

The new district councils, 26 in number, all have the same three main roles. These
are:

(a) a *direct* role in which the councils are responsible for a wide range of local services including gas supply, street cleansing, refuse collection and disposal, litter
prevention, consumer protection, environmental health, miscellaneous licensing
provisions, the provision of recreational, social and cultural facilities, the promotion of tourist development schemes and the enforcement of the new building regulations (which replace the former building bye-laws);

(b) a *representative* role in which they nominate locally elected representatives to
sit as members of the various statutory bodies set up to administer such
regional services as education and libraries, health and personal social services,
drainage, fire and electricity; and

(c) a *consultative* role in which they act as the media through which the views of
local people, through their elected representatives, are expressed on the operation in their area of other regional services notably planning, roads and con-

servation (including water supply and sewerage services) provided by those departments of central government which have a statutory obligation to consult the district councils about proposals affecting their areas.

Councillors

The councils were elected in May 1973, using the principle of proportional representation and on the basis of single transferable votes. Between them the councils muster a total of 526 councillors, equal to the total number of wards into which the districts are divided. Under the Electoral Law (N.I.) Order 1972 (as amended) each councillor is elected for a period of four years.

Borough Status

Under the provisions of the Local Government Act (N.I.) 1972 the charters of the former Belfast and Londonderry County Borough Councils have been applied, as from 1 October 1973, to the new districts of Belfast and Londonderry which will therefore continue to be known as Cities.

Additionally the Act provides that those of the new districts whose areas include former boroughs may apply the former borough charters to the new district. To date eight districts have applied former charters, and these districts are now called boroughs.

In the cases of Belfast, Londonderry and these new boroughs the Local Government Act (N.I.) 1972 also provides that not more than one-quarter of the councillors of these areas are to be designated as aldermen. The chairman of the new Belfast and Londonderry City Councils are also entitled to the rank of Lord Mayor and Mayor respectively, while the chairmen of all the new boroughs are called mayors.

Apart from enjoying certain ceremonial rights these city and borough councils have the same range of functions as the remaining districts.

Administration

Councils are empowered to delegate to committees, with or without restrictions or conditions, any of their functions except the power of making a rate, of borrowing money, or of acquiring, holding or disposing of land. The number of members of a committee and the terms under which they operate, must be fixed by the council. A council can also appoint persons who are not councillors to be members of committees; such non-elected members must not exceed one third of the total membership of any committee. Committees may, subject to any directions of their parent council, appoint sub-committees for the exercise of any function which, in the opinion of the council or committee, would be better exercised by a sub-committee. The majority of the membership of a sub-committee must be councillors.

Joint committees may be formed by two or more councils for any purpose relating to a statutory function in which there is a common interest, subject to restrictions similar to those governing committees of a council.

Every council is required to appoint a clerk and such other officers as the council thinks necessary for the efficient discharge of the council's functions. The qualifications necessary for the post of clerk and assistant clerk are prescribed by regulations and the appointment and remuneration of these officers are subject to the approval of the Department of Housing, Local Government and Planning.

. . . . . .

Staff Commissions

. . . . . .

During 1974 the Local Government Staff Commission for Northern Ireland provided for in Section 40 of the Local Government Act (Northern Ireland) 1972, will be appointed by the Head of the Department of Housing, Local Government and Planning. Its purpose will be to exercise general oversight of the recruitment, training and terms and conditions of employment of officers of District Councils. In particular, the Staff Commission will be responsible for:

(a) establishing advisory appointment panels for the purpose of giving advice to District Councils on the suitability of applicants for appointment to the office of Clerk and other offices for which qualification regulations are prescribed;

(b) establishing a code of procedure for securing fair and equal consideration by District Councils of applicants for employment and fair and equal treatment of persons who are employed by them;

(c) assessing the probable future requirements of District Councils for the recruitment of officers and securing publicity for employment opportunities with Councils;

(d) promoting co-operation between District Councils and public bodies, Government Departments and education establishments, including the temporary transfer of officers;

(e) promoting the provision of facilities for the training of officers; and

(f) promoting the establishment of negotiating machinery for standard rates of remuneration and other terms and conditions of employment of officers of District Councils.

Local Government Franchise

The Electoral Law Act (Northern Ireland) 1969 radically amended the franchise for Local Government elections in Northern Ireland by assimilating the secondary qualifications of Local Government electors to those of electors at Northern Ireland parliamentary elections. The Electoral Law (Northern Ireland) Order 1972 provided for the election and terms of office of members of district councils and for the holding of the first elections to district councils according to the principle of proportional representation.

Membership of District Councils

Members of district councils must either —
- (a) be registered electors for the district of the council; or
- (b) have during the twelve months prior to the election —
    - (1) owned or rented as occupier any land in the district of the council,
    - (2) worked during that twelve months principally in the district of the council.

. . . . . .

LOCAL GOVERNMENT FINANCE

General

The new District Councils which came into operation on 1 October 1973 have their financial powers embodied in the Local Government Act (Northern Ireland) 1972. The services administered by the Councils are financed from rates, government grants, loans and miscellaneous receipts from charges raised. The accounts of each Council are audited annually by auditors appointed by the Department of Housing, Local Government and Planning and a summary of the Councils' statements of accounts is presented each year by that Department to Parliament (the Northern Ireland Assembly).

Rates

Rates are a tax to finance services and are paid (subject to certain statutory exceptions) by all occupiers of rateable hereditaments. The sum due from each ratepayer is calculated as a specified amount in the pound on the rateable valuation of each property. Under a new rating system introduced on 1 October 1973 the District Councils strike a rate known as the District Rate. The collection of the District Rate is undertaken by the Department of Finance in conjunction with the collection of a uniform Regional Rate which is made by the Department of Finance to meet the cost of regional services administered by government departments. The District Rate is paid by the Department of Finance to District Councils in equal monthly instalments.

. . . . . .

General Consolidated Fund Grant

In addition to specific grants paid by various government departments in respect of schemes and projects carried out by District Councils, a general grant is paid to compensate for derating and to provide for additional finance for those Councils whose rateable resources per head of population is less than the average for Northern Ireland. This general grant, known as the General Consolidated Fund Grant, is calculated using a formula which takes into account the rateable valuation and population of each Council's area.

Valuation for Rating

The Rates (Northern Ireland) Order 1972 has replaced the various Valuation and Rating Acts which were passed since the early part of the last century and which have now been repealed. The Order re-enacts the basis of valuation which was laid down in the Valuation (Ireland) Act 1852. It also provides for a general revaluation of property every five years, and for a system of continuous revision to ensure that the valuation lists are corrected to take account of additions, alterations, or any other matter which may call for adjustment in order to keep the list up-to-date.

. . . . . .

Appendix V. Summary of Comparative Local Government Finances

	England and Wales	Scotland	Northern Ireland
(1) Population (Thousands, mid-1966)	48,075	5,191	1,481
(2) Local authority expenditure (£m. 1967/68)			
Borne by — Domestic ratepayers	550	46.3	9.8
Other ratepayers	626	52.8	7.8
Exchequer	1,381	165.2	56.7
Total	2,557	264.3	74.3
(3) Expenditure per head of population (£)			
Borne by — Domestic ratepayers	11.4 (21%)	8.9 (17%)	6.6 (13%)
Other ratepayers	13.0 (25%)	10.2 (20%)	5.3 (11%)
Exchequer	28.7 (54%)	31.8 (63%)	38.3 (76%)
Total	53.1	50.9	50.2
(4) Domestic hereditaments (Thousands)	15,376	1,704	419
(5) Average rate payment for domestic hereditament (£)			
(i) on the basis used above	35.8	27.2	23.4
(ii) taking into account Rate Subsidy to Housing, Trading Accounts and adjustments for balances	40.9	41.6	26.7

The New Authorities

District Name	No. of Wards	No. of District Electoral Areas	Approximate Population (based on Registrar-General's Mid-1973 Estimate)
Londonderry	27	5	87,000
Limavady	15	3	25,000
Coleraine	20	3	49,000
Ballymoney	16	3	22,000
Moyle	16	3	14,000
Larne	15	3	30,000
Ballymena	21	4	49,000
Magherafelt	15	3	32,000
Cookstown	15	3	26,000
Strabane	15	3	35,000
Omagh	20	4	41,000
Fermanagh	20	5	51,000
Dungannon	20	4	43,000
Craigavon	25	4	68,000
Armagh	20	4	47,000
Newry and Mourne	30	6	73,000
Banbridge	15	2	28,000
Down	20	3	47,000
Lisburn	23	5	73,000
Antrim	15	3	35,000
Newtownabbey	21	4	68,000
Carrickfergus	15	3	27,000
North Down	20	4	52,000
Ards	17	3	47,000
Castlereagh	19	3	64,000
Belfast	51	8	415,000
Total	526	98	1,548,000

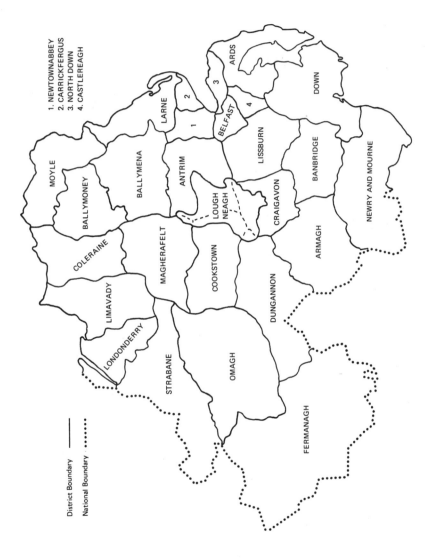

Map 7 *Northern Ireland: the New Districts*

1. NEWTOWNABBEY
2. CARRICKFERGUS
3. NORTH DOWN
4. CASTLEREAGH

District Boundary ———
National Boundary ·······

68 THE COMMISSIONER FOR COMPLAINTS

From *Commissioner for Complaints (Northern Ireland) Act, 1969*; by permission of H.M.S.O. The local authorities to which the Act has application were reconstituted by the Local Government Act (Northern Ireland) 1972, but the 1969 Act itself was subject only to minor consequential amendment.

An Act to make provision for the appointment and functions of a Commissioner to investigate complaints alleged to arise from administrative acts for which certain local or public bodies are responsible and for purposes connected therewith. [25th November 1969]

1. (1) For the purposes of this Act there shall be appointed a Commissioner, to be known as the Northern Ireland Commissioner for Complaints.

· · · · · ·

5. (1) Subject to the provisions of this Act, the Commissioner may investigate any action taken by or on behalf of a local or public body to which this Act applies, being action taken in the exercise of the administrative functions of that body . . .

· · · · · ·

[6.] (4) A complaint shall not be entertained under this Act unless it is made to the Commissioner before a day falling not later than two months from the time when the person aggrieved first had knowledge, or might reasonably be deemed to have had knowledge, of the action complained of or not later than six months of the action complained or whichever of those days shall first occur but the Commissioner may conduct an investigation of a complaint not made within the time required by this subsection where he considers that there are special circumstances which make it proper to do so and where the action complained of did not occur earlier than one year before the passing of this Act.

(5) A complaint shall not be entertained under this Act unless the person aggrieved is resident in Northern Ireland (or, if he is dead, was so resident at the time of his death) or the complaint relates to action taken in relation to him while he was present in Northern Ireland or in relation to rights or obligations which accrued or arose in Northern Ireland.

7. (1) The purposes of the investigation by the Commissioner shall be —

(*a*) to ascertain if the matters alleged in the complaint (i) may properly warrant investigation by him under this Act, (ii) are in substance, true and (iii) disclose any maladministration by or on behalf of the body against whom the complaint is made; and, where it appears to him to be desirable.

(*b*) to effect a settlement of the matter complained of or, if that is not possible, to state what action should in his opinion be taken by the body against whom the complaint is made to effect a fair settlement thereof or by that body or by the person aggrieved to remove, or have removed, the cause of the complaint.

(2) Where on an investigation made by him under this Act the Commissioner

reports that a person aggrieved has sustained injustice in consequence of maladministration, the county court may on an application made to it by that person, in accordance with county court rules and upon notice to the body against whom the complaint investigated was made, by order award that person such damages as the court may think just in all the circumstances to compensate him for any loss or injury which he may have suffered on account of —

    (*a*) expenses reasonably incurred by him in connection with the subject matter of the maladministration on which his complaint was founded; and

    (*b*) his loss of opportunity of acquiring the benefit which he might reasonably be expected to have had but for such maladministration: subject, however, to the application of the same rule concerning the duty of a person to mitigate his loss as applies in relation to damages recoverable at common law.

(3) Where on application made to it under subsection (2) it appears to the county court that justice could only be done to the person aggrieved by directing the body against whom his complaint was made to take, or to refrain from taking, any particular action, the court may, if satisfied that in all the circumstances it is reasonable so to do, make an order containing such a direction and —

    (i) for the purposes of such an order the county court shall have the like jurisdiction as the High Court to grant any mandatory or other injunction; and

    (ii) disobedience to any such order by any body on whom notice of the making thereof was duly served or by any member or officer of that body may be treated as a contempt of court to which section 141 of the County Courts Act (Northern Ireland) 1959 applies.

(4) Without prejudice to sections 2 and 7 of the County Court Appeals Act (Northern Ireland) 1964, any local or public body or any person aggrieved who is dissatisfied with an order of a county court under subsection (2) or subsection (3) may appeal from that order as if it had been made in the exercise of the jurisdiction conferred by Part III of the County Courts Act (Northern Ireland) 1959 and the appeal were brought under section 1 of the said Act of 1964.

(5) Where on an investigation made by him under this Act the Commissioner reports that a person aggrieved has sustained injustice in consequence of maladministration and it appears to the Commissioner (whether or not so stated in his report) that —

    (*a*) the local or public body against whom the investigation was made had previously engaged in conduct which was of the same kind as, or of a similar kind to, that which amounted to such maladministration; and

    (*b*) such body is likely, unless restrained by order of the High Court under this subsection, to engage in future in such conduct;

the Attorney-General may, at the request of the Commissioner, apply to the High Court for the grant of such mandatory or other injunction, or such declaration or other relief as appears to the High Court to be proper in all the circumstances, including an injunction restraining that local or public body or any member or officer of that body from engaging in, or causing or permitting others to engage in, conduct of the same kind as that which amounted to such maladministration or conduct of any similar kind specified in an order of the High Court and, where any such application is made to it, the High Court, if satisfied as to the matters mentioned in paragraphs (*a*) and (*b*), may grant such mandatory or other injunction, or such declaration or other relief.

. . . . . .

(8) For the purposes of any proceedings authorised by this section, a recommendation of the Commissioner and any report of the Commissioner relating to the complaint in connection with which the recommendation is made shall, unless the contrary is proved, be accepted as evidence of the facts stated therein.

8. (1) Where the Commissioner proposes to conduct an investigation pursuant to a complaint under this Act, he shall furnish to —

(*a*) the body concerned; and

(*b*) any person who is alleged in the complaint to have taken or authorised the action complained of or who is otherwise involved in allegations made in the complaint;

information as to the allegations made in the complaint so far as they relate to that body or (as the case may be) to that person and the substance of any evidence which the Commissioner has reason to believe may be tendered in support of those allegations and shall afford to every such body or person an opportunity to comment on those allegations and to furnish oral or other evidence respecting them.

. . . . . .

(4) The Commissioner shall not be obliged to hold any hearing, and no person shall be entitled as of right to be heard by the Commissioner but, if at any time during the course of an investigation it appears to the Commissioner that there may be sufficient grounds for making any report or recommendation that may adversely affect any local or other public body or any member or officer thereof or any Minister or department or other person, the Commissioner shall give to that body, member, officer, Minister, department or other person, as the case may be, if it or he should so desire, the opportunity of being examined . . .

. . . . . .

[**9.**] (2) It is hereby declared that nothing in this Act authorises or requires the Commissioner to question the merits of a decision taken without maladministration by a local or public body in the exercise of a discretion vested in that body.

(3) Any reference in this Act to a local or public body includes a reference to the members or officers of that body.

SCHEDULE 1

Local and Public Bodies subject to Investigation: Part I

Local Bodies
Any local body.
Any new town commission established under the New Towns Acts (Northern Ireland) 1965 to 1968 and any committee or sub-committee thereof.

Any harbour authority.

Part II

Public Bodies

Any board established under the Agricultural Marketing Acts (Northern Ireland) 1933 or 1964.

The Electricity Board for Northern Ireland.

Hospital Management Committees established pursuant to schemes made under section 28 of the Health Services Act (Northern Ireland) 1948.

Industrial Training Boards established under section 1 of the Industrial Training Act (Northern Ireland) 1964.

The Northern Ireland Fire Authority.

The Northern Ireland General Health Services Board.

The Northern Ireland Hospitals Authority.

The Northern Ireland Housing Trust.

The Northern Ireland Tourist Board.

The Northern Ireland Youth Employment Service Board.

Special Care Management Committees established pursuant to special care schemes made under section 3 of the Mental Health Act (Northern Ireland) 1961.

SCHEDULE 2

Matters not subject to Investigation

1. Action taken by or with the authority of the Minister of Home Affairs or of the Attorney-General for the purposes of investigating crime or of protecting the security of Northern Ireland or the United Kingdom.

2. The commencement or conduct of any civil or criminal proceedings before a court of law in the United Kingdom, or of proceedings before any international court or tribunal.

3. Action which is or may be investigated by the Attorney-General with a view to the institution of proceedings under section 11 of the Local Government (Members and Officers) Act (Northern Ireland) 1964:

Provided that, if, after the Attorney-General has decided not to proceed with such an investigation into such action or not to institute such proceedings in respect of it, or after the final determination of any such proceedings in respect of such action, a person aggrieved complains that such action resulted in his sustaining injustice in consequence of maladministration and that such injustice has not been remedied, the Commissioner may, if satisfied that there are reasonable grounds for that complaint investigate such action and may do so notwithstanding any limitation of time imposed by section 6 (4) so long as the action occurred not earlier than one year before the passing of this Act.

4. Action in the discharge of a professional duty by a medical or dental prac-

titioner, pharmacist, nurse, midwife or member of a profession supplementary to medicine in the course of diagnosis, treatment or care of a particular patient.

5. Action taken in respect of any matter which is within the scope of the powers of the Northern Ireland Parliamentary Commissioner for Administration.

6. Action taken in respect of any matter outside the scope of the powers of the Parliament of Northern Ireland.

69 THE 1973 LOCAL GOVERNMENT ELECTIONS

From *The Northern Ireland General Elections of 1973* (Cmnd. 5851, 1975); by permission of H.M.S.O. This commissioned study of the operation of proportional representation in the local and general elections of Northern Ireland in 1973, was produced by R. J. Lawrence, S. Elliott and M. J. Laver of Queen's University, Belfast.

Nominations

52. The long-delayed local general election took place on Wednesday, 30th May . . . Final nominations totalled 1,222.

53. In the 26 new district councils there were only 526 seats to be filled, as against some 1,300 in the old local government system. On the other hand, every area in 1973 was contested, a sharp contrast to previous elections when many seats were not fought at all . . .

54. The nominations revealed, not only a considerable degree of competition to serve the public on local authorities with much reduced powers, but an astonishing diversity of political attitudes in an area little larger than Yorkshire and with an electorate of only about 1 m. Candidates' descriptions of themselves, as published by the Chief Electoral Officer, fell into 38 groups. One group of 71 consisted of Independents. Another 71 did not identify their political outlook and were officially designated as Non-party. The rest (1,080 in all) used 36 different descriptions, including 13 varieties of Loyalist . . .

. . . . . .

56. The degree of choice reflected the extent of party fragmentation which had occurred since the last local general election in 1967. The pressure of events and the emergence of conflicting policies and personalities had combined to transform the party system. The Ulster Unionist Party remained the largest single political organisation, but the formation of the Democratic Unionist Party (DUP), the Vanguard Unionist Progressive Party (VUPP), and other Loyalist groups threatened to divide its supporters. The Nationalist Party, the main traditional opposition, had also experienced change. Dwindling support and the emergence of the Social Democratic and Labour Party (SDLP) with a developing constituency organisation provided the main challenge to it. A variety of other parties, including Republican Clubs, Unity and Republican Labour, also competed for the anti-partition vote. The Northern Ireland Labour Party (NILP), which had long sought the non-sectarian

vote, was challenged by the new Alliance Party (AP), which had rapidly built up an impressive organisation. The reader who is trying to discern some pattern in the kaleidoscope of nominations may find Table 10 helpful. We have arranged . . . 4 groups according to traditional party divisions: (1) Loyalist and Unionist, (2) Centre parties, (3) Anti-partition parties, (4) Other parties. Independent and Non-party candidates are brought together in (5).

Table 10 Nominations by party and group

	No. of Nominations
(1) Loyalist and Unionist	
Loyalist	
Democratic Unionist	39
Vanguard	25
United Loyalist/Loyalist Coalition	47
Other Loyalist	26
Official Unionist	169
Unionist	124
Unionist Unity/United Unionist	12
Independent/Unofficial Unionist	7
(2) Centre parties	
Alliance	237
Northern Ireland Labour	64
(3) Anti-partition	
Social Democratic and Labour	166
Republican Clubs	83
Republican Labour	12
Other Republican	7
Unity/Independent Unity	26
Nationalist/Independent Nationalist	16
(4) Other parties	20
(5) Independent/Non-party	142
	1,222

. . . . . .

62. Much attention during the campaign was focussed on issues that went far beyond the narrow sphere of local government. The White Paper *Northern Ireland Constitutional Proposals* had been published on 20th March. The Northern Ireland Constitution Bill, giving legislative effect to the proposals, was given its first reading on 16th May. The Northern Ireland Assembly Act, providing for elections to the Assembly, became law on 3rd May. It was hardly surprising that many people saw the local election as a test of public reaction to the Government's proposals and policies, or that political parties and groups found it necessary during the campaign to define their attitudes on these wider issues.

63. The content of the Constitution Bill, and the timing of the Assembly election, accentuated disagreement within the Unionist Party and between it and the

Loyalist Coalition of the DUP and the VUPP. Following a recommendation of the United Loyalist Council to concentrate resources on the Assembly election, both the DUP and the VUPP decided not to contest the district council election. The DUP held the election to be irrelevant and declared that the new local government structure was a farce, though it subsequently modified its decision so as to allow members already serving on local authorities to stand. It also supported United Loyalist candidates in Larne and Londonderry. But the participation of DUP and VUPP was only partial, and there was no disguising the bitter quarrel with the Unionist leadership over the White Paper's proposals.

64. On the anti-partition side, the SDLP pledged itself to participate fully in the new district councils, though it was opposed to internment. The Provisional Sinn Fein and the People's Democracy, on the other hand, urged their supporters to boycott the election. Several parties declared that elected members would only take their seats when certain conditions had been met. Thus, the Republican Clubs demanded an end to internment and Special Powers legislation, and the Republican Labour Party wanted to end internment and Army harassment of minority areas. The Unity organisation called for an amnesty for all political prisoners, disbandment of the Royal Ulster Constabulary, repeal of repressive legislation and overhaul of the judiciary, and declared that its elected members would attend their first council meeting, protest against internment, and then withdraw until their demands were met. The Nationalist Party said that its participation depended on policy decisions before October by the British Government. The Civil Rights Association urged supporters to vote for candidates pledged to take their seats only when internment and Special Powers legislation ended. Only Republican Clubs candidates signed this pledge.

. . . . . .

66. The content of the manifestos was equally diverse in respect of those local and regional matters which the new district councils were to control or might influence to a greater or lesser extent . . . Three issues attracted most attention — the role of district councils and councillors, housing, and community development and recreation. Others were: education, social welfare, industry and employment, transport, consumer protection, and the environment. Whatever else might be said about the 1973 local election, it was certainly not dull. In the course of the campaign the people of Northern Ireland were inundated by a flood of ideas and demands on a host of different themes.

. . . . . .

Turnout in the 98 electoral areas ranged from 44 per cent in Newry and Mourne E electoral area to 89 per cent in Fermanagh C. In the 26 districts it exceeded 80 per cent in 5 districts — Fermanagh 86, Magherafelt 82, Dungannon 82, Cookstown 82, and Strabane 81.

. . . Contrary to some expectations, the great majority of electors appeared to find no great difficulty in marking their preferences without ambiguity, no doubt because of the guidance given by political parties to their supporters and because an extensive campaign of official publicity had been mounted before the election . . .

Table 11 Turnout

	No.	% of electorate
Valid ballot papers	690,979	67
Rejected ballot papers	11,992	1
Totals	702,971	68

79. Lost deposits were common. Of the 1,222 candidates, no fewer than 286 (almost 23 per cent) had the misfortune to forfeit £15 because they failed to reach one quarter of the quota at any stage of the count.

. . . small parties suffered proportionately more than big ones . . . among the bigger parties or groups, NILP, Republican Clubs, Alliance, Independents and Non-party candidates fared worst and Unionists and SDLP best; and . . . the extremes on the anti-partition side did very badly indeed.

THE RESULTS

1. The Outcome of the Election

80. . . . Although . . . there is no complete statistical series of local election results for the years 1920–1967, there can be little doubt that throughout that period the great majority of local councils were controlled by Unionists and by Independents who gave them general support. At the 1973 election the Unionist Party lost some ground, but the number of its successful candidates, and their strength in relation to other parties on the new district councils, can be measured from different viewpoints: (1) the descriptions furnished by candidates themselves, (2) their party membership . . . while Loyalists and Unionists of all descriptions won rather more than half of all the 526 seats, they came out of the election with an absolute majority in only 8 of the 26 councils, of which Loyalists controlled 1, Official Unionists 4, Unionists 2 and Unionist Unity 1. In addition, Official Unionists formed the largest group, though not a majority, in another 5 councils, and Unionists in another 3. No other party won overall control of any of the new local authorities, though SDLP were the largest single group in 3 and Independent and Non-party candidates in 2 . . .

. . . If we group together as 'Unionists' all candidates nominated by Unionist constituency associations . . . we find that Unionists had an absolute majority in 12 of the 26 district councils and were the largest single party, though without a majority, in another 7. In addition, of the 24 Non-party candidates who were elected, 6 were actually nominated by local Unionist associations . . . The overall result, therefore, was that Unionists had a clear majority in 12 of the districts, while Loyalists had a majority in 1; Unionists were the largest party (though without a majority) in 9 districts and the SDLP in 3; and in 1 district no party was predominant.

81. The centre parties failed to make an impact in any way commensurate with the time, energy and money they had devoted to the campaign. The Alliance Party (AP) emerged from the election as only a minority group in each of the 20 councils on which it was represented, though its performance in winning 63 seats was impressive for a new party. NILP, with no more than 4 councillors in all, suffered a major setback. The relative lack of success of anti-partition parties other than SDLP, and of other very small parties, must also have been dispiriting to their supporters.

3. The Impact of the Elections

. . . . . .

181. We may begin with an observation on one matter of fact: the 1973 elections stimulated popular participation. At previous local government elections in Northern Ireland may seats were never contested, and even at the Stormont general election of 1969 (which aroused unusual interest) candidates in 7 of the 52 constituencies met with no competition. In 1973, by contrast, all the 526 district council seats and the 78 Assembly seats were fought by a great variety of parties and individual candidates, and a relatively high proportion of an enlarged electorate went to the polls. It does not necessarily follow that this was conducive to political health. Participatory democracy may strengthen the legitimacy of a regime, but anybody acquainted with Ireland will know that it can have the opposite effect. Free STV elections called by the British Government in 1921 resulted in the return of candidates in Southern Ireland who set themselves up an independent legislature. Nevertheless, the 1973 elections gave little support to parties which were determined to boycott the polls, or to politicians who proclaimed their intention not to take their seats if elected. One reason for this was that the largest party representing the Roman Catholic minority (the SDLP) successfully pressed for PR (as did Alliance, NILP and some other parties), and the Loyalists and Unionists who preferred the simple majority system were not intransigent. The beliefs and attitudes of the various parties were more important in making STV work than abstract arguments about its merits or demerits.

The local general election

182. The expectations of those who looked to STV to produce in the new district councils a massive block of 'moderate' opinion were not fulfilled. The Alliance Party did, indeed, win 63 (or 12 per cent) of the 526 seats, and it is virtually certain that the party would have done less well at a simple majority election. But Alliance failed to make the impact which its supporters and sympathisers had anticipated. Of its 237 candidates, 73 per cent were not elected and 30 per cent lost their deposits. The other centre party, Northern Ireland Labour, with 64 candidates and only 4 seats, failed disastrously.

183. A distinctive advantage often claimed for STV over other forms of PR is that it permits cross-voting between different parties, since supporters of one party can express second and subsequent preferences for other parties. Cross-voting did not, however, materialise on a significant scale . . .

184. The election did to some extent weaken Unionist Party control of local government. Candidates nominated by Unionist constituency associations won an overall majority on 12 of the 26 district councils and formed the largest single group on another 9. Of the other parties, Loyalists gained overall control of 1 council, and SDLP were returned as the largest single group in 3 — Londonderry, Magherafelt, and Newry and Mourne. While it is too soon to make firm judgments about the political effects of these changes, it would appear from reports of proceedings in the new councils that many elected representatives were more prepared than in the past to adopt a conciliatory attitude when they began to get down to the practical business of running the local community's affairs. It should, however, be emphasised that the scope for contention was narrower than before 1973 because local authorities had lost most of their functions and virtually all their patronage. It is easier to agree when less is at stake.

. . . . . .

Summary of issues in parliamentary manifestos

. . . . . .

1. The role of district councils and councillors

The Unionist manifesto considered that councils had many important functions, including the control of bureaucracy and the ventilation of local views, and called on people to seize the opportunity of a fresh start. The Alliance Party, which sought to control many councils, pledged itself to act as a watchdog against abuse of power, to campaign for more democratic control of Area Boards, and to use the district councils to provide new jobs through community self-help schemes. The NILP said that it would maintain advice centres and press for the holding of council meetings in the evening. The SDLP approved of the new local government structure, emphasised that the district councils had important functions and that they would also nominate up to 40 per cent of the members of the Area Boards, and promised to protect individuals against the powers of the Boards. The Republican Clubs, by contrast, sought the repeal of the Macrory Report and the creation in local government of democratic structures to defend the people's interests against international big business in the EEC. The Nationalist Party considered that local government in its new form could no longer be an arena for party politics.

. . . . . .

Select bibliography

Note. This Bibliography is in sections which have an approximate correspondence to the documentary sections. Under each heading is listed first the most relevant official publications in date order, followed by selected secondary sources, and then particularly helpful journal articles.

STRUCTURE, FUNCTIONS, LOCAL DEMOCRACY

Official publications

Local Government in England and Wales during the Period of Reconstruction (Cmnd. 6579, 1945)

Report of the Local Government Boundary Commission for 1947 (1948)

The Areas and Status of Local Authorities in England and Wales (Cmnd. 9831, 1956)

Functions of County Councils and County District Councils (Cmnd. 161, 1957)

Local Government Act, 1958

Local Government Commission for England, Reports 1–9 (1961–5)

Committee on Local Authority and Allied Personal Social Services. (Seebohm Report, Cmnd. 3703, 1968)

Royal Commission on Local Government in England, 1966–69, Vols. 1–3 (Cmnd. 4040, 1969)

Redcliffe-Maud Commission: Research Study 9. Community Attitudes Survey: England (1969)

Ministry of Housing and Local Government: Written Evidence to Redcliffe-Maud Commission (1967)

People and Planning (The Skeffington Report, 1969)

Reform of Local Government in England (Cmnd. 4276, 1970)

Local Government in England: Government Proposals for Reorganisation (Cmnd. 4585, 1971)

Local Government Act, 1972

Local Government Boundary Commission for England, First Report (Cmnd. 5148, 1972)

National Health Service Reorganisation (Cmnd. 5055, 1972)

Report of the Royal Commission on the Constitution (The Kilbrandon Report, Cmnd. 5460, 1973)

Neighbourhood Councils in England (Department of Environment, Consultative Paper, 1974)

465

Report of the Committee on Local Government Rules of Conduct (Cmnd. 5636, 1974)
Local Government Act, 1974
Local Government in England and Wales: A Guide to the New System (1974)
Local Government in Britain (Central Office of Information, 1975)
Department of Environment Circulars:
    52/72: *Planning: Publicity and Public Participation*
    107/72: *Local Government Reorganisation in England: Areas of New Counties*
    121/72: *Local Government Act, 1972*
    74/73: *Planning: Co-operation between Authorities*
    100/73: *Water Authorities and Local Authorities*
    76/74: *Local Complaints*
    45/75: *Publicity for the Work of Local Authorities*
    94/75: *Conduct in Local Government*
    113/75: *The Dobry Report on Development Control*

Other publications

The new system

Peter G. Richards: *The Reformed Local Government System* (Allen & Unwin, 2nd revised edn 1975)
    The Local Government Act, 1972: Problems of Implementation (Allen & Unwin, 1975)
Lord Redcliffe-Maud and Bruce Wood: *English Local Government Reformed* (O.U.P., 1974)
J. Brand: *Local Government Reform in England* (Croom Helm, 1974)
    'The Reform of Local Government' in K. Jones ed. *Yearbook of Social Policy in England, 1973* (Routledge & Kegan Paul, 1974)
C. Arnold-Baker: *The Local Government Act, 1972* (Butterworths, 1973)
G. W. Jones: 'The Local Government Act 1972 and the Redcliffe-Maud Commission': *Political Quarterly* 44, No. 2. April 1973
N. Boaden: 'Innovation and Change in English Local Government' *Political Studies*, Vol. 19. No. 4. (December, 1971)
L. J. Sharpe: 'Theories and Values of Local Government', *Political Studies*, 18, 1970

Introductory; Historical; Legal

K. B. Smellie: *A History of Local Government* (Allen & Unwin, 4th edn 1968)
J. Redlich & F. W. Hirst: *The History of Local Government in England* (ed. B. Keith-Lucas, Macmillan 2nd edn 1970)
B. Keith-Lucas: *The English Local Government Franchise* (Blackwell, 1952)
R. J. Buxton: *Local Government* (Penguin, 2nd edn 1973)
H. V. Wiseman: *Local Government in England, 1958–69* (Routledge & Kegan Paul, 1970)
W. Thornhill: *The Growth and Reform of English Local Government* (Weidenfeld & Nicolson, 1971)
C. A. Cross: *Principles of Local Government Law* (Sweet & Maxwell, 3rd edn 1974)
W. O. Hart & J. R. Garner: *Local Government and Administration* (Butterworths, 9th edn 1973)

Central—local relations
J. A. G. Griffiths: *Central Departments and Local Authorities* (Allen & Unwin, 1966)
   Local Authorities and Central Control (Barry Rose, 1974)
Dame Evelyn Sharp: *The Ministry of Housing and Local Government* (Allen & Unwin, 1969)
West Midlands Group: *Local Government and Central Control* (Routledge, 1956)
N. Boaden: 'Central Departments and Local Authorities: the relationship examined', *Political Studies*, 18, 2 June 1970
Owen Hartley: 'The Relations between Central and Local Authorities', *Public Administration*, Winter 1971

Politics; Democracy; Community
Dilys M. Hill: *Democratic Theory and Local Government* (Allen & Unwin, 1974)
   Participating in Local Affairs (Penguin, 1970)
W. Hampton: *Democracy and Community* (in Sheffield, O.U.P., 1970)
G. W. Jones: *Borough Politics* (in Wolverhampton, Macmillan, 1969)
Justice: *The Citizen and His Council* (Stevens, 1969)
J. K. Friend & W. N. Jessop: *Local Government and Strategic Choice* (Tavistock, 1969)
L. J. Sharpe ed: *Voting in Cities* (Macmillan, 1967)
J. G. Bulpitt: *Party Politics in English Local Government* (Longmans, 1967)
A. R. Rees & T. Smith: *Town Councillors* (Acton Society, 1964)
J. M. Lee: *Social Leaders and Public Persons* (in Cheshire, O.U.P., 1963)
A. H. Birch: *Small Town Politics* (in Glossop, O.U.P., 1959)
J. G. Bulpitt: 'Participation in Local Government' in Geraint Parry ed. *Participation in Politics* (Manchester University Press, 1972)
Theresa Brown, M. J. C. Vile & M. F. Whitemore: 'Community Studies and Decision-taking', *British Journal of Political Science*, April 1972

MANAGEMENT AND INTERNAL STRUCTURE

Official publications

Committee on Management in Local Government (Maud Report, 1967)
   Vol. 1. Report
   Vol. 2. The Local Government Elector
   Vol. 3. The Local Government Councillor
   Vol. 4. Local Government Administration Abroad
   Vol. 5. Local Government Administration in England and Wales
Committee on the Staffing of Local Government (Mallaby Report, 1967)
The New Local Authorities: Management and Structure (the Bains Report, 1972)

Other

Inlogov: *The Organisation of Local Authorities in England and Wales, 1967–75* (Institute of Local Government Studies, Birmingham University, 1976)

R. Greenwood & J. D. Stewart: *Corporate Planning in English Local Government* (C. Knight, 1974)

J. M. Lee & Bruce Wood: *The Scope for Local Initiative: Cheshire, 1961–74* (Martin Robertson, 1974)

J. Dearlove: *The Politics of Policy in English Local Government* (Cambridge University Press, 1973)

R. S. B. Knowles: *Modern Management in Local Government* (Butterworths, 1971)

B. J. Ripley: *Administration in Local Authorities* (Butterworths, 1970)

H. V. Wiseman: *Local Government at Work* (Routledge & Kegan Paul, 1967)

T. E. Headrick: *The Town Clerk in English Local Government* (Allen & Unwin, 1962)

R. Greenwood, C. R. Hemmings & S. Ranson: 'Contingency Theory and the Organisation of local authorities', *Public Administration*, Spring & Summer 1975

G. W. Jones: 'The Functions and Organisation of Councillors', *Public Administration* Winter 1973

R. Greenwood, J. D. Stewart & A. D. Smith: 'The Policy Committee in English Local Government', *Public Administration*, Summer 1972

J. Stanyer: 'Elected Representatives and Management in Local Government', *Public Administration*, Spring 1971

P. J. Self: 'Elected Representatives and Management in Local Government: an alternative analysis', *Public Administration*, Autumn 1971

Bruce Wood: 'Staffing Problems in the Reorganisation of Local Government', *Public Administration*, Autumn 1971

FINANCE

Official publications

Local Government Finance (England and Wales) (Cmnd. 209, 1957)

Committee of Inquiry into the Impact of Rates on Households (The Allen Report, Cmnd. 2582, 1965)

Local Government Act, 1966

The Future Shape of Local Government Finance (Cmnd. 4741, 1971)

Local Government Act, 1974

Local Government Finance: Report of the Committee of Enquiry (The Layfield Report, Cmnd. 6453, 1976)

Local Government Financial Statistics (annually, H.M.S.O.)

Rate Support Grant Orders (annually, H.M.S.O.)

Other

A. H. Marshall: *Financial Management in Local Government* (Allen & Unwin, 1974)

N. P. Hepworth: *The Finance of Local Government* (Allen & Unwin, 1970)

Royal Institute of Public Administration: *New Sources of Local Revenue* (R.I.P.A., 1968)

Liberal Party: *Rates – Rights and Wrongs* (1966)

A. R. Ilersic: *Rates and Local Government* (M. Joseph, 1965)

L. R. Helmore: *The District Auditor* (Macdonald & Evans, 1961)

N. P. Hepworth: 'Public Expenditure Controls and Local Government', *Local Government Studies*, January 1976
D. E. Ashford: 'The Effects of Central Finance on the British Local Government System', *British Journal of Political Science*, July 1974
K. J. Davey: 'Local Autonomy and Independent Revenue', *Public Administration*, Spring 1971

LONDON

Official publications

Royal Commission on Local Government in Greater London, Report (The Herbert Report, Cmnd. 1164, 1960)
London Government: Proposals for Reorganisation (Cmnd. 1562, 1961)
London Government Act, 1963
Committee on Housing in Greater London (The Milner-Holland Report, Cmnd. 2605, 1965)
Redcliffe-Maud: Research Study 2: The Lessons of the London Reforms (1968)

Other

G. Rhodes ed: *The New Government of London: the first five years* (Weidenfeld & Nicolson, 1972)
G. Rhodes & S. K. Ruck: *The Government of Greater London* (Allen & Unwin, 1970)
F. Smallwood: *Greater London: the politics of metropolitan reform* (Bobbs Merrill, 1965)
S. K. Ruck: *London Government and the Welfare Services* (Routledge & Kegan Paul, 1963)
W. A. Robson: *The Government and Misgovernment of London* (Allen & Unwin, 2nd edn 1948)

SCOTLAND

Official publications

The Modernisation of Local Government in Scotland (Cmnd. 2067, 1963)
Royal Commission on Local Government in Scotland, 1966–69, Report (Cmnd. 4150, 1969)
The Reform of Local Government in Scotland (Cmnd. 4583, 1971)
The New Scottish Local Authorities: organisation and management structures (The Paterson Report, 1973)
Local Government (Scotland) Act, 1973
Local Government (Scotland) Act, 1975
Royal Commission on the Constitution 1969–73 (The Kilbrandon Report, Cmnd. 5460, 1973)
Democracy and Devolution: Proposals for Scotland and Wales (Cmnd. 5732, 1974)
Our Changing Democracy: Devolution to Scotland and Wales (Cmnd. 6348, 1975)

Devolution to Scotland and Wales: Supplementary Statement (Cmnd. 6585, 1976)

Other

J. G. Kellas: *The Scottish Political System* (Cambridge University Press, 2nd edn 1975)

J. A. Brand: 'Party Organisation and the Recruitment of Councillors', *British Journal of Political Science*, October 1973

J. P. Mackintosh: 'The Royal Commission on Local Government in Scotland, 1966–69', *Public Administration*, Spring 1970

WALES

Official publications

Local Government Commission for Wales: Report and Proposals (1962)
Local Government in Wales (Cmnd. 3340, 1967)
Local Government Reorganisation in Glamorgan and Monmouthshire (1970)
The Reform of Local Government in Wales: Consultative Document (1971)
Local Government Act, 1972
Democracy and Devolution, Proposals for Scotland and Wales (Cmnd. 5732, 1974)
Our Changing Democracy: Devolution to Scotland and Wales (Cmnd. 6348, 1975)
Devolution to Scotland and Wales: Supplementary Statement (Cmnd. 6585, 1976)

Other

See under Sections 1, 2, 3,: many of these publications relate to Wales as well as England.

NORTHERN IRELAND

Official publications

The Reshaping of Local Government: Statement of Aims (Cmnd. 517, Belfast, 1967)
The Reshaping of Local Government: Further Proposals (Cmnd. 530, Belfast, 1969)
Report of the Review Body on Local Government in Northern Ireland (The Macrory Report, Cmnd. 546, Belfast, 1970)
The Northern Ireland General Elections of 1973 (Cmnd. 5851, 1975)
Commissioner for Complaints (Northern Ireland) Act, 1969
Local Government Act (Northern Ireland) 1972

Other

J. P. Mackintosh: 'The Report of the Review Body on Local Government in Northern Ireland, 1970; the Macrory Report', *Public Administration*, Spring 1971

H. J. Elcock: 'Opportunity for Ombudsman: the Northern Ireland Commissioner for Complaints', *Public Administration*, 1972, pp. 87–93.